中国金融部门评估规划系列报告

U0740141

中国金融体系稳定评估报告

CHINA FINANCIAL SYSTEM STABILITY ASSESSMENT

国际货币基金组织　编著　　中国人民银行　译

中国金融出版社

责任编辑：戴　硕　董　飞
责任校对：孙　蕊
责任印制：程　颖

图书在版编目（CIP）数据

中国金融体系稳定评估报告（Zhongguo Jinrong Tixi Wending Pinggu Baogao）/国际货币基金组织编著；中国人民银行译．—北京：中国金融出版社，2012.8
（中国金融部门评估规划系列报告）
ISBN 978－7－5049－6528－8

Ⅰ.①中…　Ⅱ.①国…②中…　Ⅲ.①金融体系—研究报告—中国　Ⅳ.①F832.1

中国版本图书馆 CIP 数据核字（2012）第 175517 号

出版
发行　中国金融出版社

社址　北京市丰台区益泽路 2 号
市场开发部　（010）63266347，63805472，63439533（传真）
网上书店　http：//www.chinafph.com　（010）63286832，63365686（传真）
读者服务部　（010）66070833，62568380
邮编　100071
经销　新华书店
印刷　北京市松源印刷有限公司
尺寸　185 毫米×260 毫米
印张　16
字数　305 千
版次　2012 年 8 月第 1 版
印次　2012 年 8 月第 1 次印刷
定价　38.00 元
ISBN 978－7－5049－6528－8/F.6088
如出现印装错误本社负责调换　联系电话（010）63263947

《中国金融部门评估规划系列报告》总序

亚洲金融危机之后，国际货币基金组织和世界银行联合推出金融部门评估规划（FSAP），致力于全面、客观地评估成员经济体金融体系的稳健状况，减少金融危机发生的可能性，并推动金融改革和发展。此次国际金融危机进一步凸显评估工作的重要性，二十国集团（G20）领导人在华盛顿和伦敦峰会上两次承诺将对本国进行FSAP评估。国际货币基金组织认真总结FSAP推出十年来的经验，并结合危机教训，进一步完善FSAP评估框架和评估方法，更加关注系统性风险、跨境溢出效应和危机管理框架等，重点评估对象也由新兴市场经济体转向了系统重要性国家和金融中心，针对性和有效性得到了进一步提升，逐渐成为国际社会广泛接受的评估机制。

中国金融管理部门一贯重视金融稳定监测与评估。早在2003年初，人民银行就牵头相关部门组成了跨部门小组，用一年多时间对我国金融体系的稳定状况开展了系统的自评估。这对于我们摸清家底、防范和化解金融风险、维护金融稳定起到了积极作用。2005年开始，人民银行定期发布《中国金融稳定报告》，在日常监测各类风险的基础上，全面分析、评估金融体系的稳健性状况。各行业监管部门也进一步加强了对相关金融行业风险状况的及时监测和评估。

与此同时，中国政府坚定不移地推进金融领域的改革，以改革促进金融业的发展和稳定。特别是2003年以来，抓住我国经济平稳较快增长的战略机遇期，果断推进和完成了主要大型金融机构财务重组、引进战略投资者、公开上市等一系列具有里程碑意义的重大金融改革。随着改革的深入，我国金融业的整体面貌发生了历史性变化，大型金融机构财务状况有了根本的好转，公司治理不断规范，抗风险能力显著提升，金融业整体实力持续增强，成功经受住了此次国际金融危机的严峻考验。在此过程中，中国金融业和金融市场实施相关国际标准的程度不断得到提升，为接受国际组织的全面评估奠定了良好基础。

在这样一种情况下，我们适时把握国际国内经济金融的最佳时机，在2009年8月启动了中国首次FSAP评估。为保障评估工作顺利进行，人民银行会同11个部门成立FSAP部际领导小组和部际工作小组，建立了相应的工作机制和工作原则。各成员单位高度重视FSAP评估，抽调精干力量，认真开展各项工作。经过人民银行和有关部门以及评估团历时两年多的精心组织和努力工作，评估于2011年11月圆满完成。随后，人民银行和国际货币基金组织在上海联合举办了"金融稳定监测与管理：来自FSAP的经验和改进FSAP的建议"国际研讨会，邀请17个亚太国家（地区）金融管理部门和主要国际金融组织的高层代表，以及美、英等一些国家驻基金组织执行董事，分享中国FSAP的成功经验，交流国际金融稳定评估的有效做法，以此促进金融稳定监测和管理的国际合作。

此次FSAP是中国金融体系首次接受国际组织进行第三方独立评估，实际上是从国际视角对我国金融体系和制度框架进行了一次全面"体检"，可以作为我国金融稳定自评估的重要补充。在符合我国有关法律法规和保密要求的前提下，我方向评估团提供了近百万字FSAP问卷答复材料，与其进行了400余场会谈，使其对我国金融体系有了更加深入、客观的认识和理解。评估团在此基础上撰写了一系列评估报告，充分肯定了中国金融业改革、发展和维护稳定的成就。报告认为，得益于中国政府推出的多项重大金融改革以及中央银行和各监管部门的有效监管，中国金融体系整体稳定，金融改革进展良好，金融机构实力不断增强，金融服务和产品日益多样化，有力支持了经济发展。

与此同时，评估报告也指出了我国金融体系的潜在风险，并就中国金融改革和发展提出了很多值得借鉴的建议。其中大部分建议，例如推进利率市场化改革、加强金融监管协调、构建逆周期宏观审慎制度框架等，在我国的"十二五"规划中已有明确表述；在2012年年初召开的全国金融工作会议上也得到了进一步强调。这说明，中外双方关于推进中国金融改革、维护金融稳定的很多观点是基本一致的。在明确改革方向的同时，作为发展中国家和经济转型国家，我们在学习借鉴国际经验做法的同时，有必要结合中国的具体国情以及国内金融业的特点，以我为主，因地制宜，在具体推进改革步骤时保持灵活性。下一步，在落实"十二五"规划和全国金融工作会议精神的过程中，我们要加快重点领域和关键环节改革，继续加强和改进金融宏观调控，推进利率和汇率改革，加快多层次金融市场体系建设，深化金融机构改革，推动存款保险制度建设，提升金融稳定和危机管理框架，进一步提高金融服务质量和效率。

FSAP评估是一项持续性工作。作为具有全球系统重要性金融体系的25个国家（地区）之一，中国今后将每五年开展一次FSAP更新评估。同时，将FSAP建议的采纳及落实情况纳入"基金组织第四条款年度磋商"范畴，并在每次评估两年后就建议落实情况接受金融稳定理事会"国家同行评估"。我们愿在此基础上加深与国际金融组织的合作与交流，借鉴国际组织的良好做法，完善自身金融稳定评估框架，提升遵守国际标准与准则的程度。同时，积极参与全球经济金融治理改革，主动参与国际金融标准与准则的制定和修订，增强标准与准则的适用性和公平性。

在中国首次FSAP圆满完成后，人民银行会同银监会、证监会和保监会将中国FSAP系列报告翻译出版。在此，我对外方评估团专家和中方参与FSAP的各部门领导和工作人员、业界专家、学者表示衷心的感谢与敬意，他们以杰出的专业精神为中国 FSAP 付出了辛勤努力。希望这套系列报告能够及时介绍国际金融组织对中国金融改革和发展的评估结论，为金融管理部门和业界人士，以及关心中国金融改革和发展的专家、学者深入研究和借鉴 FSAP 评估建议提供参考，为进一步提升中国金融体系的稳健性作出积极贡献。

周小川

2012 年 6 月 26 日

中国金融部门评估规划部际领导小组

组　长：中国人民银行行长　　　　　　　　周小川
副组长：中国人民银行副行长　　　　　　　刘士余
成　员：外交部副部长　　　　　　　　　　崔天凯
　　　　　国家发展和改革委员会副主任　　　朱之鑫
　　　　　财政部副部长　　　　　　　　　　李　勇
　　　　　人力资源和社会保障部副部长　　　胡晓义
　　　　　商务部部长助理　　　　　　　　　李荣灿
　　　　　国家统计局副局长　　　　　　　　许宪春
　　　　　国务院法制办公室副主任　　　　　安　建
　　　　　银监会副主席　　　　　　　　　　王兆星
　　　　　证监会副主席　　　　　　　　　　姚　刚
　　　　　保监会副主席　　　　　　　　　　李克穆
　　　　　国家外汇管理局局长　　　　　　　易　纲

中国金融部门评估规划部际工作小组

组　　长：中国人民银行　　　　　　宣昌能

副组长①：中国人民银行　　　　　　梁世栋　黄晓龙

成　　员：外交部　　　　　　　　　李克新

国家发展和改革委员会　　　徐　林

财政部　　　　　　　　　　孙晓霞

人力资源和社会保障部　　　张　浩

商务部　　　　　　　　　　刘景嵩

中国人民银行　　　　　　　邵伏军　张晓慧　李　波　邢毓静

　　　　　　　　　　　　　张健华　金中夏　王　煜　刘争鸣

　　　　　　　　　　　　　万存知　李晓枫　刘　荣　孙　辉

　　　　　　　　　　　　　苟文均　边志良　霍颖励　阮健宏

　　　　　　　　　　　　　李　跃　周金黄　陆书春　朱　隽

　　　　　　　　　　　　　易　诚　王关荣

国家统计局　　　　　　　　董礼华

国务院法制办公室　　　　　刘长春

银监会　　　　　　　　　　刘春航　李文泓

证监会　　　　　　　　　　韩　萍

保监会　　　　　　　　　　姜　波

国家外汇管理局　　　　　　王允贵

---

① 金荦和孙平曾先后担任工作小组副组长并兼任工作小组办公室主任，在中国首次 FSAP 的不同阶段做了大量工作，目前已不再担任此职务。

中国金融部门评估规划部际工作小组办公室

主　任：梁世栋

副主任：王素珍

成　员：范皙勇　王尊州　曲天石　那丽丽

　　　　陶　东　李敏波　林　毅　姚　斌

　　　　边永平　陈　苪　余雪扬　冯　云

　　　　陈　岩　周正清　苏宏召　王　濛

《中国金融体系稳定评估报告》

编审组：刘士余　李　勇　王兆星　姚　刚　李克穆

执行组：宣昌能　孙晓霞　刘春航　童道驰　姜　波

翻译组：梁世栋　王素珍　那丽丽　刘文中　曲天石

　　　　范智勇　陈建新　王　聪　王少群　孟　辉

　　　　洪　波　张甜甜　刘贝贝　赵冰喆　李敏波

　　　　陈　敏　王　清　陈团廷　于焘华　陈　蒂

　　　　林　毅　姚　斌　边永平　苏宏召　周正清

前　言

　　在总结 1997 年亚洲金融危机教训的基础上，国际货币基金组织和世界银行于 1999 年 5 月联合推出了"金融部门评估规划"（Financial Sector Assessment Program, FSAP），旨在通过金融稳健指标分析、压力测试和国际标准与准则评估等方法，加强对基金组织成员国（地区）金融脆弱性的监测与评估，减少金融危机发生的可能性，并推动成员国的金融改革和发展。经过不断发展和完善，FSAP 已成为国际社会广泛接受的金融稳定评估框架。截至 2011 年底，已有 130 多个国家（地区）完成了 FSAP 评估，许多国家（地区）还在初次评估的基础上进行了更新评估。

　　2008 年 2 月，温家宝总理在会见基金组织时任总裁时宣布中国将参加 FSAP 评估；此后，胡锦涛主席在二十国集团（G20）华盛顿峰会和伦敦峰会上两次做出接受 FSAP 评估的承诺。为落实我国承诺，从国际视角审视我国金融体系的稳健性，2009 年 8 月，我国正式接受国际货币基金组织和世界银行进行中国首次 FSAP 评估。中国人民银行会同外交部、发展改革委、财政部、人力资源和社会保障部、商务部、统计局、法制办、银监会、证监会、保监会、外汇局等 11 个部门成立了 FSAP 部际领导小组和部际工作小组，建立了相应的工作机制和工作原则，全力做好各项评估工作。

　　中国 FSAP 评估团由国际货币基金组织和世界银行的官员以及从其他国家聘请的财政部门、中央银行及银行、证券、保险等领域的专家组成。2010 年以来，评估团两次来华开展现场评估，部分成员多次来华进行专项评估和后续磋商，先后与国务院相关部门、部分地方政府、大型金融机构、中介机构等举行 400 余场会谈，就中国宏观金融风险和金融体系脆弱性、金融监管环境、金融体系流动性和金融稳定、金融市场基础设施建设、金融发展和金融服务可获得性、应急预案和危机管理安排等六方面内容展开深入交流。

　　经过两年多的努力，中国首次 FSAP 于 2011 年 11 月圆满完成。FSAP 评估团在中方提供的数据、信息、自评估报告和现场评估会谈的基础上撰写了一系列评估报告，主要包括《中国金融体系稳定评估报告》、《中国金融部门评估报告》、中国执行银行业、证券业、保险业、支付系统和证券结算系统等领域国际标准与准则情况的五份详细评估报告。上述报告对中国金融体系进行了系统、全面的评估，充分肯定了近年来我国金融改革和发展的巨大成就，对潜在的风险进行了提示，并提出了相应的改革建议。这些报告的英文版已在国际货币基金组织和世界银行的网站上公布。

我们及时组织翻译出版这七份报告，以期通过介绍国际金融组织对中国金融体系稳定性的评估结论，为读者深入研究 FSAP 评估建议提供有益的参考。

中国 FSAP 部际工作小组办公室

2012 年 6 月 28 日

国际货币基金组织国家报告第 11/321 号
2011 年 11 月

对中华人民共和国金融部门稳定性的评估报告由国际货币基金组织评估人员撰写，作为与成员国定期磋商的背景文件。报告基于在 2011 年 6 月 24 日完稿时的可得信息。报告所表述的是评估人员的观点，未必反映中华人民共和国政府或国际货币基金组织执行董事会的观点。

国际货币基金组织工作人员报告和其他文件的公布政策允许删除市场敏感信息。

国际货币基金组织

中华人民共和国

金融体系稳定评估

撰写：货币与资本市场部、亚洲及太平洋部

审批：José Viñals 和 Anoop Singh

2011 年 6 月 24 日

2010 年 6 – 12 月，国际货币基金组织/世界银行对中国进行了一次金融部门评估规划（FSAP）项下的评估，本报告以该评估为基础。这次评估的结论是，旨在加快金融体系商业化进程的改革取得了良好进展。但是，虽然改革取得成功，经济增长也很迅速，但中国的金融部门也面临一些近期风险、结构性挑战和政策引发的扭曲。主要的风险源是：(i) 与危机相关的信贷迅速扩张对信贷质量的影响，(ii) 日益增加的表外风险敞口和脱媒趋势，(iii) 快速上升的房地产价格出现逆转，(iv) 现有经济增长模式导致失衡加剧。中期脆弱性包括相对不灵活的宏观经济政策框架，政府在信贷配置中的重要作用，以及中央和省级政府在金融部门中的重要作用，这些脆弱性导致或有负债的积聚，并会妨害支持中国未来经济增长所需的对金融体系的重新定位。

一套稳妥设计并及时实施的改革措施将有助于应对这些挑战。这就需要在多个领域取得进一步进展，包括 (i) 深化银行和其他金融企业的商业化进程；(ii) 采取更加市场化的方式来影响货币和金融环境；(iii) 继续加强中央银行维护金融稳定的能力，并加强监管机构的能力；(iv) 进一步发展金融市场和工具以深化和加强中国金融体系；(v) 完善金融稳定、危机管理和处置安排的框架。然而，在前进的道路上还会出现新风险和新情况。为此，必须优先确立制度上和操作上的前提条件，这些前提条件对成功管理广泛的金融改革议程、实现"十二五"规划确定的目标至关重要。

FSAP 评估团成员包括：Jonathan Fiechter（国际货币基金组织，评估团联席团长），Thomas A. Rose（世界银行，评估团联席团长），Udaibir S. Das（评估团副团长，国际货币基金组织），Mario Guadamillas（评估团副团长，世界银行），César Arias, Martin Čihák, Silvia Iorgova, Yinqiu Lu, Aditya Narain, Nathan Porter, Shaun Roache, Tao Sun, Murtaza Syed（均来自国际货币基金组织）；Massimo Cirasino, Patrick Conroy, Asli Demirgüç – Kunt, Catiana Garcia – Kilroy, Haocong Ren, Heinz Rudolph, Jun Wang, Ying Wang, Luan Zhao（均来自世界银行）；Nuno Cassola, Henning Göbel, Keith Hall, Nick Le Pan, Greg Tanzer, Nancy Wentzler, Rodney Lester 和 Walter Yao（均为外部专家）。评估团先后在北京、重庆、南昌、宁波、上海和深圳等地，会见了相关政府部门的高级官员和工作人员，以及金融机构、行业组织和私人部门的代表。

FSAP 评估团访问结束以后，当局已经开始考虑各项 FSAP 建议，并针对与当前金融稳定框架相关的几个领域寻求技术合作。

本报告的主要作者是 Udaibir S. Das, Martin Čihák 和 Yinqiu Lu，FSAP 评估团也为本报告作出了贡献。

FSAP 评估旨在评估整个金融体系而不是单家机构的稳定性。这些评估意在帮助各国识别和纠正其金融部门结构中的薄弱环节，并以此增强其抵御宏观经济冲击和跨境风险传染的能力。FSAP 评估不涵盖单家机构的特定风险，如资产质量、操作或法律风险，或者欺诈。

目　　录

专栏

附录

附录表格

附件

附件表格

缩略词表

ABC	中国农业银行
ACHs	自动清算所
AIA	友邦保险公司
AMCs	资产管理公司
AML/CFT	反洗钱/反恐融资
BCP	巴塞尔有效银行监管核心原则
BEPS	小额支付系统
CAR	资本充足率
CBRC	中国银监会
CCB	中国建设银行
CCDC	中央国债登记结算有限责任公司
CCP	中央对手方
CDB	国家开发银行
CFA	中国期货业协会
CFETS	中国外汇交易系统
CFFEX	中国金融期货交易所
CIRC	中国保监会
CIS	集合投资计划
CNAPS	中国现代化支付系统
CNPS	中国支付清算体系
CPA	中国注册会计师
CPSS	支付结算体系委员会
CSD	中央证券存管
CSRC	中国证监会
CUP	中国银联
DaP	见款付券
DCE	大连商品交易所
FATF	反洗钱金融行动特别工作组
FHCs	金融控股公司
FoP	纯券过户
FSAP	金融部门评估规划

GEB	创业板
HVPS	大额支付系统
HQ	总部
IAIS	国际保险监督官协会
IASB	国际会计准则理事会
IBBM	银行间债券市场
ICBC	中国工商银行
ICP	保险核心原则
IFRS	国际财务报告准则
IMF	国际货币基金组织
IT	信息技术
JSCBs	股份制商业银行（截至 2010 年年底有 12 家）
KRI	关键风险指标
LCBs	大型商业银行（前 5 名）
LCPs	同城处理中心
LGFP	地方政府融资平台
MMOU	信息交流多边谅解备忘录
MOF	财政部
MOU	谅解备忘录
MSE	小微企业
NAO	国家审计署
NBFI	非银行金融机构
NDRC	国家发展和改革委员会
NPS	国家支付系统
NPL	不良贷款
PaD	见券付款
PBC	中国人民银行
PICC	中国人民保险集团股份有限公司
P&C	财产和意外伤害
QDII	合格境内机构投资者
QFII	合格境外机构投资者
RCSA	风险和控制自评估
RMB	人民币（元）
SAFE	国家外汇管理局
SAC	中国证券业协会
SD&C	中国证券登记结算有限责任公司
SHFE	上海期货交易所

SIPF	证券投资者保护基金
SIPS	系统重要性支付系统
SME	中小企业
SOE	国有企业
SRO	自律组织
SSE	上海证券交易所
SSS	证券结算系统
SZSE	深圳证券交易所
ZCE	郑州商品交易所

摘　要

1. 中国金融体系在商业化转型和增强财务稳健方面已经取得显著进展。金融机构和市场的结构、业绩、透明度和监管等方面也继续得到改善。因此，在国际金融危机中，中国金融部门表现良好。

潜在风险

2. 尽管改革取得了进展，财务状况良好，但中国金融部门的脆弱性依然持续积聚。金融体系正在变得日益复杂，市场、机构和国际间的相互联系正在增加。此外，非正规信贷市场、集团结构和表外活动也呈上升趋势。而且，目前的增长模式、与之相联系的相对不灵活的宏观经济政策框架以及中央和省级政府在信贷配置中的重要作用，都在导致或有负债的积聚。这些都会影响扩大内需和发展新兴产业政策的落实。然而，要量化这些脆弱性并不容易，部分原因是在监测、数据收集和部门间信息共享方面存在局限。

3. 金融体系近期面临的主要国内风险包括四个方面：（1）近期信贷急剧扩张对银行资产质量的影响；（2）表外风险敞口的上升和正规银行部门以外贷款的增长；（3）房地产价格处于相对高位；（4）当前经济增长模式导致失衡的增加。

4. 对 17 家最大的商业银行联合进行的压力测试表明，大部分银行看来能够抵御单因素冲击。这些冲击包括：资产质量的急剧恶化、房地产市场的调整、收益曲线的变动以及汇率的变化。但是，如果这些风险中有几项同时发生的话，那么，银行体系可能会受到严重影响。然而，由于数据缺口、主要金融数据缺乏足够长且连续的时间序列、信息基础设施薄弱以及对 FSAP 评估团获取机密数据的限制，还不能对这些风险的程度及其向经济和金融体系渗透的渠道进行充分评估。

加强风险监测和处置的改革措施

5. 应继续改进监管和金融稳定框架，强化银行风险管理体系，以有效应对这些风险。随着中国金融业务范围的扩大，需要相应扩大监管范围，对金融集团进行更严格的监督，强化系统性监控。这就需要增加关键部门的资源和技术人员，加强部门间的协调和数据与信息共享。人民银行（PBC）和监管机构必须加强员工能力建设，采用新的风险监测体系，强化干预框架，构建前瞻性的金融稳定评估方法。为此，首先要考虑的是继续改进会计要求、数据标准、报告要求以及信息披露质量。

6. 制度改革将有助于金融体系进一步符合国际惯例。监管机构的职责重点应该是，确保受监管机构的安全性和稳健性、风险管理以及市场行为的适当性，避免承担促进特定经济部门发展的责任，也不应负责决定资金的流向和配置。确保中央银行和金融监管机构的操作自主权至关重要。实施正式的金融稳定框架和应急预案机制十分关键。根据中国在 2008 年 6 月建立特设委员会的经验，建立一个常设的金融稳定和系统性风险委员会将是有益的一步。委员会应由一位权威高级官员担任主席，而且，委员会应有权获得所有相关的监管信息和其他财务信息。考虑到人民银行具有维护金融稳定的职责，应该由其承担秘书处职责。

7. 同时，还需要一个及时处置问题金融机构的框架。该框架的设计应有利于对问题金融机构进行有序处置和清算。应指定一个政府机构，赋予其处置权力，以处理被监管机构视为无法继续经营的机构。作为该框架的一部分，目前正在酝酿的显性存款保险制度应尽快建立起来，以便为有序处置倒闭的存款类机构提供资金支持，保护受保存款人，并使社会成本最小化。

迈向一个更加市场化的体系

8. 此外，还需要广泛的政策变革来维护金融稳定，并支持经济持续强劲、均衡增长。现行金融政策架构助长了高储蓄、结构流动性充裕以及较高的资金错配风险和资产泡沫风险，特别是在房地产行业。这些扭曲的代价随着时间的推移正在上升，加剧了宏观金融风险。到目前为止，与金融体系相关的成本已被生产力的迅速提高和对住户的隐性税收（通过存款的低收益）所吸纳，但是，不能设想这种状况会继续下去。为确保经济保持强劲、均衡增长，需要对金融体系进行以下改革：

- **改善系统流动性管理。**当前对外汇市场的高度干预、汇率浮动限制和很强的资金流入激励不利于系统流动性管理和调控。随着汇率管制的放松和汇率弹性的增强，采取措施吸收大量的结构流动性，将会降低金融稳定风险，并为中央银行货币调控提供更大的空间。

- **更多地使用市场化货币政策工具。**管理信贷扩张的主要工具应该是利率而不是对银行贷款的行政限制。这会提高资金配置的效率，增强货币政策的作用，并降低与表外贷款相关的金融稳定风险。在进行利率改革的同时，需要强化监督、完善银行风险管理和公司治理。

- **拓宽金融市场和金融服务。**发展多元化的金融中介将给银行带来竞争约束，为企业提供替代性融资渠道，并为住户提供更广阔的投融资机会。政府应优先考虑深化固定收益市场，发展多元化的国内机构投资者基础。

- **重新定位政府的角色和职责。**银行对国有企业的巨大风险敞口、利率管制带来的有保证的利差、实行差别贷款利率的能力和意愿仍然不足，再加上对新发放贷款节奏和方向的隐性指导，削弱了银行进行有效信用风险管理的动力。重要的是，银行要有相应的工具和动力来根据纯商业化目标作出贷款决定。

- **不再利用商业银行体系追求广泛的政策目标。**应该使用直接财政支出和补贴、政策性银行的直接贷款以及明确由政府资助的开发性信贷项目。政府必须着手制定防范措施和改革政策，以消除扭曲并遏制那些给公共部门资产负债表带来风险（如或有负债）的动机。

- **提升金融基础设施和法律框架。**支付和证券结算系统得到了加强，但是还需要进一步巩固，同时还要继续改进征信的覆盖范围和质量，以及对信用评级机构的监管。随着新产品的引入及其使用的增加，加强消费者保护（包括扩大金融教育计划）以及改进破产程序就显得尤为关键。鉴于近期跨境金融活动和人民币交易的增加，应该强化跨境和跨币种审慎框架。

9. 鉴于这些挑战和脆弱性的积聚，合理设计未来改革的节奏和次序很重要。合理设计并有效实施改革计划（包括上面讨论的各项要素），对中国经济的持续增长将至关重要。国际经验表明，特定的或局部改革本身有可能会给金融稳定带来风险。对中国来说，由于宏观经济政策框架和金融体系之间的紧密联系，这一点尤为重要。在加快金融深化、利率市场化以及最终实现资本账户完全开放等措施实施以前，需要具备一定的先决条件。这些先决条件包括：建立一个功能完善的法律、监管和危机管理框架；改进银行的公司治理；尽早吸收当前金融体系中的流动性；以及更多地依靠市场化的货币政策工具。因此，为了向更加市场化的体系平稳、安全地转型，认真做好筹划是关键。为帮助推动这一进程，表1列出了主要领域的优先建议，同时，表2对主要风险因素进行了评估。

表1　中国：主要建议

建议	优先度	时间框架
推进商业化		
1. 继续推进利率和汇率改革进程（¶8，11，50，51，52，68，79），同时确保金融机构能够进行适当的信用风险管理。（¶5，8，11，50，51，57，58，79）	高	中期
2. 明确区分政策性金融机构和商业性金融机构的作用和功能。（¶6，8，12，15，55）	中	中期
3. 将四家资产管理公司转型为商业化实体，作为第一步，要求其定期公布财务报表和管理报告。（¶49）	中	中期
提高机构和监管框架的效率		
4. 赋予人民银行和三个监管委员会以专责、操作自主权和灵活性，充实资金和熟练人员，并加强部门间合作，以应对快速发展的金融部门带来的挑战。（¶5，6，39，53，54）	高	中期
5. 建立针对金融控股公司、金融集团和非正规金融企业的监管框架（¶54）。过渡期内，任何受监管机构的并购活动都必须得到负责相应金融机构的监管委员会的批准。（¶54）	中	近期
6. 在中国银监会的风险评级体系中推行更具前瞻性的信用风险评估，消除与信用风险和市场风险资本框架的偏差。（¶56）	中	近期
7. 实施一个正式规划，使中国证监会得以定期对交易所进行全面的现场检查，以加强监督。（¶60）	中	近期
8. 对保险公司实行风险资本偿付能力制度，并给予其适当的过渡期，限制偿付能力水平低于100%的保险公司开展新业务。（¶61）	中	中期
9. 制订明确清晰的管理规定，为保险公司通过到期终止或资产转让而退出市场提供便利。（¶61）	中	近期
10. 制订一部"支付体系法"，为支付、衍生产品和证券结算的最终性提供全面保护。（¶63）	中	中期
11. 确保法人的受益所有权和控制信息充分、准确，且主管部门能够随时获取。（¶67）	高	中期
12. 改进人民银行和其他部门之间在反洗钱（AML）和其他监管问题方面的信息共享和协作安排。（¶39，53，54，67）	高	中期
提升金融稳定、系统性风险监测、系统流动性和危机管理的框架		
13. 建立常设的金融稳定委员会，由人民银行作为其秘书处。（¶6，39）	高	中期
14. 改进对金融机构数据的收集，包括其杠杆率、或有负债、表外头寸、未受监管产品以及跨境和部门风险敞口。（¶40）	中	近期
15. 建立宏观审慎框架来衡量并管理系统性风险，这应该包括增加人民银行和监管机构的资源、提升其监测金融稳定和定期开展压力测试的能力。（¶41）	高	近期

续表

建议	优先度	时间框架
16. 通过市场化工具加强对结构流动性的对冲,并通过间接货币政策工具管理系统流动性的溢出效应。(¶42, 51)	高	近期
17. 实行平均准备金制度,以便利流动性管理并提高稳定性和效率。(¶43)	高	近期
18. 开始试行短期回购利率目标制,作为间接流动性管理的尝试,并开始进行每日公开市场操作。(¶44, 45)	高	近期
19. 确保人民银行存贷款便利操作的即时性和自动性,对所有国内注册机构实行统一的抵押品要求。(¶46)	中	近期
20. 实行存款保险制度,为金融机构的有序关闭提供支持,并帮助理清或有负债。(¶7, 48)	中	近期
发展证券市场,将存款导向协议型和集合投资部门		
21. 确保监管规则的一致性,并明确监管责任,为固定收益市场的发展提供支持。(¶69)	中	中期
22. 继续改进财政部和人民银行的债券发行策略,以帮助改进收益率曲线上各种期限产品的现有做市活动。(¶70)	高	中期
23. 提升回购市场的管理和操作框架以提高市场流动性,加强风险管理,并强化货币和债券市场利率之间的联动。(¶68)	中	近期
24. 放宽对公司市场化债券发行累计余额不能超过净资产40%的限制,以扩大其直接融资能力。(¶72)	中	中期
25. 通过提升中央国债登记结算有限责任公司(CCDC)和中国证券登记结算有限责任公司(SD&C)之间的联系,加强银行间债券市场、上海证券交易所和深圳证券交易所之间的联动性,为这三个市场的进一步发展提供支持,并帮助其提高效率。(¶72)	中	中期
26. 巩固多支柱养老保险体系,重点关注积累制基本养老保险。(¶75)	中	中期
改善替代性融资渠道和可获得性		
27. 审视现有的政府规划,确定其在促进农村和小微企业融资方面是否有效,并制订综合且连贯的农村和小微企业融资战略。(¶76)	高	中期
28. 进一步改革农村信用合作社,增强其作为金融产品和服务的商业提供者的效率和可持续性。(¶76)	中	中期
29. 通过优化股权结构、公司化以及建立有效的公司治理,完成邮政储蓄银行的改革。(¶76)	中	中期

注:近期指3年内实施完毕;中期指3~5年内实施完毕。

表 2　中国风险评估矩阵

主要风险来源	风险爆发的可能性（未来 3 年内）	对宏观金融稳定的潜在影响
资产负债表风险 信贷总量增长的风险	**中到高** • 信贷增长非常快（2009 年增长了 33%），使信贷投放到产出率较低的投资领域的风险上升。经验表明，信贷快速增长和银行资产质量之间存在负相关关系。 • 在中国当前实用量化信贷指导的情况下，银行进行审慎风险管理的能力有限，从而可能导致潜在的信用风险。 • 表外风险转移的增加（如通过理财产品）加剧了信用风险敞口。	**中等到严重** • 不良贷款的不断累积可能损害银行的盈利能力和资本实力。贷款抵押品（在中国绝大部分为房产）价值的大幅下降将会放大银行的潜在损失。 • 银行前期进行的表外信贷活动可能会引起潜在冲击，并降低货币政策的有效性。 • 压力测试表明，如果主要的信贷冲击同时发生（在重度情景下，假设 GDP 年增长率下降至 4%），其影响将非常大，占银行体系资产 1/4 的银行将达不到 8% 的资本充足率最低要求。
宏观金融风险 跨境资本流入增加，并存在反方向流出的可能	**中到高** • 尽管中国采取广泛的资本管制，但中国的资本流动（不含直接投资）越来越多，且波动性更大。从绝对值上看，1998 年以来资本流动平均占 GDP 的 1.5%，而同期的经常项目余额和外商直接投资净额占 GDP 的比例分别为 4.7% 和 1.5%。 • 人民币升值预期增强，以及相对较高的利率（影响较小），使得投机性资本流入的可能性上升。历史数据表明，资本流入和 1 年期无本金交割远期外汇（交易最频繁的期限产品）显示的人民币升值预期具有正相关关系，且关系显著。	**中等** • 资本流动可能会通过房地产和股票市场对国内金融稳定产生不利影响。商业银行对房地产市场的大量贷款（占 GDP 的 20%）以及在房产抵押品方面的间接风险敞口，使得银行容易受资本流动波动引发的房地产泡沫及其破裂的影响。 • 大量的资本流入可能会引起银行信贷的快速扩张。尽管资本净流量和银行贷款之间的关联性被对冲操作所削弱，但国际经验表明，信贷扩张增加了银行资产质量下降的风险。 • 资本账户未开放（虽然公认可以被渗透）能起到减轻资本流入冲击的作用。
宏观金融风险 国际商品价格的大幅和持续性上涨导致输入型通货膨胀	**中到高** • 尽管一些商品市场存在大量闲置生产能力，但中国的一些关键进口商品却并非如此（特别是铜、铁矿石），这将加剧对于国际商品市场价格上升的脆弱性。 • 实证研究表明，考虑到对国内通货膨胀（和可能对货币政策）的影响，国际商品价格的上涨将给国内经济带来显著压力。	**中等** • 供给价格压力将通过旨在防止消费价格上涨的货币政策调整影响国内经济，导致国内信贷下滑，还款能力和信贷质量下降。 • 缺乏足够定价能力的借款企业利润率下降，导致不良贷款急剧上升；这些风险传递到其他部门将对经济产生第二轮影响。

	主要风险来源	风险爆发的可能性（未来3年内）	对宏观金融稳定的潜在影响
制度性风险	地方政府支持的基础设施建设项目可能违约	**中** • 受刺激政策的影响，银行对地方政府融资工具的风险敞口快速增长。大型基础设施建设项目的贷款快速增长，有些项目的回报不足以支付贷款本息，使得不良贷款累积风险加大。 • 地方政府的基础设施项目借款规模不可小视。根据市场估计，截至2010年6月底，地方政府债务约为7.7万亿元人民币，相当于全部贷款余额的16%，或2009年GDP总量的23%。	**中等到严重** • 鉴于地方政府融资平台高度依赖于以土地作为抵押品，因此，超出预期的房地产价格调整将对地方基础设施建设项目产生溢出效应，并考验银行体系的抗风险能力。 • 复杂的中央地方财政关系，以及各级政府与银行之间的潜在成本分担问题难以解决，都将加剧风险。 • 压力测试结果表明，地方政府项目的相关风险可控；但是，由于数据限制及不明确，并考虑到中央政府对地方政府的潜在支持，这一测试结果需谨慎使用。
宏观金融风险	全球经济紧缩	**中** • 由于中国经济增长高度依赖贸易和外商直接投资，因此中国出口行业以及依赖外商直接投资的行业将面临潜在冲击，从而使国内企业面临全球宏观经济冲击的风险。	**中等到严重** • 全球经济紧缩可能会削弱经济活力与就业，从而导致企业不良贷款上升，并损害银行的偿付能力。 • 由于在危机期间采取了大范围的财政刺激政策和货币刺激政策，中国政府作出进一步政策反应的余地有限。
制度性风险	对事实上的金融控股公司和产融结合型集团缺乏监管	**中** 2005年以来，随着金融业综合经营试点的稳步推进，事实上的金融控股公司发展迅速。一些产业集团投资于银行、证券公司和保险公司。 目前的监管体制中没有针对上述机构的明确监管主体。目前人民银行正在牵头起草金融控股公司管理规则。 金融控股公司增大了各金融部门间的关联性，产融结合型集团也会给实体部门和金融部门带来风险。对其缺乏有效的监测和监管容易引发系统性风险。	**中等到严重** 由于交叉持股和综合经营，可能存在跨行业、跨市场传染风险，甚至向实体经济溢出的风险。 考虑到金融控股公司的系统重要性，金融控股公司的倒闭将会影响公众对金融体系的信心，并引发更严重的风险。

主要风险来源	风险爆发的可能性（未来3年内）	对宏观金融稳定的潜在影响
资产负债表风险	**中** • 房地产价格已经大幅上升，但市场过热的情况主要在部分一线城市，没有发生全国性的系统性泡沫的迹象。 • 近期政府采取的措施将减缓房地产市场调整的潜在可能性，房地产总体价格趋于平稳，成交量近几个月有所下降。	**中等** • 房地产价格的大幅下降将通过银行在住房抵押和开发商贷款上的直接风险敞口以及对抵押品（主要是房地产形式）价值的负面影响等途径损害银行的资产质量，并使得拨备增加。 • 2010年末，对房地产和地方政府融资平台的风险敞口高达20万亿元人民币，超过贷款总额的40%。 • 房地产开发商和住房抵押贷款借款人相对较低的杠杆水平将降低对国内银行体系的影响。 • 压力测试结果表明，房地产风险是可控的；但是，因受数据限制，这一结论应谨慎对待。
房地产价格的大幅下跌以及与不动产（包括土地）贷款相关的信用风险增加		
内部关联性风险 各种冲击的汇集	**低到中** • 考虑到跨市场、跨机构关联性，此表列出的几乎所有冲击都将引发更深远的冲击。	**严重** • 例如，大量的资本流入会推升股票价格并导致房地产泡沫。由于抵押品、资本与土地价格的关联性，这将直接影响依赖房地产市场的地方政府融资平台的资产负债表。相反，资本流动的逆转会引发房地产和股票市场大幅下挫，损害银行的资产质量，包括地方基础设施相关的不良贷款累积。 • 宏观经济情景分析表明，如果一些严重的冲击同时出现，金融体系将受到严重影响。例如，在重度情景（包括GDP年增长率降至4%）下，占银行体系资产1/4的银行将达不到8%的资本充足率最低要求。

资料来源：中国FSAP评估团。

注：对于未来3年内风险爆发可能性的定性评估分为高、中、低三档。风险爆发对于金融稳定的影响分为温和、中等和严重三档。评估包含压力测试结果和其他FSAP分析的定量和定性结论。

I. 总体稳定评估

A. 宏观金融环境

10. 过去 30 年来，中国经济一直保持高速增长。 自 1978 年开始改革以来，经济年平均增长率接近 10%，而通货膨胀水平一直保持在相对低位。通过大规模投资，生产率保持快速增长，产能得到提升。商业银行部门增长迅速，并更加多元化（图 1）。自 10 年前实行住房改革以来，银行对住户的贷款急剧增加，尽管与其他国家相比仍然较低（图 2 和图 3）。

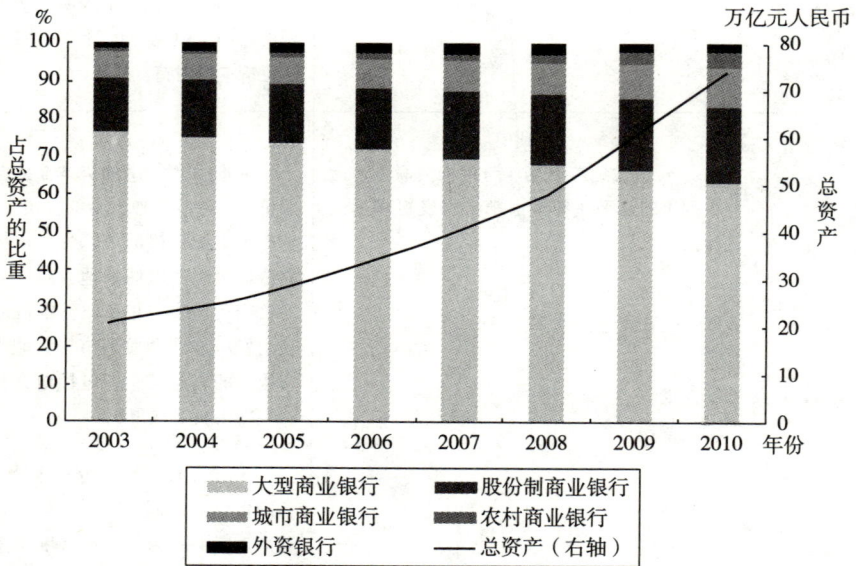

资料来源：CEIC；国际货币基金组织工作人员测算。

图 1 商业银行体系的演变

11. 然而，宏观经济和制度环境导致信贷配置缺乏效率和脆弱性的累积：

- **首先，较低的资金成本扭曲了储蓄—投资选择。** 低资金成本反映了存款利率上限限制和充裕的流动性，减少了外汇对冲交易的成本，并支持了投资和工业化。这造成了过度投资冲动，并通过存款的低回报抑制了家庭收入，从而扭曲了实体经济活动。

- **其次，不发达的资本市场限制了企业融资和家庭储蓄的选择。** 住户被限

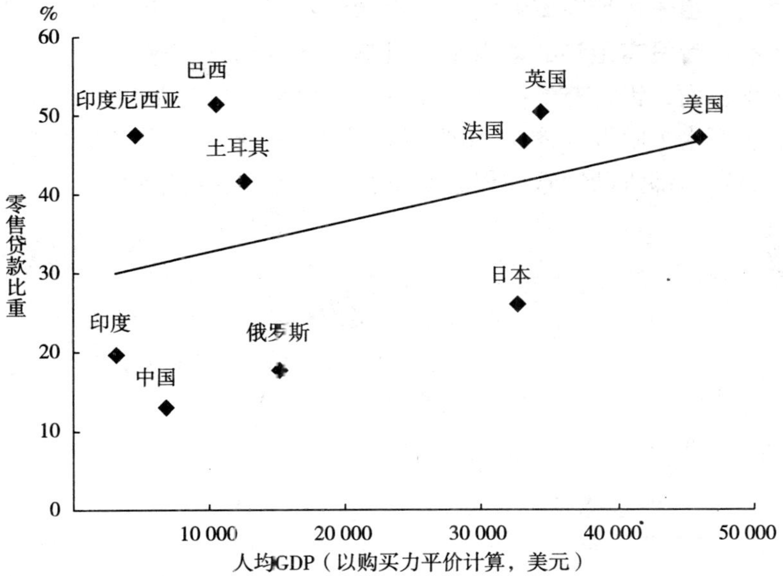

资料来源：CEIC；各国当局；国际货币基金组织《世界经济展望》；国际货币基金组织工作人员测算。

图2 部分国家银行体系中的零售贷款规模（2009年）

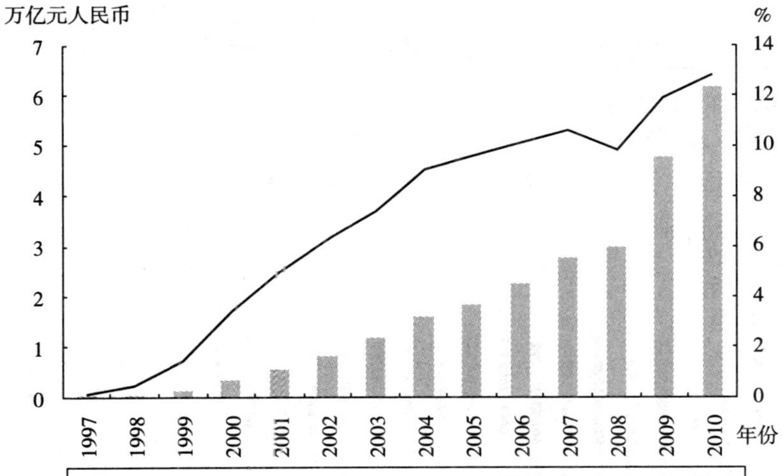

抵押贷款余额（左轴）　　占人民币贷款总额的比重（右轴）

资料来源：CEIC；国际货币基金组织工作人员测算。

图3 中国按揭贷款增长情况

于持有低收益的储蓄账户，从而抑制了收入和消费。可购买的保险产品有限也使得人们倾向于保持较高水平的预防性储蓄。在企业层面，由于很难利用资本市场融资，小企业和私营企业往往倾向于持有较高的企业储蓄。最后，由于企业和住户都追求更高收益的替代性投资，从而加大了产生资产泡沫的可能性，特别是在房地产市场（专栏1）。

- **再次，由于放松利率管制不彻底和汇率灵活性有限，造成银行和其他市场参与者没有足够的动力来改进其风险评估、管理和定价。** 在确定贷款利率方面，银行有一些灵活性，但是大部分贷款都集中在规定的贷款基准利率水平附近（图4和图5）。同时，充裕的结构流动性使大部分银行能够在内部流动性管理程序不完善的情况下继续运营。

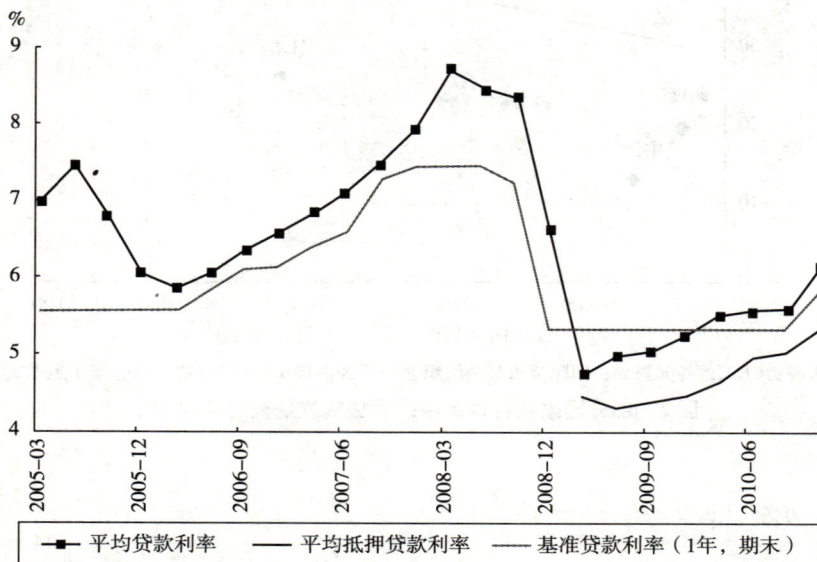

数据来源：中国人民银行；CEIC。

注：2008年12月前的平均贷款利率指6个月到1年间贷款利率。

图4　基准和平均贷款利率

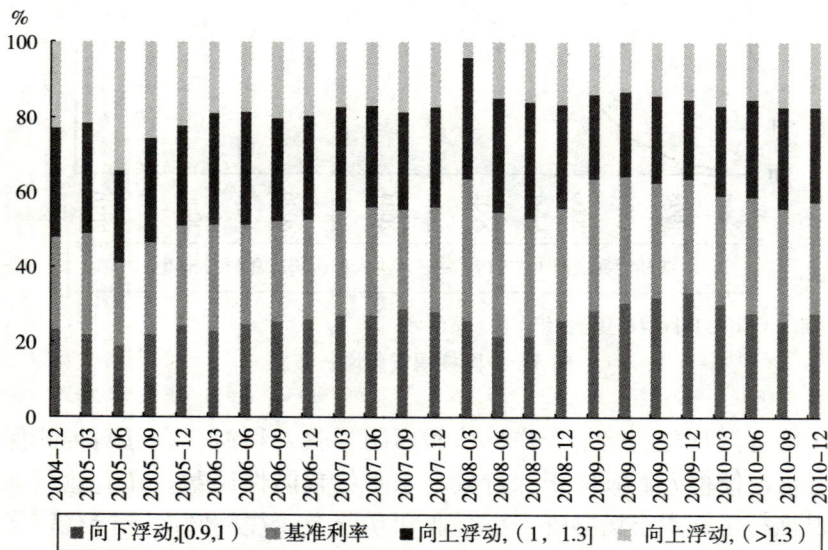

数据来源：中国人民银行；国际货币基金组织工作人员测算。

图5　贷款利率的分布（基准利率的倍数）

14

专栏 1   房地产部门和银行部门的稳健性

中国房地产价格的急剧上升，加上房地产部门的巨额银行贷款（图6和图7），加大了价格调整给中国的银行部门带来不利影响的可能性。然而，持

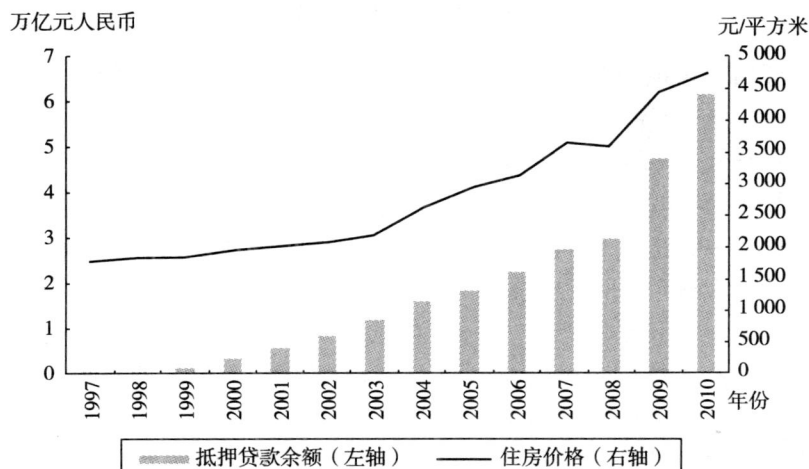

数据来源：CEIC；国际货币基金组织工作人员测算。

图6   住房价格和按揭贷款

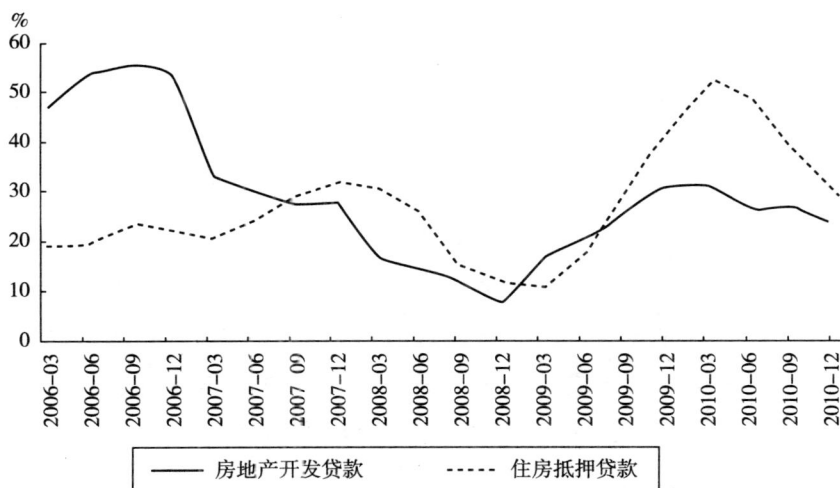

数据来源：CEIC；国际货币基金组织工作人员测算。

图7   银行向房地产部门贷款的年度变动情况

续的紧缩措施已经使房地产部门的贷款增长速度和房地产相关价格上升速度有所放缓。要遏制房地产价格调整对金融稳定的影响，持续监测、压力测试和一套综合政策措施非常必要。

几个基本因素推动了中国的房地产价格上涨。这些因素包括：收入的快速增长、存款的低回报、充裕的流动性、缺乏替代性的投资渠道、住房拥有的低成本，以及地方政府对土地出让收入的依赖。

银行部门对房地产部门的直接风险敞口有限（图8），但间接风险敞口却要高得多。与房地产部门相关的贷款大约占中国银行体系贷款总额的20%，低于香港特别行政区或美国。但是，间接风险敞口较高。贷款条件很大程度上依赖于抵押品的使用。在5家最大的银行中，有30%~45%的贷款由抵押品支持，其中大部分是房地产。房地产价格大幅回调将会降低抵押品价值，而且，如果借款人违约的话，又会降低贷款回收价值。此外，对那些与房地产部门存在"上下游关系"的产业（如建筑、水泥和钢材）提供的信贷也面临着这些风险。鉴于房地产部门对经济增长的重要性，如果因房地产价格回调而导致经济放慢，就会对银行体系的资产质量产生不利影响。最后，地方政府通过土地出让和补贴来支持地方政府融资平台的能力大大依赖于房地产市场，而这种土地出让和补贴对那些只有有限的现金流来偿还贷款的地方政府融资平台来说是必不可少的。[1]

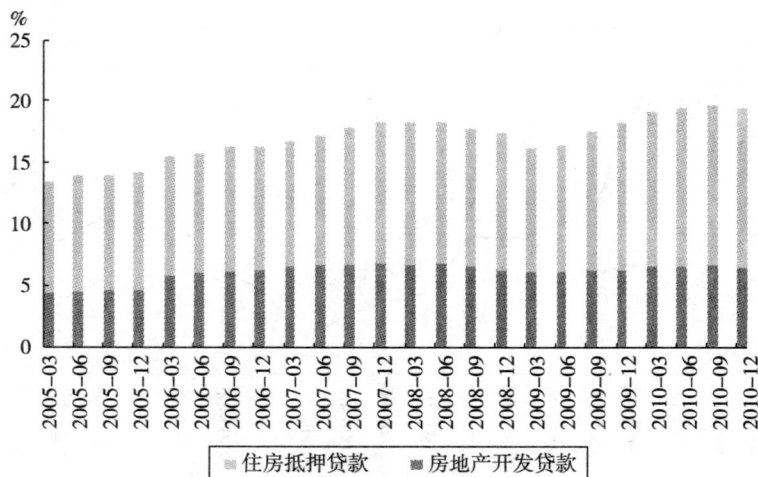

数据来源：CEIC；国际货币基金组织工作人员测算。

图8 房地产部门贷款占银行贷款的比率

从短期来看，特别是如果当前的增长势头继续保持的话，影响似乎是可控的。总体上说，中国的住宅房地产价格似乎不存在严重高估，尽管某些细分市场存在高估的迹象。同时，有限的直接风险敞口和低杠杆率（图9）将会限制房地产价格回调对银行资产质量的影响。对银行的房地产风险敞口单独进行的压力测试或结合"上下游"行业进行的联合压力测试结果（第I部分D）均表明，房地产部门的信贷质量恶化对银行的影响有限。[②]但是，如果同时出现增长放缓的冲击，对银行体系的影响及其溢出效应将十分严重。

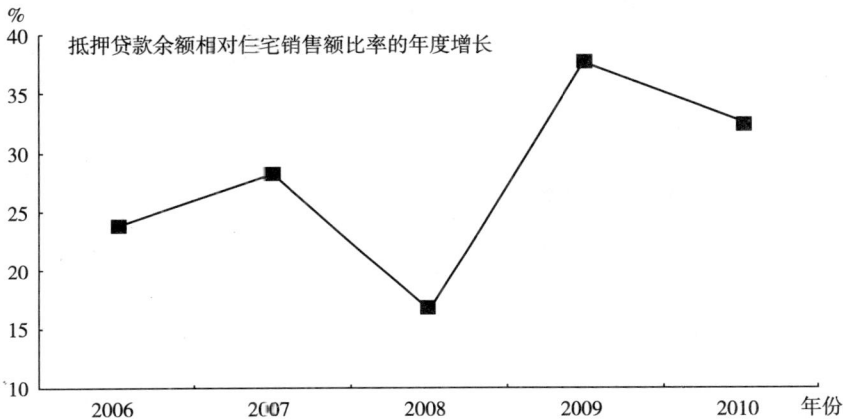

数据来源：CEIC；国际货币基金组织工作人员测算。

图9 贷款价值比代表值

从中长期看，房地产部门带来的风险大小取决于是否采取了政策措施来解决导致房地产价格上升的基本因素。要促进房地产市场的有序发展，需要一套综合措施，包括完成利率和汇率改革、进一步发展资本市场、逐步开放资本账户以及财政改革（包括开征广泛意义上的房产税）。与此同时，相关部门应该监测房地产市场动向及其对银行部门和金融稳定的潜在影响，并且在房地产价格出现上涨过度的情况下，迅速采取纠正措施。

---

① 平均来看，2010年，地方政府总收入的29%来自土地使用权的出让（瑞士联合银行，"对中国房地产泡沫的衡量"2011年3月22日）。总收入主要包括地方政府收入、中央政府转移支付和税收返还以及土地出让收入。

② 由于数据问题，在进行压力测试时没有明确将房地产市场发展的区域差异考虑进去。

12. 如果继续依赖信贷增长目标这一调控工具,即便用其他政策工具作为补充,也会削弱信贷配置的效率并扰乱货币政策传导。这种信贷目标意味着银行有强烈的冲动来扩大市场份额以增加利息收入,并使用表外渠道来绕过信贷目标,从而削弱货币调控的作用;同时,信贷目标使得公司部门往往会过度借款,因为它们知道,在到达一定程度时,将会实行信贷限制。控制利率和限定贷款数量还意味着,政策制定者无法依靠市场价格(如短期利率)来评估宏观经济和流动性状况。

13. 现行宏观金融和制度环境的一个副产品是低投资效率。据估算,自 2001 年以来,中国的 GDP 每增长 1 美元就平均需要近 5 美元的投资,与处于起飞阶段的日本和韩国相比高出 40%。[①]此外,中国的储蓄和投资总额占二十国集团总量的 20% 以上,但中国的 GDP 份额却大约只有 10%。这些可能反映出,资本被错误配置给了一些回报率低的项目。

14. 国家还直接和间接地参与了金融部门活动。银行部门大部分属于国有,银行的许多公司客户也同样是国有的。作为主要股东,国家任命所有主要银行的高级管理人员。由于没有显性存款保险制度和处置框架,国家还隐性地对所有存款进行担保。国家对金融体系许多方面的广泛参与降低了市场约束,削弱了公司治理,而且可能造成预算软约束。

15. 银行体系在财政政策实施中所起的重要作用是这种国家参与的明证。为应对 2008—2009 年全球金融危机的冲击,政府启动了一揽子经济刺激计划,并通过银行信贷扩张予以实施。地方政府热衷于基础建设项目,加上收入支出错配以及无法直接借款等因素,导致使用地方政府融资平台作为间接渠道来获得银行贷款的现象迅速增加,这通常以国有资产(如土地)作为抵押。结果,这类活动产生的公共部门或有负债大量增加。

B. 金融体系:结构和相互联系

16. 中国在提高金融体系的商业化程度方面取得了进展(表 3)。这一进展的取得与以下改革措施分不开,包括向银行体系注资、创建新的资本市场、实行审慎监管制度、在加入世贸组织后开放金融体系,并逐步改革利率和汇率政策等。股份制银行的改革促进了银行体系的商业化,而农村信用合作社的改革也已初见成效。在证券部门,主要证券公司已经得到重组,处置机制和投资者保护制度也已建立。养老金部门的改革也取得了进展,2000 年成立了全国社会保障基金。

---

① 麦金农全球研究所,2006 年,"发挥中国资本的作用:金融体制改革的价值"。

表 3 中国金融部门改革——部分标志性措施

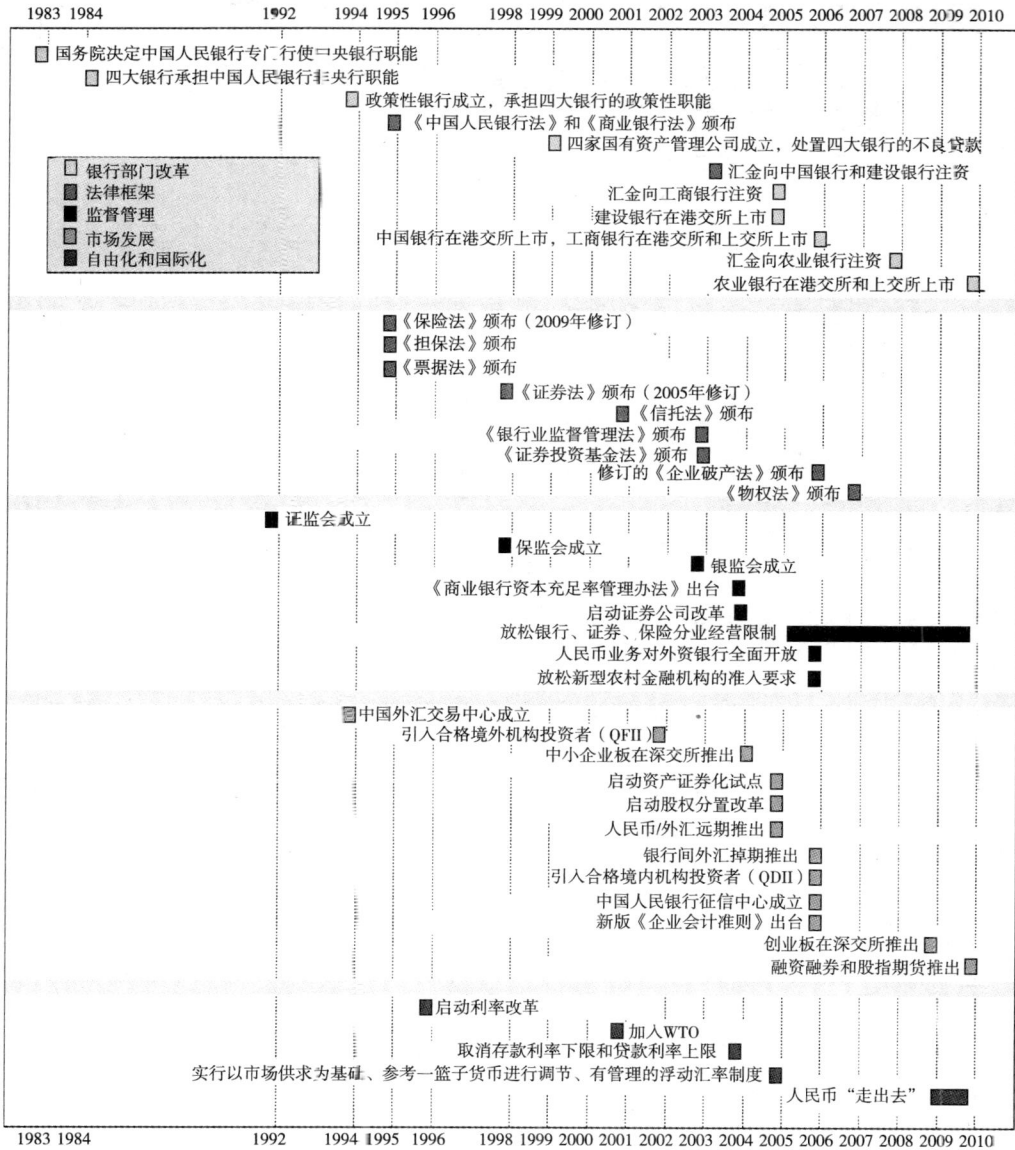

| 1983 | 1984 | 1992 | 1994 | 1995 | 1996 | 1998 | 1999 | 2000 | 2001 | 2002 | 2003 | 2004 | 2005 | 2006 | 2007 | 2008 | 2009 | 2010 |

- 国务院决定中国人民银行专门行使中央银行职能
- 四大银行承担中国人民银行非央行职能
- 政策性银行成立，承担四大银行的政策性职能
- 《中国人民银行法》和《商业银行法》颁布
- 四家国有资产管理公司成立，处置四大银行的不良贷款
- 汇金向中国银行和建设银行注资
- 汇金向工商银行注资
- 建设银行在港交所上市
- 中国银行在港交所上市，工商银行在港交所和上交所上市
- 汇金向农业银行注资
- 农业银行在港交所和上交所上市

图例：
- □ 银行部门改革
- ▨ 法律框架
- ■ 监督管理
- ▧ 市场发展
- ▦ 自由化和国际化

- 《保险法》颁布（2009年修订）
- 《担保法》颁布
- 《票据法》颁布
- 《证券法》颁布（2005年修订）
- 《信托法》颁布
- 《银行业监督管理法》颁布
- 《证券投资基金法》颁布
- 修订的《企业破产法》颁布
- 《物权法》颁布

- 证监会成立
- 保监会成立
- 银监会成立
- 《商业银行资本充足率管理办法》出台
- 启动证券公司改革
- 放松银行、证券、保险分业经营限制
- 人民币业务对外资银行全面开放
- 放松新型农村金融机构的准入要求

- 中国外汇交易中心成立
- 引入合格境外机构投资者（QFII）
- 中小企业板在深交所推出
- 启动资产证券化试点
- 启动股权分置改革
- 人民币/外汇远期推出
- 银行间外汇掉期推出
- 引入合格境内机构投资者（QDII）
- 中国人民银行征信中心成立
- 新版《企业会计准则》出台
- 创业板在深交所推出
- 融资融券和股指期货推出

- 启动利率改革
- 加入WTO
- 取消存款利率下限和贷款利率上限
- 实行以市场供求为基础、参考一篮子货币进行调节、有管理的浮动汇率制度
- 人民币"走出去"

| 1983 | 1984 | 1992 | 1994 | 1995 | 1996 | 1998 | 1999 | 2000 | 2001 | 2002 | 2003 | 2004 | 2005 | 2006 | 2007 | 2008 | 2009 | 2010 |

注：四大银行指工商银行、农业银行、中国银行和建设银行。这四家银行于近年进行了商业化改制。四大银行和交通银行一起统称为大型商业银行。

17. 尽管如此，银行（特别是几家大型银行）仍然主导着金融中介活动（**表4和表5以及图10**）。大型商业银行占商业银行总资产的近2/3（图11），四家最大银行的资产均超过了GDP的25%。固定收益市场已经发展为一个替代

表 4　中国金融部门的结构（2007—2010 年）

	2007				2008				2009				2010			
	机构数量	总资产（10亿元）	占总资产的比重	占GDP的比重	机构数量	总资产（10亿元）	占总资产的比重	占GDP的比重	机构数量	总资产（10亿元）	占总资产的比重	占GDP的比重	机构数量	总资产（10亿元）	占总资产的比重	占GDP的比重
银行机构	8 721	51 627	84.1	194.2	5 578	61 982	87.8	197.4	3 767	77 978	87.0	229.0	3 639	93 215	87.6	234.2
商业银行	187	40 459	65.9	152.2	323	47 819	67.8	152.3	336	61 513	68.6	180.7	379	74 160	69.7	186.3
大型商业银行	5	28 007	45.6	105.4	5	32 575	46.2	103.7	5	40 800	45.5	119.8	5	46 894	44.1	117.8
股份制商业银行	12	7 249	11.8	27.3	12	8 834	12.5	28.1	12	11 818	13.2	34.7	12	14 904	14.0	37.4
城市商业银行	124	3 340	5.4	12.6	136	4 136	5.9	13.2	143	5 680	6.3	16.7	147	7 853	7.4	19.7
农村商业银行	17	610	1.0	2.3	22	929	1.3	3.0	43	1 866	2.1	5.5	85	2 767	2.6	7.0
外资银行	29	1 252	2.0	4.7	148	1 345	1.9	4.3	133	1 349	1.5	4.0	130	1 742	1.6	4.4
本地注册的外资银行子行	…	…	…	…	32	996	1.4	3.2	38	1 132	1.3	3.3	40	1 522	1.4	3.8
外资银行的分行	…	…	…	…	116	349	0.5	1.1	95	217	0.2	0.6	90	220	0.2	0.6
政策性银行和国家开发银行	3	4 278	7.0	16.1	3	5 645	8.0	18.0	3	6 946	7.7	20.4	3	7 652	7.2	19.2
中国邮政储蓄银行	1	1 769	2.9	6.7	1	2 216	3.1	7.1	1	2 705	3.0	7.9	1	3 397	3.2	8.5
合作金融机构	8 503	5 121	8.3	19.3	5 150	6 295	8.9	20.0	3 263	6 789	7.6	19.9	2 870	7 893	7.4	19.8
农村合作银行	113	646	1.1	2.4	163	1 003	1.4	3.2	196	1 270	1.4	3.7	223	1 500	1.4	3.8
城市信用合作社	42	131	0.2	0.5	22	80	0.1	0.3	11	27	0.0	0.1	1	2	0.0	0.0
农村信用合作社	8 348	4 343	7.1	16.3	4 965	5 211	7.4	16.6	3 056	5 493	6.1	16.1	2 646	6 391	6.0	16.1
新型农村金融机构	27	0	0	0	101	6	0	0	164	25	0	0.1	386	113	0	0.3
村镇银行	19	0	0	0	91	6	0	0	148	25	0	0.1	349	113	0	0.3
农村互助信用合作社	8	0	0	0	10	0	0	0	16	0	0	0	37	0	0	0
非银行金融机构	690	9 744	15.9	36.7	738	8 582	12.2	27.3	772	11 666	13.0	34.3	782	13 168	12.4	33.1
保险公司	102	2 831	4.6	10.6	112	3 280	4.6	10.4	120	3 971	4.4	11.7	125	4 965	4.7	12.5
寿险公司	54	2 351	3.8	8.8	56	2 713	3.8	8.6	59	3 366	3.8	9.9	61	4 267	4.0	10.7
再保险公司	6	89	0.1	0.3	9	101	0.1	0.3	9	116	0.1	0.3	9	115	0.1	0.3
非寿险公司	42	391	0.6	1.5	47	466	0.7	1.5	52	489	0.5	1.4	55	584	0.5	1.5
养老金	39	592	1.0	2.2	39	754	1.1	2.4	39	1 030	1.1	3.0	1	1 138	1.1	2.9

续表

	2007				2008				2009				2010			
	机构数量	总资产(10亿元)	占总资产的比重	占GDP的比重	机构数量	总资产(10亿元)	占总资产的比重	占GDP的比重	机构数量	总资产(10亿元)	占总资产的比重	占GDP的比重	机构数量	总资产(10亿元)	占总资产的比重	占GDP的比重
全国社保基金	1	440	0.7	1.7	1	562	0.8	1.8	1	777	0.9	2.3	1	857	0.8	2.2
企业年金	38	152	0.2	0.6	38	191	0.3	0.6	38	253	0.3	0.7	…	281	0.3	0.7
基金管理公司	59	3 280	5.3	12.3	61	1939	2.7	6.2	60	2 677	3.0	7.9	63	2 520	2.4	6.3
证券投资基金	346	3 280	5.3	12.3	439	1939	2.7	6.2	577	2 677	3.0	7.9	704	2 520	2.4	6.3
证券公司	106	1 734	2.8	6.5	107	1 191	1.7	3.8	106	2 027	2.3	6.0	106	1 967	1.8	4.9
期货公司	177	50	0.1	0.2	171	59	0.1	0.2	167	121	0.1	0.4	164	192	0.2	0.5
合格境外机构投资者	51	286	0.5	1.1	76	179	0.3	0.6	94	290	0.3	0.9	106	297	0.3	0.7
其他非银行金融机构	152	972	1.6	3.7	168	1 181	1.7	3.8	182	1 550	1.7	4.6	213	2 089	2.0	5.2
企业集团财务公司	73	…	…	…	84	975	1.4	3.1	91	1 229	1.4	3.6	107	1 541	1.4	3.9
信托公司	54	…	…	…	54	87	0.1	0.3	58	113	0.1	0.3	63	148	0.1	0.4
金融租赁公司	10	…	…	…	12	80	0.1	0.3	12	160	0.2	0.5	17	316	0.3	0.8
货币经纪公司	2	…	…	…	3	0.1	0.0	0.0	3	0.2	0.0	0.0	4	0.3	0.0	0.0
财务公司	13	…	…	…	15	38	0.1	0.1	18	48	0.1	0.1	22	84	0.1	0.2
贷款公司	4	…	…	…	6	0	0	0	8	0	0	0	9	0.1	0.0	0
汽车金融公司	9	…	…	…	9	38	0.1	0.1	10	48	0.1	0.1	13	84	0.1	0.2
银行业资产管理公司	4	…	…	…	4	…	…	…	4	…	…	…	4	…	…	…
整个金融体系	9 411	61 370	100.0	230.9	6 316	70 564	100.0	224.7	4 539	89 644	100.0	263.3	4 421	106 383	100.0	267.3

资料来源：中国人民银行；中国银监会；中国证监会；中国保监会；中国国家统计局；人力资源和社会保障部；国际货币基金组织工作人员测算。

注：1. 由于没有一家保险公司同时从事险业与寿险业务，因此，这里提供了再保险公司的数据。2007年，保险业采用了新的会计准则，适用于2007年以后的数据。

2. 证券投资基金的收益由基金管理公司代表基金持有人进行管理。

3. 此表不包括四家资产管理公司的资产。根据 FSAP 评估团的测算，截至 2006 年底，被转移到资产管理公司的不良资产账面价值大约为 2.6 万亿元人民币（大约占金融体系总资产的 6%，或 GDP 的 12%）。由于 2006 年后资产管理公司未发布财务报表，故 2007—2010 年的可比数据尚未获得。

4. 此表未包括非正规金融，对这一块有不同的估计值。

注：2008 年、2009 年和 2010 年的数据由中国当局在 FSAP 框架下提供。2007 年的数据从公开渠道收集，特别是三家监管机构的年报和全国社保基金的财务报表。有关农村与城市信用合作社的数据来源于中国银监会的年报。

表5 中国金融发展指标（2005—2010 年）

	2005	2006	2007	2008	2009	2010
银行业						
银行机构总数	—	19 667	8 721	5 578	3 767	3 639
分行数量/百万人口	—	140	144	146	145	146
银行存款/GDP（%）	147.2	153.3	143.5	147.5	169.6	171.3
私人信贷[①]/GDP（%）	114.3	113.0	111.0	108.3	129.3	131.1
银行资产/金融体系资产总值（%）	—	—	84.1	87.8	87.0	87.6
银行资产/GDP（%）	197.1	198.3	194.2	197.4	229.0	234.2
保险						
寿险公司数量	42	48	54	56	59	61
非寿险公司数量	35	38	42	47	52	55
保险深度（保费占 GDP 的百分比）						
寿险	1.8	1.7	1.8	2.2	2.3	—
非寿险	0.9	1.0	1.1	1.0	1.1	—
保险密度（人均保费 人民币）						
寿险	250	272	336	498	554	—
非寿险	129	155	194	234	273	—
养老金						
养老金覆盖的就业人员百分比	30.1	31.5	32.8	35.4	41.2	45.7[②]
养老金资产/GDP（%）	1.5	1.7	2.2	2.4	3.0	2.9
养老金资产/金融体系总资产（%）	—	—	—	1.1	1.1	1.1
按揭						
按揭资产/金融体系总资产（%）	—	—	—	4.2	5.0	5.2
按揭债务存量/GDP（%）	—	—	—	9.4	13.1	14.0
货币市场						
银行间拆借（10 亿元人民币）	1 278	2 150	10 647	15 049	19 350	27 868
质押式回购交易额（10 亿元人民币）	15 678	26 302	44 067	56 383	67 701	84 653
买断式回购交易额（10 亿元人民币）	219	292	726	1 758	2 602	2 940
中央银行票据交易额（10 亿元人民币）	2 893	4 240	8 704	22 827	14 213	17 465
外汇市场						
外汇储备可用于进口的月份数	13.3	14.4	16.8	18.1	24.6	—
外汇储备/短期债务	4.8	5.4	6.5	8.6	9.3	7.6
外汇掉期交易额（10 亿美元）	0	51	315	441	806	1 296
外汇远期交易额（10 亿美元）	2.7	14.1	22.6	17.9	11.7	36.4

	2005	2006	2007	2008	2009	2010
资本市场						
股票市场						
上市公司数量	1 387	1 440	1 550	1 625	1 700	2 063
上市公司市值[3]/GDP（%）	17.5	41.3	123.1	38.6	71.6	66.7
股票市场交易总额/市值[3]（%）	96.4	100.4	140.8	220.1	219.7	205.6
新上市数量	15	66	124	76	99	347
新上市市值（10亿元人民币）	5.8	134.2	481.0	103.4	187.9	488.3
债券市场						
政府债券余额[4]/GDP（%）	27.3	28.9	32.4	31.3	29.3	28.1
金融债券余额/GDP（%）	10.8	12.1	12.7	13.4	15.1	15.0
公司债券余额/GDP（%）	1.7	2.6	3.0	4.1	7.1	8.6
衍生品市场						
在上海证券交易所和深圳证券交易所交易的权证总市值（10亿元人民币）	—	—	54.0	17.5	20.9	1.5
上海证券交易所和深圳证券交易所的权证年交易额（10亿元人民币）	—	—	7 783	6 969	5 365	1 499
商品期货年交易额（万亿元人民币）	—	—	20.5	36.0	65.3	113.5
人民币利率衍生品估计余额[5]（10亿元人民币）	5.0	33.3	217	529	662	1 486
人民币利率衍生品日均交易量（10亿元人民币）	0.0	0.1	0.9	2.1	1.9	6.0
集合投资基金						
持照投资基金数量	—	—	346	439	557	704
基金管理公司数量	—	—	59	61	60	63
投资基金管理的总资产/GDP（%）	—	—	12.3	6.2	7.9	6.3
投资基金中零售投资者占比（%）	—	—	89	81	82	82
备忘：						
名义GDP（10亿元人民币）	18 494	21 631	26 581	31 405	34 051	39 798
人口（百万）	1 304	1 311	1 318	1 325	1 331	1 338

数据来源：中国人民银行；中国银监会；中国证监会；中国保监会；人力资源和社会保障部；中国外汇交易中心；国际清算银行；国际金融统计；世界发展指标；瑞士再保险公司；中国债券信息网。

①包括发放给上市企业的信贷。

②2010年的劳动力数据是估计数。

③包括在上海证券交易所和深圳证券交易所上市公司的所有A股和B股。

④政府债券数据来自国际清算银行，包括国债和中央银行票据。

⑤中国外汇交易中心的估计值。

性融资渠道，但仍主要集中在公共部门证券方面（图12）。尽管最近在建立多层
次股票市场以促进对中小企业融资方面取得了一些进展，但股票市场主要满足
的还是大企业的需要。由保险部门管理的资产不到住户部门银行存款的11%。
信托公司、金融租赁公司和财务公司都在迅速发展，但其规模相对于银行来说
仍然较小。在中国，非正规金融部门也在不断发展，其中一部分向中小企业和
小型零售投资者提供融资。

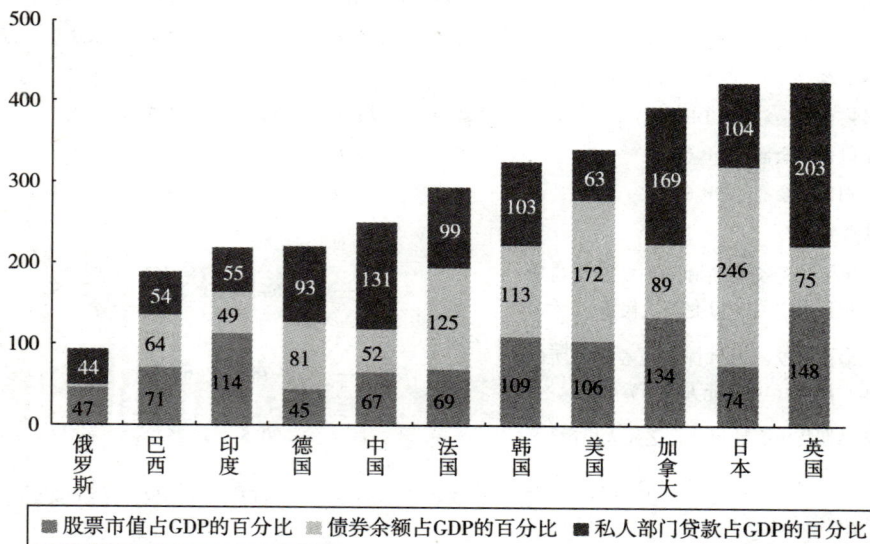

数据来源：彭博；国际货币基金组织《国际金融统计》；国际清算银行；中国银监会；中国证监会；国
际货币基金组织工作人员测算。

注：在中国，私人部门贷款指国内贷款减去对中央政府和非银行金融机构的债权。

图 10　信用中介情况（2010 年）

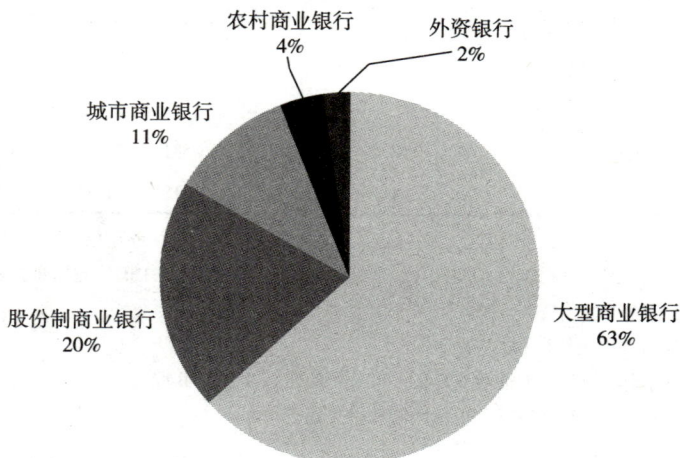

数据来源：CEIC；国际货币基金组织工作人员测算。

图 11　按资产划分的商业银行体系结构（2010 年）

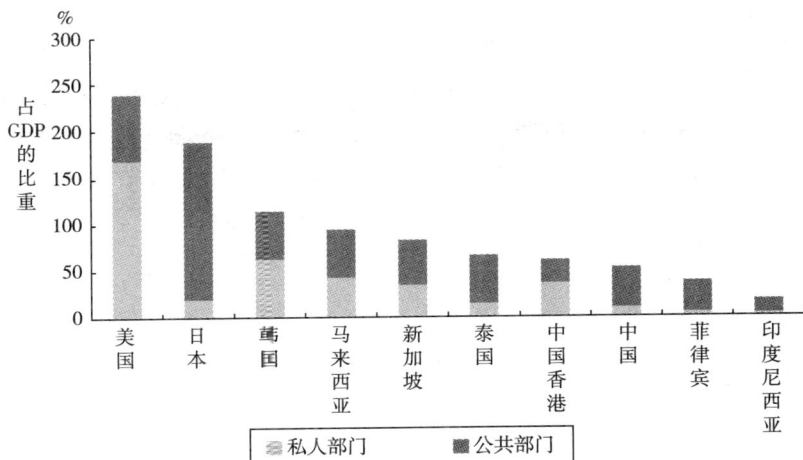

数据来源：中国债券信息网，2010 年，《中国债券市场概览》。

图 12　部分国家（地区）固定收益市场（2009 年）

18. 虽然中国金融市场仍处于发展阶段，但跨市场融合正在增加。 国内市场之间存在明显的划分（例如，国内债券市场划分为交易所交易/零售市场和银行间/批发市场），中国市场和国际金融市场之间也存在划分（部分是由于普遍实行的资本管制）。尽管如此，冲击仍然会在国内不同的市场之间进行传导，收益的正相关性便是证明。市场之间的关联性可能会迅速上升。

19. 银行之间的关联性主要通过银行间回购市场来传导。 对许多小型银行和非银行金融机构来说，要想进行融资，回购市场是必不可少的，而对较大的银行来说，也需要通过回购市场来管理盈余资金。因此，正是通过这个市场，银行体系中一部分受到挤压的流动性能够并且确实扩散到其他部分（第 I 部分 C）。

20. 银行和非银行金融机构之间的相互联系开始增加。 法律和法规允许更复杂的金融结构存在，尽管监管机构在满足并表监管原则关键要素方面面临挑战。自"十一五规划"（2006—2010 年）期间启动金融服务综合经营试点和产融结合集团获得迅速发展以来，金融控股公司发展较快，而随着金融控股公司的发展，相互关联也因此增加。与此同时，适用于影子银行及其关联机构的监管政策也需要明确和透明。为防范和管理跨市场产品和制度结构带来的系统性风险，需要采用更加结构化的监督管理方式。

21. 最后，中国和世界其他地区之间的金融联系过去十分有限，但现在正在迅速增加。 香港特别行政区的人民币存款增长很快（图 13），但相对于大陆的人民币存款而言，金额尚不大。跨境证券资本投资限于合格境内机构投资者（QDII）和合格境外机构投资者（QFII）项目。[②] B 股市场（外国投资者被允许

[②] 2010 年底，88 家 QDII 参与机构的总额度为 684 亿美元，约占国内存款的 0.6%；在 QFII 项下，106 家境外机构投资者分享 197 亿美元的总额度，约占国内债券和股票市值的 0.3%。

投资于中国股票市场的渠道）和 H 股市场（在香港交易所上市的中国公司）被 A 股市场边缘化了（图 14）。此外，A 股和 H 股之间的金融传导仍然有限（图 15）。与其他国家的银行相比，中国的银行体系的资产负债表头寸与世界主要银行业中心的相互联系还不完全相称，但在过去 10 年已经增长了 80%。

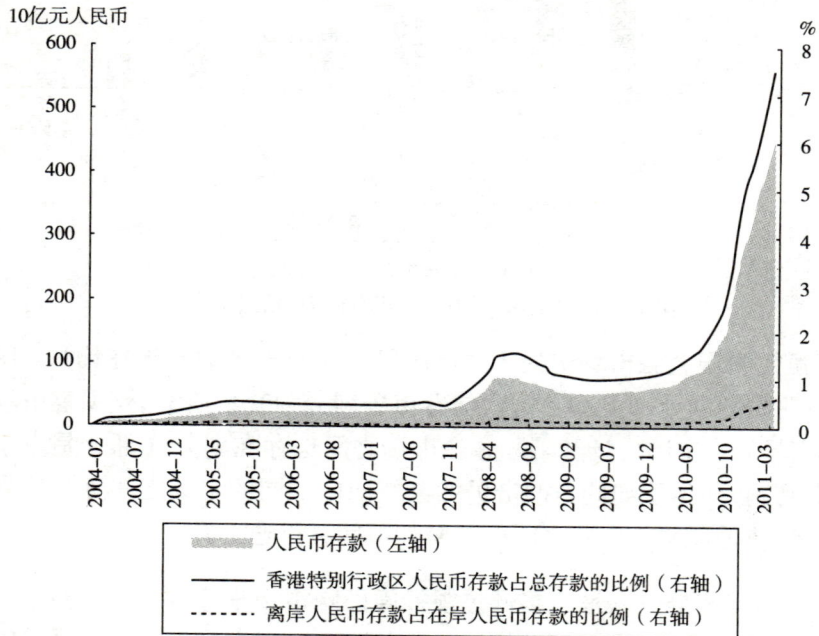

数据来源：CEIC；国际货币基金组织工作人员测算。

图 13　香港特别行政区的人民币存款

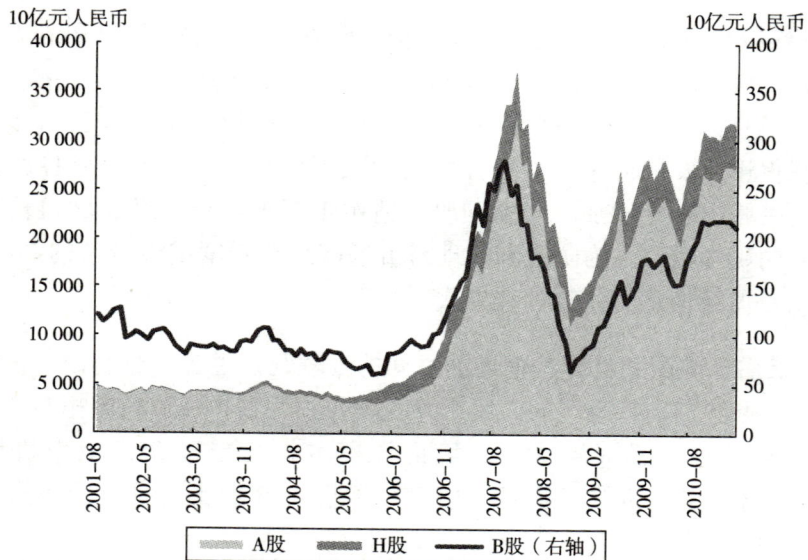

数据来源：CEIC；国际货币基金组织工作人员测算。

图 14　A 股、B 股和 H 股的市值

（指数，2007年1月=100）

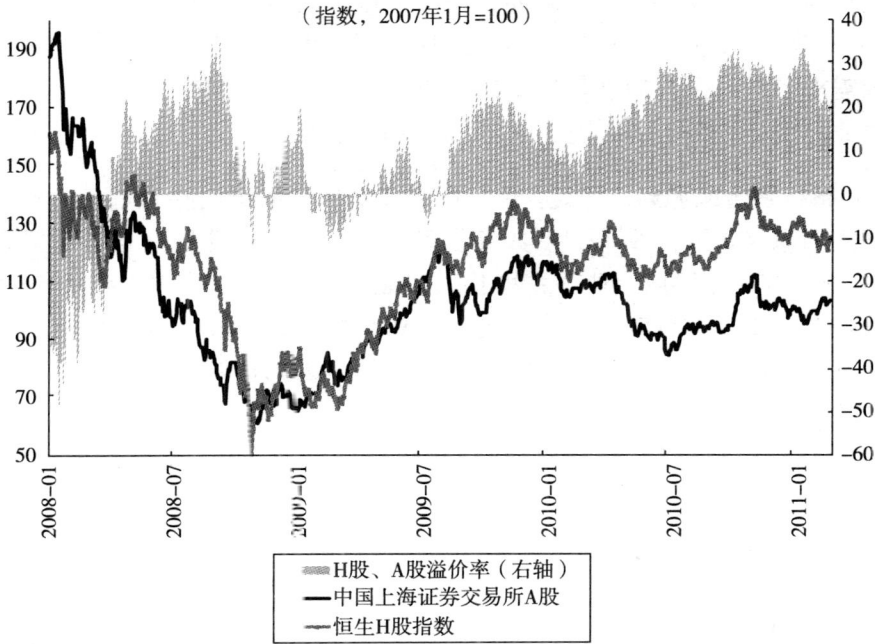

数据来源：CEIC；彭博咨讯；国际货币基金组织工作人员测算。

图 15　A 股和 H 股指数波动情况

C. 银行体系的业绩、稳健性和抗冲击能力

22. 银行部门的资产负债表迅速扩张，部分是近几年由投资驱动的刺激政策造成的。2009 年，人民币贷款总余额增长了 33%，但 2010 年的信贷增速开始放缓（图 16）。外币贷款的迅速增长可能与人民币升值预期有关。银行对基础设施

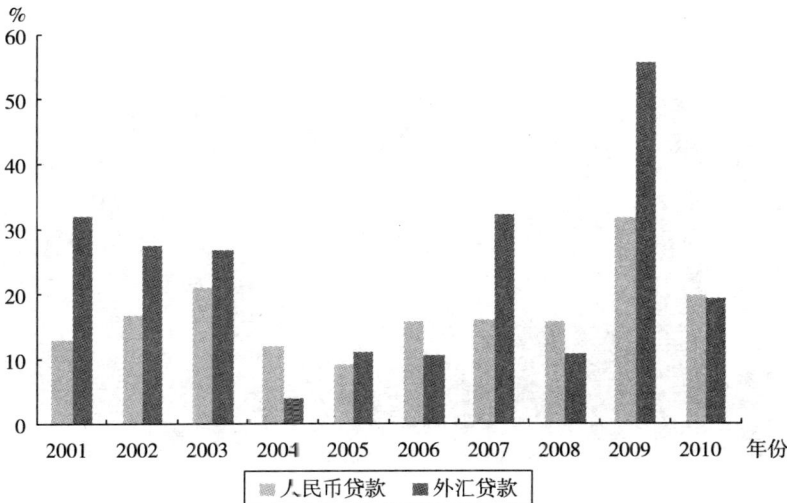

资料来源：CEIC；国际货币基金组织工作人员测算。

图 16　贷款年增长率

建设的风险敞口出现上升，这主要是由地方政府融资平台的扩张造成的，而与此同时，与制造业相关的贷款份额却出现下降。房地产市场的繁荣也刺激了按揭贷款需求上升。银行的表外风险敞口迅速扩大，这主要是随着政府开始调控贷款发放速度导致银行转而进行理财产品促销的结果。

23. **银行资金来源趋于稳定**。规模巨大和低成本的国内存款基础是银行资金来源稳定的原因。银行改革的多数年份里，虽然住户存款仍然是银行资金的主要来源，但2009年国内企业存款增长也很显著（图17）。期限错配问题也呈上升趋势。企业投资项目融资对中长期贷款的依赖日益增加，导致银行的资产平均期限（图18）变长，特别是对大型商业银行来说更是如此。

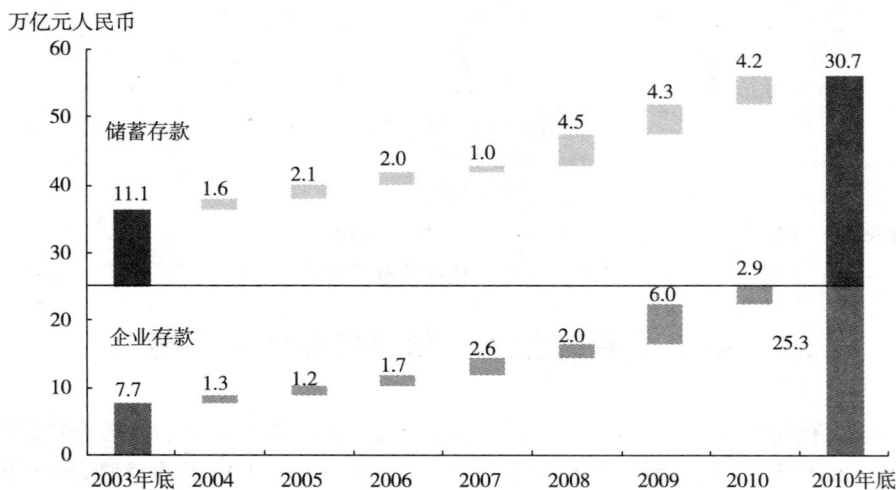

资料来源：中国银监会；国际货币基金组织工作人员测算。

图17　银行存款规模及其增长情况

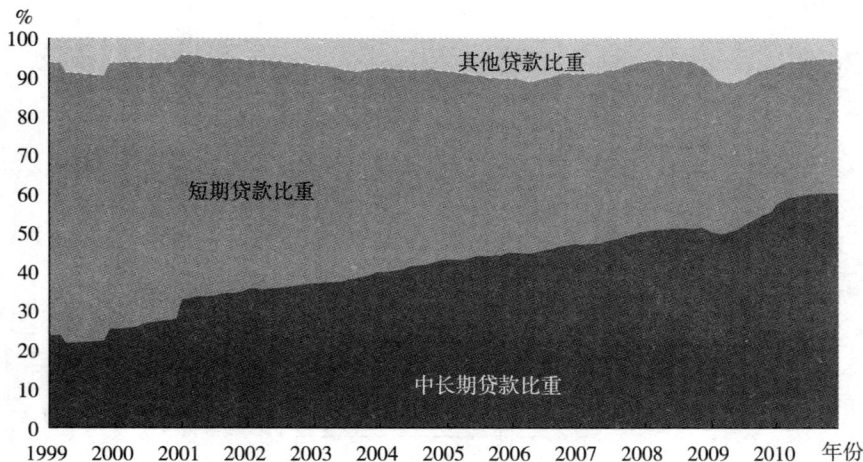

资料来源：CEIC；国际货币基金组织工作人员测算。

图18　贷款到期日结构

24. 银行利润仍保持高位（表 6）。尽管 2009 年利差部分收窄，但信贷扩张支撑了银行的盈利能力。但是，由于中国的银行利润多元化程度有限，主要依赖利息收入，因此，其利润易受管制利差和贷款总量限制的影响。

表 6　中国部分金融健康指标（2005—2010 年）[①]

	2005	2006	2007	2008	2009	2010
主要商业银行		（除另有标明外，均为百分比）				
资本充足情况						
监管资本与风险加权资产的比率[②]	2.5	4.9	8.1	12.0	11.0	12.0
监管一级资本与风险加权资产的比率	…	…	6.0	9.6	8.5	9.6
减去拨备后的不良贷款与资本的比率	…	…	55.9	4.2	1.4	-2.2
资本与资产的比率[③]	4.3	5.2	5.4	5.9	5.3	6.0
资产质量						
不良贷款与贷款总额的比率	8.9	7.5	6.4	2.4	1.6	1.1
贷款损失拨备与不良贷款的比率[③]	24.8	34.3	39.2	117.9	155.4	217.7
部门贷款与贷款总额的比率[④]						
居民	…	…	97.8	97.9	99.3	
吸收存款机构	…	…	5.1	5.7	5.7	…
中央银行	…	…	3.0	2.1	4.2	
其他金融机构	…	…	1.0	1.7	1.1	
政府	…	…	0.0	0.0	0.0	
非金融公司	…	…	70.5	69.8	68.3	
其他国内部门	…	…	18.3	18.5	20.1	
非居民	…	…	2.2	2.1	0.7	
收入与盈利情况						
资产收益率[②]	0.6	0.9	1.4	1.4	1.4	1.5
净资产收益率[②]	15.1	14.9	25.6	24.8	24.7	26.3
利差与总收入的比率[⑤]	…	…	83.6	81.1	78.0	79.1
非利息支出与总收入的比率[⑤]	…	…	41.2	37.0	38.4	35.5
净利差[⑤]	2.5	2.4	2.8	2.9	2.3	2.5
非利息支出与平均资产的比率[⑤]	1.7	1.7	1.6	1.8	1.4	1.4
成本与收入的比率[⑤]	46.3	51.7	39.2	38.1	41.7	36.8
利息收入与营运收入的比率[⑤]	87.4	90.2	87.7	87.1	84.8	84.2
存贷款参考利率差额[③]	333.0	360.0	333.0	306.0	306.0	306.0
流动性						
流动资产与总资产的比率	…	…	22.1	23.5	22.8	22.6
流动资产与短期负债的比率	…	…	37.6	44.7	41.6	41.2
外汇风险敞口						
外汇净头寸与资本的比率	…	…	22.7	12.8	7.4	7.4
非银行部门						
保险业						
覆盖率[⑥]	…	…	444.0	210.0	223.0	206.0
平均净资产收益率（寿险）	…	…	28.7	5.7	17.1	21.1

续表

	2005	2006	2007	2008	2009	2010
平均净资产收益率（非寿险）	...	...	-7.0	-26.2	2.9	21.5
国有企业公司部门						
国有企业的数量⑦	127 067	119 254	115 087	113 731	115 115.0	...
债务权益比	1.7	1.7	1.4	1.4	1.6	...
中央政府	1.4	1.4	1.2	1.3	1.4	...
地方政府	2.4	2.3	1.9	1.8	1.9	...
净资产收益率	5.6	6.2	7.2	8.7	5.7	...
中央政府	8.3	8.6	10.4	6.8	7.0	...
地方政府	2.2	3.2	6.4	4.4	4.3	...
资产收益率	2.0	2.1	3.0	3.6	2.2	...
中央政府	3.2	3.2	4.8	3.0	3.0	...
地方政府	0.6	0.9	2.2	1.5	1.5	...
债务偿还覆盖率⑧	4.12	4.43	7.25	3.72	4.3	...
中央政府	6.55	6.96	7.41	4.36	5.0	...
地方政府	2.83	3.33	4.30	2.94	3.4	...
中小企业						
中小企业的数量⑨	242 061	269 031	300 262	385 721	393 074	
债务权益比	1.45	1.42	1.38	1.31	1.26	
资产收益率	5.75	6.52	7.84	8.44	8.6	
净资产收益率	14.06	15.82	18.70	19.51	19.5	
债务偿还覆盖率⑧	6.47	7.09	7.33	7.43	8.64	
房地产部门						
商业房地产价格上涨率⑩	5.6	4.0	5.8	4.6	...	...
住房价格上涨率⑩	8.4	6.4	8.2	7.1	...	...
国内住房贷款占贷款总额的比率⑪	...	...	...	12.5	14.0	14.5

数据来源：中国人民银行，财政部，中国银监会，中国保监会，国务院国有资产监督管理委员会，国家统计局，国际货币基金组织《全球金融稳定报告》，Bankscope 全球银行与金融机构数据库，国际货币基金组织工作人员测算。

①除另有标明外，该表中的所有数据均由中国金融监管机构在 FSAP 框架下提供。以下脚注指出来源于其他公开可获得或由国际货币基金组织 FSAP 评估团测算得出的数据。

②由于覆盖面不同，跨年度数据的可比性受到限制。2005 年和 2006 年数据是指国际货币基金组织《全球金融稳定报告》中的整个银行业的数据，而 2008 年到 2010 年数据是指中国当局向 FSAP 评估团提供的 17 家主要商业银行数据。

③资本充足和资产质量指标根据中国银监会 2010 年年报的数据计算后得出。这里将资本与资产比率定义为所有者权益与资产的比率。利差是根据中国人民银行《货币政策执行报告》中的数据计算得出。

④该比率的分子与分母根据国内汇总数据计算。

⑤17 家主要商业银行的简单平均数。FSAP 评估团的计算基于银行的财务报表和 Bankscope 全球银行与金融机构数据库。

⑥实际偿付能力额度与法定偿付能力额度之比。

⑦三级以上的非金融国有企业数量。国务院国有资产监督管理委员会直接持有的国有企业称为一级企业。一级国有企业直接持有的子公司称为二级企业。二级企业直接持有的子公司称为三级企业。

⑧偿还利息和缴纳税金前的盈利占利息和本金支出的百分比。

⑨工业行业的中小企业数量。

⑩商业房地产和住房价格指数的百分比变化。

⑪中国银监会根据法人机构信贷数据获得的统计。

25. 银行体系的不良贷款（NPL）率呈持续下降趋势，2010 年底达 1.1%（图 19）。下降的主要原因包括信贷的迅速扩张、不良贷款水平的下降，以及 2008 年对一家银行的 8 160 亿元人民币不良贷款进行剥离。从更长的时间段来看，1999—2001 年和 2004—2005 年国有银行重组时进行的大规模不良贷款剥离使银行总体不良贷款率保持低位。③不良贷款的低水平也得益于强劲的经济增长和银行风险管理的改善。但是，信贷的快速增长可能会导致今后几年银行资产质量的恶化。此外，由于约有 95% 的银行贷款将在一年内进行重新定价，如果人民银行继续收紧信贷政策的话，会导致借款成本上升，实力较弱的借款人将会出现偿贷问题。

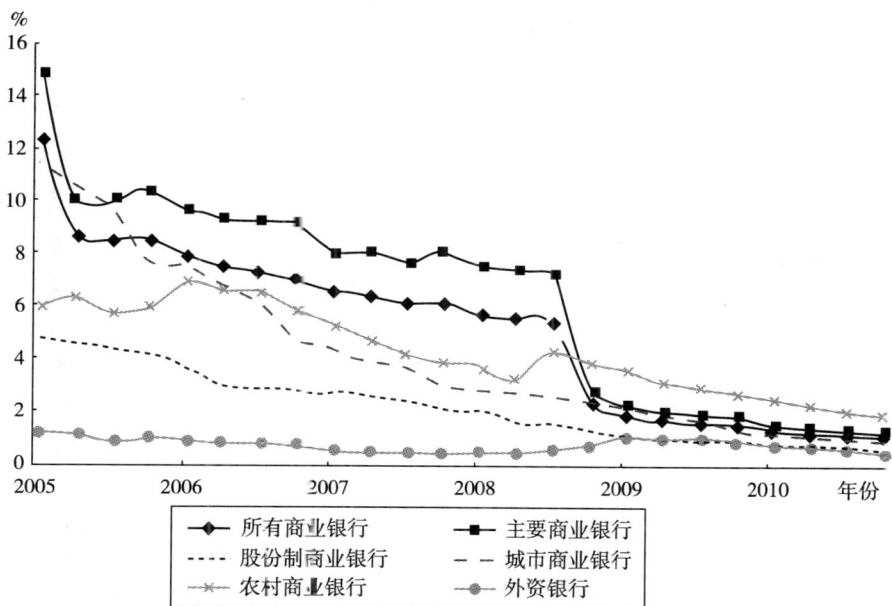

资料来源：CEIC。

图 19　不良贷款占总贷款的比率

26. 中央银行的汇率风险敞口较大。大量的经常账户盈余和有管理的浮动汇率制度共同导致了巨额外汇储备的积累和中央银行外币头寸净敞口较大。就商业银行而言，虽然规模要小得多，但从总量来看，其在外国资产方面也是多头（图 20）。

27. 近期内，流动性压力风险看来有限。银行部门的基本流动性指标较为健康。大银行一般是通过银行间市场向小银行和其他金融机构回补流动性（图 21 和图 22）。大部分银行间拆借者有抵押，且抵押品质量较高，同时流动性充裕，这些都降低了近期出现市场压力的可能性。但是，银行间市场存在着一些风险。

---

③　根据 FSAP 评估团的计算，到 2006 年年底，向资产管理公司转移的不良资产的账面价值达到了 2.6 万亿元人民币。

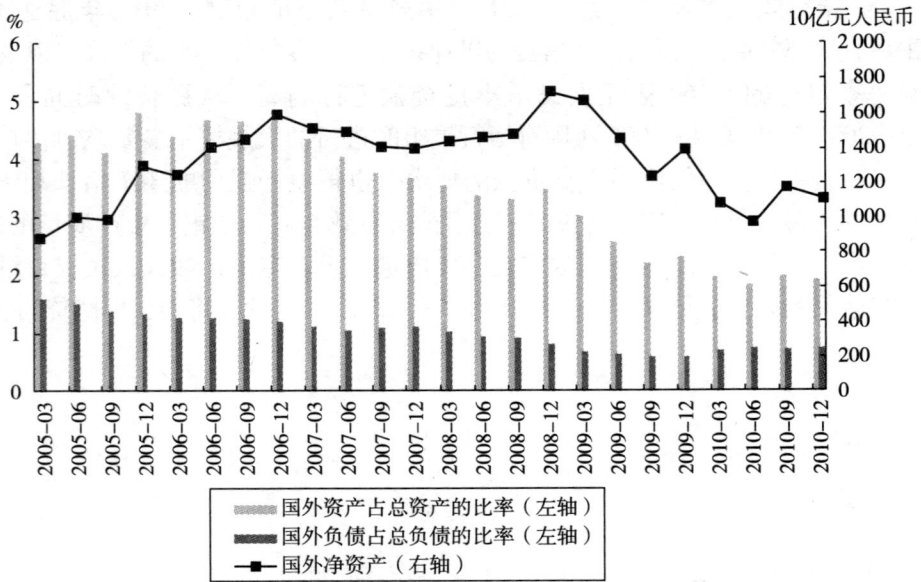

资料来源：CEIC；国际货币基金组织工作人员测算。

图20　存款性公司的国外资产和负债头寸

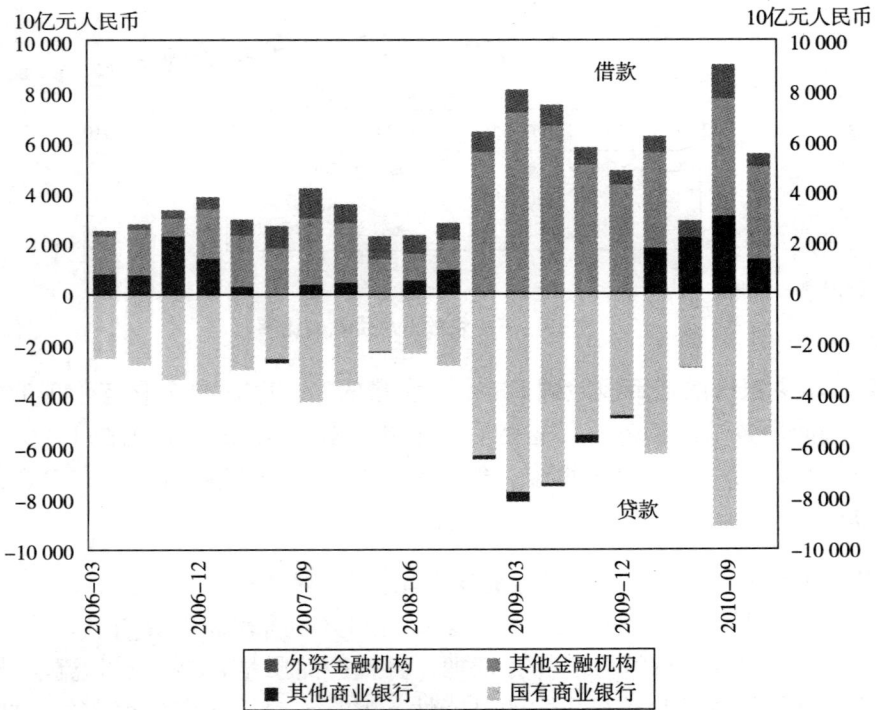

资料来源：中国人民银行。

图21　银行间市场资金流动——回购

银行间存在着持续的流动性失衡，其中小型银行和非银行金融机构特别依赖批发融资。局部的流动性紧缺可能会从面临流动性冲击时不能兑现其抵押证券面值的少数机构扩大为更广范围的流动性冲击。在无法从市场获得流动性的情况下，人民银行的存贷款便利应发挥后备作用。

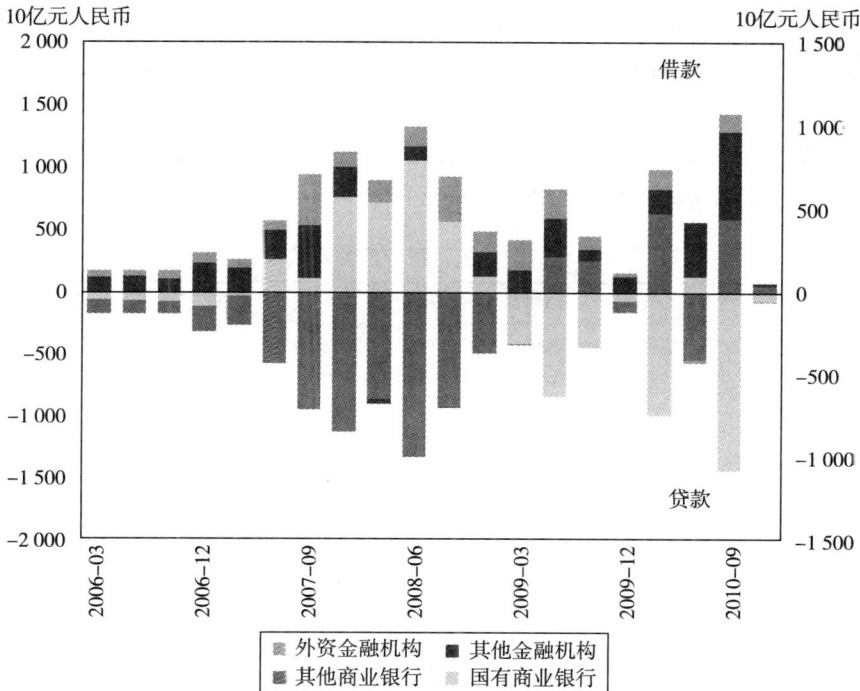

资料来源：中国人民银行。

图22　银行间市场资金流动——通知贷款

D. 压力测试结果摘要

28. 为掌握中国金融体系的主要风险，FSAP 评估团和人民银行/银监会小组联合进行了一次压力测试④。人民银行/银监会小组自上而下的测试结果和银行机构自下而上的测试结果（以 17 家银行为样本）均按总量和银行类型提供给了 FSAP 评估团。FSAP 评估团还根据公开的数据对同样 17 家银行进行了自上而下的测试。

限制条件

29. 种种因素妨碍了对风险的程度及其如何影响经济和金融体系进行充分的评估。首先，由于部门风险敞口和银行贷款企业类型方面的数据制约，无法完全

---

④　相关方法参见表7 和附录 I。

覆盖银行体系面临的所有类型的风险。同时，由于数据制约，除直接汇率风险相关的头寸外，无法对表外头寸和业务情况进行准确分析。而且，宏观情景测试多是基于主要金融数据（如不良贷款）相对较短的时间序列，且在时间序列中有结构性断点，这限制了经济计量分析的可靠性。在有些领域，由于 FSAP 评估团无法获得机密信息，所使用的公开可得信息可能不准确、不充足或缺失（如对地方政府融资平台的风险敞口和传染性风险测试），从而无法对结果进行完全的一致性验证、分析和交叉检验。最后，压力测试的假定前提是保持现状（即当前的宏观金融环境）。随着改革的深入，银行体系可能会面临现有风险放大或新的不确定性，虽然，恰当实施的改革进程和更有力的风险管理和公司治理将有助于减轻不利的金融后果。

表7　中国：银行压力测试

		偿付能力压力测试		流动性压力测试
		敏感性压力测试	情景压力测试	
1	压力测试是由谁进行的	• 三个互补方式：FSAP 评估团；人民银行/银监会小组；以及受指导样本银行 • 人民银行/银监会小组的自上而下和银行的自下而上的测试结果已经按总量水平和按银行类型分组提供给了 FSAP 评估团 • 这些结果后又由 FSAP 评估团使用公开可获得的数据进行了交叉检验		• 银行
2	覆盖的机构/市场份额	• 17 家主要银行（5 家大型商业银行和 12 家股份制商业银行）占 2010 年年底商业银行体系资产的 83%（整个银行体系的 66%） • 2010 年年底，对 5 家大型商业银行进行了传染性风险测试，它们占商业银行体系资产的 63%（整个银行体系的 50%）		• 17 家主要银行，占 2010 年年底商业银行体系资产的 83%（银行体系的 66%）
3	冲击的严重程度	• 信贷总量：不良贷款上升 100%~400%；阈值法（分别有 10%、25%、50% 的银行达不到最低资本充足率要求，2%、4%、6%GDP 的资本注入） • 信贷集中度风险：部门不良贷款率上升到 5%、10%、15% 或不良贷款上升 100%、200%、400%。包括最大的借款人违约、房地产相关的风险（两类），对地方政府融资平台的风险敞口，对"产能过剩产业"的风险敞口，对出口导向部门的风险敞口，以及对贷款增长最快的部门（行业）和地区的风险敞口 • 市场风险：利率 54 个、81 个、108 个基点的平行上移和银行资产组合中基准贷款利率 18 个、27 个、36 个基点的下降；交易组合 50 个、100 个、150 个基点的上行；汇率：5%、10% 和 15% 的升值	三种情景 • 轻度：GDP（7%），M_2（14.7%），房地产价格（-7%），利率（变动 35 个基点），人民币实际汇率（117.5） • 中度：GDP（5%），M_2（12.4%），房地产价格（-16.2%），利率（66 个基点），人民币实际汇率（119.6） • 重度：GDP（4%），M_2（10.2%），房地产价格（-25.9%），利率（95 个基点），人民币实际汇率（123.0） 说明：这三种情景是根据一组知名专家对中国经济的问卷调查结果而设计	对每一个风险时间段的三种情景： • 7 天：债券价格下降（1%、3%、5%）；存款支取（2%、4%、6%）；银行间拆借下降（5%、10%、15%）；法定准备金比率上升（0、0.5%、1%） • 30 天：（4%、7%、10%）到期贷款变成不良贷款；债券价格下降（3%、5%、8%）；存款支取（4%、6%、8%）；银行间拆借下降（5%、10%、15%）；法定准备金比率上升（0、0.5%、1%）

		偿付能力压力测试		流动性压力测试
		敏感性压力测试	情景压力测试	
4	使用的数据	• FSAP 评估团：公开可获得的数据 • 当局：监管和审计数据 • 银行：内部风险管理系统数据		• 数据来自银行的内部风险管理系统
5	风险时间段	• 1 个季度，1 年或 2 年	1 年	• 7 天和 30 天
6	衡量标准（最低比率）	• 最低资本充足率（8%）		• 流动性比率（25%） • 流动性缺口（零）
7	包括的头寸和风险因素	• 所有的表内头寸（除与直接汇率风险相关的头寸外） • 信用风险、市场风险和传染性风险	• 资产负债表表内头寸	• 资产和负债头寸
8	方法	• 资产负债表法（违约损失率＝50%） • 零信贷增长 • 零利润 • 零拨备	• 当局：经济计量模型 • 银行：经济计量模型与专家评估相结合 • FSAP 评估团：根据国际经验进行交叉核对	测试中将融资流动性与流动资产折扣合并考虑

资料来源：FSAP 压力测试小组。

30. 在考虑到这些限制条件的情况下，压力测试结果表明，主要银行能够吸纳中度潜在损失。这反映了近几年来利润率的提高和资产负债表的改善，使银行得以积累起应对损失的缓冲。单因素敏感性测试表明，该体系将能够承受一系列单独发生的特定部门的冲击。这些特定冲击包括银行对房地产部门、地方政府融资平台、出口部门和其他部门的信贷资产恶化。然而，宏观经济情景分析表明，如果几个重大冲击同时发生，则银行体系会受到严重影响。

信用风险

31. 银行体系能够承受信用风险大量增加的冲击（图 23）。假定不良贷款水平在两年内增加 400%（冲击后的不良贷款率达到约 6%），那么，以 2010 年年底数据为基础进行的测试表明，没有任何银行的资本充足率（CAR）低于最低监管要求（8%）。2008—2010 年抗冲击能力的提高反映出不良贷款水平的下降。此外，由于 2010 年银行资本状况明显改善，使得样本银行即使在重度冲击下也能够满足资本充足率的最低监管要求。

32. FSAP 评估团和人民银行/银监会联合小组进行的逆向压力测试（"阈值法"）也验证了这种抗冲击能力。例如，根据 2009 年年底的数据，若使银行体系的一半（以总资产衡量）突破资本充足率的最低监管要求，则不良资产总额与总贷款的比率需上升至近 11%。或者说，假定银行体系需要占 GDP 6% 的资本

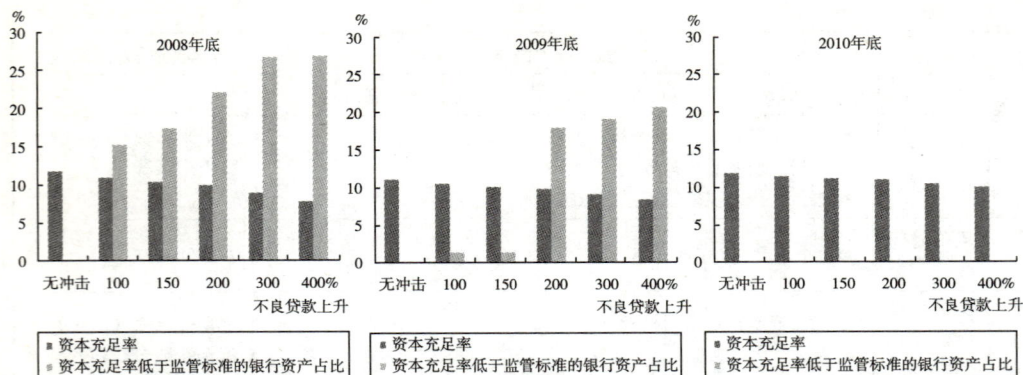

资料来源：中国人民银行，中国银监会。

图23 总体信用风险：敏感性分析

注入，那么，不良贷款率需要达到24.8%（而2009年年底的不良贷款率实际为1.6%）。

33. 人民银行/银监会联合小组和各家银行进行的压力测试表明，来自房地产部门的冲击对信贷资产质量的影响可控。一共进行了两项测试。第一项测试是由人民银行/银监会联合小组和各家银行共同进行的，假设的冲击包括个人抵押贷款、房地产开发贷款和土地储备贷款的不良贷款水平上升。以2010年年底的数据为基础，如果15%的开发商和土地储备贷款以及7.5%的抵押贷款变成不良贷款，那么，17家银行整体资本充足率水平会下降1个百分点，但没有银行会下降到最低监管要求之下（图24）。第二项测试由各银行自行完成，是第一项测试的扩展。在第二项测试中，除了上面所列三个房地产贷款细项外，还假设房

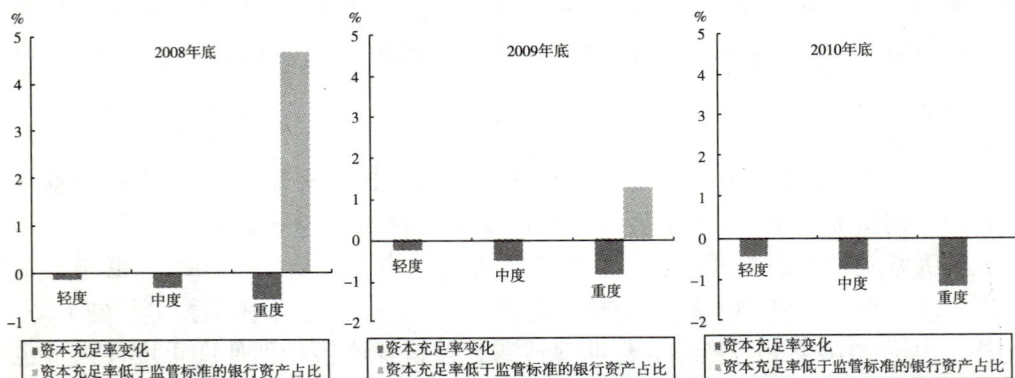

资料来源：中国人民银行，中国银监会。

注：轻度情景——5%的房地产开发贷款和土地储备贷款，以及3%的个人抵押贷款转为不良贷款；

中度情景——10%的房地产开发贷款和土地储备贷款，以及4.5%的个人抵押贷款转为不良贷款；

重度情景——15%的房地产开发贷款和土地储备贷款，以及7.5%的个人抵押贷款转为不良贷款。

图24 贷款集中度：房地产敏感性分析

地产价格下降造成与其存在"上下游关系"的 6 个相关行业⑤出现偿付困难。测试结果显示房地产价格下降 30%、利率提高和由此对相关行业产生的冲击，其影响非常小，使银行整体资本充足率下降不到 0.25 个百分点（图 25）。

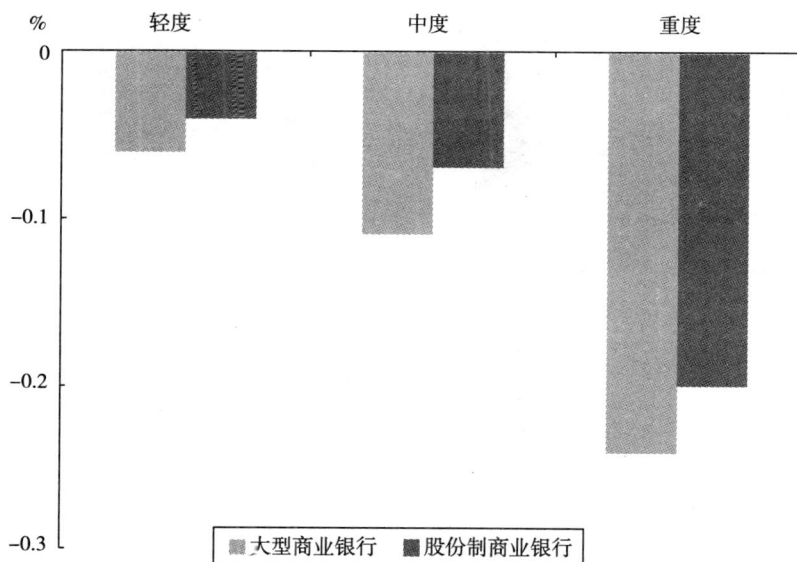

资料来源：中国人民银行，中国银监会。

注：轻度情景——房地产价格下降 10%，利率上升 27 个基点；中度情景——房地产价格下降 20%，利率上升 54 个基点；重度情景——房地产价格下降 30%，利率上升 108 个基点。

图 25 资本充足率的变化：贷款集中度：房地产—替代方法（2010 年 3 月）

34. 此次压力测试还评估了地方政府融资平台贷款的潜在损失。各家银行开展的自下而上压力测试结果表明，如果银行地方政府融资平台贷款出现 15% 的损失，将只有两家小型股份制商业银行资本充足率下降至最低监管要求以下（图 26）。

直接利率风险

35. 银行账户和交易账户的直接利率风险可控。测试中使用了存贷款利率冲击，由人民银行/银监会联合小组和各家银行对其影响（以这种冲击可能带来的资本充足率变化来衡量）进行了评估。结果表明，即使发生严重的联合冲击，所有 17 家银行的资本充足率也只会轻微下降（图 27）。交易账户收益率曲线平移风险也由各家银行进行了测试，结果再次表明，其影响非常小（图 28）。

⑤ 这些行业是（i）钢铁行业；（ii）水泥、石灰和石膏制造业；（iii）砖、石和其他建筑材料制造业；（iv）房屋建筑业；（v）家具制造业；以及（vi）家电制造业。

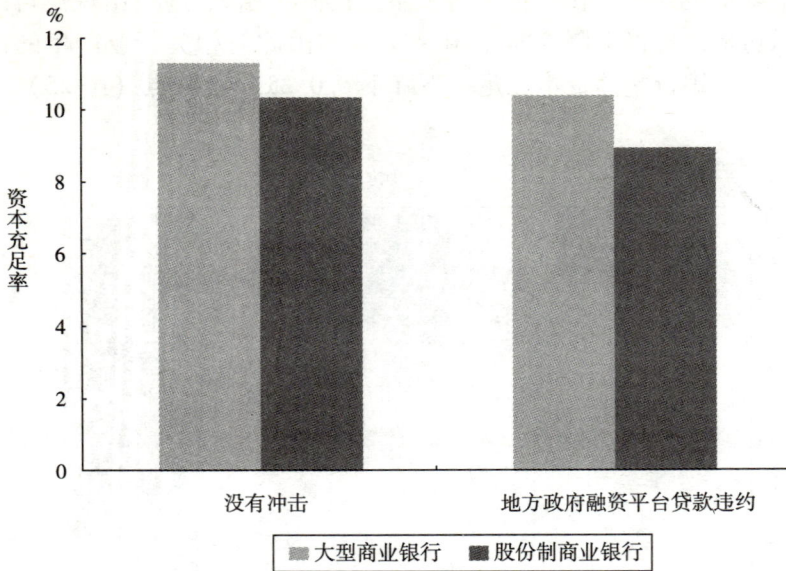

关键假设：15%的地方政府融资平台贷款违约。违约损失率为50%。

资料来源：中国人民银行，中国银监会。

注：未向FSAP压力测试小组提供银行对地方政府融资平台风险敞口数据。

图26　银行对地方政府融资平台的风险敞口测试（2009年年底）

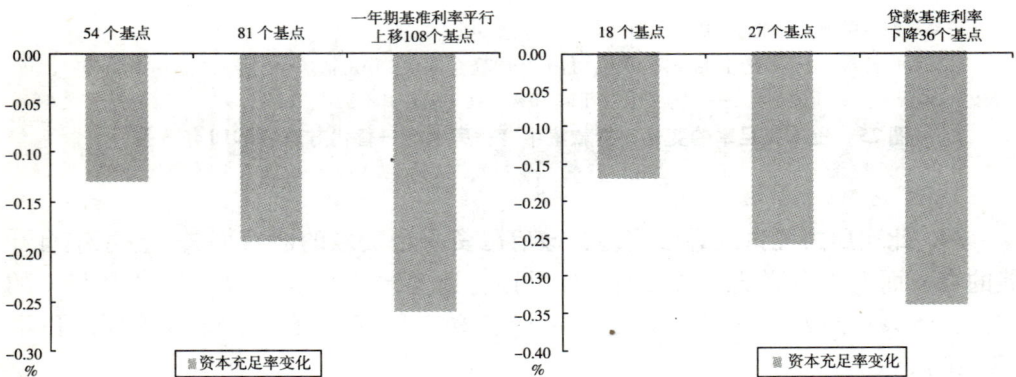

资料来源：中国人民银行，中国银监会。

图27　利率风险：银行账户（2009年年底）

直接汇率风险

36. **汇率变动对银行体系的直接影响有限。**人民银行/银监会联合小组的自上而下和各银行的自下而上的压力测试表明，在重度冲击下，银行体系的整体资本充足率下降不到0.1个百分点，所有17家银行的资本充足率仍高于最低监管要求（图29）。

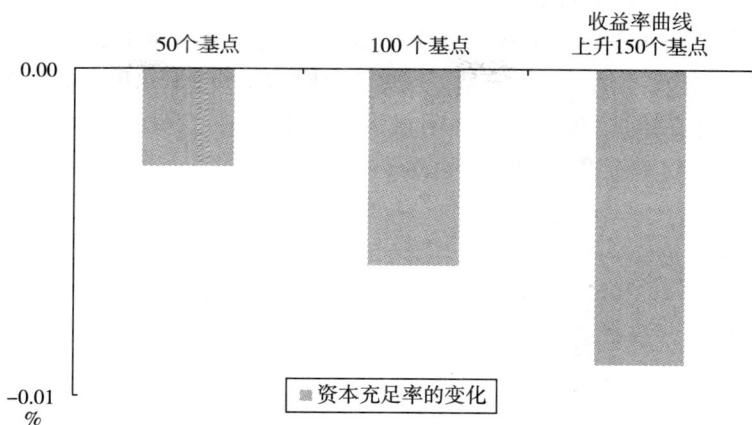

资料来源：中国人民银行，中国银监会。

注：按一个季度的时间区间评估。

图28 利率风险：交易账户（2009年年底）

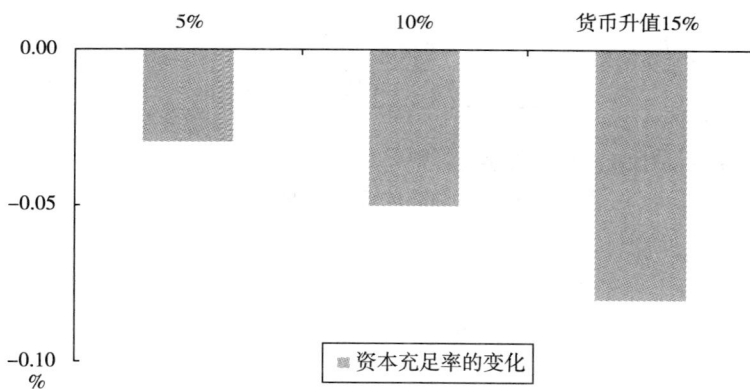

资料来源：中国人民银行，中国银监会。

注：冲击指人民币对美元升值，同时假定美元对其他货币汇率保持稳定。

图29 直接汇率风险（2009年年底）

流动性风险

37. 此次压力测试开展了两轮流动性风险压力测试。在第一轮测试中，即不考虑银行出售债券的能力，结果对流动性影响较大，例如，有6家银行在7天时间内出现了现金流负缺口。在第二轮中结果稍好，即假定银行能够折价抛售债券，30天的时间窗口内有16家银行的现金流缺口为正。

宏观情景测试

38. 宏观经济情景分析表明，如果几个重大冲击同时发生，会给银行体系带

来严重影响（图 30）。例如，重度冲击下（GDP 年增长率放缓至 4%），银行体系整体资本充足率水平约为 8%，其中，资本充足率低于 8% 的银行的资产之和约占 17 家银行总资产的 1/4。该情景分析的结果与之前 FSAP 评估问卷调查的结果基本一致，即在重度冲击（GDP 明显放缓）情况下，产出增长率每下降 1 个百分点，不良贷款率上升至少 1 个百分点。

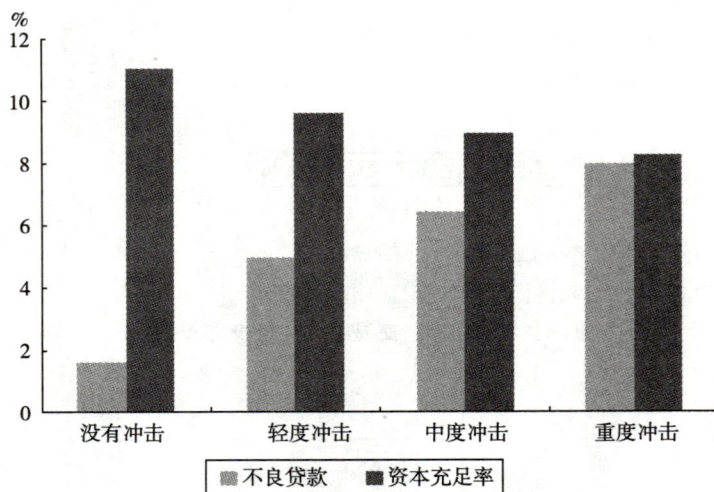

资料来源：中国人民银行，中国银监会。

图 30　宏观情景测试结果（2009 年年底）

II. 管理风险：升级危机管理工具箱

A. 金融稳定框架

39. 为加强宏观审慎监测，应该建立一个常设的金融稳定委员会，由人民银行承担其秘书处职责。委员会应由一位非常有权威的官员担任主席，并应该有明确的职责和授权来识别和监测系统性风险的发生情况，并提出解决建议。委员会成员将包括一行三会、财政部和其他相关部委或机构。作为委员会秘书处的人民银行与各监管机构将有权提供和获得必要信息，包括特定机构的机密监管信息。

40. 应该加强数据搜集，以便更好地了解金融机构的资产负债表及其联系。这些数据应该包括杠杆率水平、期限错配、大额风险敞口、或有负债、表外头寸、未受监管的产品以及跨竟和跨部门（如住房、地方政府）风险敞口，这进而要求加强对金融机构的非金融交易对手的数据搜集工作。制订一个前瞻性的早期预警系统，纳入宏观指标和金融指标、金融稳健指标、系统性风险指标以及资产负债表信息等，将有助于识别有可能威胁金融体系的宏观经济和金融发展动向。

41. 需要继续努力构建一个全面的宏观审慎管理制度框架以评估和管理系统性风险。中国已经在运用一些宏观审慎工具来处理这些风险，包括对系统重要性金融机构提出额外资本要求、动态拨备，可变资本要求、法定准备金要求，以及与贷款价值比和贷存比相关的要求。需要进一步完善这些缓冲标准和要求，明确说明这些指标是如何随着情况的变动而变化。同时，还应增加人民银行及其他监管机构用于监测金融稳定和进行定期压力测试的资源和能力。

B. 系统流动性管理

42. 人民银行应开始吸纳金融体系中的剩余流动性。这就需要大大增加公开市场操作的使用，直到人民银行不再需要依赖对银行贷款的行政性限制为止。随着流动性状况的收紧，银行将会有动力来改进其内部流动性管理，更加重视权衡贷款配置中的风险与收益。

43. **同时，可考虑引入平均准备金制度**。这样做将有利于流动性管理，并增强稳定性和效率。法定准备金按日调整的特点意味着，它主要是银行的一个总量流动性管理工具，而不是一个审慎缓冲。银行往往会为缓冲目的而持有大量低收益的超额准备金，这实际上是对银行中介活动的一种额外税收。在整个银行体系，这些准备金平均约为存款的 2% ~ 3%，但是，不同类型银行的实际持有金额有很大不同。因此，平均准备金制度将有助于降低这一额外税收，并减轻所有机构特别是小型机构的流动性管理负担，同时限制流动性压力在机构间传导的可能性。

44. **中央银行应该开始制订短期回购利率目标**。为进一步加强对短期利率的管理，中央银行可以提高对超额准备金支付的利率，以缩小该利率与贴现率之间的差异。为支持间接工具的使用，并作为结构流动性回笼的补充，人民银行可以通过更多地使用较长期回购来延长其公开市场操作的期限。

45. **随着时间的推移，人民银行应该提高其进行每日流动性操作的能力**。最近的国际经验表明，即使在流动性看似充裕的情况下，也有可能会发生流动性危机。人民银行需要进行更高频率的流动性预测，这就要求加强财政部、国家外汇管理局与人民银行之间的信息交流。

46. **人民银行存贷款便利的使用应该更加自动和透明，并通过其定价机制来解决道德风险问题**。人民银行对存贷款便利的使用拥有相当的自由裁量权，使得资金的拨付变得复杂，并有可能会延迟资金拨付。要解决这一问题，需要降低人民银行的自由裁量权，使各存贷款便利的使用自动化，并对所有国内注册的机构都实施统一的抵押要求。这样会提供一个有约束力且有效的利率通道，强化人民银行的利率指导。

C. 危机管理、处置和存款保险

47. **中国的危机管理安排由国务院负责**。随着金融体系的日趋复杂，处置工具箱需要相应的扩充。当前的工具箱实质上是对不可持续经营银行的"不关闭处置"和对存款人的隐性全额担保，实际上由人民银行承担了存款保险的责任。这就意味着存在严重的道德风险。一个更全面的工具箱应当包括安全网和有效的机制安排，赋予相关管理机构操作自主性和法律权力，以便对那些财务状况不佳、难以持续经营的金融机构进行快速干预。

48. **应该加快实施正在酝酿的显性存款保险制度，以便提供结构化的安全网**。此制度也有助于对破产银行进行有序处置。建立存款保险制度，应该吸收国际存款保险协会制订的原则。同时，妥善设计其组织结构，并考虑以下因素：大量的存款类机构、日趋复杂的结构、不同机构在处置中的作用，以及在处置倒闭机构时澄清政府特别是人民银行承担的或有负债情况。

49. **需要重新审视并加强所有部门有关金融机构破产法律**。应指定一家独立的实体单位，赋予其管理被干预机构的能力以及用于处置（包括注资、部分或全部出售或清算）这类机构的资源。该实体单位的资金应来自业内以降低（如果不是消除）对政府支持的依赖。在机制上，处理倒闭机构问题资产的能力是一个重要方面。该实体单位可以负责实施存款保险制度和管理倒闭机构的资产。同时，应为目前四家资产管理公司制订策略。第一步，应要求资产管理公司定期公布财务报表和管理报告，并最终将大部分（如果不是全部）转变为商业机构。

D. 宏观金融框架

50. **中国在金融稳定方面的一个内在特征是，宏观经济政策框架和金融部门之间是相互联系的**。正是由于这一原因，中国的金融体系尽管从审慎角度来看是稳定的，如问题贷款水平不高、贷款拨备充足以及主要借款人的杠杆率（仍然）很低等，但同时还存在着配置低效和结构脆弱性。正如前面所述，商业银行经常成为货币政策和财政政策的实施工具。因此，现行政策框架严重扭曲了激励机制，并给公共资产负债表带来了或有负债风险。在完善风险管理的同时，有必要继续强化审慎监管，但金融体系的进一步深化和成熟很大程度上需要在宏观经济政策框架的演变过程中来实现。

51. **人民银行应该更多地依靠间接货币政策工具来进行宏观经济调控**。市场化的利率应该取代信贷增长目标成为管理信贷扩张的主要工具。这会降低货币调控在面临资本流入、表外贷款和其他金融创新时，被越来越多地规避并变得无效的风险。同时，还会增强银行实施差别贷款利率和改善信贷配置的能力。

52. **一个自由、灵活的汇率市场对执行货币政策是必要的，同时可以减少人民银行流动性管理所面临的挑战**。目前这种高度的外汇干预需要显著的对冲举措。此外，对汇率波动的单向博弈的想法引发资本流入，从而使金融市场的情况变得更加复杂。增加汇率市场的灵活性将会降低与跨境资本流动和交易相联系的金融稳定风险，减轻人民银行面临的流动性管理挑战，并为间接货币政策工具的独立使用提供更大的空间。要实施这些措施，需要加强市场和系统性风险监测以及跨境监管。

III. 加强金融监管

53. 对监管框架的评估（表 8）显示，该框架与国际标准高度一致，但挑战犹存。[⑥]挑战是如何提高其效率、质量和反应能力。在加强监管与实现金融体系有效创新和发展之间应取得适当的平衡。评估的一个中心主题是增强监管机构的操作自主权，提升技能和风险监测能力，增加资源并加强机构间协调。

表 8　中国金融体系管理架构

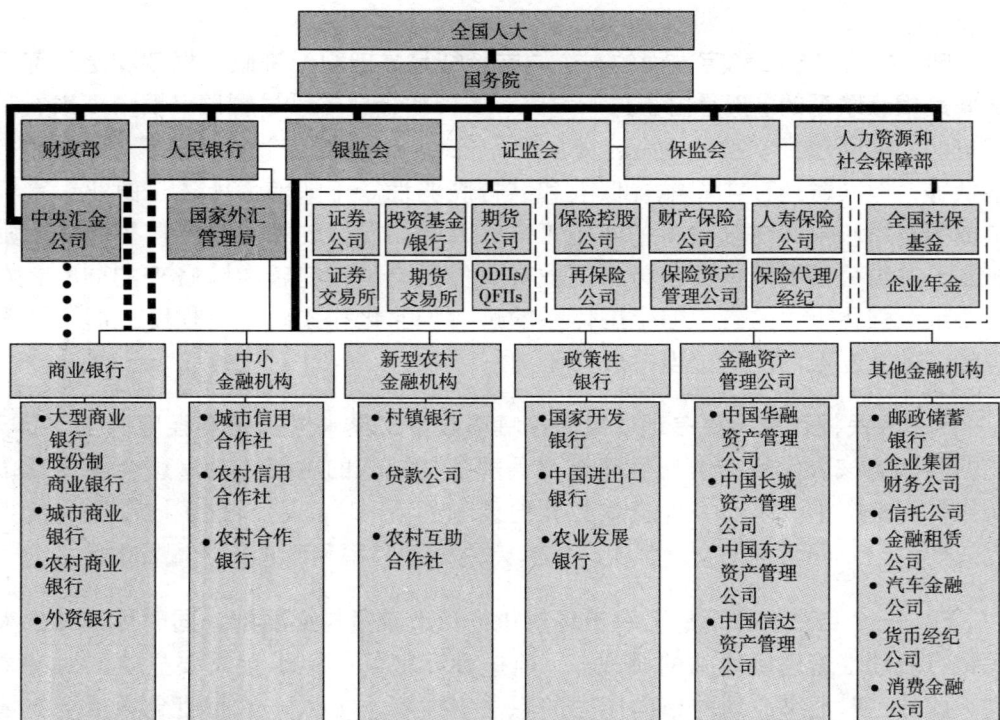

注：最粗的连结线表示制定金融政策的最高当局。全国人大颁布所有金融部门法律，国务院执行金融监管，并对所有的监管机构予以政策指导。点连线表示中国人民银行的三项主要职责：制定货币政策、维护金融稳定和提供金融服务；同时也表示财政部作为税收管理者、财政管理者和部分商业银行的所有者的三重角色。从银监会、证监会、保监会以及人力资源和社会保障部引出的较细连结线表示，这些机构主要负责对相关金融行业的监管。此外，国家外汇管理局负责监管证券和保险公司的外汇操作。国家开发银行和邮政储蓄银行正在向商业银行改制的过程中。中央汇金公司代表国家行使作为主要国有金融机构投资人的权利与义务。全国社保基金也具有机构投资人和部分大型商业银行的持股者的双重角色。

54. 中国的分业监管框架需要高度协调以避免监管"盲点"。需要制订一个

---

⑥　本节应与包括"金融部门标准和准则遵守情况报告"的附件 I 至附件 V 结合起来读。

监管框架，授权一家机构，如人民银行来监管金融控股公司，包括投资于金融企业的产业集团。国务院已经授权人民银行会同三个监管机构研究拟定监管规则。过渡期内，机构的并购活动应该得到负责监管该机构的监管委员会的批准。此外，适用于影子银行体系的监管政策需要予以明确（表9）。需要强化人民银行与三个监管机构之间以信息共享谅解备忘录为基础的协调安排，并消除这方面的任何法律限制。

表9　中国：影子银行体系

种类	金融机构	注册	调查人/监管者
非正规金融部门	典当行，贷款担保公司，微型金融公司	地方政府	由中国人民银行、银监会和公安部负责调查。另外，由银监会牵头的融资性担保业务监管部际联席会议负责制定对信用担保机构的监管政策、提供指导并进行协调。地方政府负责监管，包括发照、现场检查和非现场监管。
	地下中介活动	无	无监管者，但中国人民银行进行不定期调查。
私募基金	据估计，截至2010年中，共有3 500家私募基金，资产总额约9 000亿元人民币，其中70%属于外资。	工商行政管理局	私募基金投资按照发展改革委和商务部颁布的规定进行管理，证监会负责私募基金的数据收集和调查。此外，部分私募基金还处于监管部门的视野之外。
理财产品	截至2010年底，估计有理财产品7 049种，总金额达1.7万亿元人民币，有124家银行业机构涉足该业务。	银监会，证监会，保监会	人民银行，银监会，证监会，保监会

资料来源：中国人民银行；中国银监会；中国证监会；国家发展和改革委员会；国际货币基金组织工作人员测算。

注：（1）按照金融稳定理事会的定义，影子银行是指在银行系统外从事信用创造和期限/流动性转换的实体，并具有某种杠杆功能，包括货币市场互助基金、财务公司、资产抵押商业票据工具、特殊投资工具等。由于数据限制，本表未涵盖这些实体。（2）本表仅包括当局认可的实体，如非正规金融部门和私募基金，以及FSAP评估团选取作为影子银行的实体，如信托公司和理财产品。

A. 商业银行监管

55. 中国银监会有着明确的维护银行体系安全和稳健的职责。 但由于商业银行承担了支持经济发展的职能，银监会的操作独立性经常受到影响。银监会在改进商业银行监管框架和强调审慎目标方面取得了长足进展。尽管如此，确保该机构能够不受阻碍地履行其职责仍很重要。为此，需要赋予银监会更加稳定的资源，使其能够灵活地建立起一支熟练、专业的人员队伍，同时继续推进银行的商业化改革。

56. 银行业法律和监管框架已与国际标准进一步趋同，但仍有差距。现行法律框架缺乏对间接控制权变更申报、最终受益所有权人和银行客户身份识别的具体规定。在无法实行并表监管的情况下，应该禁止复杂的结构。识别关联方和处置银行的规则需要强化。资产分类和拨备的审慎制度运作良好，但银行的实际做法还存在不足。对巴塞尔 I 框架的微小偏离[⑦]未来可能会使银行资本出现高估。

57. 银行的风险管理能力和措施需要改进。大银行已根据简单但保守的监管标准和技巧建立了自己的风险管理体系，但某些较小银行的风险管理体系需要加强。所有银行都需要更新其风险管理做法，以跟上市场化的步伐和日益加强的国际化趋势。虽然主要银行正在制订更细致的二维分类体系，但目前这些分类体系在风险区分和贷款定价中的应用仍然有限。应改变对抵押品的强烈依赖，解决前瞻性估值措施缺失问题，以减少贷款的信用风险和顺周期性（图31）。流动性风险和市场风险管理框架在当前环境下运作良好，但是，随着市场结构和银行业的发展，该框架可能会显得不足。实施全面的、涵盖整个企业的风险管理应该是主要银行的最紧迫任务。有关国别风险和转移风险管理的指导原则刚刚出台，但鉴于中国银行业国际风险敞口和国际化程度的提高，其实施力度必须加强。中小银行需要加强操作风险管理程序。

58. 银行的风险管理框架受制于当前宏观经济和制度环境。国家对银行信用风险敞口的隐性担保使其缺乏对信用风险进行有效管理的积极性。银行的信用风险管理策略受贷款增长计划的主导，而且银行的风险管理和对其进行的监管评价都以不良贷款率为重点，而不是以信用风险的前瞻性评估为重点。

B. 证券中介和证券市场监管

59. 虽然证监会在证券市场监管方面积极主动并采取战略性举措，但法律和监管制度仍有待完善。与其他监管机构一样，由于政府对人员任命和运作结构的影响，证监会缺乏操作自主权。证监会需要有更大的预算灵活性，以便在迅速发展的市场环境下吸引合格的专业人员。在上市公司审计方面，会计和审计的专业性在短期内取得很大进展，但还需要进一步努力。应该对新实施的基于风险的净资本规则进行监测，以确保其覆盖所有风险。虽然在处置倒闭中介机构方面有充足的规定，但采取行动的门槛应该降低以便进行早期干预。

---

⑦ 这些偏离目前还不是实质性的，而且被较高的最低资本要求所抵消了。

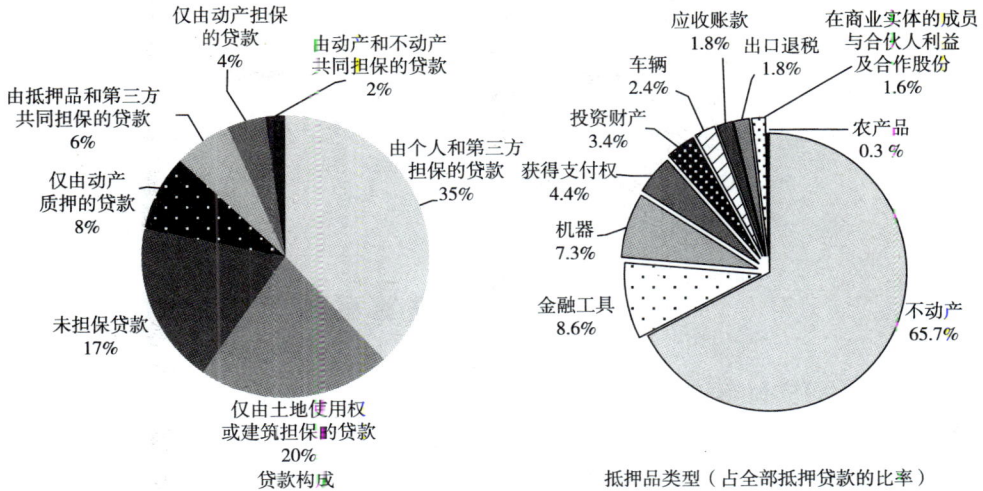

仅由动产担保的贷款 4%
由动产和不动产共同担保的贷款 2%
由抵押品和第三方共同担保的贷款 6%
仅由动产质押的贷款 8%
由个人和第三方担保的贷款 35%
未担保贷款 17%
仅由土地使用权或建筑担保的贷款 20%

贷款构成

应收账款 1.8%
出口退税 1.8%
在商业实体的成员与合伙人利益及合作股份 1.6%
车辆 2.4%
投资财产 3.4%
农产品 0.3%
获得支付权 4.4%
机器 7.3%
金融工具 8.6%
不动产 65.7%

抵押品类型（占全部抵押贷款的比率）

资料来源：国际金融公司，2007 年，《改革抵押品方面的法律与登记：国际最佳做法与中国案例》。

图 31　银行贷款对房地产抵押的依赖（2007 年）

60. 为加强监管，应制定一个对交易所进行定期全面现场检查的正式计划。要更加重视对非法投资活动的查处以及对对冲基金及私募股权基金的监测。认真监测"了解你的客户"规则的实施情况，证券公司和期货公司应保留顾客身份、交易和账户数据的全面记录，以确保投资者在信息充分的基础上作出决策。

C. 保险监管

61. 保监会已建立全面的监管框架，但需要强化偿付能力监管。最低偿付保证金应该以风险为基础来确定。偿付水平不足 100% 的公司继续开展新业务是不可取的。需要制定明确和清晰的规则，使保险公司可以通过保单责任托管或业务转移来退出市场。应恢复使用以前在保险公司报告中要求的早期预警比率，以加强非现场监测。

62. 作为监管者，保监会的发展职责应该着重于确保行业安全这一公共属性。当前基于规则的监管体系和对保险公司业务按月频繁监测，加大了监管人员的负担，应予以重新考虑。随着市场和新实施的基于风险的监管制度不断成熟，保监会应该改变目前直接参与保险公司的产品、分配和投资策略的状况。保监会的人员配备应该加强，在关键的工作领域应有合适的高技能人员。

IV. 完善金融基础设施和法律框架

A. 支付和证券结算系统

63. 对大额支付系统和证券与衍生品结算系统的评估表明，这些系统基本符合国际标准，但仍有几个方面需要完善。人民银行对中国支付清算体系进行了全面改革。今后，政府部门应确保其法律框架能充分保障支付、衍生品和证券结算的最终性。人民银行应细化支付系统监管政策，确定履职范围、主要政策和工具。人民银行还应明确系统重要性支付系统的判断标准，加强支付体系领域的机制安排和合作。同时，建议人民银行对中国外汇交易系统进行更积极主动的监管。

B. 法律和监管结构

64. 有必要对金融业法律体系所存在的差距、交叉情况和清晰性进行一次"摸底"（部分情况参见表 10）。到目前为止，对中国来说，基于规则的监管方式虽然是适合的，但中国在制订和实施法律时如能逐步采取更加基于原则的方式来处理日益复杂的新问题，将可从中获益。

表 10 中国部分金融产品的法律和监管架构

产品	发行机构	监管机构	法律和法规	任务
共同基金	基金管理公司	证监会	《证券投资基金法》	审批
集合投资计划	证券公司	证监会	《证券公司客户资产管理业务试行办法》	备案或审批
集合理财产品	商业银行	银监会	《商业银行个人理财业务管理暂行办法》	登记备案
信托计划	信托投资公司	银监会	《关于进一步规范集合资金信托业务有关问题的通知》	登记备案
投连险产品	保险公司	保监会	《投资连结保险管理暂行办法》	审批

资料来源：中国银监会，中国证监会，中国保监会。

65. 需要清晰阐明、宣传和实施关于消费者保护的法律框架。必须加强消费者保护，不仅要提高法院强制执行合同的能力，而且还要让消费者组织有效地发挥作用，增强法律对个人信息和隐私的保护，同时确立市场行为和管理守则。

66. 应重新审视债权人权利保护法律框架，提供高效、有效的退出机制。在某些部门（如保险部门），尚未制订关于金融机构破产问题的具体法律。需要继续加强对法官的培训，培训内容包括破产法的原则、《企业破产法》的具体内容以及其他相关司法解释。

C. 市场诚信

67. 2007 年 6 月金融行动特别工作组（FATF）的互评估报告指出，中国在实施反洗钱/反恐融资（AML/CFT）制度方面取得了重大进展，但还存在几项重大不足。[8]尽管中国加强了反洗钱/反恐融资制度（包括通过立法改革来加强预防性措施），特别是在顾客尽职调查和可疑交易报告领域。但是，仍然存在两处严重缺陷。首先，中国的法律和实践限制了相关部门或金融机构获知法人受益所有权人身份的能力。其次，预防性措施尚未扩大到"FATF 建议"中指定的大部分非金融业务和行业，在自我洗钱定罪和冻结恐怖主义资产方面也存在着不足。此外，还需要改进人民银行和其他机构之间在反洗钱方面的信息共享和协调安排。

---

⑧ 2007 年 6 月的报告是可以获得的关于中国反洗钱/反恐融资全面评估的最新报告。全文见 http：//www. fatf－gafi. org/infobycountry/0，3380，en＿ 32250379＿ 32236963＿ 1＿ 70342＿ 43383847＿ 1＿ 1，00. html。

V. 拓宽金融市场和金融服务

A. 固定收益市场

68. 利率未完全市场化抑制了银行利用固定收益工具管理资产负债表的积极性。市场化融资机制的缺失以及贷款业务占主导地位，使银行没有动力积极进行资产负债管理以对冲错配风险。此外，有保证的利差也降低了银行在资本市场上开展收费业务的动力。监管框架和回购市场运行框架需要改善，以增加市场流动性，强化风险管理，增强货币市场和债券市场的联系。

69. 需要采取措施确保对固定收益市场和产品的监管保持一致，并清晰地告知市场。进一步明确三家机构（人民银行、发展改革委和证监会）的职责，特别是在公司债券市场方面。对相同类型的市场参与者应适用相同的监管规定，即使其归属不同的监管机构监管。支持现行市场做法的可行方案是，对批发和零售市场进行区分，并在人民银行和证监会之间划分监管职责。

70. 对收益率曲线上的所有期限产品都应有更加积极和持续的基准构建策略。目前，财政部发行的债券，与中央银行票据在中短期无风险固定收益市场占主导，同时与流动性较高的政策性银行债券在中长期市场上占主导（图32）。应通过加强财政部和人民银行之间的协调来改进债券发行策略。为控制人民银行

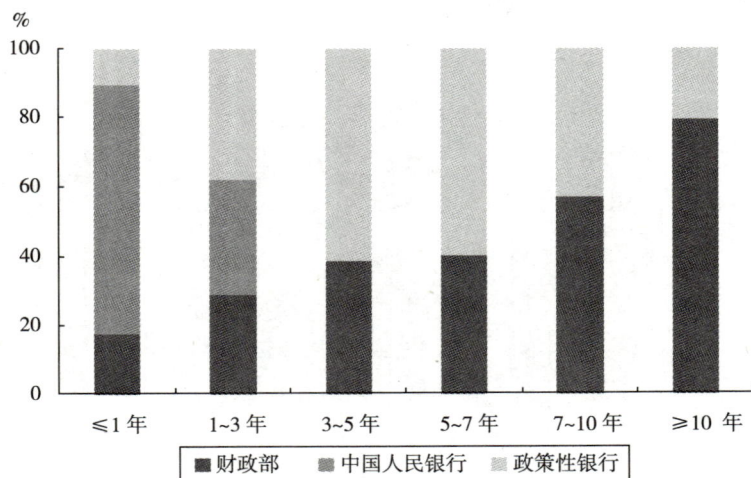

资料来源：中国债券信息网。

图32 每个公共部门债务发行人都主导着一个不同期限的细分市场（2009 年）

流动性管理活动对财政部发行债券收益的影响，人民银行应尽量发行短期票据。长期流动性回笼则通过中央银行票据展期或人民银行较长期的回购操作来进行。

71. 发展地方政府债券市场是可行的，但也存在风险。在缺乏合适的中期财政框架、债务可持续性分析及中期债务管理策略的情况下，省级政府发行的债券将很快变成或有债务，并对全国固定收益市场产生不利影响。为帮助投资者评估项目债券的风险，需及时提供足够的数据。为确保使用统一的债券评级方法，应正确界定信用评级机构的职责。

72. 在公司债券市场方面，发展细分市场，允许评级较低、信用良好但目前被排除在证券市场之外的企业能在该市场上发行债券。放宽债券发行不超过净资产40%的法定限制，将使所有公司能够更多地利用直接融资。此外，加强中央国债登记结算有限责任公司和中国证券登记结算有限责任公司之间的联系，以增强银行间债券市场、上海证券交易所和深圳证券交易所的互联互通，进一步推动市场发展，促进三个市场提高效率。

B. 股票市场

73. 解决遗留问题，更好地服务中小企业，以进一步促进股票市场发展。应全面解决包括 A 股、B 股、非流通股及上市企业流通股比例低在内的一系列遗留问题。在私募和公募市场之间建立顺畅的渠道，将为中小企业提供可持续的融资选择，并使更多的私营企业在交易所上市。2009 年启动的创业板有望为私募资金退出提供渠道。

C. 保险部门

74. 在规模和竞争之间需进行更好的平衡。过去十年获得牌照的大部分保险公司一直亏损（表 11）。应引入更全面的基于风险的资本要求，并要求股东在一定期限内达到这一要求。应加强对非寿险理赔准备金的精算监督，明确自愿关闭和退出的规则与程序。员工工资和福利、受担保借款人在公司清盘时的受偿顺序优先于寿险保单持有人的做法不符合国际最佳做法。还可以在其他方面采取措施以使保险公司获得更稳定、更高的股本回报。

表 11　保险——按规模划分的经营业绩（2009 年）　　　　单位：%

	最佳资产回报率	联合比率	股本回报率
寿险			
前 10 名	6.3		18.4
下一个 10 名	-1.1		-11.4
其他	-2.6		-11.4
多险种非寿险			
前 10 名		101.7	11.4
下一个 10 名		117.7	-5.9
其他		122.0	-5.3

资料来源：《2010 年中国保险年鉴》。

D.　养老金部门

75. 养老金体系的重点应是积累制养老保险。第一支柱的养老基金结余仍然投资于效率不高的资产组合。保本型年金作为企业年金制度最普遍的投资策略，不能产生足够的回报来满足未来合理的养老金需求。长远看，投资策略应偏重股权和长期债券。投资监管不应鼓励短期业绩评价，而应重点关注养老基金的长期精算目标。在中国人储蓄倾向较高的情况下，可通过设计有吸引力的个人所得税激励措施，或使基金缴纳额符合低收入者的情况，来扩大个人固定缴款养老金计划的范围。

E.　金融可获得性

76. 大力转变促进农村和小微企业融资的机制。政府应对现行促进农村和小微企业融资机制的有效性进行评估，并制订综合、统一的农村和小微企业融资战略，采取措施大大拓宽金融可获得性。继续推进农村信用合作社改革，提高其作为商业化金融产品和服务提供者的效率及可持续性。通过股权结构的优化，彻底的公司化改革和有效公司治理结构的建立，完成邮政储蓄银行的改革。

VI. 金融改革次序

77. **深化金融改革对中国的可持续增长至关重要，同时，为限制其对金融稳定的风险，改革需要精心筹划。**国别经验表明，虽然金融自由化能够促进增长和发展，但是，如果设计和筹划不当，也会带来风险。鉴于中国所设想的改革议程宽广，很有必要设计一项战略，把可能发生的复杂情况和不确定性预先考虑进去，并且对如何以最佳方式安排政策措施同时又不延迟必要的改革提供指导。在不具备必要前提条件的情况下贸然进行改革对金融稳定来说极其危险。

78. **虽然没有一个"放之四海而皆准"的金融自由化模式，但一些大的原则还是适用于中国的情况（图33）。**顺利转型的一个首要的压倒一切的前提条件是，要建立一个功能完善且有着充分技术能力的法律、监管和危机管理框架，这对监测金融机构和管理风险是必不可少的。另一个前提条件是，尽早吸纳当前金融体系中的剩余流动性，以防止不经意地放松货币和信贷。应该早日实施平均准备金制度和常规性公开市场操作来吸纳一些过多的流动性。同时，更多地依靠间接货币工具和更灵活的汇率制度将会增加宏观经济调控的余地。

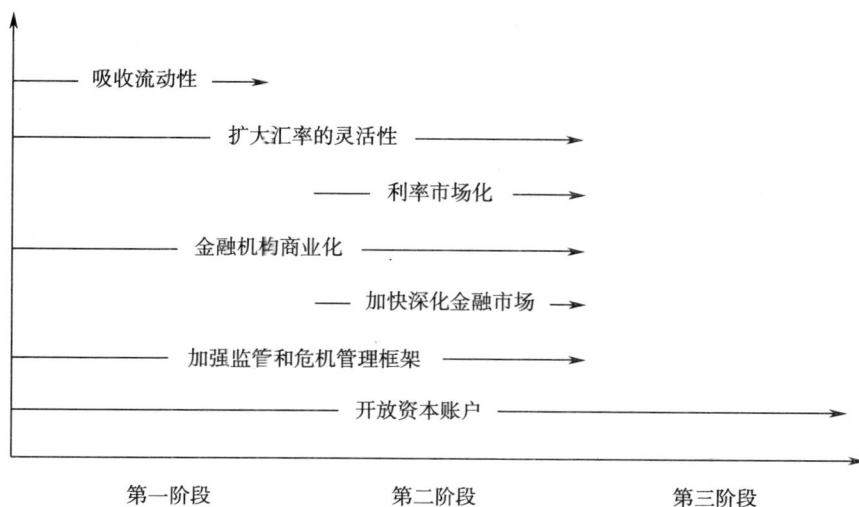

吸收流动性

扩大汇率的灵活性

利率市场化

金融机构商业化

加快深化金融市场

加强监管和危机管理框架

开放资本账户

第一阶段　　　　　　第二阶段　　　　　　第三阶段

资料来源：中国 FSAP 评估团。

图33　为金融改革排定优先顺序

79. **现代化的金融基础设施和更加市场化的金融体系将有助于与全球金融体**

系的稳步融合。银行体系需要在更加商业化的基础上运行，并应予以密切监督以避免过度冒险行为和对银行利润的不可持续的挤压。政府需要重新定位其在金融体系中的作用，以便降低其资产负债表发生直接和或有风险的可能性，并消除道德风险问题。有了这些改善，那么，存款和贷款利率的逐步市场化便可以成功地实施。随着银行体系变得更加商业化，更广泛的金融深化可以加速进行，同时不会产生无序的金融脱媒风险。当利率由供求决定，而货币调控通过短期政策利率来进行时，中国将可以进一步向资本账户完全开放转变。

附录 I. 压力测试

80. 这次压力测试由 FSAP 压力测试小组与人民银行/银监会压力测试小组合作进行。 这样做是为了：(1) 掌握中国经济和金融体系的主要方面；(2) 尽可能参照已经进行的分析工作；(3) 建立一个具有一致性的操作框架，使中国当局可以在此次 FSAP 完成之后加以利用和发展。

81. 这次压力测试包括了 5 家大型商业银行和 12 家股份制商业银行。 截至 2010 年底，这 17 家主要银行资产之和占中国银行业总资产的大约 66%，商业银行资产总额的 83%。这次压力测试不包括非银行金融机构。所有测试所依据的都是这 17 家主要银行 2009 年底的审计数据或监管数据，而且为了比较，对同样银行的 2008 年底和 2010 年底数据进行了自上而下的总体信用风险测试和房地产风险测试。由于缺乏关于这些银行的可靠市场指标，压力测试采用的方法所依靠的是各家银行的公开财务报表、审慎报告和银行的内部数据系统。

82. 这次压力测试有三个支柱：一个自下而上的支柱和两个自上而下的支柱（图 34）。

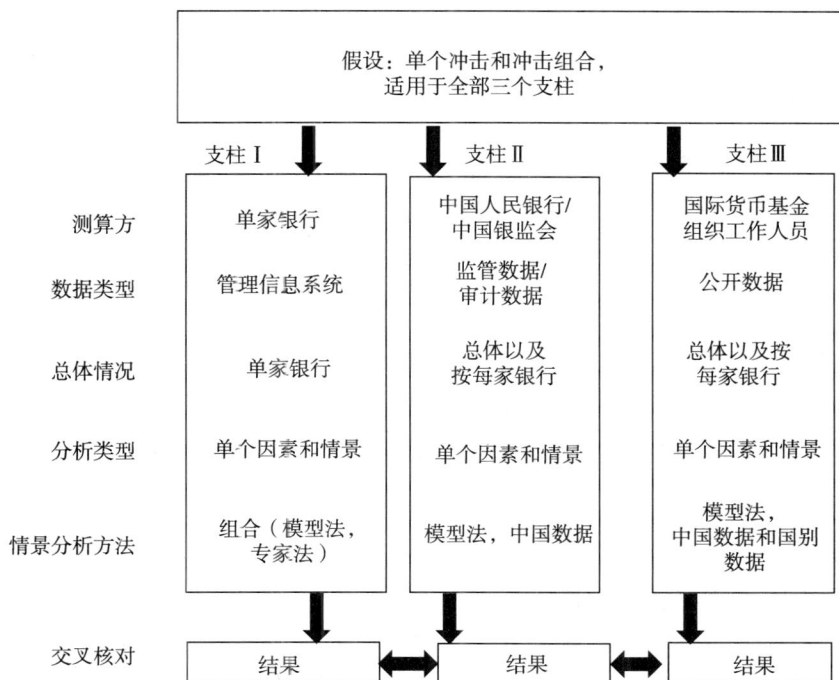

资料来源：FSAP 压力测试小组。

图 34　压力测试：三个支柱

所选定的这 17 家银行开展自下而上的测试，并采用一套相同的冲击和假设。人民银行/银监会压力测试小组使用监管数据，运用商定方法分别对每家银行进行了自上而下的计算。两组结果都是以汇总形式和按银行类型提供给 FSAP 压力测试小组。此外，还提供了没有达到监管要求的银行数目，以及这些银行在银行体系总资产中所占比重。FSAP 压力测试小组采用公开数据，自行开展了一套自上而下的测试。对这三种方法得出的结果进行了比较、分析和交叉核对。

83. 这些测试包括一系列敏感性分析和情景测算。这些分析和测算检查了总体信用风险、信用风险集中度、直接汇率和利率风险、流动性风险、通过有记录的银行同业市场传播的传染效应以及一组宏观经济冲击的总影响。

84. 敏感性测试估计了个别变量的变化对银行资产组合的影响。在敏感性分析框架内，假设冲击源于单一风险因素，且其他风险因素保持不变。冲击被假设为瞬间发生，除非另有注明。敏感性分析包括了对风险因素变化敏感的所有头寸。尽可能在这些头寸中包括了资产负债表内和表外的所有多头（买人）和空头（卖出）头寸。

85. 信用风险是压力测试关注的重点领域。对信用风险的敏感性分析包括对资产质量的总体冲击和一系列单独的冲击，后者中每个冲击的目的是检查信用风险集中度的不同方面。总体测试假设资产质量全面恶化。此外，部分测试是为了反映银行向其提供贷款的各经济部门、不同类型实体和银行集中开展业务的不同地区之间的风险差异。但是，考虑到数据限制，无法做到完全覆盖所有这些层面。有鉴于此，采用了一系列单独的冲击，对每个冲击进行单独分析，以覆盖：（1）单家最大风险敞口；（2）房地产行业的风险敞口；（3）对地方政府融资平台的风险敞口；（4）对产能过剩行业的风险敞口；（5）对出口行业的风险敞口；（6）对贷款增长最迅速的部门（行业）和地区的风险敞口。没有进行股票市场冲击分析，因为银行不得直接投资于股票市场，而间接风险敞口又无法估计。

86. 宏观情景测试是这次压力测试的重要组成部分。假设了三种不利的宏观经济情景：轻度、中度和重度。根据对中国过去实际 GDP 增长率的分析及其他国家的经验，把三种情景下的实际 GDP 年增长率分别假设为 7%、5% 和 4%。

87. 冲击情景参考一组有影响力的中国经济问题专家的意见进行了校准。为了将 GDP 增长率与其他变量结合在一起从而设计出有意义的情景，人民银行/银监会压力测试小组与 FSAP 压力测试小组协商，征求了一组专家的意见。为了提高专家们的意见的可比性，并考虑到所有银行都把 GDP 作为一个宏观经济指标，向专家们提供了 GDP 增长率，以作为每个情景中的一个关键变量，并征求他们对其他变量在各种假设下的变动的意见。表 12 概括了所选定的宏观经济情景。

表 12　中国宏观经济情景假设

单位：%

	轻度	中度	重度
GDP	7	5	4
M$_2$	14.7	12.4	10.2
房地产价格	−7.0	−16.2	−25.9
人民币贷款和存款基准利率变化（基点）	35	66	95
实际有效汇率指数	117.5	119.6	123.0

注：这些不是预测，而是关于今后可能出现的不利事态发展的假设。

资料来源：FSAP 压力测试小组和人民银行/银监会，以一组著名中国经济问题专家的意见为依据。假设是专家意见的平均值，从其中排除了两个离群值。

88. 同时采用自上而下和自下而上的方法对宏观经济情景进行了测试。为进行自下而上的分析，银行综合采用了计量经济模型和专家分析，但确切的实施取决于每个银行的能力，一些银行具备复杂的内部模型，另一些银行则更多地依靠较为基本的模型编制方法或依靠贷款人员的专业判断。人民银行/银监会压力测试小组为了进行自上而下的估计，采用了一个根据最新的中国数据估计得出的计量经济等式。FSAP 小组的自上而下估计包括根据国际经验进行的交叉核对。

表 13　中国：改进压力测试的建议

- 定期举行有各主要银行参加的宏观审慎压力测试。
- 人民银行和银监会与银行进一步合作，以确保提高银行的模型构建能力，特别是为分析宏观经济影响而构建模型的能力。
- 统一银行的压力测试方法，特别是宏观情景测试方法。
- 继续努力，把各种信用风险分析与关于市场风险、流动性风险和传染性风险的计算结合起来。
- 将压力测试范围扩展至这 17 家银行之外，并包括更多的表外风险敞口。
- 提高压力测试基础数据的质量，尤其是违约概率和违约损失率数据的质量。
- 加强数据收集能力。
- 在分析中纳入更多关于银行贷款组合的分项数据，按经济部门、交易对手类型（例如国有企业和中小企业）和集中了银行大部分业务活动的具体部门分列这些数据。
  - 这方面的一个重点部门应该是房地产。应改进数据上报系统，以便能够针对全国不同地区采用不同的冲击强度进行压力测试。
  - 另一个重点领域应该是对地方政府的风险敞口。
- 开始收集关于银行对出口导向型企业的风险敞口数据。
- 开始收集更全面的关于银行间双边敞口的数据，以改进传染效应压力测试。
- 开始收集关于银行的非金融机构交易对手（公司、住户）的数据。

资料来源：FSAP 压力测试小组。

附件：对金融领域标准和准则的遵守情况——评估意见概述

本附件概述了关于中国对金融领域国际标准和准则遵守情况的评估意见。这些评估意见有助于识别监管和市场基础设施框架在管理金融体系的潜在风险和脆弱性方面的主要优势，并提出需要加强和进一步改革的方面。

本概述是以针对下列国际标准进行的详细评估为依据：

- 巴塞尔银行监管委员会《有效银行监管核心原则》——评估人：Nicholas Le Pan（世界银行顾问）、Walter Yao（国际货币基金组织顾问）和 Aditya Narain（国际货币基金组织）

- 国际保险监督官协会（IAIS）《保险核心原则》——评估人：Henning Göbel（世界银行顾问）

- 国际证监会组织（IOSCO）《证券监管目标和原则》——评估人：Greg Tanzer（世界银行顾问）

- 支付结算体系委员会（CPSS）《系统重要性支付系统核心原则》——评估人：Massimo Cirasino（世界银行）和 Mario Guadamillas（世界银行）

- 支付结算体系委员会—国际证监会组织《证券结算系统和中央对手方建议》——评估人：Massimo Cirasino（世界银行）和 Mario Guadamillas（世界银行）

附件 I. 对金融领域标准和准则——巴塞尔《有效银行监管核心原则》的遵守情况：概述

A. 导言

89. 中国银行体系监管已经取得长足进步。风险计量和风险管理有了显著改进。这得益于要求资本和流动性保持高质量的监管制度，且往往是通过简单、基础的监管要求进行监管。然而，随着开放和创新的不断深入以及中国银行业规模的不断扩大，复杂性和风险将会增加。银监会和银行必须在短期内迅速调整，以应对挑战。总体上，中国已建立起高质量的法律和指引框架，但其中很大一部分是近期推出的。银行对法律和指引的执行需要改进，在有些方面需要重大改进。银行和监管机构需要提高警惕，不断控制中国银行体系中的风险，因为国家期望银行大规模直接参与实现各项经济和社会目标。银监会受到广泛尊重，并显示出为执行其维护银行体系安全和稳健的任务而采取行动的意愿。银监会迫切需要制订一项计划，用以增强自身经验和专业能力，确保迄今取得的进展是可持续的，并需要在这一努力中继续得到政府的支持。

90. 对中国实施《巴塞尔有效银行监管核心原则》（《巴塞尔核心原则》）情况的评估在 2010 年 6 月 7 日至 6 月 25 日期间进行。评估反映了截至评估完成之时的监管框架。按照《巴塞尔核心原则》的方法，评估侧重于各主要商业银行及其监管，原因是这些银行对于全系统非常重要。

B. 用于评估的信息和方法

91. 评估团考察了银行监管的法律框架，与银监会及两家地方银监局的工作人员进行了广泛讨论。评估人员还与中央银行（人民银行）、财政部、审计署、一些商业银行、会计师事务所、评级公司和中国银行业协会的人员举行了会谈。评估团详细了解了银监会的现场检查和非现场监管做法。评估团得益于银监会提供的全面自评估报告、会谈人员的充分配合，获取了评估所需的资料信息。

92. 为了得出结论，评估团需要作出判断。银行体系因国家而异，各国的国内情况各不相同。近年来，中国银行业发生了巨大变化，这一过程仍在继续。银监会是一个相对年轻的机构，2003 年才从人民银行分设出来，是中国当局对银行业实施重大改革举措的一部分。除了加强金融部门监管外，改革措施还包括把四家大型国有银行改造为股份制公司、改革农村信用社、改组股份制银行和证券公司以及保险业改革。

C. 体制环境和市场结构：概述

93. 迅速增长的银行业在中国金融体系中占主导地位，非银行金融机构仅占很小一部分。 每年新增贷款的近 80% 来自银行业。中国的资本市场相对而言仍然没有深度，60% 以上的债券由政府发行，其余绝大部分债券由大型金融机构发行，其中政策性银行（它们是国有银行，为支持基建、农业发展、出口保险等活动提供一系列融资服务）和国家开发银行是第二大发行主体。然而，保险业增长迅速，这也体现在银保联系的日益加强方面。

94. 虽然银行体系异常庞大，其资产超过 GDP 的 200%，但金融体系仍然相对较新、比较简单，且仍处于发展之中。 主要的金融价格仍受管制，使得银行与市场风险隔绝。尽管十多年来逐渐推行利率放开，但零售利率仍受到部分管制，存款利率有上限，贷款利率有下限。银行可使贷款利率在一定程度上高于下限，实际上也是这样做的。

95. 在银行业内部，五家大型商业银行的资产占银行体系总资产的一半以上。 第二个层次的银行是股份制商业银行；第三个层次是城市商业银行和农村商业银行，这两类银行分别由城市信用社和农村信用社改制而成。第四个层次是存款吸收机构，例如农村和城市信用社、邮政储蓄银行和村镇银行。外资银行虽然在中国有 200 多家分行和法人银行，但所占比重仍然很小，不到总资产的 2%。但是，近年来，海外金融机构对中国的银行进行了大量股权投资。

96. 银行体系的审慎比率，例如资本充足率、不良贷款率和流动性比率，已经大大改善。 银行资产中的相当一部分是对中央银行和中央及地方政府的风险敞口，而且在拓宽金融中介业务方面仍有改进余地。

D. 实现有效银行监管的先决条件

97. 中国法律体系总体秉承民法法系框架，同时也包含一些具有自身特点的法律传统。 这一法律框架的结构经历了一系列阶段性变革，首先是在 20 世纪 70 年代之前的全面国有制，最近的变化则是在社会主义政治和经济框架内朝着市场化方向发展。

98. 作为《商业法典》的替代，中国实施了一系列商业法律，以规范商业活动监管机制。 政府颁布了一系列特定措施代替商业法典，用以管理商业关系。最近通过了一系列具有重要象征意义的法律，特别是 2007 年《物权法》和 2007

年《企业破产法》，前者进一步确认了私人财产权，后者相对其他法律对有担保的债权人给予更多的保护（例如在破产清算时把有担保的债权人置于比工人工资更优先的地位）。关于银行债务强制执行情况的数据很少，但现有的数据显示，为跟上经济改革的步伐，一些中心城市法院强制执行合同的情况总体上已有大幅度改善。

99. 中国正在逐步建立起促进和支持市场纪律的基础设施。《公司法》、《商业银行法》、《银行业监督管理法》、《证券法》和《保险法》都对信息披露提出了具体要求。2003年设立了银监会，作为一个独立的审慎管理机构。人们普遍认为，银监会在建立后的短时间内取得了巨大成就，推动改进了户国各银行的风险管理、公司治理以及内部控制和披露。在实践中，所有银行都必须在年度报告中公开披露信息，包括经审计的财务报表、公司治理、资本充足率、风险敞口、风险管理策略和实践以及其他定量和定性信息。此外，上市银行还需遵守证监会的信息披露规定。中国金融监管机构为改进金融机构的公司治理付出了巨大努力。根据有关公司治理规则，银行设立了全职董事会及对董事会和高级管理层进行监督的监事会。监事会不参与战略的制定，可获取审计和控制部门的报告，以确保董事会和管理层按照规定行事并执行董事会批准的战略。

100. 2005年以来，中国的会计准则基本上与《国际财务报告准则》和《国际审计准则》趋同。2006年2月，负责制定会计和审计准则的财政部颁布了《企业会计准则》，取代了以前的《中国会计准则》，并于2007年1月生效。这套新的会计准则包括一项基本准则和38项具体准则，基本上与国际准则趋同，得到国际会计准则理事会的承认。当前，所有上市公司、金融机构和非上市大中型企业都采用了新的会计准则。同样在2006年，财政部发布了一套新的审计准则、一项审阅准则、两项其他鉴证业务准则、两项相关服务准则和一项质量控制准则。这些准则也与国际标准趋同，因此得到国际会计师联合会的承认。

101. 会计和审计行业发展迅速，但有些方面仍需改进。过去30年，中国的注册会计师（CPA）行业一直稳步发展。目前，在中国注册的会计师事务所超过7 000家，执业注册会计师超过97 000人。财政部负责监管会计和审计行业，具体包括资格审查和批准、执业质量监督和对相关行业协会的活动进行监督。银行审计的覆盖面是充分的，银监会要求所有总资产超过10亿元人民币的银行接受财务报表审计，但仍存在一些不足。以前的报告和评估人员约谈的市场参与者都提到，较小的会计师事务所的审计质量有待提高。近期，《中国注册会计师职业道德基本准则》纳入了一套标准的审计师独立性规定，如果当局在实施这一规定的过程中，能够定期和更加频繁地检查会计师事务所的审计质量，将提高审计行业的公信力。

102. 近年来，人民银行对国家支付系统（NPS）进行了重大改革，建立了中国现代化支付系统（CNAPS）。中国现代化支付系统由大额支付系统（HVPS）和小额批量支付系统组成。大额支付系统是一个实时总额结算系统，主要用于大额转账。这个系统被用来向银行业机构、私人和公共实体以及金融市场提供快捷、高效、安全、可靠的支付清算服务。该系统目前有 1 600 多个直接参与者。中国正在大力发展非现金支付工具，特别是银行卡。

103. 中国还没有显性存款保险这样的公共安全网，但正在考虑推出。由于政府对银行的参股程度很高，公众可能认为，如果银行倒闭，国家会保护所有存款者的利益。中央银行承担着银行最后贷款人职能。

104. 中国曾对几家出现严重财务困难的银行进行重组。这些重组往往采取"整体接收银行"的方式，这种持续经营解决办法是说服另一家银行接管问题机构的资产和负债（或至少是存款类负债）。尽管没有任何明确的处置框架，但当局证明有能力运用现有的《破产法》和其他法律来进行处置。《破产法》中有几个方面的问题值得考虑，以便在银行倒闭时增加系统性保护，降低风险传染。当局应考虑，建立一个专门针对银行的破产制度是否更为有利，特别是在大型银行日益国际化，而且需要建立更加协调的跨境处置框架的国际背景下。

E. 主要结论

目标、独立性、权力、透明度和合作（核心原则1）

105. 银行监管的目标和职责很明确。银监会被授予的职权使其能够集中精力执行其唯一使命，即维护银行体系的安全和稳健，从而有助于它成为一个高效的组织。银监会利用这一授权非常成功地向银行和公众阐明，必须维护银行体系的安全和稳健，以及通过银行体系促进经济发展和社会进步。实际上，安全和稳健将有助于实现发展目标。银监会推动银行开展高质量的风险管理，以之作为实现经济和社会目标的努力的一部分。根据授权，同时考虑到银行业风险管理中已有或潜在的缺陷，银监会最近出台了一系列审慎监管措施，包括加强地方政府融资平台贷款和房地产贷款信用风险管理。针对经济刺激计划实施过程中出现的贷款快速增长，银监会成功地推动银行提高了资本和拨备水平。

106. 维护银行业安全和稳健的目标与其他目标之间的潜在冲突在许多国家都存在，但在中国可能更突出，原因是中国主要运用银行体系来实现经济和社会目标，而该体系大部分是国有的。作为"十二五"规划的一部分，金融业"十二五"规划应强调银行业安全和稳健的重要地位，并加强银监会为防患于未然的早期干预。该规划还应把持续改进银行的风险管理放在首位，确保所有银行而不仅仅是最先进的银行，都作出必要的改进，并确保已作出的改进融入银行的各项业务。当局应该清醒地认识到安全和稳健以及高质量的风险管理对实现经济和社会目标的重要性。当前，银监会在促进银行审慎经营，及处理银行业安全和稳健目标与国家经济政策可能存在的冲突方面发挥了重要作用。银监会持续发挥这一作用十分重要。

107. 银监会的资源配备对其独立性具有潜在影响，并削弱了监管的有效性，尤其在银行复杂性和创新程度不断提高以及海外业务不断扩张的情况下。此外，国务院有权撤销银监会制定的规章，也会影响银监会的独立性，尽管国务院从未行使过这一权力。《银行业监督管理法》规定，银监会的决策不受任何方面干涉，银监会报告称自其成立以来从未受到干涉。然而，现有安排可能在将来引发问题。总的来说，银监会在运作时所依据的法律、规则和指导方针广泛借鉴了国际标准和《巴塞尔核心原则》，确立了一整套高质量的审慎监管标准。

108. 然而，很多指引出台时间相对较短，此次评估中发现的问题大多存在于实施环节。迄今为止，在许多方面，银监会的监管优势在于它坚持采用的简单、保守的方法，要求银行必须遵守具体的审慎比率。例如，对流动性比率和资本充足率都制定了具体要求。但随着市场和银行的发展，这种方法将不足以应对未来的挑战。银监会虽然面临一些限制，但其治理比较完善，透明度得到持续显著的提升。目前银监会需要：制定更具前瞻性的资源规划；亟需一项政府支持的战略来大幅度提升各种技能，尤其是专业技能；在编制预算和薪酬方面享有更大的灵活性，以支持这一战略并吸引和留住人才。银监会监管成效的相关信息披露已大大改善，但仍有改进的空间。

109. 在借鉴国际标准的基础上不断完善银行业监管法律框架，并涵盖法律法规、指引和条例（均具有法律效力）。银监会有权采取一系列纠正和整改措施，而且必要时能积极主动使用这些权力。银监会工作人员依法履职的行动受法律保护。银监会也有权在签署谅解备忘录的基础上与国内外监管机构进行信息共享。

发照和结构（核心原则2—5）

110. 中国界定了银行的业务经营许可范围，对银行有完整的发照和审批程序。相当数量的监管人员从事新机构、现有机构新设分支机构、新产品以及所有权变更的审批工作。对董事会成员和高级管理人员制定了适当的任职资格标准，而且把这一标准的适用范围扩大到银行的其他职位。对"银行"名称的使用受到应有控制，不允许成立空壳银行。新设银行的最低资本要求取决于银行的类型，这一点符合或高于国际标准。

111. 银监会对所有权变更和重大收购实行适当的审批程序。然而，中国经济体系正处于由国家所有制向私人所有制演变，从而可能使得银行的所有制结构变得更为复杂。在这方面，法律尚未授权银监会对受益所有权人或控制权间接变更进行审查。银监会称其一般能够通过直接收购者或其他间接方式获得关于受益所有权人/间接所有权人的信息。虽然评估团没有发现因为这个问题而削弱了监管有效性的情况，但这一法律授权应得到加强。应审查银监会关于可能更复杂的银行所有权结构的其他监管规则（例如关联方规则），以确保这些规则明确涵盖了这样的所有权结构。银行投资，包括对其海外分行的投资需要获得监管机构的批准。虽然一般情况下禁止银行投资于非银行活动，但银行投资于金融租赁公司和资产管理公司已在最近获批。银行投资于保险公司和基金管理公司直到最近才获批，有四个交叉所有权项目正在试点。在这些试点中，银监会要求银行与其他机构之间建立防火墙。此外，还明确规定这些试点非银行机构必须获得至少相当于行业平均水平的回报，否则将要求银行退出。

审慎监管和要求（核心原则6—18）

112. 有关资本充足率的法规以巴塞尔协议 I 为基础。巴塞尔协议 II 将于2011—2013 年期间对六家银行强制实施，其他银行则自愿实施。由于巴塞尔协议 II 尚未完全实施，因此没有对其进行正式评估。中国在巴塞尔协议 I 的执行工作中十分审慎，致使中国各家银行的资本比率普遍高于巴塞尔最低资本要求。银行的资本主要由高质量核心资本构成（约3/4）。最低资本要求为8%。为了建立逆周期缓冲，最新监管措施要求银行提高资本充足率，从而使五大银行的资本充足率达到11.5%，所有其他银行将达到10%。至于这些缓冲将如何发挥逆周期调节作用，并没有具体说明。银监会需要审视并向各方说明，当前要求银行所持资本高于最低要求是基于何种期望，并解释改变缓冲的标准。规章中有些方面不如巴塞尔协议 I 的规定那么保守，应对此加以检查。

113. 中国银行业的风险管理不断提高。在已经取得的巨大成就中，银监会发挥了重要作用。本次评估对某些方面未评为完全符合，主要是因为法律框架的缺陷（这些缺陷是可以纠正的），或因为银行还没有完全落实银监会的法规及指引。银监会在富有挑战、快速变化的环境中表现出色。银监会已制定行之有效的改革议程，需要沿着这个方向继续前行。为了实现为自己设定的目标，银监会需要所有其他政府部门的充分支持。大多数主要银行都已针对自身面临的主要风险建立了风险管理系统，但有些地方仍需要改进。银监会制定的指引整体上质量很高，这些指引往往是直接借鉴巴塞尔文件制定而成。一些风险领域的框架指引出台得相对较晚，其中的一些在 2009 年下半年才出台。需要一段过渡期以提高这些指引实施的有效性，使那些并非最先进的银行迎头赶上，并使银监会确保所有银行都建立与其所承担风险相适应的风险管理系统。

114. 新的风险治理、风险计量和风险管理系统尚未在压力状态下得到检验，有些方面显然需要重大改进。董事会批准的战略目标往往过度集中于各行业的贷款增长目标，对银行自身的风险管理系统关注不够，这有悖于监管要求。在一些银行，包括一些主要银行，在风险计量、管理和压力测试当中考虑到风险之间相互作用，并使资本与风险挂钩的全面风险管理方法尚处于早期阶段。对许多银行而言，需要优先考虑的不是迅速进展到这个阶段，而是确保充分建立健全风险管理框架，使其植根于本银行的文化和全行的运作，并可持续下去。虽然中国的银行业务主要是存款和贷款，但中国各家主要银行属于世界上大型银行之列，中国贷款市场由于业务范围和多样性而非常复杂，而且银行正在开展新的贷款业务和其他业务。因此，风险管理需要与这些现实相适应。中国正考虑推出显性存款保险制度，应认真考虑各种组织在破产重组中的作用。

115. 信用风险是中国银行业面临的最主要风险，且在一段时间内不会改变。这一风险受到银行和银监会的高度关注，并得到很好的控制。然而，银行、决策者和相当一部分银监会工作人员过于关注不良贷款。考虑到 21 世纪前几年的严重坏账问题，这是可以理解的。但是，这种几乎心无旁骛的关注，有时不利于对信用风险采取早期、前瞻性的措施。银监会和部分银行的高层意识到前瞻性判断的必要，但评估人员感到，这一理念还没有在机构内得到广泛宣传。关于不良资产以及上市银行准备金计提的规则和做法都非常充分。这些规则和做法均以与《国际财务报告准则》（IFRS）同等效力的会计准则和关于贷款分类的监管要求为依据。银监会定期对资产质量和准备金计提制度的实施情况进行广泛、深入的检查。绝大多数上市银行由主要会计师事务所进行审计。监管制度鼓励银行多提拨备，并要求在银行股本中持有额外缓冲。

116. 无论从整体来看，还是对主要单家银行来说，中国银行体系交易账户的市场风险都很低。随着市场的放开，这一风险可能会增加。最近宣布的汇改政策可能会增加银行及其客户的外汇风险。风险管理工具以及支持这些工具的信息技术和数据基础设施总的来说与风险水平相适应，但仍有需要改进的地方。然而，市场风险管理的先进程度在不久的将来很可能需要大幅度提高。实施巴塞尔协议Ⅱ将有所帮助。对于很多银行来说，银行账户利率风险（IRRBB）较为普遍。这种风险也可能随着利率市场化的进一步推进而上升。应尽快开发相应的风险管理工具，而不仅仅限于当前许多银行采用的以资产负债合约期限为基础的静态缺口分析。银监会还可以加强对这种风险的离群值分析。这将不仅仅对上市银行产生影响，而且这些改进不需要使用模型。

117. 多年来，操作风险一直是银行的一个关注焦点。主要有两类操作风险，一是内部控制缺陷和欺诈行为，二是信息技术风险。银行非常关注这两类风险，与评估团会谈的银行和其他人士都称，此类风险在最近几年呈明显下降趋势。现在的挑战是制定更全面的框架，以处理与银行有关的所有操作风险因素。这项工作已经开始。应该有更多的银行对风险和内控定期进行自评估，并进一步开发、监测和完善关键的操作风险指标。同样，无须改为采用复杂的用于资本分析的高级计量法（AMA）模型，便可实现这些改进。

持续监管方法（核心原则 19—21）

118. 监管方法越来越注重以风险为本。然而，由于使用 CAMELS + 评级体系和其他一些监管方法（包括在某些方面的最新做法），意味着监管评估的前瞻性不足。此外，过度依赖少数几个基本的简单比率的做法虽然是恰当的，但可能妨碍对银行内在风险及其风险管理和治理质量进行更多的基于判断的评估。应继续发挥简单的基本指标带来的好处，同时督促银行执行银监会发布的指引，这些指引要求银行采用更为复杂的方法。这也将鼓励银行形成良好的风险管理文化，而不是仅仅过度依赖于遵守监管规定。

119. 可能需要更多地关注中小银行，以确保其改进风险管理和公司治理。银监会拥有必要的现场和非现场监管工具以及经常、定期从银行获取信息的系统。但是，银行或银监会披露的有关安全性和稳健性等重要信息少于其他许多国家，如关于资本和流动性状况的信息。应该对此加以研究和改进。

会计处理和披露（核心原则22）

120. 中国已建立了与《国际财务报告准则》基本趋同的会计制度。世界银行最近的一份研究报告也高度评价了中国在这方面作出的努力，同时也指出了需要改进的一些地方。需进一步关注中国私营会计及审计行业的发展，以确保财务报表的专业编制和审计。对于被认为不适合开展可靠和独立审计的外部审计机构，银监会应有否决的权力。

监管当局纠正和整改的权力（核心原则23）

121. 银监会有权采取行动解决问题，并显示出这样做的意愿。处理问题银行一直以持续经营解决方案为基础。今后可能需要加强关闭问题银行的能力。

并表和跨境银行监管（核心原则24—25）

122. 对银行及其国内或海外直接附属公司和分行的并表监管质量很高。但是，现有法律允许并表监管可能覆盖不到的更复杂的集团结构的存在。银监会偶尔使用间接和非正式的手段来处理这种情况，对结构进行必要的改变。评估团建议（核心原则4）修订法律，正式规定最终受益所有权和间接控制权的变更需要得到银监会的批准，这项建议也将有助于解决这一问题。如果由一个监管机构依靠其他机构对综合经营集团（银行/保险/基金管理公司/试点）进行监管，在实践中可能并不总能发挥很好的作用，而且其有效性还未得到真正检验。在母国与东道国关系方面，银监会与许多国家（地区）有着广泛的正式和非正式合作安排，并且作为母国和东道国监管机构有效地利用这些安排。

表14 对《巴塞尔核心原则》的遵守情况概述

核心原则	评论
1. 目标、独立性、权力、透明度与合作	
1.1 责任和目标	法律明确规定银监会的目标是维护银行体系的安全和稳健，但当局最近也强调贷款增长，特别是某些行业的贷款增长，以促进经济发展和宏观经济复苏。银监会应继续强调其关于平衡贷款增长与审慎监管的理念。正在制定的金融业"一二五"规划，作为国民经济和社会发展第十二个五年规划的一部分，应强调银行业安全和稳健的重要性。银监会领导层应继续强调，银行在执行国家经济政策时应坚持稳健经营的做法。
1.2 独立性、问责制和透明度	预算安排、工作人员编制须经外部审批的规定和国务院能撤销银监会的规章与决定的权力（虽然迄今未使用过这项权力）削弱了银监会的监管有效性，并可能影响其操作独立性。银监会需要不断提升监管人员素质，培养更为专业化的队伍，以有效应对更为复杂、创新和国际化的环境。银监会需要得到政府的支持，为实现这一目标制定专门的战略，包括在预算、薪酬和激励机制等方面更具灵活性，以吸引和留住能够应对日益复杂的银行监管等工作的人才。银监会需要采用更具前瞻性的资源规划，并增加绩效考核的透明度。
1.3 法律框架	关于银行业监管的法律框架已在借鉴国际标准和良好实践基础上进行了修订。一些法律法规（在报告的其他部分阐述）需要加强，并在下一轮的修订中澄清某些重叠之处。
1.4 法律权力	已授权银监会采取各种纠正和整改措施，以处理银行的不审慎和违规行为。
1.5 法律保护	银监会工作人员依法履职的行动受到法律保护。
1.6 合作	国内机构之间建立了大量的信息共享和协调机制，但很多人认为，国务院牵头的跨部门金融协调机制最为有效。
2. 许可的业务范围	关于许可银行开展业务的规定很清晰，当局特别重视防止未经授权吸收存款。虽然禁止银行进行非银行活动，但允许以试点的方式进行新的尝试。最近一段时间以来，通过银信合作方式进行的个人和机构理财业务大幅增加，这反映了银行追求高收益的以及通过出售贷款来满足监管比率要求。
3. 发照标准	银监会投入大量资源用于发照和审批制度，这个制度很全面，包括对所有业务经营、服务和产品的事前审批。
4. 大笔所有权转让	在审批银行的大笔所有权转让时，银监会审查最终受益所有权人或控制股东的法律授权受到限制，因此采用间接和/或非正式的方法来达到这一目的。
5. 重大收购	对国内银行间重大收购的判断标准需要进一步明确。

核心原则	评论
6. 资本充足率	总的来说，银监会采取了相对保守的措施来实施巴塞尔协议 I，只有少数例外。银监会要求银行持有的资本高于巴塞尔最低资本要求，且 3/4 的资本由核心资本构成。银监会最近采取了逆周期资本缓冲措施，应进一步阐明其内容，以提高其有效性。银监会缺乏一个长期的、易于理解的、高于最低资本要求的资本缓冲政策。巴塞尔协议 II 的实施有助于推动各主要银行进一步改进风险管理，但根据目前的时间表，银监会用于有效实施巴塞尔协议 II 的资源可能很紧张。
7. 风险管理程序	虽然中国银行业仍以存款和贷款业务为主，但一些主要银行已跻身于世界大型银行之列，中国的贷款市场由于业务范围和多样性而非常复杂，而且银行正在涉足新的贷款领域和其他业务活动。因此，风险管理需要与这些情况相适应。银监会已经出台了高质量的符合国际标准的风险管理指引（有些指引是近期才出台的）。银行尚未完全落实这些指引，有些银行的差距还很大，可能需要一段时间才能将其付诸实践。各主要银行和中型银行都建立了信用/市场/操作风险的管理程序。然而，在一些银行，包括一些主要银行，考虑风险之间的相互作用，涵盖风险战略制定、监测、管理和压力测试的真正全面的风险管理方法尚处在初级阶段。某些风险指引（例如全面风险管理、流动性风险管理、声誉风险管理）刚出台不久，因此还不能期望它们在短时间内得到有效实施。现有的和新采用的风险管理程序从制定到充分发挥效力并得到监管机构的评估都还需假以时日。 对银行和监管机构而言，将银行所持资本与风险挂钩的程序尚不成熟。对主要银行而言，随着巴塞尔协议 II 的实施，这一情况将逐渐改观。可能需要为较小的银行制定一些更为详细的指引，说明如何使资本与风险挂钩。
8. 信用风险	这是中国银行体系中最主要的风险，在未来一段时间内将继续如此。最近在清理银行资产组合方面取得较大成就。但是，信用风险很可能会上升。银监会的指引是适当的。最近，很多银行的信用风险管理大幅改进，评估人员看到银行有很多良好的信用风险管理实践。然而，评估人员同时还发现一些明显的证据表明，并非所有银行都强化了与信用风险管理有关的治理措施（这些措施也尚未经受压力考验）。很多银行在制定信贷战略时更为依赖监管的不良贷款比率要求。银监会不得不采取各种措施来促使银行改进放贷和信用风险管理程序，而如果银行的风险管理方法更为可靠，这些措施本是不必要的。
9. 问题资产、拨备和准备	评估人员用了很多时间来评估这一原则。大多数银行都遵守了有关贷款损失拨备的会计准则和银监会的最低监管要求。银监会和主要银行的审计师付出了很大努力来确保拨备的计提符合会计和监管要求。较小的银行在遵守有关确认单项和组合减值的会计准则方面面临挑战。由于财政部规定了严格的核销标准，银行及时核销贷款的能力受到不利影响。
10. 大额风险敞口限额	银监会十分重视通过专门的非现场监督制度来识别大额风险敞口。然而，银监会还应该考虑建立一个更为全面的框架，用以评估关系方/关联方之间的风险。

核心原则	评论
11. 对关联方的风险敞口	尽管已有健全的制度来确认关联方，并规定关联方之间的交易须公平进行并有限额要求，但该制度没有考虑到，对某些地方政府持股的银行来说，地方政府作为共同所有人可能会带来关联方风险。
12. 国家风险和转移风险	国家风险和转移风险对于中国的银行来说越来越重要。尽管存在明显国家风险和转移风险敞口的主要银行已经建立了相关制度，但其他银行仍需努力。银监会最近整合了这方面的监管要求，并监测其实施情况。
13. 市场风险	考虑到市场结构和复杂产品未获批准，市场风险的规模和复杂程度都比较低，银行战略更偏重客户而不是自营交易。现有的风险管理方法符合当前的环境，但在执行中仍有缺陷。如果进一步放开利率或汇率，或是银行采取更激进的战略，这些风险管理方法将需要重大改进。
14. 流动性风险	由于采用简单的监管规则，例如贷存比上限和最低流动资产比率以及法定存款准备金要求，银行的流动性很高。应该鼓励银行采用更为先进的流动性风险管理方法，以便为进一步的市场放开做准备。
15. 操作风险	银行和监管机构长期以来一直有详细、高质量的内部控制程序（侧重于减少欺诈），而且注重信息技术风险。当前的挑战比这更进一步，是要对操作风险进行更为全面的计量和管理。各大银行已有所进展，但进展情况参差不齐。覆盖了核心原则所有内容的指引刚出台不久，需要提升银监会的监管专业技能。银行对各种业务进行风险与控制的自评估或为各业务条线制定关键风险指标的做法需进一步完善。
16. 银行账户利率风险	这一风险对各类银行来说都非常值得关注。随着利率的进一步放开，需要对利率风险进行积极的管理。当前，很多银行采用基于合约期限的静态缺口分析法来计量和管理这一风险。应该改为采用更为动态的分析方法，以预期现金流和利率非平行变动为基础，同时还应将各类资产和负债在上述情景中可能受到的影响考虑在内。银监会应加强对可能出现的离群值的分析。
17. 内部控制和审计	内部控制意识已得到强化，银监会非常注重这方面的监管。上市银行将面临执行"企业内部控制基本规范"（C–SOX）的挑战，该规范要求外部审计机构就银行内部控制自评估的充分性发表意见。
18. 防止利用金融服务从事犯罪活动	关于防止利用金融服务从事犯罪活动的监管职责由人民银行和银监会分担，其范围包括在银行实施和银行自己实施的犯罪活动。人民银行和银监会在履行这一职责时，需要改进合作和信息共享。银监会在银行欺诈监管方面取得长足进展，但还有一定的改进空间。2006年的反洗钱金融行动特别工作组（FATF）评估报告提出的与银行有关的反洗钱建议仍有待落实。
19. 监管方式	监管方式更加以风险为基础并借鉴了国际良好实践，但监管者应考虑在监管评级中更多地采纳检查人员的判断，减少对量化公式方法的依赖。

核心原则	评论
20. 监管技术	为了完善现有的以风险为基础的监管手段，银监会应重新考虑以分支机构合规性的检查为重点的策略，从而将资源用于其他更需优先考虑的监管行动上。
21. 监管报告	银监会已建立了一个全面的系统，可以经常、定期地从银行获取信息，银监会应考虑向公众提供银行的季度财务信息，以进一步提高银行业的透明度。
22. 会计处理和披露	银监会无权否决被认为不合适、无法进行可靠和独立审计的外部审计机构。2009年10月，《世界银行关于中国遵守标准与准则情况的报告——会计和审计》指出了中小型会计师事务所审计质量和会计行业监管工作的缺陷。银行业整体和单家银行的公开财务数据的缺乏降低了银行体系的透明度。
23. 监管当局纠正和整改的权力	如果银行没有遵守审慎规则，银监会有能力采取纠正行动。有关这方面的数据显示，银监会有意愿这样做。虽然银监会参与的银行重组中也有一些大规模的银行合并案例，但关于银行关闭的经验还非常有限。
24. 并表监管	对银行及其境内外附属公司和分行的并表监管质量很高。法律和法规允许更为复杂的集团结构存在，这使得银监会要符合本条原则的主要内容将面临挑战。由于银行对基金管理公司和保险公司的交叉持股（已有试点），依赖于防火墙和分业监管的做法可能是不够的。
25. 母国和东道国监管机构之间的关系	银监会重视与海外监管机构建立并保持多种形式的正式和非正式的合作机制，并且作为母国和东道国监管机构有效地运用这些机制。银监会还针对一家大型国际银行建立了监管联席会议机制，不久将针对第二家大型银行建立这样的机制。

表15　为更好地遵守《巴塞尔核心原则》的行动建议

参照的原则	行动建议
原则1.1　责任和目标	确保国务院制定的金融"十二五"规划强调安全与稳健的重要性，包括强调监管机构早期干预以解决潜在问题的重要性，并强调安全和稳健的银行为实现经济和社会目标所做的贡献。今后五年应优先考虑改进银行的风险管理（不只是主要银行，而是包括所有银行），以支持经济与社会目标。应考虑修订银监会的目标，以强调早期干预。降低对不良贷款的关注，要更加重视前瞻性的风险监测和计量。银监会领导层应继续强调审慎目标在执行国家经济政策方面的重要性。
原则1.2　独立性、问责制和透明度	赋予银监会根据大致目标决定人员编制和预算的权力。考虑改为采用直接通过行业收费的模式为银监会提供经费，以加强其独立性。制定一项由国务院支持的计划，以提升银监会工作人员的专业水平，包括更灵活的预算，允许银监会制定更灵活的薪酬政策以更好地吸引和留住专业人才。解决潜在的独立性问题。
原则4　大笔所有权转让	法律应明确规定，对所有的收购和银行大笔所有权转让，都应该对最终受益所有权人和间接控制人进行评估。

参照的原则	行动建议
原则6　资本充足率	重新考虑少数几个不及巴塞尔协议Ⅰ审慎的资本监管规定。考虑应采取何种方式来规划巴塞尔协议Ⅱ的实施，以确保取得成功，例如设置一个较长的过渡期。不断争取更多的专业人才，以对实施巴塞尔协议Ⅱ的银行进行持续有效的监管。加强银行资本状况的披露。
原则7　综合风险管理	继续督促银行遵守银监会的风险管理指引。确保充分重视银行的风险管理能力，不仅限于实行巴塞尔协议Ⅱ的银行。鼓励银行在经董事会批准的年度战略规划中采取更多与风险有关的措施。对风险管理实践进行跨银行专项检查，侧重于全行性的操作方法和评估标准，并提出改进意见。鼓励多使用全行性的压力情景进行压力测试，例如经济增速放缓将如何影响各类风险领域。鼓励银行将所持资本与风险挂钩。考虑就此对各家主要银行进行专项检查，确定评估标准，并提出改进意见。考虑为未实施巴塞尔协议Ⅱ的银行制定更为详细的指引，说明如何使资本与风险挂钩。
原则8　信用风险	在银监会的风险评级系统中增加更具前瞻性的信用风险评估内容。鼓励银行在制定其年度信用风险战略时，更多采用自己的风险评估体系。确保各主要银行都贯彻落实了银监会的信用风险管理指引。
原则9　问题资产	建立一个相对简单的机制，以方便贷款核销。
原则10、11　大额风险敞口和关联方贷款	在关于大额风险敞口和关联方交易的定义和规定中考虑地方政府对企业的共同所有权。
原则12　国家风险和转移风险	确保各主要银行执行国家风险和转移风险管理指引（2010年6月发布）。要求银行在2010年底之前提交针对有关缺陷的行动计划。在未来18个月内对这些银行的政策和实践进行一次检查。
原则13　市场风险	制定并实施一项行之有效的战略，以增加这一领域的专业人才。按照2006年的做法，定期对市场风险管理进行跨系统检查，以评估进展情况、确定评估标准并推动银行持续改进。评估市场风险资本计提豁免的门槛值是否适当。
原则14　流动性风险	应格外重视这一领域的监管，以提高2009年发布指引的实施效果。引导银行实施更先进的流动性风险管理。高度重视对各主要银行实施新指引情况的评估。
原则15　操作风险	确保各主要银行都已制订计划，至少针对各项业务进行风险和控制自评估，并制定关键风险指标体系。提高银监会监管人员的专业素质，以便能够根据2007年指引对主要银行的落实情况进行跨系统检查。操作风险的优先程度低于流动性风险和银行账户利率风险。须防范在条件不成熟的情况下过早采用高级计量法。
原则18　防止利用金融服务从事犯罪活动	银监会和人民银行应加强协调和信息共享，经常并定期地交流信息，包括反洗钱检查结果及大额可疑交易报告。建立银监会与人民银行信息共享机制。继续加强对在银行内部实施和银行自己实施的欺诈交易的处理。通过法律规定银行必须确认受益客户。

参照的原则	行动建议
原则 22　会计处理和披露	出台审计独立规定，以提高审计行业的公信力。 世界银行 2009 年 10 月公布的《关于中国遵守标准与准则情况的报告——会计和审计》建议，提高中小型会计师事务所的审计质量，加强对会计行业的监管力度。应重点实施这些政策建议。授权银监会否决被认为不合适、无法进行可靠和独立审计的外部审计机构。提高银行体系的透明度，按季公布银行业汇总数据、关键财务比率指标以及同类型机构平均数据。应提高审计监督检查的频率。
原则 24　并表监管	修订法律以授权银监会在所有情况下都可以要求银行建立适用并表监管的公司结构。运用在受益所有权和间接控制权（核心原则 4）方面新的授权，以保证公司结构允许并表监管。如果认为银行的附属基金管理公司和保险公司存在风险管理能力问题，则授权银监会对其进行检查。

F. 当局回应

123. 中国监管当局非常欢迎并积极配合此次针对《巴塞尔核心原则》的评估，以此为契机反映国际监管标准在中国的实施情况，并对照国际标准改进中国银行业监管。 评估过程中，评估团展现出令人赞叹的专业素质、敬业精神和在有限的时间内剖析复杂问题的能力，评估工作取得良好成效。中国监管当局借此机会阐述如下观点：

124. 银监会在中国政府的大力支持下，通过借鉴国际监管标准制定和颁布审慎监管框架，不断提高监管有效性，积极履行其维护银行业安全、稳健运行的法定职责。 改革开放三十年来，中国银行业的风险管理能力和公司治理水平有了显著提高，为监管工作的顺利开展提供了有利条件。评估报告充分肯定了中国银行业在风险管理和监管方面取得的进步与成绩，并认为中国银行业监管基本符合《巴塞尔核心原则》的各项要求。

125. 中国监管当局希望就评估报告中的以下问题进一步阐明观点。 评估报告指出国务院具有否决银监会规章的权力，这可能会影响到银监会的监管独立性。但是银监会并不认为这会影响其独立性或牺牲监管有效性。《银行业监督管理法》规定，银监会应依照相关法律、行政法规制定并发布银行业金融机构监督管理的规章、指引。而根据《立法法》，只有部委颁布的规章违反法律、行政法规或者不同部委的规章存在不一致时，国务院才可以修改或撤销不适当的部门规章。因此，除非银监会的规章、指引违反了相关法律、行政法规，银监会完全可以独立行使制定规章的权力。这种制度安排一方面建立了对银监会等政府机构依法行使权力的检查和制衡机制，另一方面也有助于促进中国法律体系的健全性和一致性。实践中，国务院从未修改或撤销过银监会发布的规章、指引。

126. 评估报告还指出，银监会现行的预算和编制安排可能不利于其独立地开展监管工作，影响监管有效性。自成立以来，银监会在履行银行监管职责过程中一直得到国务院及相关部委的大力支持。银监会通过海外招聘、培训和职业发展教育等措施不断提升员工素质和工作效率，信息技术的有效应用也提高了银监会的监管效率。然而，银监会承认，在竞争日益加剧、经营愈加复杂的行业背景下，银监会同世界上许多银行监管当局一样，在吸引、发展和留住监管人才方面面临挑战。通过与相关政府部门的密切合作，银监会致力于进一步增加监管资源、提升人员能力、留住高素质的一线监管人员，以便在瞬息万变的金融环境中，履行其维持银行业稳健、安全运行的职责。

127. 2006 年修订的《巴塞尔核心原则》更加强调风险管理的重要性，其评估方法要求评估者将银行的风险管理实践同监管当局的监管都纳入评估范围。银监会自成立以来，努力提升自身风险监管能力，同时督促银行提高公司治理和风险管理水平。迄今为止，中国银行业仍以传统的吸收存款、发放贷款为其主要业务。最近几年才开始在个别银行试点非银行金融业务，其业务规模也较小。因此，中国的银行体系比发达国家简单得多，不像发达国家那样由于复杂程度和关联程度较高，风险环境给银行业所带来的挑战大得多。评估报告认为银监会对银行风险管理能力方面的巨大进步起到了重要作用，不过仍有一些地方需要改进。在评估中国银行业风险管理能力与其当前所处风险环境的适应程度方面，银监会与评估团的观点有所不同。但是，银监会赞成随着金融改革的深化和金融自由化的发展，中国金融体系的关联度和复杂程度都将提高，继续提高银行的风险管理能力十分必要。比如，中国银行业未来需进一步完善将风险之间相互作用考虑在内，并将资本同风险有效挂钩的全面风险管理体系。同时，随着中国银行业蓬勃发展和经营日益复杂化，银监会将继续提高评估银行风险状况及风险管理程序的能力。

128. 评估报告提出了许多有价值的观点和建议，这将有助于提高中国银行业的监管水平。银监会十分重视并将积极采纳其中合理可行的部分。部分建议已经在实施过程中，部分建议也将作为银监会制定"提高银行业监管有效性中长期规划"的重要参考。实践证明，改革开放是促进中国银行业安全稳健运行的关键动力，银监会将继续推进中国银行业的改革开放。与此同时，银监会将继续积极参与金融稳定理事会和巴塞尔银行监管委员会的工作，进一步发展完善国际银行业监管标准，从而为增强全球银行体系抵御风险的能力作出贡献。

附件 II. 对金融领域标准和准则——
国际保险监督官协会（IAIS）
《保险核心原则与方法》的遵守情况：概述

A. 导言

129. 中国的保险公司受到密切监督，并普遍受到适当的监管。保监会采用基于规则的监管框架，被监管保险公司高度遵守监管规则。总体来看，《保险核心原则与方法》中以规则为导向的原则得到了严格遵守。相比之下，对市场退出和业务转移的监管存在不足。建议加强以下方面的监管：准备金充足情况、保险公司对偿付能力要求的遵守情况、保监会确保遵守资本要求的严格程度。为了使监管资源满足日益增长的需求，有必要从基于规则的监管转变为基于原则的监管。然而，在近期内，基于规则的方法看来是最合适的。

130. 关于中国遵守 IAIS《保险核心原则与方法》情况的评估，是 2010 年中国金融部门评估规划的一部分。本次评估以 2003 年版的 IAIS《保险核心原则与方法》为依据。除了保险核心原则外，评估还参考了 IAIS 的其他相关标准和指引。

131. 保监会通过北京总部和 35 个地区派出机构（即保监局）履行职责。保监会根据国务院颁布的条例（包括强制性汽车保险）和全国人大颁布的法律来制定保险监管规章。除了正式规章之外，保监会还根据国务院制定的保险市场商业和社会目标，发布了一系列指令、指引等。

132. 这次评估以金融部门评估规划筹备阶段和 2010 年 6 月现场评估访问期间向评估人员提供的资料为基础。保监会按要求提供了一份自评估报告，并根据评估人员在现场评估访问之前和访问期间提出的要求进一步提供了有关信息资料。所要求的文件，包括相关法律和一些主要的法规，都提供了英文版本。但在 42 个主要的保监会规章以及辅助指引和说明中，很多仅提供了中文版本。评估参照了与监管机构和市场人士的讨论内容。评估人员会晤了保监会和两个大型保监局工作人员、保险公司、保险中介以及会计和精算业内人士。评估人员感谢各方给予的积极支持和配合。

B. 体制结构和市场结构概述

133. 中国保险市场在全球排名第六。 截至 2009 年底，中国共有 59 家寿险公司、52 家非寿险（财产和意外伤害保险或财产保险）公司和 9 家再保险公司，其中包括一家专业信贷保险公司和 4 家专业农业保险公司（其中一家是相互保险公司）。4 家专业健康保险公司被列入人身（人寿等）保险业中。非寿险公司现在也可以经营短期健康保险。保险（控股）集团和控股公司有 8 家，另有 10 家保险公司设立了资产管理公司。2009 年，寿险保费达 1 092 亿美元，保险深度（即占 GDP 的比重）为 2.3%，这是相对发达经济体的典型标志。2009 年，非寿险业实现保费 539 亿美元，保险深度为 1.1%。财产和意外伤害保险业由汽车保险占主导地位（占保费总额的 70%），这是新兴市场的典型特征。这种不同寻常的模式可能反映了文化和历史根源。

134. 中国寿险市场高度集中。 前十大保险公司占保费总额的近 90%。除美国友邦保险公司（AIA）外，寿险业务未对其他外资公司开放，外资公司只能通过合资企业经营寿险业务，其中外资持股比例最高为 50%。⑨非寿险业也高度集中，中国人民财产保险公司（PICC）一直居于主导地位。

135. 最近五年寿险业务结构发生很大变化。 传统的保证收益保险业务在人寿保单中所占比重从 42% 下降到 23%，被万能寿险与投连险所取代。由于分红保险⑩为保险公司带来了持续稳定的收益，并为保单持有人提供了增加收益的可能性，近十年该业务一直占市场份额的 55% 左右。

136. 非寿险业务结构基本保持不变。 汽车和商业地产保险占产险保费收入的 80%，责任保险、海运、航空和运输保险以及意外伤害保险共占 11%。在保费收入中所占份额出现显著上升趋势的只有农业保险和健康保险。家庭财产保险仅占中国非寿险保费收入的 1%。与其他国家不同的是，中国抵押市场的发展并没有带动保费收入的激增。部分原因也许是银行没有对续保的监测和实施做好准备。

C. 主要结论

137. 有效监管的先决条件基本得到满足。 一些原则没有得到完全遵守，通常是出于以下两个原因之一：

---

⑨ 除了美国国际集团（AIG）外，还有两家外国股东由于特殊情况，持有 51% 的股份。
⑩ 分红业务的保证收益较低，但有机会参与利润分配。

- 保监会或其他得到授权的官方机构有意决定，如果完全执行相关的核心原则，将无法充分顾及中国保险市场当前的发展阶段，或不符合制度安排。这一结论可能适用于以下方面的原则：监管权力、监管目标、投资、衍生品工具和反洗钱。

- 保监会虽然制定了比较全面的规章，但在某些重要的监管领域没有足够的细则。中国采取了相当务实的监管方法，经常等到出现实际需要时才会采取行动制定新规则。这是被动的做法，而不是主动的做法，从而忽略了重要的领域。这个结论适用于以下方面原则：控制权的变化和业务转移、退出市场以及保险活动。

138. 在另一些领域，保监会制定了严格明确的规章，但评估人员发现，这些规章的应用和执行过于宽松，这也给保监会带来很大的声誉风险。这项结论适用于关于负债和偿付能力制度的原则。

- 保监会已实施一个全面的监管框架，高度重视保险公司执行适当的公司治理规则和充分建立风险管理体系。有效保险监管的先决条件基本上得到满足，但中国官方在持续反腐败和反贿赂方面存在一些不足。

- 监管体系强而有力且组织良好，但保监会迫切需要为其核心监管部门增加资源。保监会负责在一个非常庞大且多元化的市场中执行多种多样的任务。它还必须准备应对中国众多多元化保险市场规模和范围的持续迅速扩大。当今，保监会某些部门的合格人员数量可能不足以支撑其在一个不断发展的市场中履行职责。

- 关于被监管实体的原则得到大致遵守。应该颁布更多的管理规章以方便业务转移，并使营业牌照发放与法人实体注册脱钩。

- 保监会对保险公司的持续监管以及对市场和消费者的监督比较严格，显示出强有力的控制水平。这些方面的多数原则得到完全遵守。事实上，一些关于监管报告的规定似乎过于全面，报告的频率也过高。披露和消费者保护是充分的，最近得到进一步改善。

- 对审慎性原则的实施需要大大加强，尤其是关于负债和偿付能力制度。关于量化投资要求的规定也存在一些不足，但当局表示，短期内将发布更多的规章。保监会还应该审查当前与人民银行之间的反洗钱安排。反洗钱工作全部由人民银行开展，没有体现共同责任。不将反洗钱情况充分反馈给保监会的做法是不能接受的，给保监会带来声誉风险。为此，建议审查程序和职责，并作相应的结构调整，以消除这一弱点。

表16　对《保险核心原则与方法》的遵守情况概述

保险核心原则	评论
原则1-有效保险监管的条件	有效监管的先决条件基本上得到满足。需要加大执行力度，以消除对腐败行为的普遍认同，并尽量减少金融业的不道德行为。保监会的派出机构保监局最近积极开展了一场旨在减少欺诈行为、加强保险公司管理层和工作人员职业道德的行动。 中国当局对业务发展和公司战略的影响有可能妨碍市场的健康发展。中国必须解决以下二者之间的矛盾：一方面是对市场实行控制，包括严格控制外资公司的进入和扩张，另一方面需要发展寿险市场，以提供足够的保险保障和创新，从而促进中国市场的全面发展。
原则2-监管目标	保监会的监管目标规定得比较宽泛。 可以将金融稳定、消费者保护和公平竞争转变为操作目标，作为保监会职责说明的基础。该说明还可有助于新的工作人员更快地理解保监会的任务。 保监会的第二个目标和相关职责是发展国内市场（在实践中如此），这对一个监管机构来说相当独特。保监会向评估人员明确表示，对于保险业有控制的平稳增长及向消费者和国内行业提供保险保障，这两个目标都必不可少。一般来说，监管机构是通过确保公平的竞争环境以及适度且快速的监管来支持保险业的发展。因此，保监会把更多人力用于发展目标和职责不符合本条核心原则。 此外，各种商业目标和社会目标几乎将不可避免地导致与监管目标的冲突。可能发生的情况包括根据地区和社会发展情况来决定定价、产品设计和消费者保护以及发照。监管目标和商业目标所要求的观念和技能十分不同。建议将这两项目标分离开来，并指定合适的机构来负责行业发展、商业目标和社会目标。这将有助于确保监管机构有一个明确目标，并能够在没有冲突的情况下承担其责任；有助于政府和保险业更好地理解风险，以保证所采取行动的安全性和稳健性。
原则3-监管机构	保监会不是完全独立的，也不能免于行政干预。显然，中国的监管框架是建立在从国务院到保监会总部，再到各保监局的层层严格控制的基础上。此外，保监会的人力资源不足。特别是在非现场监督、检查、国际合作、会计和审计领域以及保监局关键部门，应通过适当增加人力资源予以大大增强。 与核心原则2一样，建议将保监会与商业和社会发展目标脱钩，并考虑建立一个负责整个金融业发展的机构。该机构因此可以确保银行、证券和保险领域的协调发展，同时照顾到每个领域的特定需求。
原则4-监管过程	在保险业发展的现阶段，保监会采用基于规则的监管方法是合适的，不建议保监会转向基于原则的监管体系。事实上，与保监会工作人员和保险从业人士，包括与审计师和精算师进行的会谈都表明，基于规则的监管制度在当前符合中国的商业文化。随着保险业的进一步发展，今后应该重新审视这个问题，以确定基于规则监管方法的可行性和适宜性。此外，因为基于规则导向的监管方法要求配备足够的工作人员，以完成劳动密集型监管过程，今后有必要考虑这对保监会可能造成的影响。虽然无论是基于规则的监管方法还是基于原则的监管方法，都需要增加保监会的工作人员，但在基于规则的监管方法下，为妥善应对预期庞大的市场规模以及各省和市场参与者的多元化，需要大幅增加工作人员。
原则5-监管合作和信息共享	与其他监管当局之间的信息共享以监管需求为基础。建议建立主动的信息共享机制，定期向在华从事相关业务的保险集团的监管机构提供关于中国市场的相关信息。相应地，保监会也应要求对方提供各自的信息。

保险核心原则	评论
原则6－发放牌照	发照程序不应仅限于控制保险公司的市场准入，还应当督促保险公司转变战略，增强承保业务能力。应该将公司组建与发放保险牌照更明确地分开来。保监会必须保证，一家公司可以被禁止签发新的保单，但仍有责任、有能力管理其当前的负债及合同。
原则7－人员的合适性	保险公司在变更外部审计时需要向保监会提交申请。在这方面，目前只需向保监会提交有关审计事务所的名字，而不是负责合伙人的名字。如不进一步询查，保监会将无从了解所涉保险公司的复杂程度与负责审计师的经验之间可能存在的不一致。建议保监会要求提供更详细的信息，说明有关外部审计师的背景和职业技能。这个方法将更符合监管方法中关于控制的总体态度。 保监会对关键工作人员合适性的要求很高。应密切关注保险市场的发展以及对高素质和经验丰富的管理人才的需求。不能由于没有足够适合的工作人员而限制市场的进一步发展，甚至导致不应有的折中做法。因此，保监会应确保人们普遍认识到，大学和专业机构需要培养出合适的人才，并鼓励保险公司举办适当的培训课程。
原则8－股权变更和业务转移	保监会必须制定合适的规章来方便业务转移。必须特别注意负债的转移、准备金和技术准备金的充足性、业务接受方满足适当性、牌照和内部控制要求的能力。转移不应取决于保单持有人或受益人的认可，但应将可能的转移及时通知他们。涉及人寿保险业务转移时，应要求接受转移的公司将现有的人寿保险业务与被转移业务分开。
原则9－公司治理	保监会已经颁布了足够的规章以确保将公司治理作为保险监管框架的主要组成部分。考虑到中国版图之大、市场规模之大（在现在的早期发展阶段就已经很庞大）和保险公司数量之少，公司治理监管和强制实施对于建设一个稳健安全的市场环境来说至关重要。 为准备这次评估进行的研究、与保险公司人员的会谈和深入对话，提高了人们对反腐败（包括反贿赂）体系健全性的关注。人们普遍认为，需要加大力度来减少腐败。这特别涉及到保险产品销售、保险理赔的办理、法律体系的总体信誉、诉诸法院的机会和对消费者权益的保护等方面。
原则10－内控	保监会对内控的监管以规则为基础，并制定了十分详细的规定。保险公司定期、及时地向保监会总部和各保监局提交报告。保险公司各委员会的会议记录都要提交并进行分析。 保监会可考虑聘请外部审计师将对风险管理体系和内部控制程序的检查纳入定期审计，至少对大型保险公司需要这样做。对于这些大公司，每五年开展一次全面检查的周期可能太长。
原则11－市场分析	保监会要求提交的月度报告内容庞杂且非常详细。但不清楚的是，这些数据在多大程度上得到及时、有意义的分析，特别是考虑到技术绩效的数据通常在如此短的时间内不会发生重大变化。保监会应考虑是否需大大减少月度提交的资料。正如现在对再保险公司的要求那样，一些关于技术绩效的数据可改为按季提交。
原则12－向监管机构报告和非现场监测	保监会建立了一个全面的分类监管体系，并能根据每个被监管机构的风险状况来有效分配监管资源。可以进一步完善分类监管体系的标准，以便通过内涵价值法来反映人寿保险业务的技术绩效。此外，还应更好地反映风险的影响和概率。

保险核心原则	评论
原则 13 - 现场检查	还应该利用现场检查来验证对非现场监测所作假设的准确性。将检查工作集中在一个部门有很多优点。然而，对保监会所有参与运营监管过程的人员来说，具备关于保险公司运作方式以及关于保险公司流程和业务模式等方面的经验和知识是非常重要的。
原则 14 - 预防和整改措施	预防程序很彻底、很全面。考虑到上文所述企业文化，该程序包含的规则比必要得多，且必须在所有领域执行，特别是审慎原则，其执行力度更大。整改措施以偿付能力为基础，有证据显示存在监管宽容。
原则 15 - 执行或处罚	
原则 16 - 清盘或退出市场	保监会需要制定专门的规则，以便保险公司通过托管（适用于非寿险公司）或业务转移/合并来自愿退出市场。考虑到当前的市场状况，这些规则的制定比较紧迫，包括单一保险人规则。业务转移应该经过精算核准和监管审批，而不是经过保单持有人的批准。
原则 17 - 对集团的监管	中国保险市场的发展有一个明确的目标：将公司的数量限制在可控范围内。中国保险市场已位居全球第六位。前十大保险市场中，多数发达市场的保险公司数目至少相当于中国的三倍。预计保险集团的作用将变得更为重要，保监会应进一步研究制定规章，以促进对保险集团的监管。考虑到集团的多元化经营，监管势必包括集中化的风险管理职能和集团偿付能力要求。
原则 18 - 风险评估和管理	为了履行风险管理职能，需要保险公司和保监会都付出大量努力。对风险管理体系的改进和适当性，很难通过非现场监测和监管报告来衡量。现场检查周期长达五年。保监会应同意修改监管规则，并要求保险公司提交充分的、经过审计的报告，至少要求那些所占市场份额相当大或存在特殊风险敞口的公司这样做。
原则 19 - 保险活动	关于保险活动的界定很充分。保监会对市场实行高度控制。保险公司为获得竞争优势进一步开发产品或业务的能力受到限制。 保监会应防止保险公司通过贷款和抵押资产的方式来增加资本或技术准备金。 产品审批和非现场监测必须能及早识别不足之处，并能迅速有效地进行整改。
原则 20 - 负债	保监会不应允许保险公司将准备金维持在不足的水平。保单持有人和受益人一定期望保监会确保各公司始终满足最低准备金要求。产品审批和非现场监测必须能及早识别不足之处，并能迅速有效地进行整改。保监会还应防止保险公司在准备金不足时签发新保单，并应防止保单的过度交叉补贴。 在引入新会计准则的同时应采取预防措施。重新计量结果应延期作为股权的一部分纳入总收益，至少三年内不得支付给股东。
原则 21 - 投资	保险公司的投资类别和机会十分有限。这种定量和定性方面的限制措施似乎确保了安全与稳健的市场环境，但也使保险公司过度面临国内利率风险和信用风险。如第22条保险核心原则所述，保监会应发布关于允许宏观对冲和组合对冲的规定。保监会应该认定投资管理者能够进行对冲活动。对中国保险公司财务状况进行的分析显示，投资收益波动很大。特别值得注意的是，传统盈利产品的业绩依赖于可靠且稳定的投资收益。保险公司应有更大的灵活性来实现这些收益。微观对冲不充分，且不够灵活，无法提供适当的保护。 保监会应对计入技术准备金和资本要求的资产质量进行明确规定。不应允许使用这类资产进行关联方交易。

保险核心原则	评论
原则 22 – 衍生产品和类似产品	在进行本次评估时，尚不允许保险公司从事衍生品业务。因此，对冲投资风险的手段有限。不过，有六家内控完善的国内保险公司获得例外许可进行试点。作为试点研究的一部分，允许这六家保险公司购买人民币利率掉期。保监会现已发布一项关于股指期货的规则，并正在考虑制定实施细则。
原则 23 – 资本充足和偿付能力	偿付能力规定在很大程度上是静态的，没有完全以风险为基础。国际上讨论的主要有两种偿付能力框架：偿付能力 II（Solvency II）是欧盟制定的一个标准，考虑到了保险公司业务模式的具体细节，并允许根据充分经济价值概念重新计算资产和负债。第二个概念是对风险资本方法的改进，在美国市场得到应用。从概念上看，偿付能力 II 可能更加先进，但是对保险公司和监管机构来说，在应用时也复杂得多。中国当前正在研究，以在这两大方法之间作出选择。考虑到保监会当前基于规则和控制的监管方法，可能不适于采用偿付能力 II。根据当前的发展阶段，应在以下现行原则的基础上完善目前的偿付能力制度：对理赔和保费趋势进行静态分析、资产风险评估、发展确认以及为通货膨胀预留的款项和各项业务条线的具体情况。此外，强烈建议重新计算负债以确定偿付能力。 目前有 8 家公司的偿付能力低于 100%。保监会仍然允许这些公司开展新业务，但可能会限制其增设分支机构。其中一些公司的偿付能力不足情况已经持续了两个季度以上。 作为一条监管原则，不应允许任何偿付能力不足 100% 的持照机构开展新业务。如果管理层或股东无法在非常有限的时间内注入资本，应宣布公司偿付能力不足，并由监管机构来管理。当前有 8 家公司的偿付能力不足 100% 的情况向市场发出这样的信号：违反资本要求不会导致吊销牌照或公开警告等严重后果。 对于保险公司存放于资本充足率不达标银行的存款认可为资产的做法是自相矛盾的。适当的做法应该是要求保险公司立即取出存款，以维护保单持有人和公司的利益。 保监会应该认识到，由于没有充分的偿付能力监管，将使其面临声誉风险。而由于过度的监管宽容，没有充分的强制执行措施，也使其面临声誉风险。监管宽容与对保险公司的全面实际控制方法是矛盾的。 保监会应该防止保险公司通过贷款和抵押资产的方式来增加资本或技术准备金。
原则 24 – 中介	
原则 25 – 消费者保护	保监会可引入公司投诉披露机制，以进一步强化公司自律，并提高对消费者满意度的认识。应该把投诉职能从保险协会移交给更加独立的机构，以加强这项工作的公信力。
原则 26 – 面向市场的信息、披露和透明度	由于关于披露的法规最近才出台，应该建立一审查程序，以便在今后两年内进行修订和完善。
原则 27 – 欺诈	保监会在打击欺诈方面已做了相当多工作。应增加人员配备水平，以更好地打击欺诈行为。腐败和贿赂也是值得关注的问题。应加大努力并补充足够的工作人员，这将使保监会能够为金融业市场纪律的总体规范作出更大贡献。
原则 28 – 反洗钱和反恐融资	当前，人民银行和保监会共同担负保险业反洗钱职责，由于保监会没有积极参与和影响这项工作，给保监会带来相当大的声誉风险，尤其在当前人民银行实行的反洗钱制度尚不完善的情况下。需要建立明确的问责制，以便根据反洗钱方面的具体需要及时采取应对措施。保监会在反洗钱方面职责模糊以及在检查和处罚方面缺乏影响和参与，这种情况难以令人满意。需要确定负责反洗钱职责的部门，然后确保该职责得到有效的履行。如果不是由保监会承担这一职责，则必须向其提供充分的信息，以便其对保险业进行适当的监管。此外，报告可疑交易的门槛值应该与关于收入的门槛值更加一致。

D. 主要建议

139. 评估团发现若干有待改进之处，在表 17 中加以概述：

表 17　为更好地遵守《保险核心原则与方法》的行动建议

原则	行动建议
原则 2 – 监管目标	可以将金融稳定、消费者保护和公平竞争转变为操作目标，作为保监会职责说明的基础。该说明有助于新的工作人员更快地理解保监会的任务。 保监会的第二个目标和相关职责是发展国内市场（在实践中如此），这对一个主流监管机构来说相当独特。建议把这两项目标分离开来，并指定一个合适的机构来负责行业发展、商业目标和社会目标。这将有助于确保监管机构有一个明确目标，并能够在没有冲突的情况下承担其责任。
原则 3 – 监管机构	保监会的人力资源不足。特别是在非现场监督、检查、国际合作、会计和审计领域以及保监局关键部门，应通过增加适当人力资源予以大大增强。
原则 6 – 发放牌照	发照程序不应仅限于控制保险公司的市场准入，还应当督促保险公司转变战略，增强承保业务能力。保监会必须保证，一个公司可以被禁止签发新保单，但仍有责任、有能力管理其当前的负债及合同。
原则 8 – 股权变更和业务转移	保监会必须制定合适的规章来方便业务转移。必须特别注意负债的转移、准备金和技术准备金的充足性以及业务接受方满足适当性、牌照和内部控制要求的能力。 转移不应取决于保单持有人或受益人的认可，但应将可能的转移及时通知他们。 涉及人寿保险业务转移时，应要求接受转移公司将现有的人寿保险业务与被转移的业务分开。
原则 14 – 预防和整改措施	需要加大力度，对违反偿付能力规定的保险公司采取《保险法》第 6 章规定的整改措施。
原则 16 – 清盘或退出市场	保监会应该制定专门的规章，以便保险公司能够通过业务转移或合并来退出市场，并允许非寿险业务的托管。
原则 20 – 负债	产品审批和非现场监测必须能及早识别不足之处，并能迅速有效地进行整改。保监会还应防止保险公司在准备金不足时开展新业务，并应防止对保单的交叉补贴。 在引入新会计准则的同时应采取预防措施。重新计量结果应延期作为股权的一部分纳入总收益，至少三年内不得作为股息支付给股东。
原则 23 – 资本充足和偿付能力	保监会应督促 8 家偿付能力低于 100% 的保险公司进行整改。作为一条监管原则，不允许任何偿付能力不足 100% 的持照机构开展新业务。 如果管理层或股东无法在非常有限的时间内安排注入资本，应宣布公司偿付能力不足，并由监管机构来管理。 对于保险公司存放于资本充足率不达标银行的存款认可为资产的做法是自相矛盾的。适当的做法应该是要求公司立即取出存款，以维护保单持有人和公司的利益。
原则 28 – 反洗钱和反恐融资	需要建立明确的问责制，以便根据反洗钱方面的具体需要及时采取应对措施。保监会在反洗钱方面职责模糊以及在检查和处罚方面缺乏影响和参与，这种情况难以令人满意。需要确定承担反洗钱职责的部门，然后确保该职责得到有效的履行。 如果不是由保监会承担这一职责，则必须向其提供充分的信息，以便其对保险业进行适当的监管。

E. 当局回应

140. 感谢评估团专家对保监会在监管执行力、分类监管、市场分析研究、监管合作、信息共享和消费者保护等方面取得成绩的认可。

141. 评估团专家同样看到，保监会在公司治理、内控、集团监管、偿付能力监管、风险管理、非现场监管方面所作的努力和取得的进步。

142. 评估团专家能够理解，在个别没有完全遵守国际原则的领域，保监会是根据中国国情，针对特有的市场环境和发展阶段，选择了适当的监管措施和手段。我们遵循的监管理念和 IAIS《保险核心原则与方法》是一致的。我们着眼于审慎监管，重视加强风险防范，大力维护市场秩序，保护消费者权益，有效地维护了市场稳定。

143. 关于偿付能力监管，保监会高度重视偿付能力监管，在研究欧盟、美国等偿付能力监管标准的基础上，建立了符合中国国情的偿付能力监管体系。现行的偿付能力监管制度，符合中国新兴市场的发展状况，有利于维护保险市场稳定。事实证明，在全球金融危机中，我们的偿付能力体系有效发挥了风险防范作用，中国保险业成功抵御了国际市场动荡的冲击。现行偿付能力监管制度关注了保险公司的承保风险、投资风险、利率风险、信用风险、资产负债匹配风险，具备以风险为基础的偿付能力监管的基本特征，为向全面的风险监管过渡奠定了良好的基础。保监会正全面研究国际偿付能力监管制度，积极制定更为完善的偿付能力监管制度。

144. 关于反洗钱监管，中国有其独特的反洗钱工作机制。中国《反洗钱法》规定，人民银行是全国反洗钱工作的主管部门，各监管机构积极配合。中国有关部门的反洗钱职责划分是清晰的。保监会也承担着不可或缺的反洗钱职责，并通过其日常监管予以实现。从反洗钱监管实践看，保险业金融机构能够认真接受人民银行和保监会共同实施的反洗钱监管，建立完善的内控制度和措施，自觉主动地履行反洗钱义务。保监会与人民银行（反洗钱局）建立了充分的信息沟通渠道，同时也对保险机构包括反洗钱在内的各项内控制度进行检查，全面掌握其风险状况。

145. 针对发展过程中出现的新问题、新局面，保监会一直大力推动完善规章制度建设，努力提高监管执行力。自 2009 年 10 月 1 日新修订的《保险法》出台后，保监会制定、修订、颁布了一系列部门规章，从任职资格、信息披露、资金运用、股权管理等多个方面进一步规范行业秩序，加强公司治理与内控，力求促进保险公司提高风险管理能力，从根本上保障被保险人的合法利益。

146. 对评估专家提出的建议，我们将在监管实践中、在法规制度制定过程中认真研究和借鉴。

附件 III. 对金融领域标准和准则—— 国际证监会组织（IOSCO）《证券监管目标与原则》的遵守情况：概述

A. 导言

147. **这项评估是作为中国金融部门评估规划的一部分于 2010 年进行的。** 评估工作采用了 IOSCO 的《证券监管目标与原则》（2003 年 5 月）和《证券监管目标与原则实施状况评估方法》（2008 年 2 月）。在评估中参考了证监会提供的自评估报告、证监会网站和中国其他部门网站上的公开信息以及中国相关法律法规。

B. 体制结构和市场结构 – 概述

148. **证监会对中国大陆的证券和期货市场实行集中监管。** 中国对金融业实行分业监管模式，证券市场由证监会负责监管。证监会根据法律和国务院授权，对中国证券期货市场实行集中统一的监管，目标是促进市场稳健和推动市场发展。

149. **在该体制下，证监会总部负责履行下列职责：** 制定、修改和完善证券期货市场规章和条例；拟定市场发展规划；办理重大审核事项；指导和协调无偿付能力证券期货公司的风险处置；组织查处证券期货市场重大违法违规案件；指导、检查、促进和协调全国的监管工作。在证监会总部的监督下，36 个派出机构负责各自辖区内的一线监管工作。

150. **自律组织是监管体系的重要组成部分。** 作为证监会监管工作的补充，自律组织包括各证券和期货交易所、中国证券登记结算公司、中国证券业协会和中国期货业协会，负责对其会员和上市公司的证券期货交易活动进行自律监管和一线监督。此外，成立于 2007 年的中国银行间市场交易商协会（NAFMII），对银行同业拆借市场和债券市场的定期金融工具交易进行监督。

151. **证监会受国务院的统一领导，并由国务院任命证监会主席。** 证监会主席是中国政府部长级官员，与银监会和保监会主席平级。《证券法》、《证券投资基金法》明确规定了证监会的职责，还有一系列相关法律对证监会的职责和权力进行了扩充。

152. **证监会对各股票和期货交易所、中国证券登记结算公司及其他清算和结算机构、证券公司、期货公司以及集合投资计划运营商拥有广泛的监管权。**其他政府机构各自履行 IOSCO 原则所述的部分监管职责。其中主要机构描述如下，其他机构将在逐项原则评估中提到。与 IOSCO 的评估工作特别有关的机构是人民银行，它负责中国反洗钱的监管，指导和组织金融部门和包括证监会在内的监管机构的反洗钱工作，并监测相关的资金流动。人民银行还负责管理银行间同业拆借市场和银行间债券市场，是为证券投资者保护基金提供初始资金的政府部门，建立该基金的目的是为了帮助处置本世纪初大量倒闭的证券公司并向投资者提供补偿。

153. **上海证券交易所（上交所）成立于 1990 年。**截至 2009 年底，上交所总共有 870 家上市公司，1 351 只上市股票，总市值达 2.78 万亿美元，股票成交额达 5.22 万亿美元。上交所有 107 家证券公司会员以及 7 个国内和海外特别会员。在上交所采用电子竞价交易系统，该系统通过上交所的主机按照价格优先和时间优先的原则进行自动价格撮合。深圳证券交易所（深交所）也成立于 1990 年，设有主板、中小企业板、创业板和代办股份转让系统。上交所和深交所的交易和业务规则须经证监会审批。

154. **中国境内有三家商品期货交易所和一家金融期货交易所。**它们是：上海期货交易所（上海期交所）、大连商品交易所（大连商交所）、郑州商品交易所（郑州商交所）和中国金融期货交易所（中金所）。中金所由其他商品期货交易所出资组建，最近开始交易股指期货，这是中国的第一个金融衍生工具。中国计划今后推出其他市场化的金融衍生工具，例如期权，并有可能推出国债和外汇期货和期权，以丰富金融衍生品市场。商品交易所的交易和业务规则须经证监会审批。

155. **中国证券登记结算公司成立于 2001 年，负责制定清算和结算参与人规则，特别是清算和结算账户的管理规则。**按照规定，作为一个证券登记和清算机构，中国证券登记结算公司应建立证券和清算账户，清算、结算证券以及证券交易资金，并根据发行人的指令派发证券权益（《证券法》第 157 条）。中国证券登记结算公司制定了详细规则，以确保其会员遵守相关法律法规，包括证券账户管理规则、清算参与人管理办法和证券结算备付金管理规则，这些规则均须经证监会审批。其处罚权包括限制或撤销参与账户的使用权，暂停或终止清算参与人的清算权。

156. **中国主要有两类集合投资计划业务：基金管理人管理的证券投资基金和证券公司开展的集合资产管理业务。**近年来，理财产品的规模大幅增长，截至

2009 年底，银行理财产品总额达 1 476 亿美元，其中投资级产品超过 964 亿美元。此外，一些基金，特别是通过信托公司管理的私募股权基金，由银监会负责监管。其他一些基金，尤其是与产业发展有关的私募股权基金，由发展改革委负责监管。

157. **中国证券业协会和中国期货业协会分别是证券业和期货业的全国性自律组织。** 这两个组织的目标，是在证监会的集中监督管理下对证券业和期货业实行自律管理；发挥政府与证券业和期货业之间的桥梁和纽带作用；保持证券业和期货业的公平竞争，促进市场的透明、公正与公平，并促进市场的健康、稳定发展。中国证券业协会和中国期货业协会负责对其会员进行一线监督，并受证监会委托对证券业和期货业会员进行初步资格审查。

158. **中国证券业的发展经历曲折，但总的来说增长非常迅速，最近五年尤其如此。** 在监管层面，已经进行了一系列重要的监管改革，以推动发展一个更为现代化的资本市场。股权分置改革为政府和准政府机构在上市公司持有的所谓非流通股建立了一个市场定价系统。在 21 世纪前十年早期，继证券公司和基金公司发生偿付能力普遍不足问题和挪用客户资金的情况后，证券业进行了一次重大整顿。这次整顿包括对客户资产普遍要求按第三方存管规定进行处理，并对证券公司提出风险资本要求。这些改革有力地加强了证券公司的稳定性，保护了客户资产。

C. 有效证券监管的先决条件

159. **中国监管制度采用了一套清晰的会计和审计准则。** 这些准则与《国际财务报告准则》和《国际会计准则》高度趋同，质量很高，得到国际认可。会计和审计行业正在发展中，专业素质和能力不断提高。同样，私人法律行业和司法系统处理商业争端的能力也在持续增强，但是，机构股东和散户股东在公司治理中的参与度还不够。因此，与那些股东较为活跃、而且比较易于通过诉讼来解决严重争端的国家和地区相比，中国证监会在处理因违规行为引起的企业倒闭方面任务较重。

160. **中国的立法有多个层级。** 最高一级是全国人民代表大会或其常务委员会制定的法律，其中包括《证券法》和《证券投资基金法》。第二层级是国务院根据《宪法》和其他法律颁布的行政法规。第三层级是证监会根据法律和国务院的法规制定并颁布的（从属于这些法规的）规章和指引。证监会的这些规章和指引如果是新的监管要求或与创新有关，则会冠以"暂行"或"试行"等字样，但是享有与证监会颁布的其他规章和指引同等的地位和同等的执行力。

161. 在有些情况下，最高人民法院会出台相关意见来强化法律的严格规定，这种做法富有成效。例如，最高法院出台意见确立了《证券法》第139条的合法性和可执行性，并作出类似规定，明确如果证券公司破产，其代客户持有的资金不应作为清算资金的一部分，而应继续作为客户的财产〔见《最高人民法院关于冻结、划拨证券或期货交易所、证券登记结算机构、证券经营或期货经纪机构清算账户资金等问题的通知》（1997年）〕。在闽发证券公司破产案件中，破产管理人提议将价值约1 129万美元的客户交易结算资产认定为清算财产。最高人民法院的裁决是，这些资金不在清算之列，应该用来弥补客户交易结算资金的缺口。

D. 主要结论

162. 如上所述，自证监会成立以来不到20年间，中国证券期货业及其监管得到了很大发展。近年来的改革，特别是股权分置改革、2010年推出的股指期货交易、建立第三方存管制度和对证券公司基于风险的净资本要求等，提高了市场透明度，拓宽了产品范围，增强了中介机构的财务稳健性，对投资者保护非常有益。这些改革经过精心规划和实施，受到市场参与者的欢迎。这证明证监会和其他相关机构采取了积极、战略性的方式来监管中国的证券市场。这些改革依据一套广泛的监管规定，这些规定参考了其他较为发达的证券市场，包括美国和中国香港市场的经验。为完全符合IOSCO的标准，还需要在监管框架的个别方面加以改进。本报告指出的某些有待改进的方面有赖于法律和会计环境的进一步改善。

163. 监管机构：证监会负责证券业的监管，其职责由以下三大法律明确界定：《证券法》、《证券投资基金法》和《期货交易管理条例》。中国实行分业监管，银监会负责银行业和银行业机构的监管，保监会负责保险业和保险公司的监管。如果银行或保险公司从事证券类活动，例如开发销售理财产品，银监会和保监会分别对其具有相应的监管权限。此外，有些实体，例如对冲基金和私募股权基金，不受其他实体的监管或监管不足。为了避免监管套利，对具有相似功能的产品应该以相似的方式监管，在这方面，当局应该特别关注对理财产品的监管。关于对冲基金和私募股权基金，在这次评估之前，IOSCO原则不要求对其进行监管。然而，考虑到这些基金增长迅速（特别是私募股权基金），而且有可能被用作散户的投资工具，当局应考虑将其置于证监会的监管范畴。证监会为了履行其职责，有权在《立法法》和相关法律赋予的权力范围内制定规章和规范性文件。实践中，证监会作为一个独立机构行事，不受政治或商业利益干扰，但是作为国务院的直属事业单位，按规定需遵守公务员制度下的人事程序和预算程序，这不一定跟得上受监管对象的发展步伐。如果在这方面增加灵活性，将有助于证监会行使监管职能。考虑到市场的迅速增长和其他市场约束机制在中国资本市场发展现阶段的性质，证监会的预算对其行使权力和履行职责来说是不够的。中国非常注重投资者教育，但需进一步加大努力，以增强散户投资者对市场和风险的认识。

164. 自律组织： 中国的监管制度在很大程度上依靠自律组织在证监会的领导和监督下行使监管职能。这些自律组织包括交易所、清算和结算机构以及行业协会。考虑到中国资本市场的成长，特别是上市公司、散户投资者和监管对象的增加，自律组织需要不断关注其监管职能，并为之提供资源。虽然证监会对自律组织行使重要的监督管理并定期与其沟通，但应考虑制定一个正式的规划，定期对各交易所进行全面检查。

165. 执法： 证监会拥有全面的检查、调查、监察和执行权力，特别是在案件调查期间，有权通过行政命令冻结保护资产。在违规行为对投资人造成损失的情况下，相关法律规章规定了私人采取追偿行动和其他行动的权利，但在中国，由法律制度（特别是商业法庭）以及机构投资者和其他参与者形成的市场约束对公司治理的影响不如在其他国家或地区那样大。私人执法行动虽然不能取代公共执法行动、监督和管理，但可以对后者进行补充和支持。这些因素综合在一起，削弱了私人采取法律行动的能力，使其无法对遵纪守法产生有意义的实际影响。考虑到市场的散户参与程度非常高，与其他市场相比，证监会和其他相关部门在确保合规方面承担的任务较重。关于异常交易的监督范围甚广，并已采取一些重大的执法行动，以遏制市场操纵行为和内幕交易，但还需要不断努力，加强在非法投资活动（包括庞氏骗局和非法投机券商）方面的法律，并增加这方面的人力资源。

166. 合作： 为行使管理和监督职能，证监会能够与国内外同行分享公开和非公开信息，无须经过其他外部程序。证监会与银监会和保监会以及很多外国证券期货监管机构正式签署了信息共享协议。证监会和其他国内监管机构应该更多考虑其合作协议的功效，特别是在确保具有相似功能的产品和活动受到相似监管方面的功效，以避免可能出现的监管套利。作为 IOSCO《关于信息交流的多边谅解备忘录》的签署方，证监会积极要求外国监管机构提供信息和协助，并应对方要求向其提供信息和协助。

167. 发行人： 现有监管制度包含证监会和各交易所制定的详细规定和后续机制，以保证上市公司和其他投资计划披露有关财务结果和风险的全面信息。证监会应针对广告活动制定更明确的规定，与关于集合投资计划的规定相似，要求广告中载明请潜在投资者参阅招股说明书的表述。监管制度在股东权利和公平对待股东方面有充分的规定，包括与并购有关的这些问题。然而，与其他主要市场实行的标准相比，提供年度和半年度财务报表的时限太长以及报告重大持股变化的门槛值太高，应该对其进行审查。监管制度采用了一套明确的会计和审计准则，这些准则与《国际财务报告准则》高度趋同，质量很高，得到国际认可。需继续关注私人会计和审计行业的发展，并重新考虑针对提供虚假或不实财务报表规定的罚款数额，以保证财务报表的编制和审计符合专业水准。

168. 集合型投资计划：中国针对那些希望运营或销售集合投资计划的主体制定了明确的监管规定，包括合理的准入要求、持续的资质条件和操作规范以及旨在管理利益冲突的规定。监管制度就集合投资计划的法律形式和结构制定了充分的规定。通过强制性第三方存管制度对客户资产进行隔离和保护，并作出了全面的披露规定，以使潜在投资者能够评估计划的适当性和前景。监管制度包含充分的估值规定，包括审计规定，并就认购或赎回基金时的定价作出了具体规定。然而，随着这个行业的发展，应对有关与基金管理人专业资格和经验的规定进行评估。考虑到市场中的散户参与程度很高，必须用简单明确的语言提供所有信息，证监会需要对此进行密切监督。证监会应该警惕可能出现的无照集合投资计划活动，例如庞氏骗局，并注意识别和阻止这类活动。

169. 市场中介机构：中国监管制度规定，市场中介机构必须获得证监会颁发的牌照，并遵守初始和持续的资本、资历和资格要求。证监会应考虑修订关于投资顾问的规则，要求这些顾问向客户详细披露其个人背景和职业履历、工作经验、合规记录、投资策略和费用结构，这是因为，在一个有大量散户参与的市场中，发展独立财务顾问能力是其重要组成部分。中国监管制度为市场中介机构规定了适当的审慎控制措施，这些措施与市场中介机构从事的具体行业中的风险密切相关。初始的注册资本要求和持续的基于风险的净资本要求提供了重要的风险缓冲。由于基于风险的净资本制度还比较新，证监会应继续对其进行认真监测，以确保该制度覆盖所有相关风险。监管制度要求市场中介机构必须具备内部风险管理功能并制定相关控制措施，以保护客户利益。证监会可考虑在一定程度上延伸监管制度的技术性内容，以覆盖该行业现有的组成部分，例如，鉴于中国资本市场有大量散户参与和需要向投资者说明适合其自身情况的产品的风险，可考虑是否更广泛地应用股指期货交易规定中的适当性概念，并考虑对目前由期货公司管理的客户保证金实行某种形式的第三方存管制度。根据 21 世纪前几年处理大量证券公司倒闭的经验，中国监管制度就处置中介机构的倒闭作出了充分规定。然而，当局应考虑修改有关"严重威胁市场秩序"的门槛规定，以确保证监会可在问题严重恶化之前迅速采取行动。

170. 二级市场：中国监管制度作出了充分的规定，以对那些希望运营证券或期货交易所的实体进行授权和监督，这些规定涉及交易所本身、交易品种的准入、交易信息和执行程序。监管制度规定，市场主管部门须监测那些对市场或清算构成风险的大额未平仓头寸。如果发生违约，有相应的程序确保问题得到隔离，使其不影响其他市场参与者，并合理分配相关损失。证监会工作人员与证券交易所保持定期对话，特别是关于上市公司的披露和交易事宜，而且交易所的会员和交易规则须经证监会审批，但是，还应考虑推出一个正式的规划，以像对其他交易所那样定期进行全面现场检查。证监会和各交易所实行了相应制度，对交易进行持续监测和监督，以确保市场的诚信，并投入了大量人力和技术资源来查处并制止内幕交易和操纵市场的行为。同时，考虑到市场的规模及其迅速增长以及新股上市引发的巨大热情，所监测到的异常交易数量和采取的相应行动似乎较少。证监会应考虑继续加大努力以发现并制止不公平交易行为。

表 18　对 IOSCO 原则的遵守情况概述

原则	评论
原则 1　对监管机构责任的规定应明确、客观	证监会作为证券监管机构的职责明确载于以下三部主要法律：《证券法》、《证券投资基金法》和《期货交易管理条例》。为了履行其职能，证监会有权在《立法法》和相关法律赋予的权力范围内制定规章和规范性文件。证监会须遵守《立法法》和《中华人民共和国宪法》确立的法律原则，包括透明度原则。在实践中，证监会制定了若干与其职能相关的规章、规则、指引或指导意见。市场参与者对咨询过程的透明度表示满意。 中国实行分业监管，银监会负责银行业和银行业机构的监管，保监会负责保险业和保险公司的监管。如果这些机构从事证券类活动，例如开发和销售理财产品，银监会和保监会分别对其具有相应的监管权限。如果具有相似特点的产品没有受到相似监管，可能会导致监管真空和不公平现象，因此应对银行、保险和证券业的理财产品规定进行一次审查，以确保监管方法的一致性，避免任何不公正的区别对待。
原则 2　监管机构在行使职权时应独立、负责	在实践中，证监会作为一个独立机构行事，不受政治或商业利益干扰。近年来推行的改革，包括股权分置改革、推出股指期货以及旨在解决证券公司和基金管理公司的偿付能力和操守问题的改革，都彰显了证监会的独立性。然而从形式上看，证监会在操作上并非完全独立于政治影响。证监会主席由国务院任命，证监会的运作体制和治理结构须受国务院的监督。关于工作人员可能承担的法律责任的规定应更加明确，工作人员如果正当执行公务，将无须为此承担任何法律责任，而且对工作人员的保护不受证监会的影响。尽管会计和法律框架取得长足发展，但考虑到市场的迅速增长和其他市场约束机制在中国资本市场发展现阶段的性质，证监会的预算对其行使权力和履行职责来说是不够的。目前已针对监管和行政决策建立了问责制度。

原则	评论
原则3　监管机构应拥有充分权力、适当资源和能力以行使其职权	考虑到中国资本市场的性质，证监会拥有的权力和授权是充分的。然而，证监会的预算与其监管对象和活动的增长速度不匹配，工资水平远远没有达到可比的行业标准，这限制了证监会留住富有经验专业人员的能力。
原则4　监管机构应采用明确、一致的监管程序	证监会在制定监管和行政决策时采用明确、一致的程序，提供了足够的审查机会。证监会十分重视投资者教育，但还需进一步努力，以使散户投资者更好地了解市场和风险。
原则5　监管机构的工作人员应遵守最高职业准则	证监会工作人员遵守高职业标准，包括避免利益冲突以及对在履职中获得的信息进行保密。证监会工作人员须遵守立法规定和书面行为守则，包括不得持有或交易证券和期货，不得在任何受监管机构中担任职务，不得滥用信息。
原则6　监管制度应根据市场规模和复杂程度适当使用自律组织，在其各自专长领域行使直接监督职责	中国的监管制度在很大程度上依靠自律组织在证监会的领导和监督下行使监管职能。这些自律组织包括交易所、清算和结算机构以及行业协会。
原则7　自律组织应受监管机构的监督，在行使权力和代行责任时应遵守公平准则和保密原则	自律组织服从证监会的适当授权和监督安排，以确保自律组织有能力履行职能。考虑到中国资本市场的增长，特别是上市公司和受监管对象的增加，自律组织需要不断关注其监管职能，并为之提供资源。证监会应考虑制定一个正式的规划，定期对各交易所进行全面的现场检查。
原则8　监管机构应具备全面的检查、调查和监察权力	证监会具备全面的检查、调查和监察权力。
原则9　监管机构应具备全面的执行权力	证监会具有全面的执行权力，特别是在案件调查期间，有权通过行政命令冻结保护资产。应该修订行使正式调查权力的条件，以使监管机构在何时动用这些权力方面有更大的自由裁量权。在由违规行为对投资人造成损失的情况下，相关法律法规规定了私人采取追偿行动和其他行动的权利，但在中国，法律制度（特别是商业法庭）以及机构投资者和其他参与者形成的市场约束对公司治理的影响不如在其他国家和地区那么明显。这些因素综合在一起，削弱了私人采取法律行动的能力，使其无法对遵纪守法产生有意义的实际影响。考虑到市场的散户参与程度非常高，与其他市场相比，证监会和其他相关部门在确保合规方面肩负着更大的责任。
原则10　监管制度应确保以有效、可信的方式行使检查、调查、监察和执行权力，并实施有效的合规计划	证监会监管着一个可信且活跃的检查、监督和调查体系，以对市场进行充分的监督。证监会应考虑采取措施鼓励遇到问题的投资者向其反映自己的关切，以增加这个来源的市场情报，并提高投资者对监管框架的信心。异常交易的监督范围甚广，并已采取一些重大的执法行动，以遏制市场操纵行为和内幕交易，但需要不断努力，加强在非法投资活动（包括庞氏骗局和非法投机券商）方面的法律，并增加这方面的人力资源。

原则	评论
原则11 监管机构应有权与国内外同行分享公开和非公开信息	为行使监管职能，证监会能够与国内外同行分享公开和非公开信息，无需经过其他外部程序。
原则12 监管机构应建立信息共享机制，规定何时及以何种方式与国内外同行分享公开和非公开信息	证监会与银监会和保监会以及很多外国证券期货监管机构正式签署了信息共享协议。证监会和其他国内监管机构应该更多考虑其合作协议的功效，特别是在确保具有相似功能的产品或活动受到相似监管方面的功效，以避免可能出现的监管套利。
原则13 外国监管机构为履行职责和行使权力需要进行调查时，监管系统应允许向其提供协助	作为IOSCO《多边谅解备忘录》的签署方，证监会积极要求外国监管机构提供信息和协助，并应对方要求向其提供信息和协助。
原则14 应完整、及时、准确地披露对投资者决策关系重大的财务状况和其他信息	现有监管制度包含证监会和各交易所制定的详细规定和后续机制，以保证上市公司和其他投资计划披露有关财务结果和风险的全面信息。证监会应考虑针对广告活动制定更明确的规定，与关于集合投资计划的规定相似，禁止广告活动，除非在广告中载明请潜在投资者参阅招股说明书。与其他主要市场实行的标准相比，提供年度和半年度财务报表的时限看来太长，应该对其进行审查。此外，需继续关注私人会计和审计行业的发展，并重新考虑针对提供虚假或不实财务报表规定的罚款数额，以保证财务报表的编制和审计符合专业水准。
原则15 应公正、公平地对待公司证券持有人	监管制度在股东权利和公平对待股东方面有充分的规定，包括与并购有关的这些问题。虽然法律就这些问题作出了适当规定，但一个私人机构股东或一群散户股东可以在多大程度上通过法院系统采取实际行动，看来受到成本和法院能力的制约。因此，实际结果是，市场约束不足，无法强制行使这些权利，也无法强制履行这些义务，这增加了证监会或自律组织处理违规案件的负担。应审查关于报告重大持股变化（当前适用于幅度超过5%的变化）的要求，以与其他主要市场中的标准保持一致。
原则16 会计和审计准则应达到国际认可的高水准	中国监管制度采用了一套明确的会计和审计准则，这些准则与《国际财务报告准则》高度趋同，质量很高，得到国际认可。考虑到会计师和审计师在确保上市公司和其他投资工具的财务报表的准确性和完整性方面的重要作用，中国会计和审计行业的规模和经验都需要进一步发展。
原则17 监管制度应为希望销售或运营集合投资计划的主体制定资质标准和监管标准	中国针对那些希望运营或销售集合投资计划的主体制定了明确的监管规定，包括合理的准入要求、持续的资质条件和操作规范以及旨在管理利益冲突的规定。随着这个行业的发展，应对有关与基金管理人专业资格和经验的规定进行评估。证监会应警惕可能出现的无照集合投资计划活动，如庞氏骗局，并注意识别和制止这类活动。有关委托的规定，特别是关于基金管理人、托管人和证券公司对受委托者进行充分监督的规定，应予以进一步明确。

原则	评论
原则18 监管制度应对集合投资计划的法律形式和结构以及客户资产的隔离与保护作出规定	监管制度对管理集合投资计划的法律形式和结构作出充分的规定。通过强制性第三方存管制度对客户资产进行隔离和保护。
原则19 与有关发行人的原则要求相同，监管制度应提出披露要求，这对于评估集合投资计划是否适合具体投资人以及投资人在计划中所持权益的价值十分必要	监管制度对披露作出全面的规定，要求集合投资计划提供必要信息，以使潜在投资者能够评估计划的适当性和前景。制定了充分的估值规定，使投资者能够判断其投资的价值。考虑到市场中的散户参与程度很高，必须用简单明确的语言提供所有信息，证监会需要对此进行密切监督。
原则20 监管制度应确保集合投资计划中的资产评估以及单位的定价和赎回建立在适当、公开的基础之上	关于集合投资计划资产的评估已有详细的监管要求，其中包括审计要求，并对基金份额的申购或赎回定价作出了具体规定。
原则21 监管制度应为市场中介机构设定最低准入标准	中国监管制度规定，市场中介机构必须获得证监会颁发的牌照，并遵守初始和持续的资本、资历和资格要求。证监会应考虑修订关于证券期货投资顾问的规则，要求这些顾问向客户详细披露其个人背景和职业履历、工作经验、合规记录、投资策略和费用结构，这是因为，在一个有大量散户参与的市场中，发展独立财务顾问能力是其重要组成部分。
原则22 应该根据市场中介机构所承担的风险，对其提出相应的初始和持续的资本要求及其他审慎要求	中国监管制度为市场中介机构规定了适当的审慎控制措施，这些措施与市场中介机构从事的具体行业中的风险密切相关。初始的注册资本要求和持续的基于风险的净资本要求提供了重要的风险缓冲。由于基于风险的净资本制度还比较新，证监会应继续对其进行认真监测，以确保该制度覆盖所有相关风险。
原则23 市场中介机构应遵守内部组织和运营行为准则，以保护客户利益，确保合理管理风险，中介机构管理层承担与此相应的主要责任	监管制度要求市场中介机构必须具备内部风险管理功能并制定相关控制措施，以保护客户利益。考虑到需要向散户投资者提供关于产品和服务的充分信息，使其能够作出知情的投资决定，应将股指期货交易规定中的适当性概念更广泛地应用于期货交易和证券交易。考虑到市场的增长和散户的参与水平，应仔细监测最近针对证券公司推出的"了解你的客户"规定，以确保这些规定帮助投资者更好地作出知情的投资决定。鉴于针对证券公司和基金管理公司的第三方存管规定在防止挪用客户资产方面的明显成效，证监会应考虑是否对目前由期货公司管理的客户保证金实行某种形式的第三方存管制度。
原则24 应该制定处置市场中介机构倒闭的程序，尽量减少投资者损失，控制系统性风险	根据本世纪前几年处置大量证券公司倒闭的经验，中国监管制度就处置中介机构的倒闭作出了充分规定。然而，当局应考虑修改有关"严重威胁市场秩序"的门槛规定，以确保证监会可在问题严重恶化之前迅速采取行动。

续表

原则	评论
原则 25 设立交易系统，包括证券交易所，须获得监管部门授权并接受其监督	中国监管制度作出了充分的规定，以对那些希望运营证券或期货交易所的实体进行授权和监督，这些规定涉及交易所本身、交易品种的准入、交易信息和执行程序。虽然证监会工作人员与证券交易所保持定期对话，特别是关于上市公司的披露和交易事宜，但还应考虑像对其他交易所那样进行年度检查。证监会还应考虑在选择高管方面给予证券交易所更大的自主权。
原则 26 对交易所和交易系统应进行持续监管，以确保通过公平、公正的规则平衡不同市场参与者的需求，实现诚信交易	证监会和各交易所对交易实行持续监测和监督制度，以确保市场的诚信。交易所的会员和交易规则须经证监会审批。
原则 27 监管应提高交易的透明度	监管规则要求及时向市场参与者提供交易前和交易后信息，包括要求公平地向所有参与者提供这些信息。
原则 28 监管应能够发现并制止操纵行为和其他不公平的交易行为	证监会和各交易所投入了大量人力和技术资源来查处并制止内幕交易和操纵市场的行为。与此同时，考虑到市场的规模及其迅速增长以及新股上市引发的巨大兴趣，所监测到的异常交易数量和采取的相应行动似乎较少。证监会应考虑继续加大努力以发现并制止不公平交易行为。
原则 29 监管应确保对大额持仓风险、违约风险和市场中断进行适当管理	监管制度规定，市场主管部门须监测那些对市场或清算构成风险的大额未平仓头寸。如果发生违约，有相应的程序确保问题得到隔离，使其不影响其他市场参与者，并合理分配相关损失。
原则 30 证券清算和结算系统应受到监管，确保其公平、有效和高效率并减少系统性风险	未评估。请参阅支付结算体系委员会/国际证监会组织分别对支付、清算和结算系统进行的评估。

E. 主要建议

171. 评估团发现若干有待改进之处，在表 19 中加以概述：

表 19 为更好地遵守 IOSCO 原则的行动建议

原则	行动建议
原则 1	如果银行或保险公司从事证券类活动，例如开发和销售理财产品，适用的监管方法应与证监会对理财产品的监管方法一致，以避免监管套利。应该对银行、保险和证券业的理财产品的监管要求进行审查，以确保监管方法的一致性，避免监管真空或任何不公正的区别对待。

原则	行动建议
原则 2 和 3	应该根据受监管对象的规模调整证监会的业务预算，并给予证监会一定的自由度，使其能够安排自己的结构，调整工资水平，从而留住具备适当资质和行业经验的工作人员。关于工作人员可能承担的法律责任的规定应予以明确，以确保工作人员不因为正当执行公务而承担法律责任。
原则 4	证监会、证券投资者保护基金和自律组织应加大努力开展投资者教育，增强其对市场和风险的认识。
原则 7	考虑到中国资本市场的增长，特别是上市公司和受监管对象的增加，自律组织需要不断关注其监管职能，并为之提供资源。证监会应考虑制定一个正式的规划，定期对各交易所进行全面的现场检查。
原则 9	如果修订证监会行使正式法定调查权的门槛，以赋予证监会更大的自由裁量权来确定何时使用这些权力，将是有益的，并使证监会的执法具有更大的法律确定性。
原则 10	证监会应考虑采取措施鼓励遇到问题的投资者向其反映自己的关切，以增加来自投资者的市场情报，并增强投资者对监管框架的信心。此外，证监会需要继续努力，加强与非法投资活动（包括庞氏骗局和非法投机券商）方面的法律，并增加这方面的人力资源。
原则 12	证监会和其他国内监管机构应该更多考虑其合作协议的功效，特别是在确保具有相似功能的产品或活动受到相似监管方面的功效，以避免可能出现的监管套利。
原则 14	证监会应考虑针对广告活动制定更明确的规定，禁止广告活动，除非在广告中标明请潜在投资者参阅招股说明书。应重新考虑针对提供虚假或不实财务报表规定的罚款数额。应该审查上市公司提供年度和半年度财务报告的法定时限。
原则 15	应该审查关于报告重大持股变化（当前适用于幅度超过 5% 的变化）的要求，以与其他主要市场中的标准保持一致。
原则 16	需要继续关注私人会计和审计行业的发展，以确保财务报表的编制和审计符合专业水准。
原则 17	随着这个行业的发展，应对有关与基金管理人专业资格和经验的规定进行评估。证监会应警惕可能出现的无照集合投资计划活动，如庞氏骗局，并注意识别和制止这类活动。有关委托的规定，特别是关于基金管理人、托管人和证券公司对受委托者进行充分监督的规定，应予以进一步明确。
原则 21	证监会应考虑修订关于证券期货投资顾问的规则，要求这些顾问向客户详细披露其个人背景和职业履历、工作经验、合规记录、投资策略和费用结构，这是因为，在一个有大量散户参与的市场中，发展独立财务顾问能力是其重要组成部分。
原则 22	由于基于风险的净资本制度还比较新，证监会应继续对其进行认真监测，以确保该制度覆盖所有相关风险。

原则	行动建议
原则23	考虑到需要向散户投资者提供关于产品和服务的充足信息，使其能够作出知情的投资决定，应将股指期货交易规定中的适当性概念更广泛地应用于期货交易和证券交易。鉴于针对证券公司和基金管理公司的第三方存管规定在防止挪用客户资产方面取得明显成效，证监会应考虑是否对目前由期货公司管理的客户保证金实行某种形式的第三方存管制度。考虑到市场的增长和散户的参与水平，应仔细监测最近针对证券公司推出的"了解你的客户"规定，以确保这些规定帮助投资者更好地作出知情的投资决定。
原则24	当局应考虑修改有关"严重威胁市场秩序"的门槛规定，即对市场中介机构倒闭的干预，以确保证监会可在问题严重恶化之前迅速采取行动。
原则25	应像对期货交易所那样，对股票交易所也采用年检制度。证监会应考虑在选择高管方面给予证券交易所更大的自主权。
原则28	证监会应考虑继续加大努力以发现并制止不公平交易行为，包括： • 教育公司职员、证券和期货公司的职员以及相关各方，向其说明，内幕交易和其他操纵市场的行为是刑事犯罪； • 教育检察官和法官，使其了解内幕交易给投资者对市场的信心造成的影响； • 加倍努力，对可能涉及可疑交易的事件（例如首次公开发行和并购声明）进行调查，并降低调查或质询的门槛； • 考虑是否应该制定专门的规定，对可疑交易的收入进行冻结或隔离检查，包括考虑降低可疑程度的门槛（用于冻结或隔离检查行动），或改变违规交易和可疑交易的定义，以便于民事诉讼或惩处行动的开展； • 审议有关产品设计的措施，特别是有关期货产品的设计，使其覆盖面足够广泛，从而使得内幕交易或操纵市场的行为难以得逞。

F. 当局回应

172. 中国证监会感谢 FSAP 评估员、国际货币基金组织及世界银行专家在《中国遵守标准和准则情况的报告：IOSCO 证券市场评估》（以下简称《报告》）上所投入的时间、精力和资源。总体而言，《报告》反映了中国证券期货监管系统实施国际证监会组织（IOSCO）目标和原则的状况。我们充分理解对中国这样一个资本市场——世界上最大的新兴加转轨的市场，进行评估，是件极富挑战、非常复杂的工程。我们非常感动，评估专家们在有限的时间内做了大量的工作：在数周内与中国证监会总部及派出机构、受监管实体、自律组织、服务提供机构以及地方政府官员等举行了密集的会谈，并参阅了大量的资料。他们不仅对中国资本市场及其监管情况做出了全面的评估，并提出了诸多有价值的建议和意见。

173. 我们感谢有机会对《报告》做出正式的回应。我们接受《报告》所含大部分内容,包括主要的结论和部分建议。在《报告》中,评估专家高度认可过去 20 年来中国资本市场所取得的发展与成就以及监管方面做出的努力。《报告》认为,近年来的改革,特别是股权分置改革、2010 年股指期货交易的推出、第三方存管的整治以及证券公司基于风险的净资本要求等,加强了市场透明度,扩大了市场产品的范围,提高了中介机构的财务稳健性,在很大程度上有利于在中国对投资者的保护。我们赞同《报告》的相关结论,即这些改革都进行了周密安排和谨慎执行,受到了广大市场参与者的欢迎;这证明证监会及其他相关机构在监管中国证券市场时采取了积极的战略措施。同时,《报告》指出这些改革所依据的一整套广泛的监管规定吸取了更为发达的证券市场的经验。其中几乎没有任何方面的监管框架是不符合 IOSCO 标准的。此外,《报告》也认可,中国的监管机制采用了一套清晰的会计审计标准,在与《国际财务报告准则》和《国际会计准则》接轨方面取得了长足的进步,并具有国际认可的较高质量。

174. 对于《报告》中 FSAP 评估专家们提出的行动计划建议,证监会均予以高度关注,并将其中部分建议纳入我们的工作规划。例如:

a. 涉及监管机构

175. 汲取此轮国际金融危机的教训,我们认同《报告》中关于提高监管当局(即证监会、银监会和保监会)间监管合作,加强对不受监管市场和产品的监管,提高监管机构在人员配备和预算方面的灵活性,以及明确监管机构员工不应为正当执行公务而承担责任等内容。作为回应,中国监管当局将进一步完善制度或采取相关措施,提高"三会"间监管合作备忘录的效力,避免监管套利。同时,中国监管当局已积极考虑将私募股权基金等此前未受监管的机构和产品纳入监管范畴。此外,关于增加监管资源及正当执行公务免责等问题,我们将进一步与国内其他政府部门以及立法、司法部门沟通。我们相信更多的监管资源应与中国政治体制、国家经济水平和金融行业整体收入水平相匹配,以更好适应不断增长的市场及监管需求。

b. 涉及自律组织

176. 我们认同《报告》所言,自律组织需要对其监管职能持续投入关注和资源;中国证监会、证券投资者保护基金和自律组织应加大投资者教育方面的努力,增强投资者对市场和风险的意识。随着中国资本市场的快速成长,尤其是上市公司、散户投资者和中介机构等监管对象的成长,自律组织的作用有待进一步发挥。证监会将加强对各自律组织的监督管理并定期与其沟通,并认真考虑《报告》的建议,安排对证券交易所定期进行全面的现场检查。

177. 然而,我们对《报告》中某些结论和建议方案并不完全赞同。我们认为之所以产生如下所示的一些误解和错误结论，一方面是此次评估忽略了中国资本市场的特性，缺乏对中国资本市场及其运行制度的了解，导致了错误的结论；另一方面是评估人员对中国监管当局已经采取的改进措施认识不足，对相关制度实施的效果抱着怀疑态度，甚至在没有足够证据证明中国监管方式无效的情况下，否定了若干业经中国实践证明行之非常有效的做法。主要表现在如下几方面：

c. 关于执法

178. 我们认为，《报告》并未全面反映证监会在打击非法投资行为和打击内幕交易等方面所做的努力及监管成绩。2006 年，证监会与公安部等有关部门成立了"整治非法证券活动领导小组"，组织、协调和领导全国打击非法证券活动，工作非常有效。在日常工作中，证监会重视对网络等新闻媒体的监测，注意及时发现和及时处理非法证券活动，早在 2001 年就发布了《关于做好非法证券期货交易和证券期货诈骗有奖举报工作的通知》，鼓励投资者反映非法证券期货行为的问题。由于按照中国法律规定，非法证券期货活动金额达到 30 万元人民币就属于犯罪，中国证监会依法将相关案件移送公安机关处理。总之，近年来类似庞氏骗局和投机商号的非法投资活动得到了有效惩处。

d. 关于中介机构

179. 《报告》建议：应根据市场中介机构所承担的风险，对市场中介机构提出相应的初始和持续资本要求及其他审慎要求。《报告》还建议：鉴于基于风险的净资本制度相对较新，证监会应对其继续进行认真监控，以确保该制度涵盖全部相关的风险。我们认为，证监会目前对净资本的监管、对中介机构进行的非现场监管以及现场检查、对存在问题的中介机构及时采取监管措施等方面，做法是充分的、适当的，能够确保该制度涵盖全部相关的风险。事实上，证监会已从 2007 年开始，对以净资本为核心的风险监管制度以信息技术监控平台为基础进行持续监控和评估，并要求定期进行压力测试。

180. 近年来，证监会对市场基础设施采取了一系列的改进措施，期货市场已取得很大的进展。对期货保证金安全存管的监测系统充分考虑了期货交易的特征和市场现状，对确保期货市场的健康、稳健发展发挥了不可或缺的重要作用。我们希望与其他国家的同行分享我们的创新监管体系，并通过加强交流来强化金融监管。

e. 关于会计和审计准则

181. 我们遗憾地表示，不能同意 IOSCO 原则 16 下的评级。为确保对上市公司和其他市场参与方的审计质量，证监会已建立资格准入制度，只允许已获得资格准入的会计师事务所对上市公司和其他市场参与方进行审计。证监会对具有相关资质的会计师事务所（目前有53家）、上市公司和其他主要市场参与方进行全方位的监管，包括现场检查。事实上，目前会计师和审计师的现状、规模和专业能力足以满足资本市场的需要。

f. 结论

182. 尽管我们并不完全同意《报告》的结论，但我们完全同意评估团的善意提醒，我们绝不会自满或者骄傲于以往的成绩。FSAP评估的过程为我们提供了认真总结过去和清醒面对未来的好机会。作为监管者，我们清醒地认识到，当今世界正处在大发展、大变革、大调整时期。在这种时代背景下，中国资本市场面临的内外部环境正不断发生深刻变化，市场运行更加复杂，维护资本市场稳定、健康发展的任务更加艰巨。如何进一步完善法律法规，并加强执法，威慑违法违规行为，更好地保护投资者的合法权益；如何强化对面向公众发行的理财类产品的监管协调和功能监管，减少"监管套利"和"监管真空"；如何监管以前未受监管的金融市场和产品，平衡金融创新和金融监管的关系；如何防范化解系统性风险，加强对资本跨境流动的监管，有效预警和处置国际市场风险；如何培育多元化投资者队伍……这些都是我们面临的困难和挑战，需要我们不懈努力。作为中国资本市场的监管者，我们前方的路仍然很长，但充满希望。

附件 IV. 对金融领域标准和准则的遵守情况—— 支付结算体系委员会（CPSS） 《系统重要性支付系统核心原则》 的遵守情况评估：概述

A. 导言

183. 这项评估于 **2010 年 6 月进行。** 除了 2001 年的 CPSS《系统重要性支付系统核心原则》外，评估方法还遵循国际货币基金组织和世界银行与 CPSS 合作，于 2001 年 8 月编写的《系统重要性支付系统核心原则评估指南》。

184. 评估中使用的信息包括所有相关法律、法规和系统管理程序以及中央银行内外可获得的大量资料。[11]此外，评估团与以下方面进行了广泛讨论：监管机构，包括人民银行、财政部、证监会、银监会和外汇管理局；中国支付系统的部分参与者，包括四大商业银行、股份制商业银行、城市商业银行、政策性银行、外资银行、农村银行、[12] 基金管理公司，银行卡公司（中国银联）、中国外汇交易中心（外汇交易中心）和证券登记公司，即中央国债登记结算有限责任公司（中债登）和中国证券登记结算有限责任公司（中证登）。人民银行对中国的重要支付系统对支付结算体系委员会核心原则的遵守情况，以及人民银行在应用核心原则时的责任进行了自评估，并在现场评估之前提供了自评估报告。该自评估报告由人民银行支付结算司会同中国支付清算体系（CNPS）的主要参与者编写。

B. 体制结构和市场结构

185. 近年来，人民银行对中国支付清算体系进行了重大且全面的改革。人民银行推出了中国现代化支付系统（CNAPS），该系统包括大额实时支付系统（大额支付系统）和小额批量支付系统（小额支付系统）。大额实时支付系统目前以分层方式运作（多点接入），建有两级处理中心，即国家处理中心和 32 个地方处理中心。该系统与许多交易、支付和证券结算系统连接，以便能够执行中央银行货币结算。此外，全国各地还建有很多票据清算所，由人民银行当地

---

[11] 特别重要的是人民银行支付结算司编写的 2007 年、2008 年和 2009 年《中国支付体系发展报告》。

[12] 中国银行、中国工商银行、中国建设银行、中国农业银行、北京银行、国家开发银行、交通银行、上海浦东发展银行、渣打银行、汇丰银行、东亚银行、摩根大通银行和山东农村信用社联社。

分支行进行管理，或授权商业银行管理。中国银联（银联）通过大额实时支付系统完成银行卡交易资金清算。此外，自动清算所和其他系统处理各种支付工具的清算和结算。

186. 大额支付系统是中国国家支付系统的核心，是具有系统重要性的支付系统。 2009 年，大额实时支付系统处理的交易总值达 804 万亿元人民币，大约相当于 GDP 的 24 倍。因此，根据 CPSS 的 10 项系统重要性支付系统核心原则和中央银行在应用核心原则时的 4 项责任对大额支付系统进行了评估。小额支付系统目前不是具有系统重要性的支付系统，但其对于银行间支付系统的高效结算的重要性正在持续上升。

187. 全国各地的票据清算所也处理大量交易。 2009 年签发的支票总值达到 248 万亿元人民币，大约相当于 GDP 的 7.4 倍。然而，其中有 3.5 亿张支票是银行间支票，金额大约为 62.5 万亿元人民币。这意味着在中国签发的支票大多数是"本行付款"支票。此外，自动清算所在 2009 年处理了 69 万亿元人民币的票据，大约相当于 GDP 的两倍，对于中国这样一个大国来说还是比较重要的（虽然不是最主要的）。因此，无论是支票清算所还是自动清算所，在本次评估中都不被视为具有系统重要性，但是在评估中央银行责任 B 和 C 的时候考虑到了它们的相对重要性。

188. 关于支付工具的使用，中国正积极推进非现金支付工具的广泛使用，尤其是银行卡。 现金（M_0）的使用量与 GDP 的比率一直在下降，从 2000 年的 14.8% 下降到 2009 年的 11.2%。银行卡的发行量也在迅速上升，截至 2009 年底，银行卡的发卡量约 20.7 亿张，其中 18.8 亿张是借记卡。因此，银行卡在中国已成为最主要的非现金支付工具，占 2009 年非现金支付总额的 90% 以上。

189. 国内的外汇交易主要是在中国外汇交易中心进行。 截至 2010 年底，大部分参与者通过双边模式进行结算，另外还有 26 个参与者使用净额结算模式，以中国外汇交易中心作为中央对手方。外汇交易中，人民币头寸的结算通过大额支付系统进行，外汇头寸的结算通过参与者在其中开立了外汇账户的国内结算银行进行。中方没有向评估团提供通过多边安排清算和结算的交易明细数据，人民银行也没有对这个支付系统进行自评估。然而，鉴于这些交易的性质和该系统的潜在系统重要性，强烈建议人民银行尽快评估该系统对国际标准的遵守情况。

190. 中国境内外币支付系统于 2008 年 4 月上线运行，以处理境内外币交易的清算和结算。 境内外币支付系统是一个实时全额结算系统，目前负责处理 7 种外币的支付交易。该系统处理的交易金额表明，它不具备系统重要性。

C. 支付系统监管

191. 人民银行对支付和结算系统的监管权有明确的法律依据，证监会对证

券结算系统拥有交叉监管权。人民银行对零售支付、银行间支付、证券结算和相关职能的监管权力在法律框架中得到确认。这些权力在《中国人民银行法》第4条得到明确阐述。根据《证券法》第179条，证监会对包括政府证券在内的证券结算拥有监管权。关于人民银行、财政部和其他主管部门（例如证监会和银监会）之间的总体合作安排通过一项正式的谅解备忘录予以明确。目前还没有具体的谅解备忘录来界定这些主管部门在支付和结算系统方面的合作模式，但在技术层面经常采取协调行动和定期会晤。

192. **人民银行对全国所有的支付安排行使监管职能。**除了监管具有系统重要性的支付系统外，人民银行还在改革中国的银行间支付安排方面发挥了积极作用。最近，人民银行扩大了监管范围，对非银行支付服务提供者进行监管。然而，人民银行尚未就此发布文件，以说明其监管的目标、范围、工具和制度安排。

193. **人民银行已建成一个数据分析平台，用来协助其监管活动。**支付管理信息系统从大额支付系统和小额支付系统等各个系统采集支付和结算信息。该系统提供各种标准的分析报告和专题分析报告，这有助于人民银行开展监管活动，还使人民银行能够实时监测参与者的流动性状况。

194. **人民银行尚未正式成立任何形式的国家支付委员会。**虽然人民银行拥有法律授权并正在筹备建立自律监管组织中国支付清算协会，但至今尚未建立（中国支付清算协会已于2011年5月成立——译者注）。

195. **人民银行积极与其他部门和相关参与者开展合作，以进一步提高中国支付清算体系的安全性和效率。**合作项目包括：建立第二代中国现代化支付系统；从主要方面入手改革法律和监管框架；采取措施进一步提高零售支付服务的渗透率，特别是利用创新的渠道和方式提高农村地区的渗透率。

D. 主要结论

196. **评估团认为，中国各支付系统运行安全。**同时也存在一些有待改进之处，表20对此进行了概述。

表20　为更好地遵守CPSS核心原则和央行在
应用核心原则时的责任的行动计划建议

原则	行动建议
法律基础 核心原则1	中国当局应加快立法进程，以完成支付和证券结算法规框架的改革。包括： ● 颁布一项支付系统法，以为结算的最终性和净额结算安排等提供充分的法律保护； ● 发布《企业破产法》释义，或修订《企业破产法》，以使支付系统领域享有对"零点规则"的豁免。 ● 提升支付系统法则的层级，使其符合人民银行的监管需要。

原则	行动建议
了解和管理风险 核心原则 2 和 3	由于目前尚不清楚参与者是否充分认识到与结算最终性有关的潜在法律风险，建议人民银行向参与者说明它为减轻这一风险所采取的措施以及为消除这一风险所开展的项目。 人民银行应通过完善法规、建设第二代支付系统来进一步监测支付系统的信用风险和流动性风险。有关行动主要包括： • 为参与者提供更为全面的排队和账户监测功能、"打包"流动性实时查询功能和大额支付系统排队撮合功能； • 对日间流动性贷款使用的抵押物实行更为积极的"盯市机制"； • 随着流动性条件的变化，对日间流动性贷款的条件保持一定的灵活性，并考虑取消对抵押信贷的收费。
结算 核心原则 4、5 和 6	——
系统的安全性和运行的可靠性以及应急安排 核心原则 7	第二代支付系统应有一个更高效的运行和维护机制，实现系统应用软件的自动升级；这将： • 改善对系统运行的实时监测功能，对支付系统的信息技术资源进行全面、自动的监测； • 提高风险预警能力，有效分析系统的潜在风险并及时发出警告； • 最大限度地实现系统故障的自动处理； • 减少系统维护工作量，提高运行监测效率并提升运行维护水平。 第二代支付系统将在生产中心、远程备份中心和同城数据备份中心的框架内建立备份系统，使其具备全面的生产恢复能力、业务切换能力和数据查找能力，以确保在出现紧急情况时持续处理支付业务并保证信息和数据的安全和完整。 强烈建议采取上述措施。
系统的效率和实用性 核心原则 8	尽管自从建立中国现代化支付系统以来取得了重要进展，但需调整一些性能，以提高系统的效率和实用性，例如： （1）系统的"多点接入"性能会影响流动性的高效率管理，并增加了参与成本； （2）大额电子交易与大额支票交易相比费用仍然较高，尽管各商业银行正逐渐引导客户改为采用其他电子支付手段； （3）可以延长每天的运行时间，以体现支付系统的重要性日益增加。
准入标准 核心原则 9	为了进一步加强对支付系统参与者的监督和管理，保证支付系统的安全、稳定运行，人民银行计划修订《银行业金融机构加入、退出支付系统管理办法》。例如，人民银行计划在《管理办法》中具体规定和详细说明对申请加入者进行审查的方式： • 对有关人员进行支付系统知识方面的测验； • 对支付结算处理环境进行现场检查； • 召集高层管理人员进行审慎谈话，以提高加入申请审批工作的可操作性。 强烈建议采取上述措施。
支付系统的治理 核心原则 10	如前所述，人民银行已经在着手解决该系统的大部分缺陷，并为建立和运行一个先进、可靠的支付系统，使之成为中国金融体系的支柱做出了非凡的努力，这是值得赞赏的。 使越来越多的系统参与者加入"第二代"项目，并最终建立一个正式的用户组织，这将有助于逐步促进合作并提升系统性能。 此外，通过定期在人民银行各个部门内以及与系统参与者之间，针对所有类型的紧急事件，而不仅仅是针对操作问题，开展突发事件应急演练，无疑将增强人民银行应对意外事件的能力。 随着时间的推移，人民银行应努力实现对其他核心原则的完全遵守。

续表

原则	行动建议
央行在应用核心原则时的责任 央行职责 A、B、C 和 D	人民银行应在公开文件中详细说明其关于支付系统监督的政策立场，详细阐述人民银行为实现其支付系统公共政策目标所采取行动及实施计划的范围。关于政策目标，建议人民银行清楚阐明，其监管目标不局限于两个传统的主要目标，即支付系统的效率和可靠性，进而延伸至包括促进支付服务市场的竞争和保护消费者利益等更广泛的领域。关于人民银行监管职责的范围，文件应明确阐述，人民银行决定对中国所有具有系统重要性的支付系统和证券结算系统进行监管，并对零售系统进行监管，因为零售系统在支持经济活动、扩大支付服务的提供和增强公众对货币的信心方面特别重要。 该文件还应详细说明人民银行的主要政策和工具。主要政策将涉及支付系统的各主要方面，包括风险控制、准入、治理、透明度、定价、系统可靠性和业务连续性、效率等。工具的范围很广，既包括道义劝说，又包括现场检查；既包括监管，又包括合作；既包括处罚措施，又包括直接提供支付服务。 此外，该文件应详细说明用来确定一个系统具有系统重要性的标准。应该提供这些系统的清单，并不断对其进行监测和更新。 最后，该文件应详细阐述在支付系统领域的制度安排与合作（见下文职责 D）。 大额支付系统没有完全遵守所有系统重要性支付系统核心原则，人民银行应优先采取行动使其完全遵守这些原则。 作为一个紧迫事项，应该对支票清算的相关风险进行一次彻底的评估，并采取积极行动以在支票清算所中消除大额支付项目。 人民银行有必要澄清支付结算司和内审司在人民银行运营的支付系统中的监督作用。 评估团认为，人民银行应对中国外汇交易系统和自动清算所进行更积极的监督。尤其建议根据相关国际标准对这些系统的安全性和效率进行一次评估。 人民银行应考虑进一步完善国内合作框架，启动并落实关于支付结算的谅解备忘录，与所有相关部门建立结构化监管机制，同时推动建立中国支付清算协会（中国支付清算协会已于 2011 年 5 月成立——译者注）。 在国际层面，人民银行做的努力值得赞赏，建议人民银行继续加强与国外有关中央银行和国际组织的合作。 此外，建议全面采用 CPSS 的跨境合作框架。

E. 当局回应

197. 中国当局欢迎并支持针对 CPSS 核心原则的评估，并以此为契机对照国际标准来反思、改进中国支付结算系统。评估团出色地完成了任务，展现出高度的敬业精神、献身精神和在有限的时间内解析复杂问题的能力。当局感谢有机会发表以下意见。

198. 过去十年来，中国不断推进中国支付结算系统的发展，该系统是中国金融体系的支柱。我们已经建立了一个由人民银行的银行间支付系统、商业银行行内支付系统、证券结算系统、外汇结算系统、银行卡支付系统和其他第三方机构的零售支付系统构成的支付网络。非现金支付工具已得到广泛使用，满足了各种支付需求。商业汇票签发后可以以电子方式转账。银行卡的渗透率正在快速增长，并已成为中国居民使用最广泛的支付工具。网上支付、移动支付和电话支付取得较快发展。非现金工具的使用大大方便了经济生产和人民生活，减少了现金流通量，降低了交易成本。多元化发展的支付服务提供者包括中央银行、银行业金融机构、非银行业金融机构和证券结算机构。支付服务日益市场化。现代支付方式也进入了农村地区。跨境贸易人民币结算试点在有序推进。人民银行颁布了《银行结算账户管理办法》，建立了银行结算账户管理系统并不断加以完善。与此同时，人民银行会同公安部门建立了一个全国范围的联网核查公民身份系统，以落实"了解你的客户"计划。支付系统监督工作得到了加强，重点关注安全性和效率。人民银行还改进了监督技术，实现债券市场的券款对付（DVP）结算。

199. 人民银行运营的大额支付系统（LVPS）被确定为具有系统重要性，根据核心原则进行了评估。评估得出的结论是，除了核心原则 1（法律基础）外，该系统遵守或大致遵守了所有其他核心原则。人民银行高度重视评估结论，感谢国际货币基金组织和世界银行提出的宝贵建议。人民银行已在第一代支付系统中实现了一点接入，如国库集中核算系统和中国邮政储蓄银行的行内支付系统已经实现与第一代支付系统"一点接入、一点结算"。

200. 我们将采取措施增强中国支付系统的法律基础，加强对支付系统的管理和监督，提高支付系统实用性和效率。

- 核心原则 1，法律基础。人民银行已意识到法律框架的不足之处，并决定起草《支付系统条例》，以避免"零点法则"的影响，并在法律上认可净额结算安排和结算的最终性。但是，立法工作需要时间，并可能涉及多个部门。

- 核心原则 8，实用性和效率。人民银行正在建设第二代现代化支付系统，以提高效率和实用性。第二代支付系统在设计上将延长结算营业时间，以满足不同地区和各金融市场用户的需求。

- 核心原则 10，治理。人民银行决定改进管理，升级支付系统并定期进行应急演练，以实现对各项核心原则的完全遵守。

201. 中央银行的责任 A、B、C 和 D。人民银行完全同意各项建议，将采取适当措施确保证完全遵守所有核心原则。人民银行将在公开文件中详细阐明对支付系统监督管理的政策立场，并将监督范围延伸至所有支付和证券结算系统，包括具有系统重要性的系统和零售支付系统。人民银行将根据有关国际标准评估中国外汇交易系统和自动清算所系统的安全性和效率。此外，人民银行即将建立中国支付清算协会，并加强与有关部门、国外中央银行和国际组织的合作。

附件 V. 对金融领域标准和准则的遵守情况——CPSS – IOSCO 《证券结算系统和中央对手方建议》的遵守情况评估：概述

A. 导言

202. 本概述基于对支付结算体系委员会（CPSS）和国际证监会组织（IOSCO）联合颁布的《证券结算系统建议》和《中央对手方建议》遵守情况的评估。这次评估于 2010 年 9 月进行。

203. 这次评估采用的信息包括有关证券结算系统的法律、法规和操作程序以及其他可获得的材料等信息。[13]此外，评估人员还与人民银行、证监会、上交所、上海期交所、大连商交所、郑州商交所、金融期交所、中债登、中证登、中国证券业协会、中国期货业协会等监督管理机构进行了广泛讨论，与证券结算系统的部分参与方进行了座谈，其中包括参与上交所、上海期交所和银行间债券市场活动的银行、经纪商或交易商，中债登和中证登系统的参与者；为证券和期货交易提供结算和资金托管服务的银行。中债登、上海期交所、证监会市场监管部分别就中央国债登记结算系统、上海期货交易所清算与结算系统、中国证券登记结算系统进行了自评估并提供了自评估报告。还有一些信息来自于对重要支付系统的评估。

204. 这次评估的对象是证券结算系统的程序和功能，而不是机构。考虑到债券交易主要通过场外交易（OTC）进行，因此对证券交易所以外的交易程序也进行了检查。

B. 体制结构和市场结构

205. 中国证券结算系统围绕三种不同类型的市场而组成，这三类市场是债

---

[13] 证监会 2008 年和 2009 年《年报》、中债登关于 2009 年中国债券市场的《年度报告》、人民银行对 FSAP 关于支付系统以及证券清算和结算系统问卷的答复；证监会、上交所、深交所、上海期交所、中债登/中国债券信息网的网站；其他有关文件。

券市场、股票市场和期货市场。债券市场包括银行间债券市场、交易所债券市场和银行柜台市场。银行间债券市场居于主导地位，其债券交易量占比超过97%。上交所和深交所两家证券交易所成立于1990年，均提供同样类型的证券交易，这些证券包括股票、债券、基金和认股权证。这两家证券交易所的交易额相对较高，且在过去十年间增长迅猛。据世界证券交易所联合会统计，2009年，上交所交易额达34万亿元人民币，居全球第三；深交所交易额达18万亿元人民币，居全球第六。中国还有三家商品交易所，即上海期交所、大连商交所和郑州商交所。按交易的合约数量衡量，上海期交所是全球第十大衍生品交易所，也是全球第二大商品交易所。金融期交所成立于2006年，由上交所、深交所、上海期交所、大连商交所和郑州商交所合资组建，但交易量和交易金额相对而言仍然不大。

206. **中债登既是证券结算系统，也是中央证券存管机构**。中债登是唯一一家受财政部委托托管国债的机构。该公司作为政府的一个实体成立于1996年，由人民银行负责管理，由人民银行和财政部负责监督，银监会负责任命中债登的总经理。中债登以全额结算方式结算债券交易的券和款（包括现货、回购和远期交易），目前该公司在人民银行的指导下也正考虑推出净额结算机制。多数情况下，证券由最终投资者持有，这种情况约占98%。中债登簿记系统与中国外汇交易中心运营的银行间交易系统相联接。现金结算可通过中央银行大额支付系统进行。大部分交易的结算采用 T + 0 方式，2009年 T + 0 方式结算额占结算总额的82.9%。除了经常使用的券款对付（DvP）结算方法外，中债登还允许采用其他结算方式，包括见券付款（PaD）、见款付券（DaP）和纯券过户（FoP）。

207. **中证登是中央对手方、证券结算系统和所有在上交所和深交所交易的金融工具的中央证券存管机构**。中证登成立于2001年，上交所和深交所各自拥有其50%的股份。上交所和深交所的证券结算安排基于前端的证券和资金的可获得性，否则交易不会达成。在这一证券结算系统中，证券由投资者直接开户持有，资金则通过第三方存管制度安排由银行持有，中证登担任结算代理人。

208. **四家期货交易所都有自己的清算和结算部门，这些部门发挥着中央对手方功能**。四家期货交易所可以每天按市值进行现金结算，也可以到期时通过实物交割进行结算。这四家期货交易所实行初始保证金制度，即只有在存入了足够保证金的情况下才可以购买期货合约。除了初始保证金制度外，期货交易所还建立了其他风险管控制度，包括：限价、限制投机性持仓、限制大额持仓、强制平仓、预警指标系统和结算准备金。现金结算通过五家"结算"银行的账户进行。五家"结算"银行只是负责对保证金进行管理，并为资金转账提供便利，结算功能由交易所承担。此外，为保障期货保证金的安全，2006年三家期货交易所发起建立了中国期货保证金监控中心。该中心为非营利机构。

209. 中债登、中证登和上海期交所、大连商交所、郑州商交所所运营的证券和衍生品结算系统都很重要，因为这些系统交易量大、交易值高（与 GDP 相比较），而且支持着主要的金融市场（包括银行间债券市场、交易所市场和期货市场）。因此，下面根据《证券结算系统建议》中的 19 条建议对中债登和中证登进行评估，根据《中央对手方建议》中的 15 条建议对上海期交所进行评估。中证登在大部分市场交易中发挥着中央对手方的功能，但考虑到其结算程序的独特性（证券和资金的前端控制），将根据《证券结算系统建议》对其进行评估。另外两家商品期货交易所（即大连商交所和郑州商交所）采用的结算程序与上海期交所的非常相似，因此，对后者的评估结论和建议也适用于这两家商交所。

C. 主要结论

210. 评估团认为，中国各证券结算系统运行安全，但是也存在一些有待改进之处，表 21、表 22 和表 23 对此进行了概括。

表 21　为更好地遵守 CPSS – IOSCO《证券结算系统建议》的行动建议
——场外债券市场—中债登

有关建议	行动建议
法律风险	
建议 1. 证券结算系统应在相关的司法管辖范围内具有稳健的、清晰的和透明的法律基础。	人民银行和财政部应考虑对法律和监管框架进行一次全面审查，以便为银行间货币市场、场外债券市场和中债登的清算和结算奠定坚实的法律基础。该框架不仅包含部委层面的程序规范，还应包括法律层面的主要内容。 应尽快分析抵押物的处置效率，并加以改善。 目前，对于中国证券结算系统来说，跨境结算方面的法律冲突并不是重要的风险来源。然而，随着中国金融市场与外国金融市场的互动日益增加，中国的法律和监管框架解决任何潜在的法律冲突至关重要。
结算前风险	
建议 2. 市场直接参与者之间的交易应在成交后尽快进行确认，不应迟于交易当日（T + 0）。市场间接参与者（如机构投资者）参与的交易需确认的，应在成交后尽快确认，最好在 T + 0 日，但不应迟于 T + 1 日。	应努力确保所有场外交易都在 T + 0 日得到真正确认。
建议 4. 应对中央对手方的收益和成本进行评估。如采用这种机制，中央对手方应严格控制其承担的风险。	人民银行应综合考虑金融市场类型以及法律、制度和市场因素，对是否应该建立中央对手方机制作出最终决策。

有关建议	行动建议
建议 5. 证券借出和借入（或回购协议和其他经济上与此对等的交易），应作为加速证券交易结算的方法予以提倡。阻碍以此为目的开展证券借贷业务的障碍，应当消除。	中债登应在现有的双边安排之外考虑改进证券借出和借入机制。 需要改进会计办法和税务规则，以便利证券的借出和借入。
结算风险	
建议 7. 中央证券存管机构应通过证券转账和资金转账的联网实现券款对付（DvP），以消除本金风险。	自 2008 年以来，使用券款对付方式进行的交易结算迅猛增加。应鼓励中债登进一步增加使用券款对付方式进行的结算，尽快实现 100% 的以券款对付方式结算。
建议 8. 最终结算应不迟于结算日日终。在需要降低风险的情况下，应当提供日间或实时最终结算。	应将对结算最终性的保护纳入法律框架。
其他事项	
建议 13. 中央证券存管机构和中央对手方治理安排的设计应当能够满足公共利益要求，并提升所有者和用户的目标。	应该明确区分人民银行的监管职能、银监会和财政部的监督职责以及人民银行的运营责任。 应明确考虑到中债登系统参与者的利益。
建议 16. 证券结算系统应当采用或遵循相关的国际通信程序和标准，以便跨境交易的高效结算。	中债登应努力提高对相关国际通信程序和标准的应用水平，促进跨境交易。
建议 17. 中央证券存管机构和中央对手方应向市场参与者提供充分的信息，使其能够准确判断使用中央证券存管机构或中央对手方服务的风险和成本。	中债登应披露对 CPSS/IOSCO 披露框架中的调查问卷的答复，或披露对《证券结算系统建议》评估方法中所提出的主要问题的答复。
建议 18. 证券结算系统应接受透明有效的管理和监督。中央银行和证券监管机构应相互合作，并与其他相关部门进行合作。	监管机构应继续有效地采取行动。 人民银行应将其对中债登的监管职责与参与该系统治理区分开来，以明确职责定位。 需进一步完善不同监管机构在清算和结算方面的合作安排。
建议 19. 联网结算跨境交易的中央证券存管机构，在设计和运行跨境联网时，应当有效降低与跨境结算相关的风险。	对跨境结算风险似乎缺乏全面、标准化的分析程序，中债登及其监管部门应尽快解决这一问题。

D. 主要建议

211. 评估团发现了一些有待改进之处，表 22 对其进行了概括。

表 22　为更好地遵守 CPSS – IOSCO《证券结算系统建议》的行动建议
——证券交易所（上交所和深交所）—中证登

有关建议	行动建议
结算前风险	
建议 4. 应对中央对手方的收益和成本进行评估。如采用这种机制，中央对手方应严格控制其承担的风险。	目前，中证登主要依靠其清算和结算系统的设计以及一些额外的风险控制措施来确保控制风险。 今后，中证登可考虑通过审视风险敞口监测、压力测试、财务资源可获得性等因素来评估和加强其作为中央对手方的稳健性，在这方面可借鉴海外同行的经验。 如果中证登希望顺应日具批发性质的市场发展趋势，这项工作将显得更大紧迫。因为对于更具批发性质的市场，当前的清算和结算设计（主要针对零售市场）可能不够有效。
结算风险	
建议 7. 中央证券存管机构应通过证券转账和资金转账的联网实现券款对付（DvP），以消除本金风险。	证监会和中证登应考虑公开说明中证登的清算和结算安排，以避免人们由于该系统没有实行更加"规范"的券款对付结构而以为可以不遵守券款对付原则。
建议 9. 向参与者提供日间信贷的中央证券存管机构，其中包括采用净额结算系统的中央证券存管机构，应制定风险控制措施，至少要确保在具有最大支付义务的参与者不能结算的情况下，系统可实现及时结算。最可靠的控制措施是抵押品要求和限额的结合。	中证登应尽快对其信用风险敞口进行一次全面、深入的评估，包括对多重违约可能性的评估。
建议 10. 用来结算源于证券交易的最终支付义务的资产，应当没有或几乎没有信用风险或流动性风险。如果不使用中央银行货币，由于代理人的资产是用于资金结算的，因此必须采取措施确保中央证券存管机构成员免受现金结算代理人违约所产生的潜在的损失和流动性压力。	用于资金转账的支付系统应该完全遵守《系统重要性支付系统核心原则》，以确保支付系统中的流动性风险和信用风险不会引发清算和结算过程中的结算风险。然而，中证登结算安排的性质等同于券款对付，最终能将风险限制于市场风险。

有关建议	行动建议
其他事项	
建议 13. 中央证券存管机构和中央对手方治理安排的设计应当能够满足公共利益要求，并提升所有者和用户的目标。	建议中证登制订行动计划，以符合所有关于证券结算系统的建议，系统治理机制须承担相应责任，并采取必要行动达到全面符合。
建议 16. 证券结算系统应当采用或遵循相关的国际通信程序和标准，以便跨境交易的高效结算。	建议中证登与交易所、市场参与者、证监会协商合作，启动对相关国际通信程序和标准的发展效益的持续评估程序，并迅速进行必要的改进，以满足市场需求。
建议 17. 中央证券存管机构和中央对手方应向市场参与者提供充分的信息，使其能够准确地识别和评估使用中央证券存管机构或中央对手方服务的风险和成本。	中证登应披露对 CPSS/IOSCO 披露框架中的调查问卷的答复，或披露对《证券结算系统建议》评估方法中所提出的主要问题的答复。
建议 18. 证券结算系统应接受透明有效的管理和监督。中央银行和证券监管机构应相互合作，并与其他相关部门进行合作。	监管机构应继续采取有效行动。 尽管有关部门之间已建立了高层次合作框架，但技术层面的合作架构也许应该更为正式。 除了现有机制外，当局还应促进与私人部门和其他利益相关方之间的合作，为此可通过建立适当的论坛来共同讨论支付结算问题。
建议 19. 联网结算跨境交易的中央证券存管机构，在设计和运行跨境联网时，应当有效降低与跨境结算相关的风险。	鉴于中国市场潜在的国际化，跨境联系很可能变成常态而非例外。建议中证登、各交易所和市场监管机构着手建立一个标准化框架，以在必要时评估这些联系带来的风险。

表 23　为更好地遵守 CPSS–IOSCO《中央对手方建议》的行动建议
——上海期交所

建议 1. 法律风险	行动建议
在所有相关的司法管辖区内，中央对手方的各项业务活动应具有稳健的、透明的和可执行的法律框架。	有关清算和结算的主要概念体现在上海期交所的规则和自律性文件中，但未形成成文法。为遵守该项建议，成文法应该载有关于衍生品交易的条款，例如关于交易的可执行性、最终性、净额结算、合约更新、投资者保护和抵押品保护的规定。
建议 4. 保证金要求	
中央对手方如果依靠保证金要求来限制其对参与者的信用风险敞口，保证金要求应足以覆盖常态市场状况下的潜在风险敞口。测算保证金要求的模型和参数应以风险为基础，并需定期审查。	没有明确的法律依据支持接受仓单作为存交保证金的抵押物，以覆盖市场风险敞口，这种情况对中央对手方的稳定构成威胁。

续表

建议 13. 治理	行动建议
中央对手方的治理安排应当明确和透明，以满足公共利益需要并支持所有者和参与者的目标。特别是，这些安排应有助于提升中央对手方风险管理程序的有效性。	强烈建议上海期交所按照 CPSS 和 IOSCO 正在编写并将于 2011 年公布的新准则进行一次自评估。可针对这些准则组织一次专题研讨会，邀请地方主管部门、市场参与者以及国际上来自公共部门和私人部门的从业人员共同参加。
建议 14. 透明度	
中央对手方应向市场参与者提供充分的信息，使其能够准确地识别和评估使用中央对手方服务的风险和成本。	为遵守这项建议，上海期交所应按 CPSS 和 IOSCO《中央对手方建议》公布信息披露框架。
建议 15. 管理和监督	
中央对手方应接受透明有效的管理和监督。国内外中央银行和证券监管机构应相互合作，并与其他相关部门展开合作。	考虑到中央对手方的风险集中程度及其对金融稳定的潜在影响，证监会和人民银行应该针对中央对手方建立合作性监督框架。

E. 当局回应

212. 人民银行和证监会感谢国际货币基金组织和世界银行在 FSAP 评估中，根据 CPSS—IOSCO《证券结算系统建议》和《中央对手方建议》，对中证登、中债登和上海期交所进行全面评估。我们对参加这一评估工作的各方付出的巨大努力和评估人员的专业素质表示敬意。相信这次评估对系统重要性支付系统以及清算和结算系统的稳定和有效管理将产生积极而深远的影响。

213. 这次评估客观地反映了中国股票市场、债券市场和期货市场结算系统的现状，中证登和中债登对《证券结算系统建议》的遵守情况、上海期交所对《中央对手方建议》的遵守情况。人民银行和证监会将与中证登、中债登和上海期交所分享并分析这次评估的意见和建议，并考虑在今后的工作中予以吸收和借鉴。有关各方将共同努力，确保中国证券结算系统具有安全、高效、透明的运行环境。

214. 与此同时，证监会仍对关于上海期交所对《中央对手方建议》的遵守情况的部分评估意见持有保留意见，涉及建议 1 和建议 4，理由如下：

- **关于法律基础问题**。根据中国的立法体系，法律由全国人民代表大会颁布，行政法规由国务院颁布。行政法规是中国法律体系的重要组成部分，不仅为行政管理提供了法律依据，而且为司法机关处理纠纷和案件提供了依据。然而，行政法规毕竟不是一项明确的法律条款。《期货交易管理条例》作为规范期货交易的行政法规，是中国期货市场的法律基础。我们并不认为中国期货结算系统存在法律缺陷。

- **关于无纸化仓单作为保证金的法律认可问题。**关于使用标准仓单作为保证金的问题，《期货交易管理条例》、《期货交易所管理办法》和各期货交易所的有关业务规则都有明确规定。《物权法》也就抵押权作出明确规定。在实践中，上海期交所指定交割仓库履行无纸化仓单出质登记职责。操作过程中从未出现过任何争议或纠纷。

215. 人民银行对部分关于中债登的评估意见持有保留，这些评估意见涉及中债登对《证券结算系统建议》建议 1 和建议 8 的遵守情况。由于债券是一种证券，《证券法》适用于银行间债券市场。此外，最终性也具有法律确定性。人民银行发布的文件规定："债券结算一旦完成不可撤销"；"已进入证券结算过程处于待付状态的资金和债券以及该笔结算涉及的担保物只能用于该笔结算，不能被强制执行"。尽管《证券法》的具体规定更多地针对交易所市场，但是其精神和原则适用于中国国内所有证券市场，包括银行间债券市场。人民银行颁布的管理规定符合《证券法》的精神和原则，主要适用于银行间债券市场，是中国法律体系中关于证券的具体规定。根据《立法法》，人民银行颁布的管理规定属于广义的法律，具有法律可执行性。因此，银行间债券市场自建立以来，运行一直平稳、安全。

216. 人民银行将会同中债登认真分析评估报告中的意见和建议，不断改进中国银行间债券市场的存管和结算制度。

November 2011
IMF Country Report No. 11/321

People's Republic of China: Financial System Stability Assessment

This financial sector stability assessment on the People's Republic of China was prepared by a staff team of the International Monetary Fund as background documentation for the periodic consultation with the member country. It is based on the information available at the time it was completed on June 24, 2011. The views expressed in this document are those of the staff team and do not necessarily reflect the views of the government of the People's Republic of China or the Executive Board of the IMF.

The policy of publication of staff reports and other documents by the IMF allows for the deletion of market-sensitive information.

Copies of this report are available to the public from

International Monetary Fund•Publication Services
700 19th Street, N.W.•Washington, D.C. 20431
Telephone: (202) 623-7430 • Telefax: (202) 623-7201
E-mail: publications@imf.org Internet: http://www.imf.org

International Monetary Fund
Washington, D.C.

INTERNATIONAL MONETARY FUND

PEOPLE'S REPUBLIC OF CHINA

Financial System Stability Assessment

Prepared by the Monetary and Capital Markets and Asia and Pacific Departments

Approved by José Viñals and Anoop Singh

June 24, 2011

This report is based on the IMF/World Bank Financial Sector Assessment Program (FSAP) exercise for China undertaken during June–December 2010. The assessment concluded that reforms have progressed well in moving to a more commercially-oriented financial system. Despite success and rapid growth, China's financial sector is confronting several near-term risks, structural challenges, and policy-induced distortions. The main sources of risks are: (i) the effects of a rapid crisis-related credit expansion on credit quality, (ii) growing off-balance sheet exposures and disintermediation, (iii) a reversal in rapidly rising real estate prices, and (iv) an increase in imbalances due to the current economic growth pattern. Medium-term vulnerabilities—the relatively inflexible macroeconomic policy framework, and the government's important role in credit allocation and in the financial sector at the central and provincial levels—are building up contingent liabilities and could impair the needed reorientation of the financial system to support China's future growth.

A properly composed and timely implemented set of reforms would help address these challenges. This will require further progress in multiple areas, including (i) deepening the commercial orientation of banks and other financial firms; (ii) moving to more market-based means of influencing monetary and financial conditions; (iii) continued strengthening of the capacity of the central bank on financial stability issues, and that of the supervisory commissions; (iv) further development of financial markets and instruments to deepen and strengthen China's financial system; and (v) upgrading the framework for financial stability, crisis management, and resolution arrangement. Moving along this path, however, will pose additional risks and new situations. Hence, priority must be given to establishing the institutional and operational preconditions that are crucial to successfully managing a wide-ranging financial reform agenda, and the intent outlined in the latest 12th Five-Year Plan.

The FSAP team comprised Jonathan Fiechter (IMF, Mission Co-Chief), Thomas A. Rose (World Bank, Mission Co-Chief), Udaibir S. Das (Deputy Mission Chief, IMF), Mario Guadamillas (Deputy Mission Chief, World Bank), César Arias, Martin Čihák, Silvia Iorgova, Yinqiu Lu, Aditya Narain, Nathan Porter, Shaun Roache, Tao Sun, Murtaza Syed (all IMF); Massimo Cirasino, Patrick Conroy, Asli Demirgüç-Kunt, Catiana Garcia-Kilroy, Haocong Ren, Heinz Rudolph, Jun Wang, Ying Wang, Luan Zhao (all World Bank); Nuno Cassola, Henning Göbel, Keith Hall, Nick Le Pan, Greg Tanzer, Nancy Wentzler, Rodney Lester, and Walter Yao (all experts). The team met senior officials and staff from relevant government agencies, as well as representatives from financial institutions, industry organizations, and private sector representatives in Beijing, Chongqing, Nanchang, Ningbo, Shanghai, and Shenzhen.

Subsequent to the FSAP mission, the authorities have begun to move on the various FSAP recommendations, and have asked for technical cooperation in several areas relating to the existing financial stability framework.

The main authors of this report are Udaibir S. Das, Martin Čihák, and Yinqiu Lu with contributions from the FSAP team.

FSAP assessments are designed to assess the stability of the financial system as a whole and not that of individual institutions. They have been developed to help countries identify and remedy weaknesses in their financial sector structure, thereby enhancing their resilience to macroeconomic shocks and cross-border contagion. FSAP assessments do not cover risks that are specific to individual institutions such as asset quality, operational or legal risks, or fraud.

CONTENTS Page

Tables

GLOSSARY

ABC	Agricultural Bank of China
ACHs	Automated Clearinghouses
AIA	International Assurance Company
AMCs	Asset Management Companies
AML/CFT	Anti-Money Laundering/Combating the Financing of Terrorism
BCP	Basel Core Principles for Effective Banking Supervision
BEPS	Bulk Electronic Payment System
CAR	Capital Adequacy Ratio
CBRC	China Banking Regulatory Commission
CCB	China Construction Bank
CCDC	China Central Depositary Trust & Clearing Co., Ltd.
CCP	Central Counterparty
CDB	China Development Bank
CFA	China Futures Association
CFETS	China Foreign Exchange Trading System
CFFEX	China Financial Futures Exchange
CIRC	China Insurance Regulatory Commission
CIS	Collective Investment Scheme
CNAPS	China National Advanced Payment System
CNPS	China National Payment System
CPA	China's Certified Professional Accountant
CPSS	Committee on Payment and Settlement Systems
CSD	Central Securities Depository
CSRC	China Securities Regulatory Commission
CUP	China Union Pay
DaP	Delivery after Payment
DCE	Dalian Commodity Exchange
FATF	Financial Action Task Force
FHCs	Financial Holding Companies
FoP	Free of Payment
FSAP	Financial Sector Assessment Program
GEB	Growth Enterprise Board
HVPS	High Value Payment System
HQ	Headquarters
IAIS	International Association of Insurance Supervisors
IASB	International Accounting Standards Board
IBBM	Interbank Bond Market
ICBC	Industrial Commercial Bank of China
ICP	Insurance Core Principles
IFRS	International Financial Reporting Standards
IMF	International Monetary Fund
IT	Information Technology

JSCBs	Joint-Stock Commercial Banks (12 banks as of end-2010)
KRI	Key Risk Indicators
LCBs	Large Commercial Banks (Top 5)
LCPs	Local Processing Centers
LGFP	Local Government Financing Platform
MMOU	Multilateral Memorandum of Understanding on Exchange of Information
MOF	Ministry of Finance
MOU	Memorandum of Understanding
MSE	Micro and Small Enterprise
NAO	National Audit Office
NBFI	Nonbank Financial Institution
NDRC	National Development and Reform Commission
NPS	National Payment System
NPL	Nonperforming Loan
PaD	Payment after Delivery
PBC	People's Bank of China
PICC	People's Insurance Company of China
P&C	Property and Casualty
QDII	Qualified Domestic Institutional Investor
QFII	Qualified Foreign Institutional Investor
RCSA	Risk and Control Self Assessment
RMB	Renminbi (yuan)
SAFE	State Administration of Foreign Exchange
SAC	Securities Association of China
SD&C	China Securities Depository and Clearing Corporation Limited
SHFE	Shanghai Futures Exchange
SIPF	Securities Investment Protection Fund
SIPS	Systemically Important Payment System
SME	Small and Medium Enterprise
SOE	State-Owned Enterprise
SRO	Self-Regulatory Organizations
SSE	Shanghai Stock Exchange
SSS	Securities Settlement Systems
SZSE	Shenzhen Stock Exchange
ZCE	Zhengzhou Commodity Exchange

Executive Summary

1. China has made remarkable progress in its transition toward a more commercially-oriented and financially sound system. Improvements continue to be made to the structure, performance, transparency, and oversight of financial institutions and markets. As a result, the financial sector entered the global financial crisis from a position of relative strength.

Potential risks

2. Despite ongoing reform and financial strength, China confronts a steady build-up of financial sector vulnerabilities. The system is becoming more complex and inter-linkages between markets, institutions, and across international borders are growing. In addition, informal credit markets, conglomerate structures, and off-balance sheet activities are on the rise. Furthermore, the current growth model, the associated and relatively inflexible macroeconomic policy framework, and the government's important role in credit allocation at the central and provincial levels are leading to a build-up of contingent liabilities. These could affect the needed reorientation toward domestic demand and new sectors of growth. These vulnerabilities are not easily quantified, however, in part due to limitations on monitoring, data collection, and inter-agency information exchange.

3. The main near-term domestic risks to the financial system are four-fold: (i) the impact of the recent sharp credit expansion on banks' asset quality; (ii) the rise of off-balance sheet exposures and of lending outside of the formal banking sector; (iii) the relatively high level of real estate prices; and (iv) the increase in imbalances due to the current economic growth pattern.

4. Jointly conducted stress tests of the largest 17 commercial banks indicate that most of the banks appear to be resilient to isolated shocks. Such shocks included a sharp deterioration in asset quality, a correction in the real estate markets, shifts in the yield curve, and changes in the exchange rate. If several of these risks were to occur at the same time, however, the banking system could be severely impacted. A full assessment of the extent of these risks and how they could permeate through the economic and financial system, however, was hindered by data gaps, the lack of sufficiently long and consistent time series of key financial data, weaknesses in the informational infrastructure, and constraints on the FSAP team's access to confidential data.

Reforms to strengthen the monitoring and resolution of risks

5. Continued advances in supervision and regulation, and the financial stability framework, together with the upgrading of banks' risk management systems are required to effectively respond to these risks. As the range of financial activities offered in China grows, there is a need for a concomitant expansion of the regulatory and supervisory perimeter, combined with stronger supervision of financial groups and robust systemic oversight. This will require augmenting resources and skilled personnel, and improved coordination and information and data exchanges among the key agencies. The People's Bank of China (PBC) and the various supervisory commissions must build staff capacity, adopt new risk monitoring systems, strengthen their intervention frameworks, and establish more forward-looking approaches to assessing financial stability conditions. In support of this, continuing improvements in accounting requirements, data standards, reporting requirements, and meaningful disclosure should be an immediate priority.

6. Institutional reforms will help bring the system more in line with international practices. The mandates of the supervisory agencies should focus on ensuring the safety and soundness of regulated institutions, risk management, and proper market conduct and avoid taking on the responsibility for promoting the development of specific economic sectors or for making decisions on how capital should be intermediated and allocated. Ensuring the operational autonomy of the central bank and the financial supervisors is crucial. Implementation of a formalized financial stability framework and mechanisms for contingency planning is essential. Establishing a permanent committee on financial stability and systemic risk that builds on China's recent experience with an ad-hoc committee set up in June 2008, would be a useful step. Chaired by a senior official with authority, the committee should have access to all relevant supervisory and other financial information. Consistent with its financial stability mandate, the PBC should serve as its secretariat.

7. A framework to resolve weak financial institutions on a timely basis is also needed. The framework would be designed to facilitate the orderly resolution and winding up of distressed financial institutions. A designated government entity should be vested with resolution powers to address institutions determined to be nonviable by their supervisor. As part of this framework, an explicit deposit insurance scheme presently under consideration should be established promptly to finance the orderly resolution of failed depository institutions and protect insured depositors, while minimizing the cost to the public purse.

Towards a more market-based system

8. In addition, broad policy changes will be needed to safeguard financial stability and to support continued strong and balanced growth. The existing configuration of financial policies fosters high savings, structurally high levels of liquidity, and a high risk of capital misallocation and asset bubbles, particularly in real estate. The cost of these distortions is rising over time, posing increasing macro-financial risks. So far, costs relating to the financial system have been absorbed by rapid productivity gains, and by an implicit tax on households through low remuneration on deposits, but these cannot be presumed to continue. To ensure strong and balanced growth going forward, needed financial system reforms include:

- *Improved management of systemic liquidity.* The current high levels of foreign exchange intervention, limited exchange rate movements, and strong incentives for capital inflows hamper systemic liquidity management and control. Steps to drain large amounts of structural liquidity along with moves towards a liberalized and flexible exchange market will reduce financial stability risks and afford the central bank with greater levers for monetary control.

- *Greater use of market-oriented monetary policy instruments.* Interest rates should be the primary instrument to govern credit expansion rather than administrative limits on bank lending. This would enhance the efficiency of capital allocation, strengthen the role of monetary policy, and reduce financial stability risks associated with off-balance sheet lending. Interest rate reform needs to be accompanied by strengthened supervision and improved bank risk management and corporate governance.

- *Broadening financial markets and services.* Developing diversified modalities for financial intermediation would create competitive discipline on the banks, offer enterprises alternative avenues for financing, and provide households with a broader range of financing and investment possibilities. The government must move ahead with its priority to deepen fixed income markets and develop a diversified domestic institutional investor base.

- *A reorientation in the role and responsibilities of government.* Banks' large exposures to state-owned enterprises, guaranteed margins provided by interest rate regulations, still limited ability and willingness to differentiate loan rates, coupled with the implicit guidance on the pace and direction of new lending, undermine development of effective credit risk management in the banks. It is important that banks have the tools and incentives to make lending decisions based upon purely commercial goals.

- *Replacing the use of the commercial banking system to pursue broader policy goals.* The use should be made of direct fiscal expenditures and subsidies, direct lending by policy banks, and explicit government-sponsored credit programs for developmental credit. The government must start establishing safeguards and policy reforms that remove distortions and curb those incentives that place risks on the public sector balance sheet as contingent liabilities.

- *An upgrading of the financial infrastructure and legal framework.* Payments and securities settlement systems have been strengthened, but further progress is required along with continued improvements in the coverage and quality of the Credit Reference Center and oversight of credit rating agencies. As new products are introduced and access is increased, stronger consumer protection, including an expanded financial literacy program, together with improved insolvency proceedings are critical. Cross border and cross currency prudential framework should be strengthened given recent growth in cross-border financial activity and RMB transactions.

9. Given these challenges and build-up of vulnerabilities, calibrating the

appropriate pace and order of future reforms will be key. A well-composed and properly implemented plan, including the various elements discussed above, will make an important contribution to sustaining China's growth. International experience suggests that ad hoc or partial reforms could themselves pose a risk to financial stability. In the case of China this will be all the more critical given the close association between the macroeconomic policy framework and the financial system. Certain pre-conditions have to be made before broader acceleration of financial deepening, liberalization of interest rates, and, finally, full liberalization of the capital account. Such pre-conditions include putting in place a well functioning legal, regulatory, supervisory, and crisis management framework; improving the corporate governance in banks; early absorption of the current liquidity overhang in the financial system; and greater reliance on market-oriented monetary policy instruments. Therefore, careful planning will be critical to smoothly and safely transition to a more market-based system. To help with this process, a prioritized list of recommendations in key areas is presented in Table 1 along with an assessment of the main risk factors in Table 2.

Table 1. China: Key Recommendations

Recommendations	Priority	Time-Frame
Improving commercialization		
1. Continue to advance the process of interest rate and exchange rate reform (¶8, 11, 50, 51, 52, 68, 79), while ensuring that appropriate credit risk management practices in financial institutions are in place. (¶5, 8, 11, 50, 51, 57, 58, 79)	High	MT
2. Clearly delineate the roles and functioning of policy financial institutions from commercial financial institutions. (¶6, 8, 12, 15, 55)	Medium	MT
3. Transform the four Asset Management Companies (AMCs) into commercial entities and, as a first step, require them to publish periodic financial statements and management reports. (¶49)	Medium	MT
Increasing efficiency of the institutional, regulatory, and supervisory framework		
4. Empower the PBC and three supervisory commissions with focused mandates, operational autonomy and flexibility, increased resources and skilled personnel, and strengthen interagency coordination to meet the challenges of a rapidly evolving financial sector. (¶5, 6, 39, 53, 54)	High	MT
5. Develop a framework for regulation and supervision of financial holding companies (FHCs), financial conglomerates, and informal financial firms (¶54). In the interim, acquisition of a regulated institution should be approved by the regulatory commission responsible for the underlying financial institution. (¶54)	Medium	NT
6. Introduce a more forward-looking assessment of credit risk in the China Banking Regulatory Commission (CBRC) risk rating system and eliminate deviations from the capital framework for credit and market risk. (¶56)	Medium	NT
7. Introduce a formal program whereby the China Securities Regulatory Commission (CSRC) conducts regular comprehensive on-site inspections of the exchanges to improve oversight. (¶60)	Medium	NT
8. Introduce a risk-based capital (RBC) solvency regime for insurance firms with suitable transition period and restrict new businesses by insurance companies operating below the 100 percent solvency level. (¶61)	Medium	MT
9. Develop explicit and clear regulation for facilitating the exit of insurance companies from the market via run off or portfolio transfers. (¶61)	Medium	NT
10. Enact a payment system law to give full protection to payments, derivatives and securities settlement finality. (¶63)	High	MT
11. Ensure that beneficial ownership and control information of legal persons is adequate, accurate, and readily accessible to competent authorities. (¶67)	High	MT
12. Improve information sharing and coordination arrangements among the PBC and other agencies on anti-money laundering (AML) and other supervisory issues. (¶39, 53, 54, 67)	High	MT
Upgrading the framework for financial stability, systemic risk monitoring, systemic liquidity, and crisis management		
13. Establish a permanent committee of financial stability, with the PBC as its secretariat. (¶6, 39)	High	MT
14. Upgrade data collection on financial institutions including their leverage, contingent liabilities, off-balance sheet positions, unregulated products, and cross-border and sectoral exposures. (¶40)	Medium	NT

Recommendations	Priority	Time-Frame
15. Build a macro prudential framework for measurement and management of systemic risks; this should include increasing the resources and capacity of the PBC and regulatory agencies to monitor financial stability and to carry out regular stress tests. (¶41)	High	NT
16. Enhance the sterilization of structural liquidity through market-based instruments and manage systemic liquidity spillovers via indirect monetary policy instruments. (¶42, 51)	High	NT
17. Introduce reserve averaging to facilitate liquidity management and enhance stability and efficiency. (¶43)	High	NT
18. Start targeting a short-term repo rate on a pilot basis, as a trial of indirect liquidity management, and commence daily open market operations. (¶44, 45)	High	NT
19. Ensure that PBC's standing facilities operate immediately and automatically, with specified collateral requirement identical across all domestically incorporated institutions. (¶46)	Medium	NT
20. Introduce a deposit insurance scheme to assist in the orderly wind-down of financial institutions and to help clarify the contingent liability. (¶7, 48)	Medium	NT
Developing securities markets and redirecting savings to contractual and collective investment sectors		
21. Ensure regulations are consistent and clarify regulatory responsibilities to support fixed income market development. (¶69)	Medium	MT
22. Continue to improve bond issuance strategies between Ministry of Finance (MOF) and the PBC to help improve the existing market-making across all maturities of the yield curve. (¶70)	High	MT
23. Upgrade regulatory and operational repo market framework to increase market liquidity, enhance risk management and reinforce the money and bond market interest rate nexus. (¶68)	Medium	NT
24. Ease the 40 percent of net assets limit applicable to corporation's market based debt issuance to expand their direct funding capacity. (¶72)	Medium	MT
25. Upgrade links between China Central Depository Trust & Clearing Co., Ltd. (CCDC) and Securities Depository and Clearing Corporation Limited (SD&C) to enhance connectivity among Interbank Bond Market (IBBM), Shanghai Stock Exchange (SSE), and Shenzhen Stock Exchange (SZSE), support further development, and contribute to efficiency in all three markets. (¶72)	Medium	MT
26. Consolidate the multi-pillar pension system, with emphasis on the funded component. (¶75)	Medium	MT
Improving alternative financing channels and access		
27. Review existing government programs to determine their effectiveness in promoting rural and micro and small enterprise (MSE) finance and formulate an integrated and coherent rural and MSE finance strategy. (¶76)	High	MT
28. Further reform the rural credit cooperatives to enhance their efficiency and sustainability as commercial providers of financial products and services. (¶76)	Medium	MT
29. Complete the reform of the Postal Savings Bank (PSB) by optimizing equity ownership, overhauling the bank to become a corporation, and building effective corporate governance. (¶76)	Medium	MT

Notes: NT (Near Term) means implementation completed within three years; MT (Medium Term) means implementation completed in three to five years.

Table 2. China: Risk Assessment Matrix

	Principal Sources of Risk	Likelihood of Realization (next three years)	Potential Impact on Macro-Financial Stability
BALANCE SHEET RISKS	Growing aggregate credit risks	**Medium to High** • Very rapid credit growth—up by 33 percent in 2009—raises the risk of credit being directed to less productive investments. Empirically, there is an inverse relationship between rapid credit growth and bank asset quality. • Under the quantitative lending guidance used in China banks have limited ability to apply prudent risk management practices, suggesting potential credit risks. • Increasing shift of risks off-balance sheet—for example via wealth management products (WMPs)—augment credit risk exposures.	**Moderate to Severe** • NPL accumulation would impair banks' profitability and capital positions. A sizeable decrease of loan collateral values—which in China predominantly takes the form of real estate—would amplify potential bank losses. • A potential shock may be augmented by banks' previous shifts of credit off-balance sheet, which could undermine monetary policy effectiveness. • Stress tests show that the impact of concurrent major credit shocks (a severe scenario includes a slowdown in annual GDP growth to 4 percent) could be sizable, with 25 percent of banking system assets dropping below the 8 percent minimum CAR.
MACRO-FINANCIAL RISKS	An increase of cross-border capital inflows, and a potential flow reversal	**Medium to high** • Capital flows (excluding direct investment) to and from China are becoming large and more volatile, despite extensive capital controls. In absolute terms, flows have averaged about $1^1/_2$ percent of GDP since 1998, compared to a current account balance and net FDI flows at 4.7percent and $1^1/_2$percent of GDP, respectively. • Rising RMB appreciation expectations, and to a lesser degree, higher relative interest rates, suggest potentially stronger speculative capital inflows. The historical relationship between inflows and RMB appreciation expectations embedded in NDFs with a 12-month maturity—typically the most traded maturity—has been positive and significant.	**Moderate** • Capital flows would affect adversely domestic financial stability via real estate and equity markets. High real estate-related bank lending exposures (20 percent of GDP), and indirect exposures via property collateral, make banks vulnerable to real estate booms and busts related to more volatile capital flows. • Large capital inflows could lead to a rapid credit expansion. While the link between net flows and bank lending is weakened by sterilization, international experience shows that lending booms raise the risk of sizable asset quality deterioration. • The closed capital account, albeit admittedly porous, has a mitigating effect against a capital inflow shock.
MACRO-FINANCIAL RISKS	A large and persistent increase in international commodity prices with a pass-through to domestic inflation	**Medium to High** • While some commodity markets have large spare capacity buffers, a number of key imports in China—particularly copper and iron ore—do not, exacerbating vulnerabilities to price upswings in international commodity markets. • Empirical studies suggest that rising commodity prices could exert a significant pressure on the domestic economy, in view of the pass-through to domestic inflation (and possibly monetary policy).	**Moderate** • Supply price pressures could affect the domestic economy via a monetary policy adjustment to counteract consumer price inflation, resulting in a slowdown of domestic lending, lower repayment capacity and credit quality deterioration. • Borrowing firms without sufficient pricing power would suffer from lower profit margins, resulting in a potential upsurge of NPL accumulation; transmission of these risks could lead to second-round economic effects.

	Principal Sources of Risk	Likelihood of Realization (next three years)	Potential Impact on Macro-Financial Stability
INSTITUTIONAL RISKS	Default of infrastructure projects supported by local governments	**Medium** • Banks' exposures to local government financing vehicles increased rapidly as a result of the stimulus. The very rapid expansion of borrowing for large infrastructure projects creates sizable risks of NPL buildup, as some project may not generate sufficient returns to make loan payments. • The size of infrastructure-related lending to local governments is non-trivial. At market estimated RMB 7.7 trillion as of end-June 2010, it is equivalent to 16 percent of outstanding loans and 23 percent of GDP at end-2009.	**Moderate to Severe** • A sharper-than-anticipated correction in real estate prices would spill over to local infrastructure projects and test banking system resilience, given high dependence on land collateral in LGFP funding. • Complex fiscal federal relations and potential difficulty in resolving potential burden-sharing between different levels of government and the banks could enhance risks. • Stress test results point to manageable risks related to local government projects; however, these results need to be used carefully due to data limitations and ambiguity, regarding potential central government's support of local governments.
MACRO-FINANCIAL RISKS	A contraction in the global economy	**Medium** • In view of China's high dependence on trade and FDI for economic growth, domestic enterprises are exposed to a global macroeconomic shock via the potential negative impact on China's export sector and on industries that depend on FDI flows.	**Moderate to Severe** • A global contraction could lead to a weakening of economic activity and rising unemployment, with an increase of corporate NPLs and an adverse impact on banks' solvency. • Scope for policy response is likely more limited in view of the already sizable government-led fiscal and monetary stimulus during the past crisis.
INSTITUTIONAL RISKS	Lack of regulation and supervision on de facto financial holding companies and industrial conglomerates holding financial institutions	**Medium** • Since 2005, with a pilot program of integrated financial services progressing steadily, de facto financial holding companies are developing fast. Some industrial conglomerates are investing in banks, securities firms, and insurance companies. • Current regulatory regime has no explicit agency assigned to oversee the above institutions. The PBC is taking the lead in drafting administrative rules. • Financial holding companies increased inter linkages across financial sectors, and industrial conglomerates holdings could pose risks to both the industrial sector and financial sector. Lack of effective monitoring and oversight might trigger systemic risks.	**Moderate to Severe** • There are potential contagious risks across different sectors and markets via cross share holding and integrated financial services, and may spill over to the real economy. • In view of financial holding companies' systemic importance, failure of financial holding companies could negatively impact public confidence to the financial system which could lead to more serious risks.

Cont

	Principal Sources of Risk	Likelihood of Realization (next three years)	Potential Impact on Macro-Financial Stability
BALANCE SHEET RISKS	A substantial decline in real estate prices, and an increase in credit risk related to property-related credit, including land	**Medium** • While real estate prices have risen significantly, market overheating has been constrained to select Tier 1 cities, with no evidence of systematic nationwide bubble. • Recent government measures would mitigate the likelihood of a potential real estate market correction, with aggregate property prices leveling off and transaction values declining in recent months.	**Moderate** • A sizable downward correction in real estate prices would impair asset quality due to banks' exposures to mortgage and developer loans, and collateral values (mostly in the form of real estate), leading to loan quality downgrades and higher provisioning. • Aggregate exposures to real estate and local government financing platforms are significant at upward of RMB 20 trillion, equivalent to more than 40 percent of the total loans at end-2010. • Relatively low leverage of real estate developers and mortgage borrowers would have a mitigating impact. • Stress test results point to manageable real estate risks; however, these results should be interpreted cautiously due to data limitations.
INTERLINKAGE RISKS	A confluence of various shocks	**Low to Medium** • Almost all shocks listed in the RAM would trigger further shocks in view of the linkages across markets and institutions.	**Severe** • For example, significant capital inflows can drive up equity prices and cause a real estate bubble. This could have a direct impact on the balance sheets of local government financing platforms, who are directly dependent on the real estate market, due to the link of collateral and capital to land prices. Conversely, a sharp reversal of capital flows, would lead to sizable downward corrections in the real estate and equity markets, impairing banks' asset quality, including a potential accumulation of local infrastructure-related NPLs. • Macroeconomic scenario analysis shows that the system could be severely impacted if several major shocks materialized concurrently. For example, a severe scenario (involving a slowdown of GDP growth to 4 percent year-on-year) implies a system-wide CAR of about 8 percent, with banks accounting for some ¼ of the total banking system assets falling below the 8 percent CAR.

Source: China FSAP team.

Note: Qualitative assessment is based on ratings of *high, medium, or low* for likelihood that the vulnerabilities will be exposed by shocks over athree-year horizon. Assessment of the impact on financial stability if the threat is realized is classified with ratings *of mild, moderate, and severe.* The assessment incorporates stress test results as well as other quantitative and qualitative elements of the FSAP analysis.

I. Overall Stability Assessment

A. The Macro-Financial Environment

10. China has maintained high growth rates over the past three decades. Since the start of reforms in 1978, growth has averaged close to 10 percent and inflation has remained relatively subdued. Productivity growth has been rapid and capacity has been expanded by very high levels of investment. The commercial banking sector has also grown rapidly and become more diversified (Figure 1). Banks' lending to households, though low compared with other countries, has picked up sharply following the housing sector reform a decade ago (Figures 2 and 3).

Figure 1. China: Evolution of the Commercial Banking System

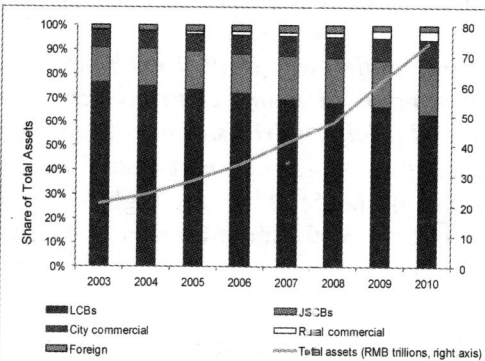

Sources: CEIC; and IMF staff calculations.

Figure 2. China: Scale of Retail Lending in Selected Banking Systems, 2009

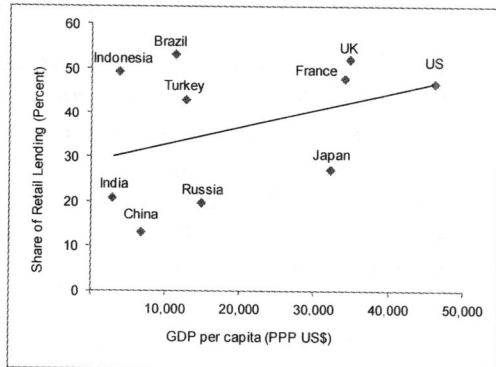

Sources: CEIC; national authorities; IMF WEO; and IMF staff calculations.

Figure 3. China: Growth of Mortgage Lending

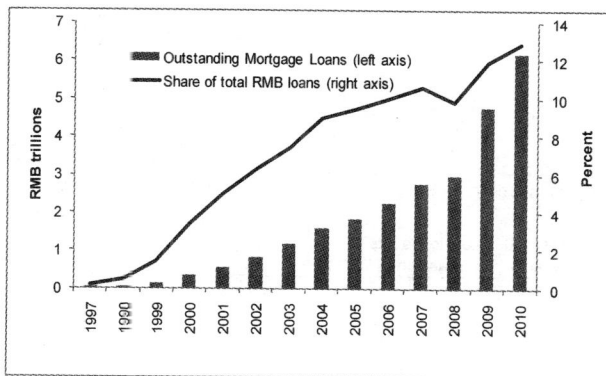

Sources: CEIC; and IMF staff calculations.

11. The macroeconomic and institutional environment, however, has contributed to credit allocation inefficiencies and a build-up of vulnerabilities:

- *First, the relatively low cost of capital distorts saving-investment decisions.* The low cost of capital reflects the ceiling on deposit rates and abundant liquidity, lessens foreign exchange sterilization costs, and supports investment and industrialization. It distorts real activity by generating incentives to over-invest and by suppressing household income through low returns on deposits.

- *Second, underdeveloped capital markets limit the alternatives for corporate funding and household savings.* Households are limited to holding low yielding savings accounts, suppressing income and consumption. The limited availability of insurance products also creates incentives for higher precautionary savings. At the corporate level, lack of access to capital markets by small, private enterprises creates incentives for higher corporate savings. Finally, the search for higher yielding alternative investments by both firms and households adds to the likelihood that asset bubbles may develop, particularly in real estate (Box 1).

- *Third, due to incomplete interest rate deregulation and limited exchange rate flexibility, banks and other market participants lack sufficient incentives to improve their assessment, management, and pricing of risks.* Banks have some flexibility in setting interest rates on loans, but most lending is clustered around the regulated benchmark loan rate (Figures 4 and 5). Also, the high levels of structural liquidity allow most banks to operate with underdeveloped internal liquidity management processes.

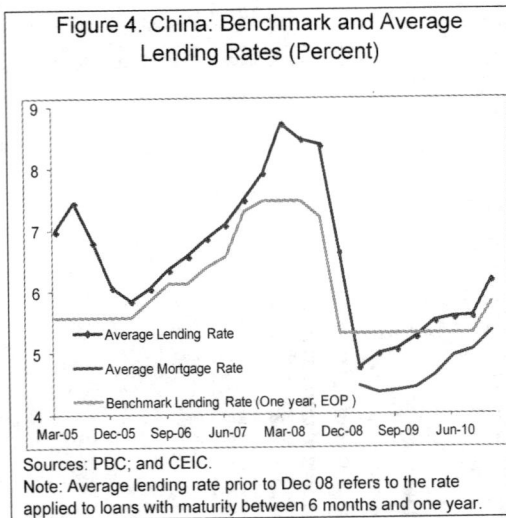

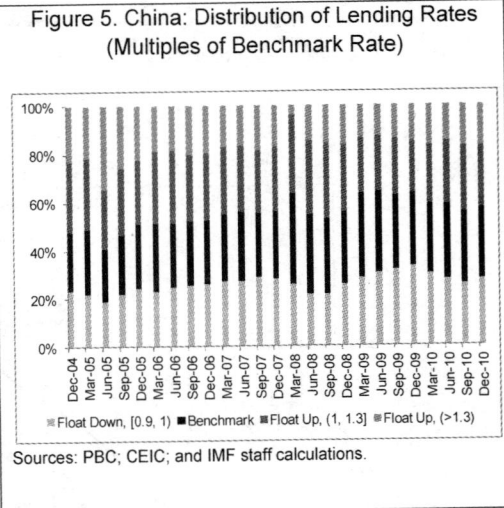

Figure 4. China: Benchmark and Average Lending Rates (Percent)

Figure 5. China: Distribution of Lending Rates (Multiples of Benchmark Rate)

Sources: PBC; and CEIC.
Note: Average lending rate prior to Dec 08 refers to the rate applied to loans with maturity between 6 months and one year.

Sources: PBC; CEIC; and IMF staff calculations.

130

Box 1. Real Estate Sector and Banking Sector Soundness

The sharp increase in China's real estate prices combined with extraordinarily high bank lending to the real estate sector (Figures 6 and 7) has heightened the prospects of a negative impact of price corrections on China's banking sector. The ongoing tightening measures, however, have slowed down loan growth to the real estate sector and the related price increases. Continuous monitoring, stress test, and a comprehensive set of policies are needed to contain the impact of a real estate price correction on financial stability.

Several fundamental factors are driving the real estate prices in China. These include rapid income growth, low return on deposits, abundant liquidity, lack of alternative investment vehicles, low cost of home ownership, and local governments' reliance on land sales revenues.

The banking sector's direct exposure to the real estate sector is moderate (Figure 8) but the indirect exposure is much higher. Real estate sector related loans account for some 20 percent of the Chinese banking system's total loans, relatively low compared with, for example, Hong Kong SAR or the United States. However, indirect exposure is higher. Loan terms in China depend heavily on collateral use. In the five largest banks, 30–45 percent of loans are backed by collateral, the majority of which is real estate. A large real estate price correction would reduce collateral values, and hence loan recovery value should borrowers default. In addition, credit to industries that are "vertically integrated" with the real estate sector (such as construction, cement, and steel) are also exposed to these risks. Given the importance of the real estate sector for economic growth, an economic slowdown as a result of a real estate price correction could adversely affect the banking system's asset quality. Last but not least, local governments' ability to support local government financing platforms (LGFPs) via land sale and subsidies—essential for those LGFPs with limited cash flows to repay the loans—heavily depends on the real estate market.[1]

In the short-term, the impact appears manageable especially if the current growth momentum continues. There does not appear to be significant over-valuation of residential real estate prices in China as a whole, though there are signs of overvaluation in some market segments. Also, the moderate direct exposure and low leverage ratio (Figure 9) would limit the impact of a real estate price correction on banks' asset quality. Stress testing banks' exposure to the real estate sector alone, or in combination with the "vertically integrated" sectors (Section I. D), suggests a modest impact on banks from credit quality deterioration in the real estate sector.[2] However, if a growth shock materialized concurrently then the impact on the banking system and its spillovers would be severe.

Over the medium- to long-term, the risk posed by the real estate sector

depends on whether the fundamentals behind the real estate price increases are addressed by policy measures. A comprehensive set of measures—including the completion of the interest rate and exchange rate reforms, further capital market development, gradual opening of the capital account, and fiscal reforms, including initiating a broad-based property tax—is needed to promote the orderly development of the real estate market. In the meantime, the authorities should monitor real estate market developments and their potential impact on the banking sector and financial stability, and take prompt corrective steps in case of real estate price overshooting.

---

[1] On average, 29 percent of their total revenues were from the sale of land use rights in 2010 (UBS, 2011, "Measuring Property Bubble in China," March 22, 2011). Ttotal revenues include mainly local government revenues, transfer and tax refunds from central government, and land sales revenues.

[2] Due to data issues, the stress testing exercise did not explicitly take into account regional differences in real estate market developments.

Figure 6. China: Residential Housing Prices and Mortgage Lending

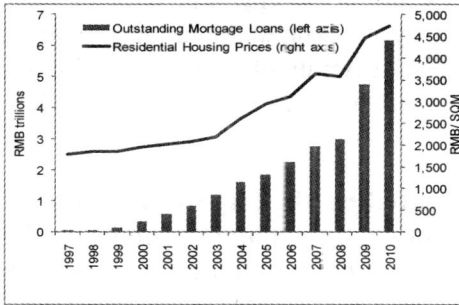

Figure 7. China: Bank Loans to the Real Estate Sector, Year-on-Year Changes (Percent)

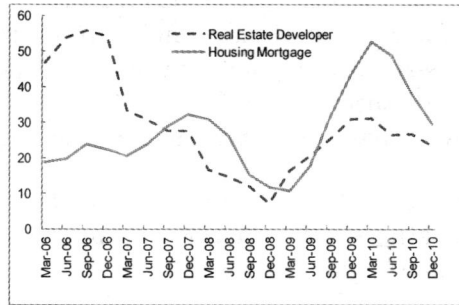

Sources: CEIC; and IMF staff calculations.

Sources: CEIC; and IMF staff calculations.

Figure 8. China: Share of Real Estate Sector Loans in Bank Loans (Percent)

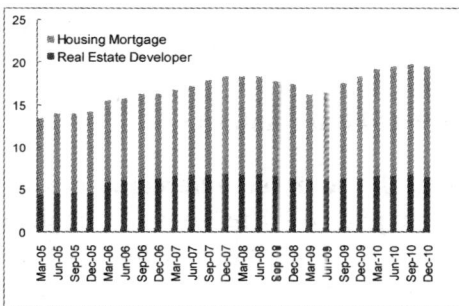

Figure 9. China: A Proxy for Loan-to-Value Ratio (Percent)

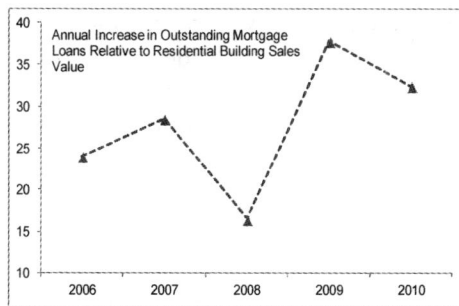

Sources: CEIC; and IMF staff calculations.

Sources: CEIC; and IMF staff calculations.

12. Continued reliance on credit growth targets, even if supplemented by other policy instruments, undermines the efficiency of credit allocation and disrupts monetary policy transmission. Such credit targets have meant that banks have strong incentives to expand market share to boost interest income and use off-balance sheet channels to circumvent credit targets, compromising monetary control; and that the corporate sector tends to over-borrow, knowing that at some point credit will be rationed. Controlling interest rates and determining quantities of lending also mean that policy makers cannot rely on market prices (such as short-term interest rates) to assess macroeconomic and liquidity conditions.

13. A by-product of the existing macro-financial and institutional environment is low investment efficiency. Since 2001, it is estimated that every US$ 1 of Chinese GDP growth has required, on average, nearly US$ 5 of investment, 40 percent more than in Japan and Korea during their take-off periods.[1] In addition, while the share of China's total savings and investment in G-20 aggregates is more than 20 percent, its GDP share is about 10 percent. These may be a reflection of misallocation of capital to some projects with low rates of return.

---

[1] McKinsey Global Institute, 2006, "Putting China's Capital to Work: The Value of Financial System Reform."

14. The state is also directly and indirectly involved in the financial sector. A large share of the banking sector is state-owned, as is much of banks' corporate client base. As the principal shareholder, the state appoints senior management in all major banks. In the absence of an explicit deposit insurance system and a resolution framework, the state also implicitly insures all deposits. The heavy involvement by the state in many aspects of the financial system reduces market discipline, weakens corporate governance, and is likely to create soft budget constraints.

15. Such state involvement has been illustrated by the important role of the banking system in the conduct of fiscal policy. To counter the impact of the 2008–09 global financial crisis the authorities launched a stimulus package that was implemented through bank credit expansion. Local governments' eagerness to undertake infrastructure projects coupled with revenue-expenditure mismatches and their inability to borrow directly, resulted in a rapid increase in using LGFPs to serve as indirect vehicles to collect bank loans, often using state-owned assets such as land as collateral. As a result, the contingent liabilities of the public sector from such activities increased considerably.

B. Financial System: Structure and Inter-linkages

16. China has made progress in moving toward a more commercially-oriented financial system (Table 3). This has been underpinned by reforms that included recapitalizing the banking system, creating new capital markets, introducing a prudential regulatory regime, opening the financial system following accession to the World Trade Organization, and taking steps to reform interest rate and the exchange rate policies. Reform of the joint-stock banks has boosted the commercial orientation of the banking system and reform of the rural credit cooperatives has yielded some initial results. In the securities sector, key companies have been restructured, and a resolution mechanism and investor protection scheme set up. Pension sector reform has also progressed, with National Social Security Fund established in 2000.

17. Nonetheless, banks, particularly the largest ones, dominate financial intermediation (Tables 4 and 5, and Figure 10). The large commercial banks (LCBs)

Table 3. China: Financial Sector Reforms—Selected Benchmarks

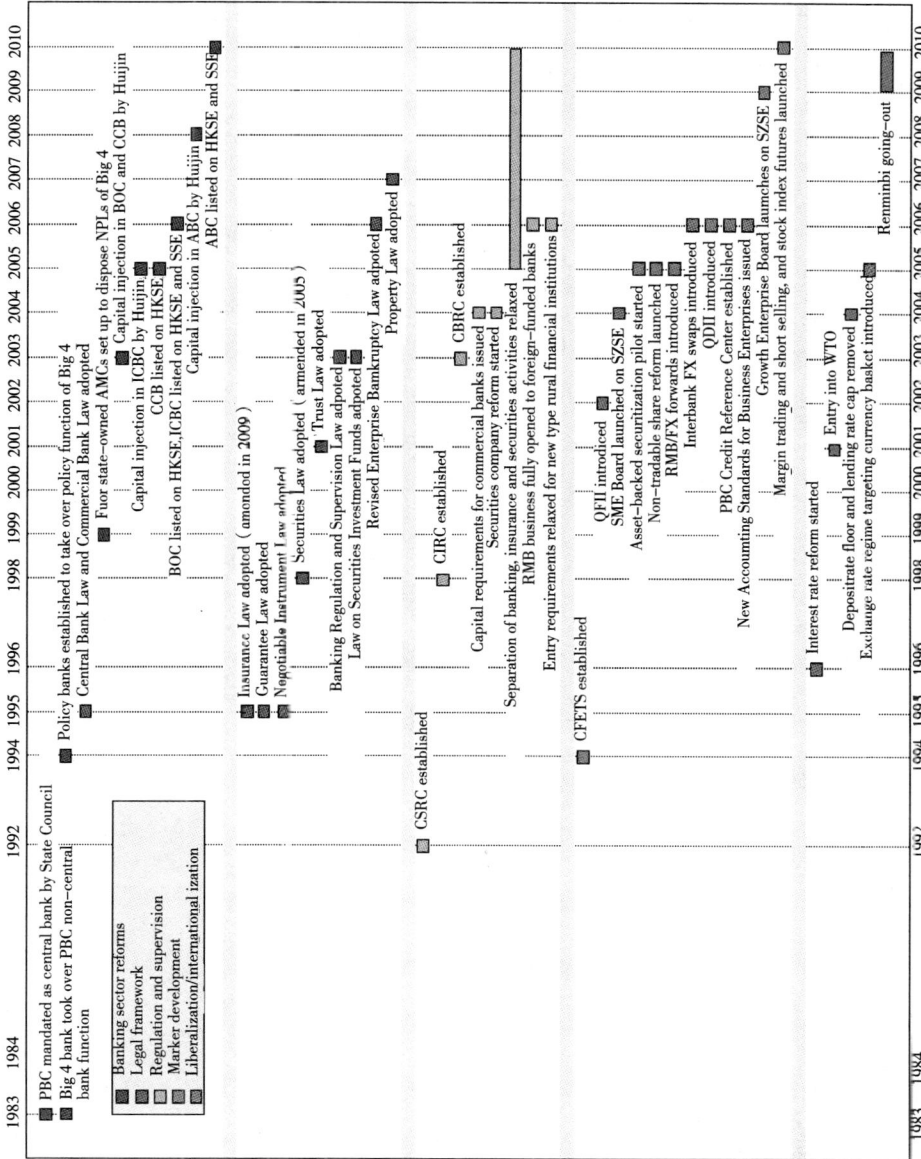

Legend:
- Banking sector reforms
- Legal framework
- Regulation and supervision
- Market development
- Liberalization/internationalization

Timeline years: 1983 1984 1992 1994 1995 1996 1998 1999 2000 2001 2002 2003 2004 2005 2006 2007 2008 2009 2010

Benchmark events:

- PBC mandated as central bank by State Council
- Big 4 bank took over PBC non-central bank function
- Policy banks established to take over policy function of Big 4
- Central Bank Law and Commercial Bank Law adopted
- Fuor state-owned AMCs set up to dispose NPLs of Big 4
- Capital injection in ICBC by Huijin
- Capital injection in BOC and CCB by Huijin
- CCB listed on HKSE
- BOC listed on HKSE,ICBC listed on HKSE and SSE
- Capital injection in ABC by Huijin
- ABC listed on HKSE and SSE
- Insurance Law adopted (amended in 2009)
- Guarantee Law adopted
- Negotiable Instrument Law adopted
- Securities Law adopted (amended in 2005)
- Trust Law adopted
- Banking Regulation and Supervision Law adopted
- Law on Securities Investment Funds adopted
- Revised Enterprise Bankruptcy Law adopted
- Property Law adopted
- CSRC established
- CIRC established
- Capital requirements for commercial banks issued
- Securities company reform started
- CBRC established
- Separation of banking, insurance and securities activities relaxed
- RMB business fully opened to foreign-funded banks
- Entry requirements relaxed for new type rural financial institutions
- CFETS established
- QFII introduced
- SME Board launched on SZSE
- Asset-backed securitization pilot started
- Non-tradable share reform launched
- RMB/FX forwards introduced
- Interbank FX swaps introduced
- QDII introduced
- PBC Credit Reference Center established
- New Accounting Standards for Business Enterprises issued
- Growth Enterprise Board launches on SZSE
- Margin trading and short selling, and stock index futures launched
- Interest rate reform started
- Entry into WTO
- Deposirate floor and lending rate cap removed
- Exchange rate regime targeting currency basket introduced
- Renminbi going-out

Note: The Big 4 banks are ICBC,CCB,ABC and BOC,which have been commercialized in recent years.The Big 4 and Bank of communications together are referred to as large commercial banks.

135

Table 4. China: Structure of the Financial Sector, 2007–10

	2007				2008				2009				2010			
	Number of Institutions	Total Assets (in bln RMB)	Share of Total Assets	Share of GDP	Number of Institutions	Total Assets (in bln RMB)	Share of Total Assets	Share of GDP	Number of Institutions	Total Assets (in bln RMB)	Share of Total Assets	Share of GDP	Number of Institutions	Total Assets (in bln RMB)	Share of Total Assets	Share of GDP
Banking Institutions	**8,721**	**51,627**	**84.1**	**194.2**	**5,578**	**61,982**	**87.8**	**197.4**	**3,767**	**77,978**	**87.0**	**229.0**	**3,639**	**93,215**	**87.6**	**234.2**
Commercial banks	187	40,459	65.9	152.2	323	47,819	67.8	152.3	336	61,513	68.6	180.7	379	74,160	69.7	186.3
Large commercial banks	5	28,007	45.6	105.4	5	32,575	46.2	103.7	5	40,800	45.5	119.8	5	46,894	44.1	117.8
Joint-stock commercial banks	12	7,249	11.8	27.3	12	8,834	12.5	28.1	12	11,818	13.2	34.7	12	14,904	14.0	37.4
City commercial banks	124	3,340	5.4	12.6	136	4,136	5.9	13.2	143	5,680	6.3	16.7	147	7,853	7.4	19.7
Rural commercial banks	17	610	1.0	2.3	22	929	1.3	3.0	43	1,866	2.1	5.5	85	2,767	2.6	70.
Foreign banks	29	1,252	2.0	4.7	148	1,345	1.9	4.3	133	1,349	1.5	4.0	130	1,742	1.6	4.4
Locally incorporated foreign subsidiaries	...	...	...	...	32	996	1.4	3.2	38	1,132	1.3	3.3	40	1,522	1.4	3.8
Branches of foreign banks	...	...	...	...	116	349	0.5	1.1	95	217	0.2	0.6	90	220	0.2	0.6
Policy banks and China Development Bank	3	4,278	7.0	16.1	3	5,645	8.0	18.0	3	6,946	7.7	20.4	3	7,652	7.2	19.2

Cont

	2007				2008				2009				2010			
	Number of Institutions	Total Assets (in bln RMB)	Share of Total Assets	Share of GDP	Number of Institutions	Total Assets (in bln RMB)	Share of Total Assets	Share of GDP	Number of Institutions	Total Assets (in bln RMB)	Share of Total Assets	Share of GDP	Number of Institutions	Total Assets (in bln RMB)	Share of Total Assets	Share of GDP
China Postal Savings Bank	1	1,769	2.9	6.7	1	2,216	3.1	7.1	1	2,705	3.0	7.9	1	3,397	3.2	8.5
Cooperative financial institutions	8,503	5,121	8.3	19.3	5,150	6,295	8.9	20.0	3,263	6,789	7.6	19.9	2,870	7,893	7.4	19.8
Rural cooperative banks	113	646	1.1	2.4	163	1,003	1.4	3.2	196	1,270	1.4	3.7	223	1,500	1.4	3.8
Urban credit cooperatives [1]	42	131	0.2	0.5	22	80	0.1	0.3	11	27	0.0	0.1	1	2	0.0	0.0
Rural credit cooperatives [1]	8,348	4,343	7.1	16.3	4,965	5,211	7.4	16.6	3,056	5,493	6.1	16.1	2,646	6,391	6.0	16.1
New-type rural financial institutions	27	0	0	0	101	6	0	0	164	25	0	0.1	386	113	0	0.3
Village or township banks	19	0	0	0	91	6	0	0	148	25	0	0.1	349	113	0	0.3
Rural mutual credit cooperatives	8	0	0	0	10	0	0	0	16	0	0	0	37	0	0	0
Non-Bank Financial Institutions	**690**	**9,744**	**15.9**	**36.7**	**738**	**8,582**	**12.2**	**27.3**	**772**	**11,666**	**13.0**	**34.3**	**782**	**13,168**	**12.4**	**33.1**
Insurance companies	102	2,831	4.6	10.6	112	3,280	4.6	10.4	120	3,971	4.4	11.7	125	4,965	4.7	12.5
Life	54	2,351	3.8	8.8	56	2,713	3.8	8.6	59	3,366	3.8	9.9	61	4,267	4.0	10.7
Re-insurance [1]	6	89	0.1	0.3	9	101	0.1	0.3	9	116	0.1	0.3	9	115	0.1	0.3

Cont

	2007				2008				2009				2010			
	Number of Institutions	Total Assets (in bln RMB)	Share of Total Assets	Share of GDP	Number of Institutions	Total Assets (in bln RMB)	Share of Total Assets	Share of GDP	Number of Institutions	Total Assets (in bln RMB)	Share of Total Assets	Share of GDP	Number of Institutions	Total Assets (in bln RMB)	Share of Total Assets	Share of GDP
Non-life	42	391	0.6	1.5	47	466	0.7	1.5	52	489	0.5	1.4	55	584	0.5	1.5
Pension funds	39	592	1.0	2.2	39	754	1.1	2.4	39	1,030	1.1	3.0	1	1,138	1.1	2.9
National Social Security Fund	1	440	0.7	1.7	1	562	0.8	1.8	1	777	0.9	2.3	1	857	0.8	2.2
Enterprise annuities	38	152	0.2	0.6	38	191	0.3	0.6	38	253	0.3	0.7	...	281	0.3	0.7
Fund management companies	59	3,280	5.3	12.3	61	1,939	2.7	6.2	60	2,677	3.0	7.9	63	2,520	2.4	6.3
Securities investment funds 2/	346	3,280	5.3	12.3	439	1,939	2.7	6.2	577	2,677	3.0	7.9	704	2,520	2.4	6.3
Securities firms	106	1,734	2.8	6.5	107	1,191	1.7	3.8	106	2,027	2.3	6.0	106	1,967	1.8	4.9
Futures companies	177	50	0.1	0.2	171	59	0.1	0.2	167	121	0.1	0.4	164	192	0.2	0.5
Qualified Foreign Institutional Investors	51	286	0.5	1.1	76	179	0.3	0.6	94	290	0.3	0.9	106	297	0.3	0.7
Other non-bank financial institutions	152	972	1.6	3.7	168	1,181	1.7	3.8	182	1,550	1.7	4.6	213	2,089	2.0	5.2
Finance companies of enterprise groups	73	...	...	...	84	975	1.4	3.1	91	1,229	1.4	3.6	107	1,541	1.4	3.9
Trust companies	54	...	...	...	54	87	0.1	0.3	58	113	0.1	0.3	63	148	0.1	0.4

Cont

	2007				2008				2009				2010			
	Number of Institutions	Total Assets (in bln RMB)	Share of Total Assets	Share of GDP	Number of Institutions	Total Assets (in bln RMB)	Share of Total Assets	Share of GDP	Number of Institutions	Total Assets (in bln RMB)	Share of Total Assets	Share of GDP	Number of Institutions	Total Assets (in bln RMB)	Share of Total Assets	Share of GDP
Finance leasing companies	10	…	…	…	12	80	0.1	0.3	12	160	0.2	0.5	17	316	0.3	0.8
Money brokerage firms	2	…	…	…	3	0.1	0.0	0.0	3	0.2	0.0	0.0	4	0.3	0.0	0.0
Finance companies	13	…	…	…	15	38	0.1	0.1	18	48	0.1	0.1	22	84	0.1	0.2
Lending companies	4	…	…	…	6	0	0	0	8	0	0	0	9	0.1	0.0	0
Auto financing companies	9	…	…	…	9	38	0.1	0.1	10	48	0.1	0.1	13	84	0.1	0.2
Banking asset management companies[3]	4	…	…	…	4	…	…	…	4	…	…	…	4	…	…	…
Total Financial System[4]	9,411	61,370	100.0	230.9	6,316	70,564	100.0	224.7	4,539	89,644	100.0	263.3	4,421	106,383	100.0	267.3

Sources: PBC; CBRC; CIRC; CSRC; NBS of China; and Ministry of Human Resource and Social Security; and IMF staff calculations.

[1] As there is no insurance company engaged in both life and non-life business, data of reinsurance companies are provided instead. In 2007 the insurance sector adopted new accounting principles which areapplied to the data starting from 2007.

[2] Proceeds raised by securities investment funds are managed by fund management companies on behalf of fund unit holders.

[3] The table excludes assets of the four AMCs. According to the FSAP team's calculations, the book value of the non-performing assets transferred to the AMCs amounted to about RMB2.6 trillion as of end 2006 (about 6 percent of total financial system assets or 12 percent of GDP). Comparable data for 2007–10 are not available, as the AMCs have not released financial statements since 2006.

[4] This table does not include informal finance, the estimates of which vary.

Notes: Data for 2008, 2009, and 2010 were provided by the Chinese authorities in the context of the FSAP. Data for 2007 were collected from publically available sources, particularly the annual reports of the three financial regulatory commissions and the financial statements of the NSSF. Data on rural and urban credit cooperatives were collected from the CBRC's annual reports.

Table 5. China: Financial Development Indicators, 2005–10

	2005	2006	2007	2008	2009	2010
Banking						
Total number of banking institutions	-	19,667	8,721	5,578	3,767	3,639
Number of branches/million population	-	140	144	146	145	146
Bank deposits/GDP (%)	147.2	153.3	143.5	147.5	169.6	171.3
Private credit[1]/GDP (%)	114.3	113.0	111.0	108.3	129.3	131.1
Bank assets/total financial system assets (%)	-	-	84.1	87.8	87.0	87.6
Bank assets/GDP (%)	197.1	198.3	194.2	197.4	229.0	234.2
Insurance						
Number of life insurers	42	48	54	56	59	61
Number of non-life insurers	35	38	42	47	52	55
Insurance Penetration (premiums in % of GDP)						
Life	1.8	1.7	1.8	2.2	2.3	-
Non-life	0.9	1.0	1.1	1.0	1.1	-
Insurance Density (premiums per capita, RMB) Life						
Life	250	272	336	498	554	-
Non-life	129	155	194	234	273	-
Pension						
Percentage of labor force covered by pensions	30.1	31.5	32.8	35.4	41.2	45.7[2]
Pension fund assets/GDP (%)	1.5	1.7	2.2	2.4	3.0	2.9
Pension fund assets/total financial system assets (%)	-	-	-	1.1	1.1	1.1
Mortgage						
Mortgage assets/total financial system assets (%)	-	-	-	4.2	5.0	5.2
Mortgage debt stock/GDP (%)	-	-	-	9.4	13.1	14.0
Money markets						
Interbank lending (RMB billion)	1,278	2,150	10,647	15,049	19,350	27,868
Pledged repo value of transactions (RMB billion)	15,678	26,302	44,067	56,383	67,701	84,653
Outright repo value of transactions (RMB billion)	219	292	726	1,758	2,602	2,940
Central bank bill value traded (RMB billion)	2,893	4,240	8,704	22,827	14,213	17,465
Foreign exchange markets						
Foreign exchange reserves in months of imports	13.3	14.4	16.8	18.1	24.6	-
Foreign exchange reserves/short-term debt	4.8	5.4	6.5	8.6	9.3	7.6
Value of transactions in FX swap (USD billion)	0	51	315	441	806	1,296
Value of transactions in FX forward (USD billion)	2.7	14.1	22.6	17.9	11.7	36.4
Capital Markets						
Equity market						
Number of listed companies	1,381	1,434	1,550	1,625	1,718	2,063
Market capitalization of listed companies[3]/GDP (%)	17.5	41.3	123.1	38.6	71.6	66.7
Stock market value traded/market capitalization[3](%)	96.4	100.4	140.8	220.1	219.7	205.6
Number of new offers	15	66	124	76	99	347
Value of new offers (RMB billion)	5.8	134.2	481.0	103.4	187.9	488.3
Bond market						
Government bonds outstanding[4]/GDP (%)	27.3	28.9	32.4	31.3	29.3	28.1
Financial bonds outstanding/GDP (%)	10.8	12.1	12.7	13.4	15.1	15.0

Cont

	2005	2006	2007	2008	2009	2010
Corporate bonds outstanding/GDP (%)	1.7	2.6	3.0	4.1	7.1	8.6
Derivatives market						
Total market value of warrants traded on SSE and SZSE (RMB billion)	-	-	54.0	17.5	20.9	1.5
Annual turnover of warrants on SSE and SZSE (RMB billion)	-	-	7,783	6,969	5,365	1,499
Annual turnover of commodity futures (RMB trillion)	-	-	20.5	36.0	65.3	113.5
Total notional outstanding of RMB interest rate derivatives[5](RMB billion)	5.0	33.3	217	529	662	1,486
Average daily trading volume of RMB interest rate derivatives (RMB billion)	0.0	0.1	0.9	2.1	1.9	6.0
Collective investment funds						
Number of licensed investment funds	-	-	346	439	557	704
Number of fund management companies	-	-	59	61	60	63
Total assets under management by investment funds/GDP (%)	-	-	12.3	6.2	7.9	6.3
Share of retail investors in investment funds (%)	-	-	89	81	82	82
Memo:						
Nominal GDP (RMB billion)	18,494	21,631	26,581	31,405	34,051	39,798
Population (million)	1,304	1,311	1,318	1,325	1,331	1,338

Sources: PBC; CBRC; CIRC; CSRC; MOHRSS; CFETS; BIS; IFS; WDI; Swiss Re Sigma; and ChinaBond.com.cn.
[1] Including credit to public enterprises.
[2] Labor force data for 2010 is an estimate.
[3] Including all the A and B shares of companies listed on SSE and SZSE.
[4] Data for government bonds are from the BIS and include both treasury securities and central bank bills/notes.
[5] Estimates by CFETS.

make up almost two-thirds of commercial bank assets (Figure 11) with the assets of the four largest banks each exceeding 25 percent of GDP. The fixed income market has grown as an alternative funding channel, but remains heavily concentrated in public sector securities (Figure 12). The equity market mainly meets the needs of large enterprises, in spite of recent progress in establishing a multilayer equity market to facilitate funding to SMEs. Assets under management by the insurance sector corresponded to less than 11 percent of household bank deposits. Trust, financial leasing, and finance companies have all been growing rapidly but remain small relative to banks. China also has a flourishing informal financial sector, parts of which provide funding to SMEs and small retail investors.

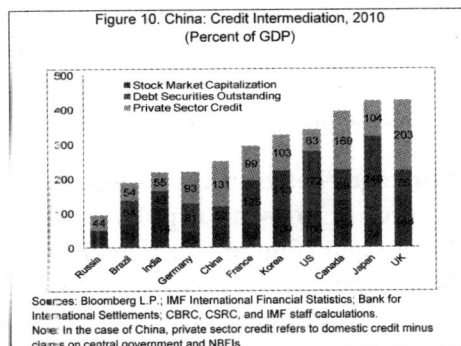

Figure 10. China: Credit Intermediation, 2010
(Percent of GDP)

Sources: Bloomberg L.P.; IMF International Financial Statistics; Bank for International Settlements; CBRC, CSRC, and IMF staff calculations.
Note: In the case of China, private sector credit refers to domestic credit minus claims on central government and NBFIs.

Figure 11. China: Commercial Banking System Structure by Assets, 2010	Figure 12. China: Fixed Income Markets in Selected Countries, 2009

Sources: CEIC; and IMF staff calculations.

Source: Chinabond, 2010, "China's Bond Market—the View."

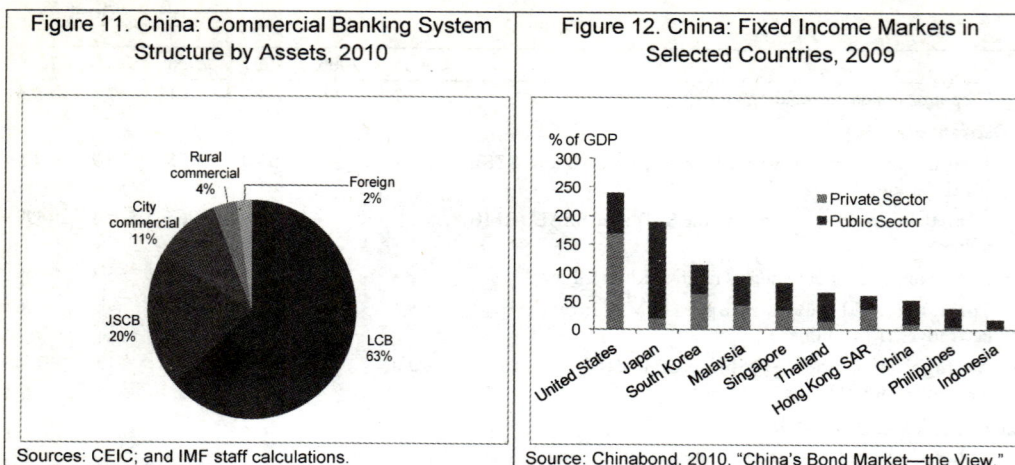

18. While China's financial markets are still in a development phase, cross-market integration has been increasing. There is distinct separation within domestic markets (for example, the domestic bond market is divided into exchange traded/retail and interbank/wholesale markets) and between Chinese markets and the international financial markets (in part, due to widespread capital controls). Nonetheless, shocks do get transmitted across different domestic markets, as illustrated by a positive correlation of yields. Connectivity between markets is likely to grow fast.

19. Linkages among the banks are mainly transmitted through the interbank repo market. The repo market is necessary for many small banks and nonbanks to fund their activities, and for larger banks to place their surplus funds. Consequently, it is the market through which a liquidity squeeze in one part of the banking system can and does spread to others (Section I.C).

20. Inter-connections between banks and nonbank financial institutions (NBFI) have begun to grow. Laws and rules permit more complex structures even though supervisors are challenged to meet the key elements of the principle of consolidated supervision. Interlinkages are increasing with the rise of FHCs, which have expanded considerably since the initiation of a pilot program on integrated financial services under the 11th Five-Year Plan (2006–10) and industrial-financial integrated groups have developed rapidly. At the same time, regulatory policies applying to shadow banking and their interconnections needs to be clarified and made transparent. A more structured oversight, regulatory, and supervisory approach is needed to prevent and to manage systemic risks via cross-market products and institutional structures.

21. Finally, the financial linkages between China and the rest of the world have historically been limited, but are growing rapidly. The growth in RMB deposits in Hong Kong SAR has been rapid (Figure 13), though the amount is insignificant relative to the RMB onshore deposits. Cross-border portfolio capital investment is subject to Qualified Domestic Institutional Investor (QDII) and Qualified Foreign

Institutional Investor (QFII) programs.[2] The markets for B shares, through which foreign investors are allowed to invest in China's stock exchange markets, and H shares (China companies listed in Hong Kong Stock Exchange) are eclipsed by the markets for A shares (Figure 14). In addition, the financial transmission between A share and H share is still limited (Figure 15). While the balance sheet positions of China's banking system vis-à-vis banks located in other countries do not yet fully match the interlinkages of the world's leading banking centers, they have increased by 80 percent in the last ten years.

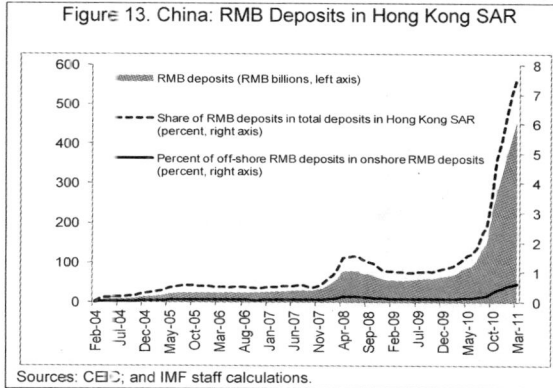

Figure 13. China: RMB Deposits in Hong Kong SAR

RMB deposits (RMB billions, left axis)

Share of RMB deposits in total deposits in Hong Kong SAR (percent, right axis)

Percent of off-shore RMB deposits in onshore RMB deposits (percent, right axis)

Sources: CEIC; and IMF staff calculations.

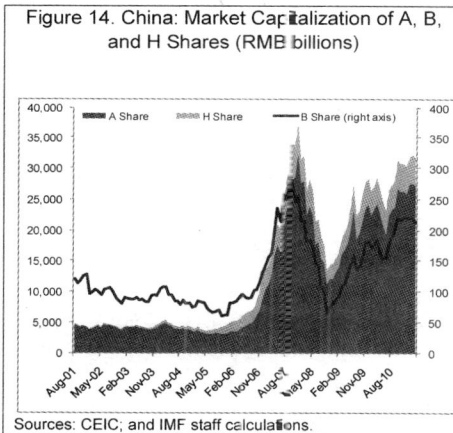

Figure 14. China: Market Capitalization of A, B, and H Shares (RMB billions)

A Share   H Share   B Share (right axis)

Sources: CEIC; and IMF staff calculations.

Figure 15. China: Hong Kong SAR Market Premium for Chinese Equity

(Index, January 2007 = 100)

Gap between H&A Shares (right axis)
China SE Shanghai A
Hang Seng H-share Index

Sources: CEIC; Bloomberg; and IMF staff calculations.

C. Banking System Performance, Soundness, and Resilience

22. The banking sector's balance sheet has expanded rapidly, in part due to the investment-driven stimulus policies of recent years. In 2009, the total amount of outstanding RMB loans expanded by 33 percent although credit growth slowed down in 2010 (Figure 16).The rapid growth in foreign currency loans is likely linked to

---

[2] The aggregate quota for the 88 QDII participants was US$68.4 billion at end-2010, which accounted for about 0.6 percent of domestic deposits. Under the QFII, 106 foreign institutional investors shared the aggregate quota of US$ 19.7 billion at end-2010, which accounted for about 0.3 percent of domestic bond and equity market capitalization.

the expectation of RMB appreciation. Bank exposure to infrastructure construction increased, driven largely by an expansion of LGFPs, while the share of manufacturing-related loans declined. The upswing in the real estate market also fueled demand for mortgage loans. Banks' off-balance sheet exposures expanded rapidly, mostly as a result of banks' promoting wealth-management products as the government began to limit the pace of new lending.

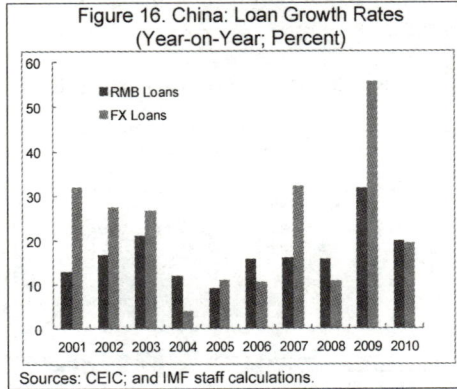

Figure 16. China: Loan Growth Rates (Year-on-Year; Percent)

Sources: CEIC; and IMF staff calculations.

23. Banks' funding appears stable. The sizable and low-cost domestic deposit base has contributed to stable bank funding. While household deposits remained critical to the growth of banks' funding base for most of the reform years, the incremental growth in domestic corporate deposits in 2009 has been significant (Figure 17). Maturity mismatches have also risen. Increasing reliance on medium- and long-term loans for investment project financing has lengthened banks' average asset maturities (Figures 18), particularly for large commercial banks.

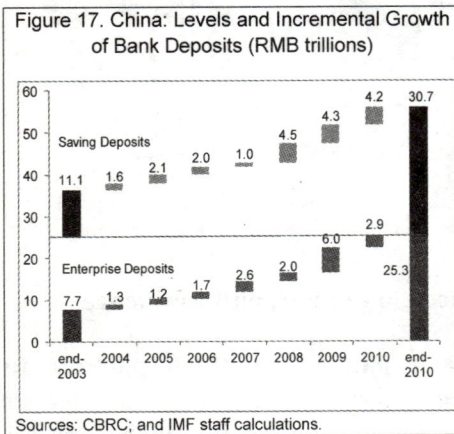

Figure 17. China: Levels and Incremental Growth of Bank Deposits (RMB trillions)

Sources: CBRC; and IMF staff calculations.

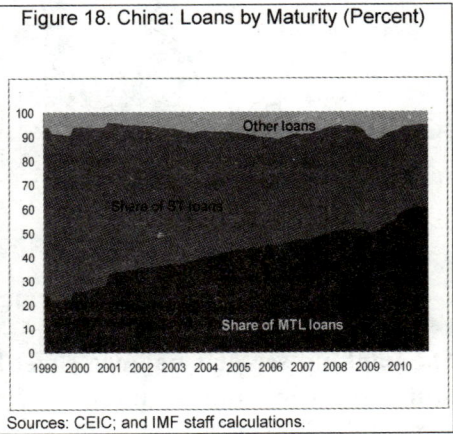

Figure 18. China: Loans by Maturity (Percent)

Sources: CEIC; and IMF staff calculations.

24. Bank profits remain high (Table 6). The credit expansion has supported bank profitability, despite a partial contraction of the interest rate margins in 2009. Chinese banks' limited earning diversification and strong reliance on interest income, however, makes their porfits prone to changes in regulated interest rate margins and limits on lending volumes.

Table 6. China: Selected Indicators of Financial Health, 2005–10[1]

	2005	2006	2007	2008	2009	2010
Major Commercial Banks			(In percent, unless otherwise indicated)			
Capital Adequacy						
Regulatory capital to risk-weighted assets[2]	2.5	4.9	8.1	12.0	11.0	12.0
Regulatory Tier I capital to risk-weighted assets	...	...	6.0	9.6	8.5	9.6
Nonperforming loans net of provisions to capital	...	...	55.9	4.2	1.4	-2.2
Capital to assets[3]	4.3	5.2	5.4	5.9	5.3	6.0
Asset Quality						
Nonperforming loans to total gross loans	8.9	7.5	6.4	2.4	1.6	1.1
Loan loss provisions to non-performing loans[3]	24.8	34.3	39.2	117.9	155.4	217.7
Sectoral distribution of loans to total loans[4]						
Residents	...	...	97.8	97.9	99.3	...
Deposit takers	...	...	5.1	5.7	5.7	...
Central bank	...	...	3.0	2.1	4.2	...
Other financial corporations	...	...	1.0	1.7	1.1	...
General government	...	...	0.0	0.0	0.0	...
Non-financial corporations	...	...	70.5	69.8	68.3	...
Other domestic sectors	...	...	18.3	18.5	20.1	...
Non-residents	...	...	2.2	2.1	0.7	...
Earnings and Profitability						
Return on assets[2]	0.6	0.9	1.4	1.4	1.4	1.5
Return on equity[2]	15.1	14.9	25.6	24.8	24.7	26.3
Interest margin to gross income[5]	...	...	83.6	81.1	78.0	79.1
Noninterest expenses to gross income[5]	...	...	41.2	37.0	38.4	35.5
Net interest margin[5]	2.5	2.4	2.8	2.9	2.3	2.5
Noninterest expenses to average assets[5]	1.7	1.7	1.6	1.8	1.4	1.4
Cost to income ratio[5]	46.3	51.7	39.2	38.1	41.7	36.8
Interest income to operating income[5]	87.4	90.2	87.7	87.1	84.8	84.2
Spread between reference lending and deposit rates[3]	333.0	360.0	333.0	306.0	306.0	306.0
Liquidity						
Liquid assets to total assets	...	...	22.1	23.5	22.8	22.6
Liquid assets to short-term liabilities	...	...	37.6	44.7	41.6	41.2
Exposure to foreign exchange risk						
Net open position in foreign exchange to capital	...	...	22.7	12.8	7.4	7.4
Non-Bank Sectors						
Insurance sector						
Coverage ratio[6]	...	...	444.0	210.0	223.0	206.0
Return on average equity (Life)	...	...	28.7	5.7	17.1	21.1
Return on average equity (Non-life)	...	...	-7.0	-26.2	2.9	21.5
State-owned enterprise corporate sector						
Number of SOEs[7]	127,067	119,254	115,087	113,731	115,115.0	...
Total debt to equity ratio	1.7	1.7	1.4	1.4	1.6	...

Cont

	2005	2006	2007	2008	2009	2010
Central government	1.4	1.4	1.2	1.3	1.4	...
Local government	2.4	2.3	1.9	1.8	1.9	...
Return on equity	5.6	6.2	7.2	8.7	5.7	...
Central government	8.3	8.6	10.4	6.8	7.0	...
Local government	2.2	3.2	6.4	4.4	4.3	...
Return on assets	2.0	2.1	3.0	3.6	2.2	...
Central government	3.2	3.2	4.8	3.0	3.0	...
Local government	0.6	0.9	2.2	1.5	1.5	...
Debt service coverage ratio[8]	4.12	4.43	7.25	3.72	4.3	...
Central government	6.55	6.96	7.41	4.36	5.0	...
Local government	2.83	3.33	4.30	2.94	3.4	...
Small-and medium-sized enterprises						
Number of SMEs[9]	242,061	269,031	300,262	385,721	393,074	...
Total debt to equity ratio	1.45	1.42	1.38	1.31	1.26	...
Return on assets	5.75	6.52	7.84	8.44	8.6	...
Return on equity	14.06	15.82	18.70	19.51	19.5	...
Debt service coverage ratio[8]	6.47	7.09	7.33	7.43	8.64	...
Real estate sector						
Commercial property inflation[10]	5.6	4.0	5.8	4.6	...	...
House price inflation[10]	8.4	6.4	8.2	7.1	...	...
Domestic residential house purchasing loans as percent of total loans[11]	...	...	...	12.5	14.0	14.5

Sources: PBC; MOF; CBRC; CIRC; State -Owned Asset Administration Commission; NBS of China; IMF *Global Financial Stability Report;* Bankscope; and IMF staff calculations.

[1] All data for this table unless noted otherwise were provided by the Chinese financial regulatory and supervisory commissions in the context of the FSAP. The following footnotes describe some cases in which the figures were obtained from other publically available sources or calculated by the FSAP team.

[2] Comparability across years is limited due to differences in data coverage. Data for 2005 and 2006 refer to the total banking industry as reported in the IMF Global Financial Stability Report, whereas data from 2008 to 2010 refer to the 17 major commercial banks as reported by Chinese authorities to the FSAP team.

[3] Capital adequacy and asset quality indicators were calculated with data from CBRC's 2010 annual report. Capital to assets ratio is defined as equity to assets ratio. Interest rate spreads were calculated with data from PBC's Monetary Policy Reports.

[4] Ratios where the numerator and denominator were compiled on a domestically consolidated basis (DC).

[5] Simple averages of 17 major commercial banks. FSAP team's calculations based on the banks' financial statements and Bankscope.

[6] Available solvency margin over required solvency margin.

[7] Number of non-financial State-Owned Enterprises (SOEs) above Grade Three. The State-Owned Assets Supervision and Administration Commission directly held SOEs are Grade One. Grade One SOEs directly held subsidiaries are Grade Two. Grade Two enterprises directly held subsidiaries are Grade Three.

[8] Earnings before interest and tax as a percentage of interest and principal expenses.

[9] Number of SMEs in the industrial sector.

[10] Percent change in commercial real estate and house price indices.

[11] CBRC's statistics based on credit data on institution (legal person).

25. The banking systems' nonperforming loan (NPL) ratio has been on a downward trend, reaching 1.1 percent at end-2010 (Figure 19). This decline was driven by the rapid expansion of credit, a decline in NPL levels, and a RMB 816 billion NPL carve-out from one major bank in 2008. Over a longer horizon, large scale NPL carve-outs associated with the 1999–2001 and 2004–05 state-owned bank restructurings have kept overall NPL ratios low.[3] The low level of reported NPLs has also been helped by strong economic growth and some improvements in risk management in banks. The rapid credit growth, however, could result in a deterioration of bank asset quality in the coming years. In addition, about 95 percent of bank loans re-price in under one year; this could lead to higher borrowing costs and loan servicing problems for weak borrowers if the PBC moves along a tightening cycle.

26. Exchange rate exposure is large at the central bank. Large current account surpluses and the management of the exchange rate regime result in the accumulation of sizeable foreign exchange reserves and a large net open foreign currency position for the central bank. Commercial banks, in aggregate, are also long in foreign assets (Figure 20) though in a much smaller scale.

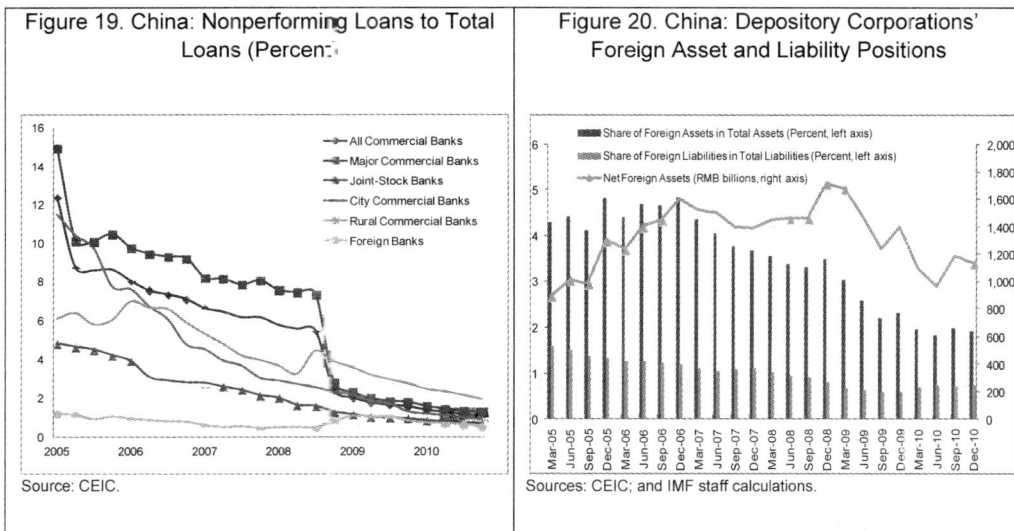

Figure 19. China: Nonperforming Loans to Total Loans (Percent)	Figure 20. China: Depository Corporations' Foreign Asset and Liability Positions
Source: CEIC.	Sources: CEIC; and IMF staff calculations.

27. The near-term risks of liquidity stress appear limited. The banking sector's basic liquidity indicators appear healthy. Larger banks typically recycle liquidity through the interbank markets to smaller banks and other financial institutions (Figures 21 and 22). The dominant share of secured interbank lending, high quality collateral, and abundant liquidity limit the prospects of market stress in the near term. Interbank markets, however, are subject to some risks. There are persistent liquidity imbalances among the banks, with small banks and non-banks particularly reliant on wholesale funding. A localized liquidity squeeze could spread from a small set of institutions that

---

[3] According to the FSAP team's calculations, as of end-2006, the book value of the non-performing assets transferred to the AMCs amounted to about RMB2.6 trillion.

face a liquidity shock and cannot realize the face value of their pledged security to a broader liquidity shock. The PBC standing facilities should act as a liquidity backstop when liquidity is unavailable from the market.

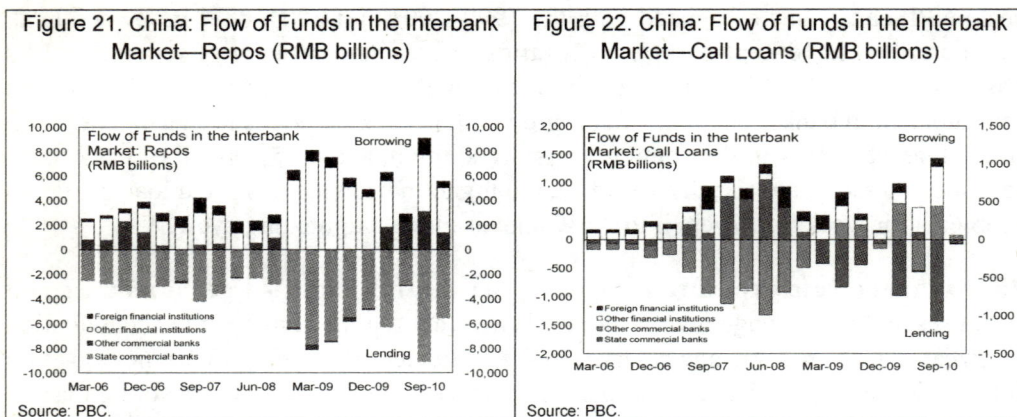

Figure 21. China: Flow of Funds in the Interbank Market—Repos (RMB billions)	Figure 22. China: Flow of Funds in the Interbank Market—Call Loans (RMB billions)
Source: PBC.	Source: PBC.

D. Stress-Testing Results Summary

28. To capture the key risks of the Chinese financial system, a stress testing exercise was jointly conducted by the FSAP team and PBC/CBRC team.[4] The results of the PBC/CBRC team's top-down and banks' bottom-up calculations—based on a sample of 17 banks—were provided to the FSAP team at the aggregate level and by bank type. The FSAP team also carried out its own set of top-down calculations, based on publicly available data on the same set of 17 banks.

Caveats

29. A full assessment of the extent of the risks and how they could permeate through the economic and financial system was hindered by various factors. First, it was not feasible to fully cover all the differentiated risks confronting the banking system due to data constraints on the sectoral exposures and types of entities that banks lend to. Also, data constraints prevented an explicit analysis of off-balance sheet positions and operations, except for those relating to the direct exchange rate risk. Moreover, much of the calibration in the macro-scenario tests was based on relatively short time series of key financial data (e.g., for NPLs) with structural breaks in the series; this limited a solid econometric analysis. Full-fledged comparison, analysis, and cross-check of the results were not possible in areas where publicly available information is imprecise, insufficient, or nonexistent (e.g., exposures to LGFPs and the contagion risk exercise) due to the constraints on the FSAP team's access to confidential data. Finally, the stress tests assumed the status quo (i.e., current macro-

---

[4] See Table 7 and Appendix I for the methodology.

Table 7. China: Stress Tests for Banks

		Solvency Stress Tests		Liquidity Stress Tests
		Sensitivity Stress Tests	Scenario Stress Tests	
1	Who performed the stress tests	• Three complementary approaches: FSAP team; PBC/CBRC team; and banks following the guidelines • The results of the PBC/CBRC team's top-down and banks' bottom-up calculations were provided to the FSAP team at the aggregate level, as well as disaggregated by bank type • These were then cross-checked by the FSAP team using publicly available data		• Banks
2	Institutions covered/ market share	• 17 major banks (5 large commercial banks and 12 joint stock commercial banks), accounting for 83 percent of commercial banking system (66 percent of banking system) assets at end-2010 • Contagion risk analysis was done on 5 large commercial banks, accounting for 63 percent of commercial banking system (50 percent of banking system) assets at end-2010		• 17 major banks, accounting for 83 percent of commercial banking system (66 percent of banking system) assets at end-2010
3	Severity of shocks	• Aggregate credit: 100–400 percent increase of NPLs; threshold approach (10, 25, 50 percent of banks below minimum CAR, 2, 4, 6 percent GDP capital injection) • Concentration credit risk: Sectoral NPL ratio increases to 5, 10, 15 percent or NPLs increase by 100, 200, 400 percent. Sectors include largest borrowers default, real-estate related risk (two types), exposures to LGFPs, exposures to "overcapacity industries", exposures to export-oriented sector, and exposures to sectors (industries) and regions with the most rapid loan growth • Market risk: Interest rates: 54, 81, 108bps parallel shift up and 18, 27, 36bps fall in benchmark loan rate in banking portfolio; 50, 100, 150bps shift up in trading portfolio; exchange rate: 5, 10, and 15 percent appreciation	Three scenarios • Mild: GDP (7 percent), M2 (14.7 percent), real estate price (-7 percent), interest rate (35bps change), REER (117.5) • Medium: GDP (5 percent), M2 (12.4 percent), real estate price (-16.2 percent), interest rate (66bps), REER (119.6) • Severe: GDP (4 percent), M2 (10.2 percent), real estate price (-25.9 percent), interest rate (95bps), REER (123.0) • Note: calibration reflects a survey among a panel of prominent experts on Chinese economy	Three scenarios for each risk horizon: • 7-day: bond prices drop (1, 3, 5 percent); deposit draw-down (2, 4, 6 percent); interbank down (5, 10, 15 percent); required reserve ratio up (0, 0.5, 1pp) • 30-day: (4, 7, 10 percent) maturing loans become NPLs; bond prices drop (3, 5, 8 percent); deposit draw-down (4, 6, 8 percent); interbank down (5, 10, 15); required reserve ratio up (0, 0.5, 1pp)
4	Data used	• FSAP team: publicly available data • Authorities: supervisory and audited data • Banks: data from the internal risk management systems		• Data from the banks' internal risk management systems
5	Risk horizon	One quarter, 1 or 2 years	1 year	• 7 days and 30 days
6	Metrics (hurdles rates)	• Minimum capital adequacy ratio (8 percent)		• Liquidity ratio (25 percent) • Liquidity gap (zero)
7	Positions and risk factors included	• On-balance sheet position for all positions except for those related to the direct exchange rate risk • Credit risk, market risk, and contagion risk	On-balance sheet position	• Assets and liability positions
8	Methodology	• Balance sheet approach (LGD=50 percent) • Zero credit growth • Zero profits • Zero provisions	• Authorities: econometric model • Bank: a combination of econometric models and expert-based approaches • FSAP team: cross-checks based on international experience	Tests combine funding liquidity with haircut on liquid assets

Source: FSAP stress testing team.

financial environment). As reforms begin in earnest, the banking system may face an amplification of existing risks or new uncertainties—although a properly implemented reform process and stronger risk management and corporate governance practices will help mitigate adverse financial consequences.

30. Keeping these caveats in mind, the stress testing results suggest that major banks can absorb moderate potential losses. This reflects improved profitability and balance sheets in recent years, which allowed banks to build up buffers. The single-factor sensitivity calculations indicate that the system would be able to withstand a range of sector-specific shocks occurring in isolation. These specific shocks include asset deterioration in bank credit to the real estate sector, LGFPs, export sector, and other sectors. The macroeconomic scenario analysis suggests, however, that the system could be severely impacted if several major shocks materialized concurrently.

Credit risks

31. The system appears able to withstand relatively sizeable aggregate increases in credit risk (Figure 23). If NPL levels were to increase by 400 percent in two years (i.e., post-shock NPL ratio reaching about 6 percent), calculations based on end-2010 data suggest that no banks would have capital adequacy ratio (CAR) below the regulatory minimum (i.e., 8 percent). The improvement in resilience from 2008 to 2010 reflects the decline in NPL levels. In addition, the buffer provided by stronger bank capital positions in 2010 helped prevent participating banks from failing to meet the regulatory minimum CAR under the most severe assumptions.

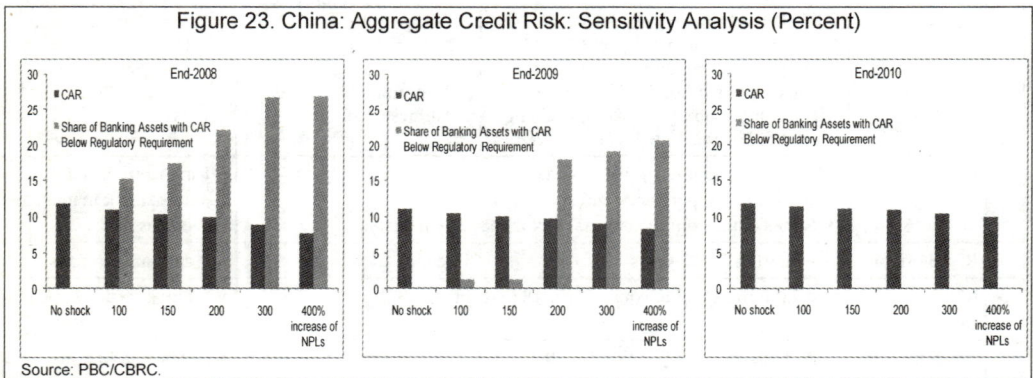

Figure 23. China: Aggregate Credit Risk: Sensitivity Analysis (Percent)

Source: PBC/CBRC.

32. The resilience was also confirmed by a reverse stress test ("threshold approach") conducted by the FSAP team and PBC/CBRC team. For instance, based on end-2009 data, for half of the banking system (in terms of total assets) to breach the regulatory minimum CAR, the ratio of gross NPLs to total loans would have to increase to almost 11 percent. Or, assuming that the banking system requires a capital injection of 6 percent of GDP, the NPL ratio would need to reach 24.8 percent (compared with 1.6 percent at end-2009).

33. Stress tests conducted by the PBC/CBRC team and the banks indicate the

impact of credit quality deterioration from a shock to the real estate sector would be contained. Two tests were conducted. The first test, conducted by the PBC/CBRC team and individual banks, involved assuming NPLs increase in the segments of personal mortgage loans, real estate development loans, and land reserve loans. Based on end-2010 data, if 15 percent of developer and land reserve loans, as well as $7^{1}/_{2}$ percent of mortgages become nonperforming, the aggregate CAR falls by about 1 percentage point but no banks fall below the regulatory minimum (Figure 24). The second test, conducted by individual banks, was an expanded version of this first exercise whereby—in addition to the three segments listed above—the impact of the real estate price decline was carried through to create insolvencies in six industries that are "vertically integrated" with the real estate.[5] A 30 percent decline in property prices, higher interest rates, and the resulting impact on related industries has only a minimal impact, lowering the aggregate CAR by less than $^{1}/_{4}$ percentage point (Figure 25).

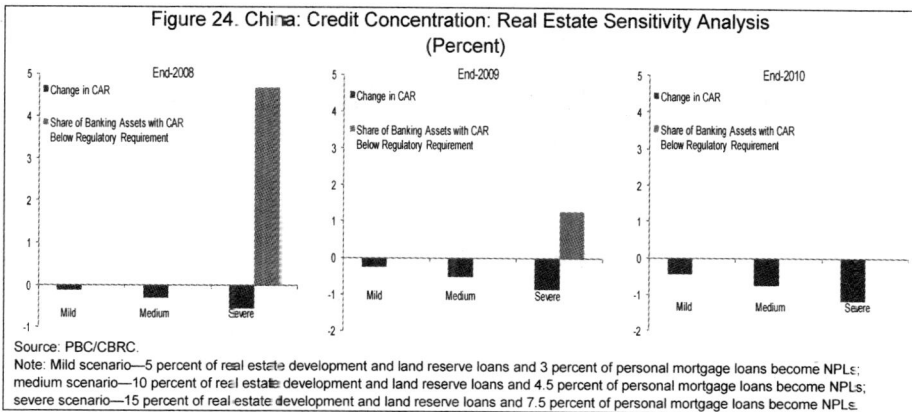

Figure 24. China: Credit Concentration: Real Estate Sensitivity Analysis
(Percent)

Source: PBC/CBRC.
Note: Mild scenario—5 percent of real estate development and land reserve loans and 3 percent of personal mortgage loans become NPLs; medium scenario—10 percent of real estate development and land reserve loans and 4.5 percent of personal mortgage loans become NPLs; severe scenario—15 percent of real estate development and land reserve loans and 7.5 percent of personal mortgage loans become NPLs.

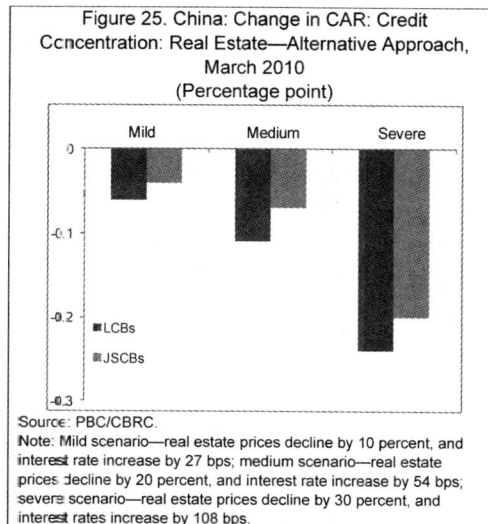

Figure 25. China: Change in CAR: Credit Concentration: Real Estate—Alternative Approach, March 2010
(Percentage point)

Source: PBC/CBRC.
Note: Mild scenario—real estate prices decline by 10 percent, and interest rate increase by 27 bps; medium scenario—real estate prices decline by 20 percent, and interest rate increase by 54 bps; severe scenario—real estate prices decline by 30 percent, and interest rates increase by 108 bps.

---

[5] The industries are (i) steel-making; (ii) cement, lime and plaster manufacturing; (iii) brick, stone and other building materials manufacturing; (iv) building construction; (v) furniture making; and (vi) household electrical apparatus manufacturing.

151

34. The stress testing exercise has also assessed the potential losses on LGFP lending. The results show that, based on a bottom-up stress test conducted by individual banks, losses equivalent to15 percent of the banks' LGFP loans would result in a fall in the CAR to below the regulatory minimum for only two small joint-stock commercial banks (JSCBs) (Figure 26).

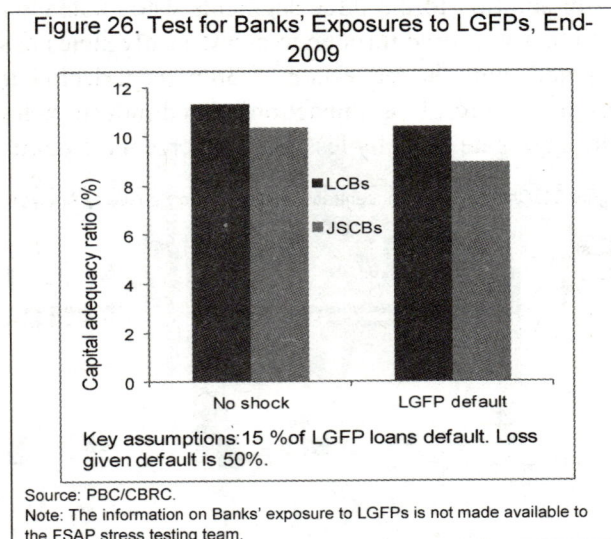

Figure 26. Test for Banks' Exposures to LGFPs, End-2009

Key assumptions:15 %of LGFP loans default. Loss given default is 50%.

Source: PBC/CBRC.
Note: The information on Banks' exposure to LGFPs is not made available to the FSAP stress testing team.

Direct interest rate risk

35. Direct interest rate risks on banking book and trading book appear manageable. Shocks to loan and deposit rates were used in the analysis, and their impacts were evaluated by the PBC/CBRC team and individual banks in terms of the implied change in the CAR. The results suggest that even under the severe combination of shocks, the CARs for all the 17 banks declined slightly (Figure 27). The risk of a parallel shift of yield curve on trading accounts was also tested by individual banks and the results again suggest the impact would be very small (Figure 28).

Direct exchange rate risk

36. The direct impact of exchange rate movements on the banking system would be limited. The results of the PBC/CBRC team's top down and individual banks' bottom-up stress tests suggest that under the severe stress scenario, the CAR for the system as a whole falls by less than 0.1 percentage point and the CARs for all 17 banks would still exceed the minimum requirement (Figure 29).

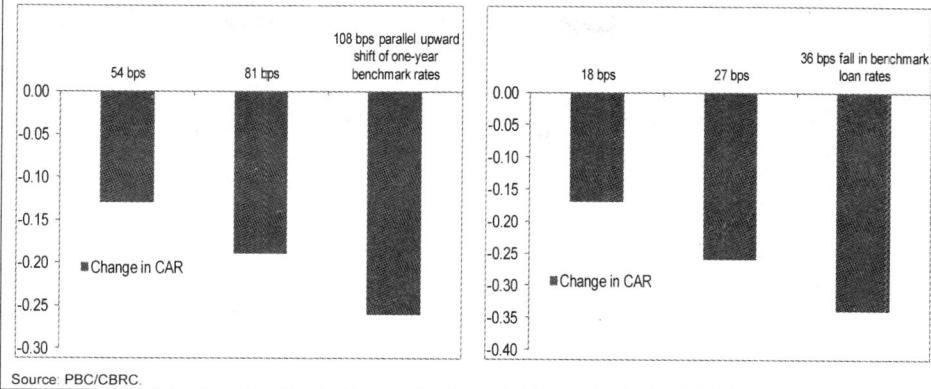

Figure 27. China: Interest Rate Risk: Banking Book, End-2009
(Percentage point)

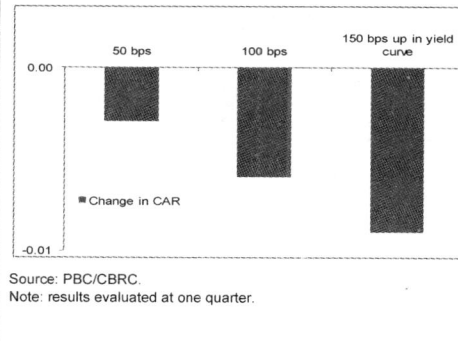

Figure 28. China: Interest Rate Risk: Trading Accounts, End-2009
(Percentage point)

Source: PBC/CBRC.
Note: results evaluated at one quarter.

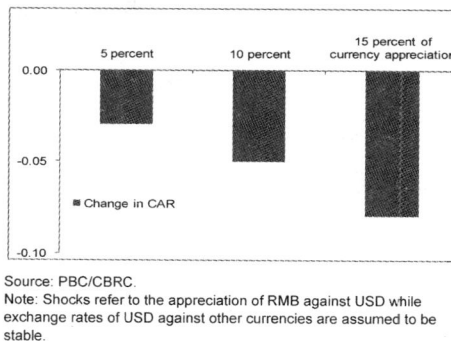

Figure 29. China: Direct Exchange Rate Risk, End-2009
(Percentage point)

Source: PBC/CBRC.
Note: Shocks refer to the appreciation of RMB against USD while exchange rates of USD against other currencies are assumed to be stable.

Liquidity risk

37. Two rounds of liquidity risk stress tests have been conducted. The results suggest that in the first round (i.e., without considering banks' ability to sell off bonds) the impact could be substantial, with, for instance, six banks having a negative cash flow gap at the seven day horizon. The results of the second round, which assume that banks are able to sell off bonds at a discount, are more benign, with all banks except one (at the 30 day horizon) having positive cash flow gaps.

Macro-scenario tests

38. The macroeconomic scenario analysis suggests a severe impact on the system if several major shocks materialized concurrently (Figure 30). For example, a severe scenario (involving a slowdown in GDP growth to 4 percent year-on-year) implies a system-wide CAR of about 8 percent, with banks accounting for some $1/4$ of the total assets of the 17 banks covered by the stress tests falling below the 8 percent minimum CAR. It is encouraging also that the results of the scenario analysis were broadly consistent with the suggestive conclusions drawn from a survey of available results in previous FSAPs (i.e., in a major slowdown of GDP), NPL ratios tend to increase by at least one percentage point for each one percentage point decrease in the rate of output growth.

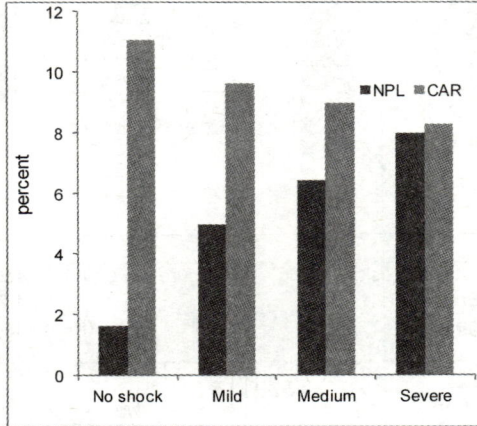

Figure 30. China: Macro-scenario Results, End-2009

Source: PBC/CBRC.

II. Managing Risks: Upgrading the Crisis Toolkit

A. Financial Stability Framework

39. To enhance macro-prudential surveillance, a permanent Financial Stability Committee should be established, with the PBC as its secretariat. It should be chaired by a very senior official and have a clear mandate and authority to identify and monitor the emergence of systemic risks and to make recommendations to address them. Members would include the PBC, the three supervisory commissions, the MOF, and other relevant ministries or agencies. The PBC, as the Committee's secretariat, along with each of the commissions would be empowered to provide and to receive necessary information, including confidential institution-specific supervisory information.

40. Data collection should be enhanced to facilitate a good understanding of financial institutions' balance sheets and linkages. Such data should include the level of leverage, maturity mismatches, large exposures, contingent liabilities, off-balance sheet positions, unregulated products, and cross-border and sectoral (e.g., housing, local government) exposures, which in turn requires improving data collection on financial institutions' non-financial counterparts. Development of a forward-looking early warning system incorporating macro and financial indicators, financial soundness indicators, systemic risk indicators, and balance sheet information would help identify macroeconomic and financial developments with a potential to threaten the financial system.

41. Continued efforts are needed to build a comprehensive macro-prudential framework for measuring and managing systemic risks. China already has several macro-prudential tools to handle these risks, including capital surcharges for systemically important financial institutions (SIFIs), dynamic provisioning, variable capital requirements, reserve requirements, and requirements related to loan-to-value and loan-to-deposit ratios. A clear indication of how these buffers and requirements may vary as conditions change needs to be developed. Increasing the PBC's and the regulators' resources and capacity to monitor financial stability and carry out regular stress tests is also needed.

B. Systemic Liquidity Management

42. The PBC should begin to absorb the significant liquidity overhang that is currently present in the financial system. This will involve a much more aggressive use of open market operations to reach a point where the PBC no longer needs to rely on administrative limits on bank lending. As liquidity conditions tighten, banks will have incentives to improve their internal liquidity management functions and focus more on assessing risk-return trade-offs in allocating loans.

43. At the same time, considering reserve averaging would be a useful step. Its introduction could facilitate liquidity management and enhance stability and efficiency.

The daily nature of the reserve requirement means that it is principally an aggregate liquidity management tool rather than a prudential buffer for banks. Banks end up holding substantial under-remunerated excess reserves for buffer purposes—effectively an additional tax on intermediation. Across the banking system these reserves have averaged around 2–3 percent of deposits, but the actual holdings vary substantially by type of bank. Therefore, reserve averaging could help reduce this additional tax and make liquidity management for all, particularly smaller, institutions easier, and limit the possibility for liquidity stresses to transmit across institutions.

44. The central bank should begin by targeting a short-term repo rate. To further strengthen the management of short-term interest rates, the central bank could raise the rate paid on excess reserves to narrow the corridor implied by the difference with its discount rate. To support the use of indirect instruments and supplement structural liquidity withdrawal, the PBC could lengthen the maturity of its open market operations through greater use of longer-term repos.

45. Overtime, the PBC should enhance its capacity to undertake daily liquidity operations. Recent international experience has demonstrated the potential for a liquidity crisis to occur even when liquidity appears abundant. The PBC needs to implement higher frequency liquidity forecasting, which in turn requires an increased flow of information among the MOF, State Administration of Foreign Exchange (SAFE), and the PBC.

46. Access to the PBC's standing facilities should be made more automatic and transparent, with moral hazard concerns addressed through pricing of the facilities. The PBC exercises considerable discretion over access to standing facilities, complicating and potentially delaying the disbursement of funds. This could be addressed by reducing PBC's discretion and making the use of each facility automatic, with collateral requirements identical across all domestically incorporated institutions. This would also strengthen PBC interest rate guidance by providing a binding and effective interest rate corridor.

C. Crisis Management, Resolution, and Deposit Insurance

47. China's crisis management arrangements fall under the purview of the State Council (SC). The resolution toolkit needs to be expanded as the financial system is becoming complex. The current toolkit is essentially based on an "open resolution" approach towards nonviable banks and an implicit blanket guarantee for depositors, with the PBC in practice taking responsibility for backing up deposits. This implies significant moral hazard. A more comprehensive toolkit would comprise a safety net and an effective institutional arrangement in which relevant authorities have operational autonomy and legal authority to intervene promptly in weak and nonviable financial institutions.

48. The introduction of an explicit deposit insurance scheme, which is under consideration, should be accelerated to provide a structured safety net. It will also help facilitate the orderly resolution of failing banks. The design features should incorporate the principles being developed by the International Association of Deposit Insurers. Its institutional structure should be appropriately designed taking into account the large number of depository institutions, growing complex structures, existing roles of various organizations in a resolution, and the need to clarify the contingent liability of the government, particularly of the PBC, when resolving failed institutions.

49. Laws concerning the insolvency of financial institutions need to be reviewed and strengthened in all sectors. A designated separate entity should be provided with the capacity to manage the intervened institution and with resources to resolve the institution through recapitalization, sale, in whole or in part, or liquidation. The entity should be funded by industry to reduce if not eliminate the need to rely on government support. The institutional capacity to deal with troubled assets in failed institutions is an important component. The entity could assume responsibility for administering the deposit insurance scheme and assets of failed institutions. As for the existing four public AMCs, a strategy is needed. As a first step, the AMCs should be required to publish periodic financial statements and management reports and eventually, most, if not all, should be converted into commercial entities.

D. Macro-Financial Framework

50. The linkages between the macroeconomic policy framework and financial sector are intrinsic to financial stability in China. It is for this reason that while the financial system looks stable in prudential terms, with a small level of problem loans, extensive credit provisioning, and (still) low leverage of main borrowers, allocative inefficiencies, and structural vulnerabilities still remain. As stated earlier, commercial banks often act as the channel of monetary policy and as facilitators of fiscal policy. The existing policy framework thus creates large distortions to incentives and places risk on the public balance sheet as contingent liabilities. While improvements in risk management, prudential regulation, and supervision remain necessary, and need to be strengthened, the further deepening and maturation of the financial system will be addressed in a large part by the process by which the macroeconomic policy framework evolves.

51. The PBC should rely more on indirect monetary policy instruments to exercise macroeconomic control. Instead of credit growth targets, market-based interest rates should become the primary instrument for managing credit expansion. This will reduce the risks that monetary control will be increasingly circumvented and ineffective in the face of capital inflows, off-balance sheet lending, and other financial innovations. It will also enhance banks' scope to differentiate loan rates and improve the credit allocation.

52. A liberalized and flexible exchange market is necessary for the conduct of monetary policy by reducing PBC's liquidity management challenges. The current high levels of foreign currency intervention require significant sterilization efforts. In addition, the perception of a one-way bet on the currency provides incentives for capital inflows that serve to complicate financial market outcomes. Moving to a more flexible exchange market would reduce the financial stability risks associated with cross-border flows and transactions; lessen the liquidity management challenges faced by the PBC; and give greater scope for independent use of indirect instruments of monetary policy. These measures would require the strengthening of market and systemic risk monitoring, and cross-border regulation and supervision.

III. Bolstering Financial Sector Oversight

53. An assessment of the regulatory and supervisory framework (Table 8) reveals a high degree of adherence to international standards, but challenges remain.[6] The challenge is to increase its efficiency, quality, and responsiveness. The appropriate balance has to be struck between the degree of regulatory control and the need to enable useful innovation and development of the financial system. A central theme of the assessments is to improve operational autonomy of the regulators, upgrade skills and risk monitoring capabilities, increase resources, and strengthen interagency coordination.

54. China's sector-based regulatory and supervisory framework demands a high degree of coordination to limit supervisory "blind spots." There is a need to develop a framework for regulation and supervision, by a single entity such as the PBC, of FHCs including industrial conglomerates investing in financial firms. The PBC has been authorized by the SC to draft administrative rules working with the three other regulatory commissions. In the interim, acquisition of a regulated institution should be approved by the relevant regulatory commission responsible for the underlying financial institution. In addition, the regulatory policies applying to the shadow banking system need to be clarified (Table 9). Interagency coordination arrangements among the PBC and three commissions backed by memoranda of understanding for information sharing need to be strengthened along with the removal of any legal restrictions on such sharing.

---

[6] This section should be read along with Annexes I to V containing the *Reports on the Observance of Financial Sector Standards and Codes.*

Table 8. China: Financial System Architecture

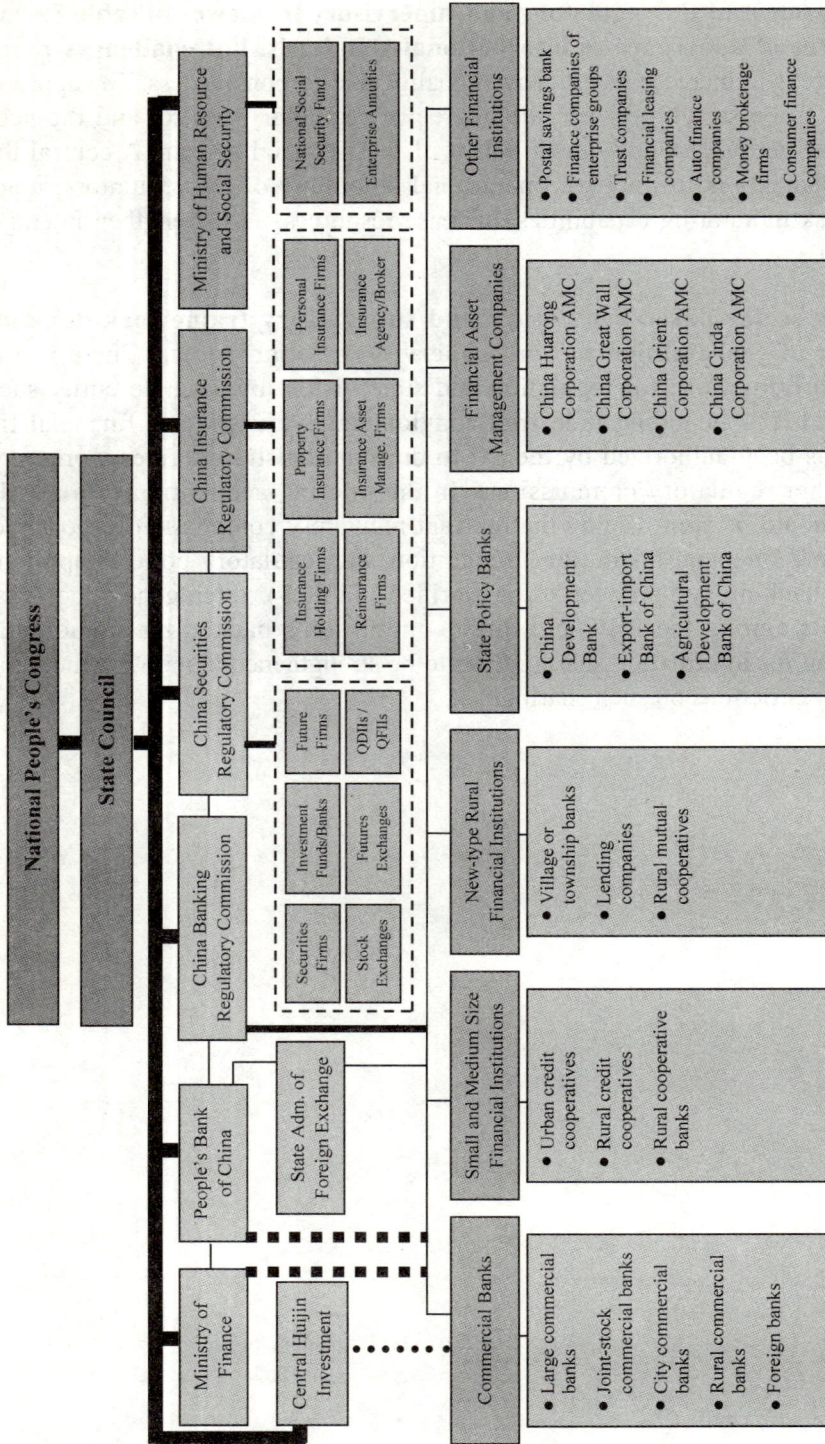

National People's Congress

State Council

- Ministry of Finance
- Central Huijin Investment
- People's Bank of China
- State Adm. of Foreign Exchange
- China Banking Regulatory Commission
- China Securities Regulatory Commission
- China Insurance Regulatory Commission
- Ministry of Human Resource and Social Security

Securities Firms | Stock Exchanges | Investment Funds/Banks | Futures Exchanges | Future Firms | QDIIs / QFIIs

Insurance Holding Firms | Reinsurance Firms | Property Insurance Firms | Insurance Asset Manage. Firms | Personal Insurance Firms | Insurance Agency/Broker

National Social Security Fund | Enterprise Annuities

Commercial Banks
- Large commercial banks
- Joint-stock commercial banks
- City commercial banks
- Rural commercial banks
- Foreign banks

Small and Medium Size Financial Institutions
- Urban credit cooperatives
- Rural credit cooperatives
- Rural cooperative banks

New-type Rural Financial Institutions
- Village or township banks
- Lending companies
- Rural mutual cooperatives

State Policy Banks
- China Development Bank
- Export-import Bank of China
- Agricultural Development Bank of China

Financial Asset Management Companies
- China Huarong Corporation AMC
- China Great Wall Corporation AMC
- China Orient Corporation AMC
- China Cinda Corporation AMC

Other Financial Institutions
- Postal savings bank
- Finance companies of enterprise groups
- Trust companies
- Financial leasing companies
- Auto finance companies
- Money brokerage firms
- Consumer finance companies

Notes: The thickest connecting lines correspond to the highest levels of authority in financial policy making. The NPC promulgates all financial sector laws and the State Council executes financial regulation and issues mandatory policy directives to all the financial regulatory and supervisory agencies. The dotted connecting lines indicate the three primary functions of PBC —formulating monetary policy, maintaining financial stability, and providing financial services— and the triple role of the MOF as tax administrator, treasurer, and owner of several commercial banks. The thinner connecting lines emerging from CBRC, CSRC, CIRC, and MHRSS reflect that these entities are mostly responsible for regulating and conducting supervision and oversight of their respective financial sectors. **Additional notes:** The SAFE is responsible for foreign exchange operations of securities and insurance companies. The China Development Bank and the Postal Savings Bank are in the process of reforming into commercial banks. Central Huijin exercise rights and obligations as an investor in major state-owned financial enterprises on behalf of the State. The National Social Security Fund has also a dual role as an institutional investor and a stakeholder in some of the largest commercial banks.

Table 9. China: Shadow Banking

Category	Financial institutions	Registration	Investigators/Regulators
Informal financial sector	Pawn shops, credit guarantee companies, micro-finance companies	Local governments	Investigated by the PBC, CBRC, and the Ministry of Public Security. In addition, Financing Guarantee Regulatory Inter-ministerial Joint committee led by the CBRC is responsible for making the regulation and policy of credit guarantee institutions, providing guidance and conducting coordination. The local government is responsible for the supervision including licensing, on-site examination and off-site surveillance.
	underground intermediation	No	No regulators, although the PBC implements survey or investigation occasionally.
Private equity	Estimated 3,500 PE funds have been established with assets of around RMB900 billion as of mid-2010 of which around 70 per cent is funded from overseas	Industrial and Commercial Bureau	The PE investment is governed by rules and regulation issued by both NDRC and MOC, whereas the CSRC performs survey and collects data of PE funds. In addition, some PE funds are not yet in regulators'radar screen.
Wealth management products	Estimated 7,049 Wealth Management products were outstanding at the end of 2010, totaling RMB 1.7 trillion, and 124 banking institutions were involved in the practice.	CBRC, CSRC, and CIRC	PBC, CBRC,CSRC, and CIRC

Sources: The PBC; CBRC; CSRC; NDRC; and IMF staff.

Note:(1) According to the FSB definition, shadow banks are those entities that engages in credit creation and maturity/liquidity transformation outside the banking system and that have an element of leverage, and that includes MMMFs, finance companies,ABCP vehicles, SIVs etc. Due to limited data, this table does not include these entities. (2) This table only includes those that are identified by the authorities (informal financial sector and private equity) and those that are taken as shadow banks by the FSAP team(trust companies and wealth management products).

A. Commercial Bank Regulation and Supervision

55. The CBRC has a clear safety and soundness mandate. However, its operational autonomy is often undermined by the use of commercial banking system for development purposes. The CBRC has made strides in improving its framework for supervising commercial banks and emphasizing prudential goals. Nonetheless, it will be important to ensure the agency's ability to pursue its mandate is unencumbered. This will be facilitated by ensuring more stable resourcing arrangements that permit greater flexibility in building up a skilled and professional staff and continued commercialization of the banks.

56. The legal and regulatory framework for banking has been brought closer in

line with international standards, but gaps remain. There is no legal requirement to be informed of changes in indirect control and to identify ultimately beneficial owners and clients of banks. Complex structures should be prohibited where consolidated supervision may not be possible. Rules for identifying related parties and rules underpinning bank resolution need to be strengthened. The prudential regime for asset classification and provisioning works well, but there are limitations in actual bank practices. Minor deviations from the Basel I framework[7] may potentially overstate bank capital in the future.

57. Banks' risk management techniques and practices need to be upgraded. Large banks have built their risk management systems around simple yet conservative regulatory metrics and techniques but systems in some of the smaller banks need to be strengthened. All banks will need to update their risk management practices to keep pace with the ongoing market orientation and increasing international presence. While the major banks are developing more granular two-dimensional classification systems, their uses in risk differentiation and loan pricing is currently limited. The strong dependence on collateral and the lack of forward-looking valuation practices need to be addressed to mitigate credit risk and pro-cyclicality in lending (Figure 31). The liquidity and market risk management framework works efficiently in the current environment, but may be inadequate as the market configuration and banking conditions change. Implementing comprehensive, enterprise-wide risk management should be a top priority for the major banks. Country and transfer risk management guidance has only recently been consolidated, and its implementation has to be strengthened in view of increasing international exposure and presence. Operational risk management processes need to be strengthened by the small and medium-sized banks.

58. The risk management framework of banks is hampered by the current macroeconomic and institutional environment. Effective credit risk management in banks is discouraged by the implicit backstop of the state for their credit exposures. Banks' credit risk strategies are dominated by loan growth guidelines, and both bank risk management and supervisory assessments focus more on NPL ratios than on forward looking assessments of credit risk.

B. Securities Intermediaries and Securities Market Regulation

59. While the CSRC has taken an active and strategic approach to regulate securities markets, the legal and regulatory system needs improvement. Similar to other commissions, the CSRC is not operationally autonomous given the state's role

---

[7] These deviations are currently not material and are offset by the higher minimum requirement.

in staff appointments and its influence over CSRC's operating structure. The CSRC needs greater budgetary flexibility to acquire qualified experts in an environment of rapidly growing markets. The accounting and auditing profession has made great strides in a short time frame in auditing listed companies and this needs to develop further. The newly introduced risk-based net capital rule should be monitored to ensure that it captures all risks. While there are adequate provisions for dealing with failed intermediaries, the threshold for action should be lowered to allow for early intervention.

Figure 31. China: Reliance on Real Estate Collateral in Bank Lending, 2007

Components of Lending

Types of Collateral (Proportion in Total Secured Lending)

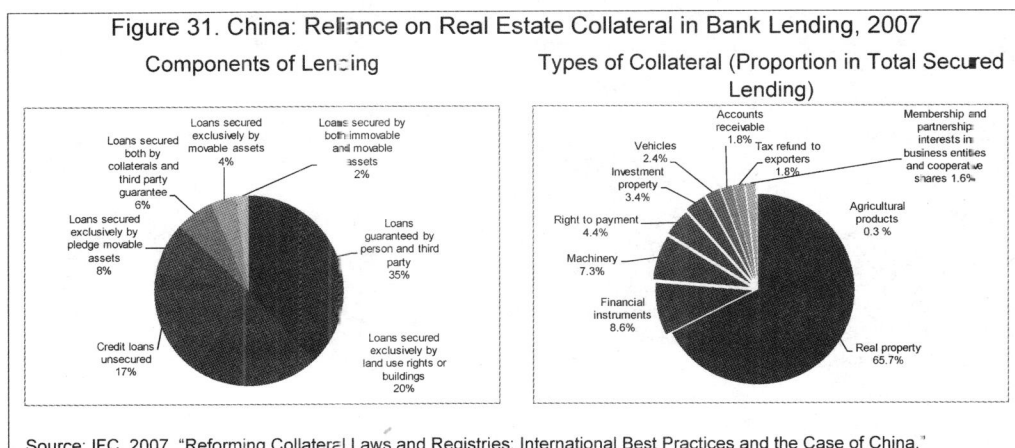

Source: IFC, 2007, "Reforming Collateral Laws and Registries: International Best Practices and the Case of China."

60. To bolster oversight, it would be beneficial to introduce a formal program of regular comprehensive on-site inspections of the exchanges. Stronger emphasis is needed on illegal investment activities and monitoring of hedge funds and private equity funds. Implementation of the "know-your-client" rules that require securities and futures companies to maintain comprehensive records of customers' identity, transaction records, and account data could be more carefully monitored to ensure that they result in investors making more informed decisions.

C. Insurance Regulation and Supervision

61. The CIRC has a comprehensive supervisory framework in place but the solvency regimes need to be strengthened. The minimum solvency margin should be risk-based. The continued issuance of new business by companies operating below the 100 percent solvency level is undesirable. Explicit and clear regulation is needed for facilitating the exit of insurance companies from the market via policy liability run off or portfolio transfers. Off-site monitoring could be strengthened through reinstatement of the early warning ratios previously required in insurer returns.

62. The developmental mandate for the CIRC should focus on its broad public good nature as a regulator to ensure safe practices. The current prescriptive, rules-based system, and close monitoring of insurance company activities on a monthly basis place a strong burden on staffing, and should be reconsidered. As the market and the newly introduced risk-based supervisory regime mature, the CIRC should move away from its current direct involvement in insurers' product, distribution, and investment strategies. CIRC's staffing levels need to be reinforced with suitably skilled personnel in key operational areas.

IV. Upgrading the Financial Infrastructure and Legal Framework

A. Payment and Securities Settlements Systems

63. The assessments of the High Value Payment System and securities and derivatives settlements systems suggest broad compliance with international standards but identify room for improvement in several areas. The PBC has carried out a comprehensive reform of the China National Payments System. Going forward, the authorities should ensure that the legal framework gives full protection to payments, derivatives, and securities settlement finality. The PBC should clarify in detail its policy stance in payment system oversight and determine the scope, major policies, and instruments of the function. It should also clarify the criteria for determining the systemic importance of a system, and strengthen institutional arrangements and cooperation in the payment system arena. A more proactive oversight by the PBC over the China Foreign Exchange Trade System is advisable.

B. Legal and Regulatory Structure

64. A "stock-take" of the gaps, overlaps, and clarity in the body of laws governing the financial sector is necessary (for a partial overview, see Table 10). While the rule-based approach to regulation has been appropriate for China thus far, China would benefit from gradually applying a more principle-based approach in the formulation and implementation of laws to deal with increasingly complex and new issues.

Table 10. China: Legal and Regulatory Structure for Selected Financial Products

Products	Issuers	Regulators	Laws and regulations	Tasks
Mutual funds	Fund management companies	CSRC	*Securities Investment Fund Law*	Approval
Collective investment plans	Securities firms	CSRC	*Trial Provisions on the Client Asset Management Business of Securities Companies*	Filing or Approval
Collective wealth management products	Commercial banks	CBRC	*Interim Measures for the Administration of Commercial Banks' Personal Financial Management Services*	Registration and filing
Trust plans	Trust investment companies	CBRC	*Notice on Relevant Issues concerning Further Regulating the Trust Plans of Assembles Funds*	Registration and filing
Unit-linked insurance products	Insurance companies	CIRC	*Provisional Measure for the Administration of the Investment-linked Insurance*	Approval

Sources: CBRC; CIRC; and CSRC.

65. The legal framework for consumer protection needs to be clearly enunciated, advocated, and implemented. Consumer protection must be strengthened not only in terms of courts' capacity to enforce contracts but also in empowering consumer organizations to play an effective role, enhancing personal data and privacy protection in the law as well as requiring market practices and codes of conduct to be in place.

66. The framework for creditors' rights also should be reviewed to provide for efficient and effective exit mechanisms. Detailed laws concerning the insolvency of financial institutions have not been developed for some sectors (e.g., insurance sector). Measures are needed to provide for a continued training of judges in principles of insolvency law as well as in the specifics of the Enterprise Insolvency Law and other relevant judicial interpretations.

C. Market Integrity

67. The June 2007 Financial Action Task Force (FATF) mutual evaluation report indicated that China made significant progress in implementing its AML/CFT system, but it also highlighted important shortcomings.[8] The AML/CFT system has since been strengthened, including through legislative changes to bolster preventive measures, notably in the areas of customer due diligence and suspicious transaction reporting. However, two significant shortcomings remain. First, Chinese law and practice provides limited ability for authorities or financial institutions to have access to the identity of the beneficial owners of legal persons. Second, preventive measures have not been extended to the majority of the non-financial businesses and professions designated by the FATF Recommendations. Deficiencies also remain with respect to the criminalization of self-laundering, and the freezing of terrorist assets. In addition, there is a need to improve information sharing and coordination arrangements among the PBC and other agencies on AML.

---

[8] The June 2007 report is the latest available comprehensive AML/CFT assessment of China. For the full text, see http://www.fatf-gafi.org/infobycountry/0,3380,en_32250379_32236963_1_70342_43383847_1_1,00.html.

V. Broadening Financial Markets and Services

A. Fixed Income Markets

68. The incentive for banks to use fixed income instruments to manage their balance sheets has been held back by partial interest rate liberalization. The absence of market-based funding and dominance of lending activities act as disincentives for banks to become active in asset liability management to hedge mismatches in their balance sheet. In addition, guaranteed interest margins reduce banks' incentives to engage in fee-generating businesses in the capital market. The regulatory and operational repo market framework would need to be upgraded to increase market liquidity, enhance risk management, and reinforce the money and bond market nexus.

69. Steps should be taken to ensure regulations of fixed income markets and products are consistent, and clearly communicated to the market. Respective roles of three agencies (PBC, National Development and Reform Commission (NDRC), and CSRC), particularly in the corporate bond market, should be further clarified. Equivalent regulations should apply to similar types of participants even when coming under different regulators. A possible option that would support existing market practices would be to delineate a division between wholesale and retail markets and divide regulatory responsibilities between the PBC and CSRC, respectively.

70. A more proactive and sustained benchmark-building strategy is required across all maturities of the yield curve. Currently, the MOF's treasury securities share the risk-free fixed income markets with the PBC bills in the short-to-medium terms and with the more liquid policy bank bonds in the medium-to-long term (Figure 32). There is a need to improve debt issuance strategy through the further strengthening of coordination between the MOF and PBC. To limit the impact of the PBC's liquidity management activities on the yields in the MOF issuances, the PBC should seek to limit the issuance of its paper to the short end of the yield curve. Longer term liquidity withdrawal could then be undertaken by rolling over these securities, or by PBC undertaking longer-term repo operations.

Figure 32. China: Each Public Sector Debt Issue Dominates in a Different Maturity Segment, 2009

Source: Chinabond.

71. The development of a proposed sub-national debt market where local governments can issue debt is a welcome step but carries associated risks. In the

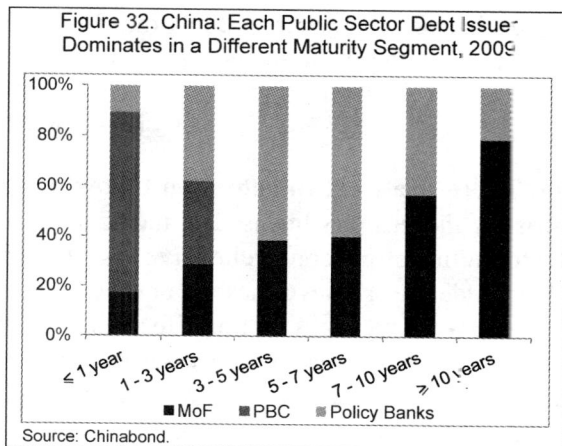

absence of a proper medium-term fiscal framework, debt sustainability analysis (DSA), and a medium-term debt management strategy (MTDS), debt issuance by provincial government could rapidly become a contingent liability and adversely affect the development of the national fixed income market. Timely and adequate data will need to be provided on projects for which bonds are issued to help investors assess risks. The role of rating agencies would also have to be properly defined so that a consistent bond rating methodology could be applied.

72. In the corporate bond market, developing a segment that accommodates lower, yet credible credit rating standards might allow enterprises, currently excluded from the securities markets, to access corporate debt markets. Easing the legal limit of 40 percent of net assets on bond issuance will enable a more extensive use of direct funding to all corporations. In addition, upgrading links between CCDC and SD&C to enhance connectivity between IBBM, SSE, and SZSE, support further development, and contribute to efficiency in all three markets.

B. Equity Markets

73. Further development in equity markets hinges on addressing legacy issues and better servicing the needs of SMEs. Residual legacy constraints and anomalies relating to nontradable, "A" and "B" shares should be addressed and the current free float of shares in public companies expanded. The build-up of a smooth conduit between the private and public offer segments is critical as this could make sustainable funding options available to SMEs and increase the presence of private companies on the exchanges. Launched in 2009, the Growth Enterprise Board is expected to provide exit channels to private financing.

C. Insurance Sector

74. There is a need to achieve a better trade-off between scale and competition. Most of the insurers licensed in the past decade continue to lose money (Table 11). Introducing more comprehensive risk-based capital requirements and requiring shareholders to achieve these over a suitable period is recommended. Strengthening the actuarial oversight of non-life claims provisioning and clarifying the voluntary wind up and exit rules and processes are also desirable steps. The fact that staff salaries and benefits and secured borrowers rank ahead of life policyholders in the event of a wind up is contrary to international best practice. Other strategies could involve taking action to enable insurers to generate more stable but higher returns to equity.

Table 11. China: Insurance—Operating Performance by Size, 2009 (In Percent)

	Op. Return on Assets	Combined Ratio	ROE
Life			
Top 10	6.3		18.4
Next 10	-1.1		-11.4
Remainder	-2.6		-1 .4
Multi Line Non Life			
Top 10		101.7	11.4
Next 10		117.7	-5.9
Remainder		122.0	-5.3

Source: Insurance Yearbook 2010.

D. Pension Sector

75. The emphasis of the pension system should be on the funded component. Pension reserves of the first pillar remain invested in inefficient portfolio. Capital protection— enterprise annuity system's most popular investment strategy—will not be able to generate sufficient returns to obtain reasonable pensions in the future. Longer-term horizon strategies require greater allocations in equity and longer-term bonds than the ones that are currently in place. Investment regulation should discourage short-term evaluation of performance and focus on the long-term actuarial objectives of the fund. Given China's strong culture of saving, one option is to expand the scope of personal defined-contribution pension plans by designing attractive personal income tax incentives or matching fund contributions for low income individuals.

E. Access to Finance

76. The approach thus far in promoting rural and MSE finance may need a paradigm shift. An evaluation of the existing government programs is needed to determine their effectiveness in promoting rural and MSE finance and the government should formulate an integrated and coherent rural and MSE finance strategy. Several steps can be taken to substantially broaden access to finance. Government should continue to reform rural credit cooperatives to enhance their efficiency and sustainability as commercial providers of financial products and services. It is also important to complete the reform of the Postal Savings Bank by optimizing equity ownership, overhauling the bank to become a corporation, and building effective corporate governance.

VI. Sequencing Financial Reforms

77. Further financial reforms are crucial for sustaining China's growth and will need to be carefully crafted to limit risks to financial stability. Country experiences have shown that while financial liberalization can spur growth and development, it also entails risks if not properly designed and composed. Given the breadth of China's envisaged reform agenda, it is important to devise a strategy that anticipates the complications and uncertainties that may arise, and provide guidance on how best to arrange the policy measures without delaying necessary changes. Reform without the necessary preconditions in place can be extremely perilous for financial stability.

78. While there is no "one size fits all" approach towards financial liberalization, some broad principles apply in the case of China (Figure 33). A key overarching precondition for a smooth transition would be to put in place a well functioning legal, regulatory, supervisory, and crisis management framework with adequate technical capacity. This is essential to monitor financial institutions and manage risks. Another precondition is an early absorption of the current liquidity overhang in the financial system to prevent an unintentional loosening of monetary and credit conditions. Reserve averaging and regular open market operations should be introduced early to help absorb some of the liquidity overhang. At the same time, greater reliance on indirect monetary instruments and more flexible exchange rate would increase the scope for macroeconomic control.

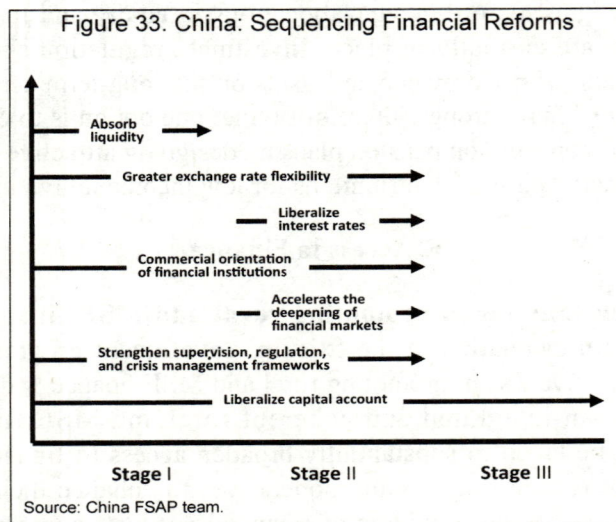

Figure 33. China: Sequencing Financial Reforms

Absorb liquidity

Greater exchange rate flexibility

Liberalize interest rates

Commercial orientation of financial institutions

Accelerate the deepening of financial markets

Strengthen supervision, regulation, and crisis management frameworks

Liberalize capital account

Stage I   Stage II   Stage III

Source: China FSAP team.

79. A modern financial infrastructure and a more market-based financial system will enhance a steady integration with the global financial system. The banking system needs to operate on a more commercial basis and be closely supervised to avoid overly risky behavior and an unsustainable compression of bank margins. The government would need to reorient its role in the financial system so as to reduce the incidence of direct and contingent risks on its balance sheet and remove the moral hazard problem. Alongside such improvements, the gradual liberalization of deposit and loan rates can be successfully implemented. As the banking system becomes more commercially-oriented, broader financial deepening could be accelerated without the risk of disorderly disintermediation. With interest rates set by supply and demand and monetary control exercised through short-term policy rates, China could then move more toward full liberalization of the capital account.

Appendix I. Stress Testing

80. The stress testing exercise was a collaborative effort between the FSAP stress testing team and a PBC/CBRC stress testing team. This was to ensure that the stress test work (i) captures the key aspects of the Chinese economy and the financial system; (ii) builds, to the extent possible, on relevant analytical work already being carried out; and (iii) establishes a coherent operational framework that the authorities could use, and build upon, following the completion of the FSAP.

81. The tests covered 5 LCBs and 12 JSCBs. Taken together, these 17 major banks accounted for about 66 percent of China's banking sector assets and 83 percent of China's commercial banking sector assets as of end-2010. The tests did not cover non-banking financial institutions. All the tests were carried out on end-2009 audited or supervisory financial positions of the 17 major banks and, for comparison purposes, top-down aggregate credit risk and real estate risk analysis was carried out for end-2008 and end-2010 positions of the same banks. In the absence of reliable market-based indicators for these banks, the approaches used in the stress tests relied on data from the banks' public financial statements, prudential reports and banks' internal data systems.

82. The exercise built on three pillars: a bottom-up pillar and two top-down pillars (Figure 34). The 17 banks selected to participate in the exercise implemented the bottom-up calculations, using the same set of shocks and assumptions. The PBC/CBRC team implemented top-down calculations on a bank-by-bank basis using supervisory data and applying an agreed methodology. Both sets of results were provided to the FSAP team at the aggregate level and by bank type. The number of banks that fall below regulatory requirements and their share in the overall banking system's total assets was also provided. The FSAP stress testing team carried out its own set of top-down calculations, based on publicly available data. The results of the three approaches were compared, analyzed, and cross-checked.

83. The tests included a range of sensitivity analyses and scenario calculations. They examined aggregate credit risk, concentration of credit risk, direct exchange rate and interest rate risks, liquidity risks, contagion effects via the documented interbank market, and the joint effect of a set of macroeconomic shocks.

84. Sensitivity tests estimated the impact of changes in individual variables on banks' portfolios. In a sensitivity analysis framework, shocks are assumed to stem from a single risk factor, holding other risk factors constant. Shocks are assumed to occur instantaneously, unless indicated otherwise. The sensitivity analysis covers all positions sensitive to risk factor changes. To the extent possible, these included all long (buy) and short (sell) positions, both on-and off- balance sheet.

Figure 34. China: Stress Testing Exercise: Three Pillars

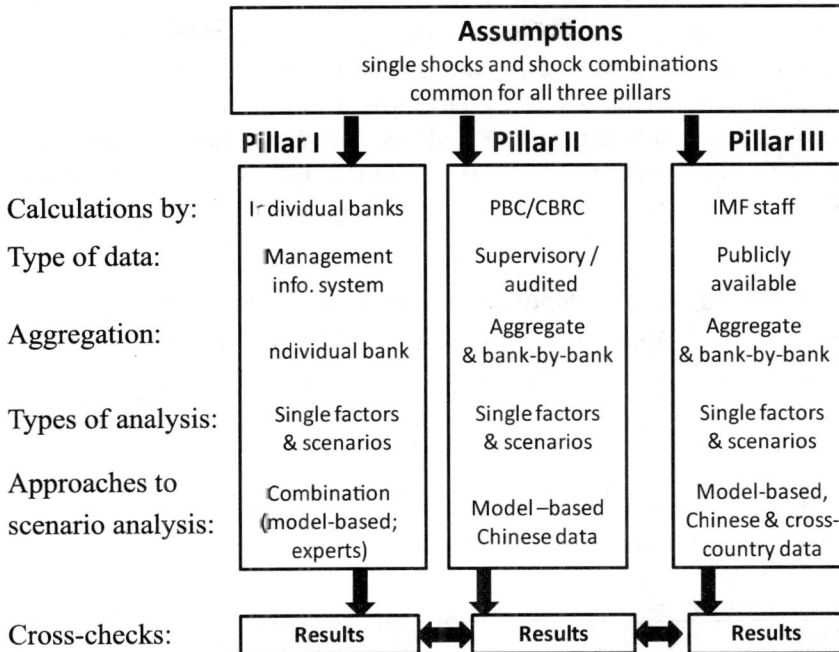

Assumptions		
single shocks and shock combinations common for all three pillars		

	Pillar I	Pillar II	Pillar III
Calculations by:	Individual banks	PBC/CBRC	IMF staff
Type of data:	Management info. system	Supervisory / audited	Publicly available
Aggregation:	individual bank	Aggregate & bank-by-bank	Aggregate & bank-by-bank
Types of analysis:	Single factors & scenarios	Single factors & scenarios	Single factors & scenarios
Approaches to scenario analysis:	Combination (model-based; experts)	Model–based Chinese data	Model-based, Chinese & cross-country data
Cross-checks:	Results	Results	Results

Source: FSAP stress testing team.

85. Credit risk was a key area of focus. The sensitivity analysis for credit risk included an aggregate shock to asset quality, and a set of separate shocks, each aiming to examine a different aspect of credit risk concentration. The aggregate test assumed an overall deterioration in asset quality. In addition, part of the exercise was carried out to pick up the differentiated risks based on the economic sectors and types of entities to which banks lend, as well as the regions in which banks concentrate their operations. However, it was not feasible to fully cover all these dimensions given data constraints. In light of this, a set of separate shocks, each run separately, covered: (i) largest individual exposures; (ii) real estate sector exposures; (iii) exposures to LGFPs; (iv) exposures to overcapacity industries; (v) exposures to export sectors; and (vi) exposures to sectors (industries) and regions with the most rapid loan growth. The equity market shock was not conducted on as banks are prohibited from directly investing in equity markets and the indirect exposure is infeasible to estimate.

86. Macro-scenario tests were a key part of the exercise. Three adverse macroeconomic scenarios were assumed: mild, medium, and severe. Based on an analysis of past growth rates of real GDP in China, as well as the experience of other countries, the assumed annual real GDP growth rates under the three scenarios were 7 percent, 5 percent, and 4 percent, respectively.

87. The scenarios were calibrated with inputs from a panel of leading experts

on Chinese economy. To arrive at meaningful scenarios combining GDP growth rates with other variables, the PBC/CBRC stress testing team, in coordination with the FSAP stress testing team, solicited opinions from an expert panel. To increase the comparability of experts' views, and given that all the banks use GDP as one of the macroeconomic indicators, the GDP growth rate was provided to experts as a key variable for each scenario and their views were solicited on the behavior of other variables under the assumptions. Table 12 summarizes the selected macroeconomic scenarios.

Table 12. China: Macroeconomic Scenario Assumptions
(Changes in Percent, unless Indicated Otherwise)

	Mild	Medium	Severe
GDP	7	5	4
M2	14.7	12.4	10.2
Real estate price	-7.0	-16.2	-25.9
Change in benchmark interest rates for lending and deposits in RMB (basis points)	35	66	95
Real effective exchange rate index	117.5	119.6	123.0

Note: These are not forecasts, but assumptions about potential adverse developments in the future.
Source: FSAP stress testing team and PBC/CBRC, based on inputs from a panel of leading experts on Chinese economy. The assumptions are derived from the averages of the experts' inputs, excluding two outliers.

88. The macroeconomic scenarios were examined using both top-down and bottom-up approaches. For the bottom-up exercise, banks relied on a combination of econometric models and expert-based approaches, although the exact implementation depended on the capacity of individual banks, with some having sophisticated internal models, while others relying on more basic modeling approaches or on loan officers' expert judgment. For their top-down estimate, the PBC/CBRC team used an econometric equation estimated on recent data for China. The top-down estimate done by the FSAP team included cross-checks based on international experience.

Table 13. China: Recommendations for Improvements in Stress Testing

- Conduct regular macro-prudential stress tests with participation of the major banks.
- The PBC and CBRC to work further with banks to ensure that they improve their modeling capacity, in particular in relation to modeling impacts of macro-economic scenarios.
- Harmonize banks' approaches to stress testing, in particular for macro-scenario tests.
- Continue working towards integrating the various exercises for credit risk with the calculations for market risks, liquidity risk and contagion risk.
- Extend the stress tests beyond the 17 banks and include more off-balance sheet exposures.
- Improve quality of the underlying data on stress testing, in particular on PDs and LGDs.
- Strengthen the capacity for data collection.
- Incorporate into the analysis more granular data on banks' loan portfolios, by economic sector, types of counterparty (e.g., SOEs and SMEs), as well as the specific sector in which banks concentrate most of their operations.
  - One sector that should be priority in this respect is real estate. Improve the data reporting systems to enable carrying out a stress test with differentiated shock sizes in different parts of the country.
  - Another sector of focus should be exposures to local government.
- Start collecting data on banks' exposures to export-oriented counterparts.
- Start collecting more comprehensive data on bilateral interbank exposures, so as to carry out an improved contagion stress test.
- Start collecting data on banks' non-financial counterparts (firms, households).

Source: FSAP stress testing team

Annes: Observance of Financial Sector Standards and Codes—Summary of Assessments

This Annex contains the summary assessments of China's observance of international standards and codes in the financial sector.

These assessments have helped to identify the main strengths of the supervisory, regulatory, and market infrastructure framework in managing potential risks and vulnerabilities in the financial system. They also suggest areas that need strengthening and further reform.

The summaries are based on detailed assessments of the following international standards:

- Basel Core Principles for Effective Banking Supervision—by Nicholas Le Pan (World Bank consultant), Walter Yao (IMF consultant), and Aditya Narain (IMF)
- IAIS Insurance Core Principles—by Henning Göbel (World Bank consultant)
- IOSCO Objectives and Principles of Securities Regulation—by Greg Tanzer (World Bank consultant)
- CPSS Core Principles for Systemically Important Payment Systems—by Massimo Cirasino (World Bank), and Mario Guadamillas (World Bank)
- CPSS-IOSCO Recommendations for Central Counterparties—by Massimo Cirasino (World Bank), and Mario Guadamillas (World Bank)

Annex I. Observance of Financial Sector Standards and Codes—Basel Core Principles for Effective Banking Supervision: A Summary

A. Introduction

89. Regulation and supervision of China's banking system has made impressive progress. Significant improvements in risk measurement and risk management have occurred. These are backed up by a regulatory system that demands high-quality capital and liquidity, often through simple and basic regulatory requirements. However, as further opening up and innovation occurs, and China's banks expand, complexity and risks will increase. The CBRC and banks must evolve quickly in the short term to be ready to meet those challenges. The framework of laws and guidance is generally of high quality, but much of it is relatively recent. Implementation by banks needs to be improved, in some cases materially. Enhanced vigilance is required by banks and the regulator to keep risks under control in China's system, in which banks are looked on by the State to be heavily, directly involved in achieving economic and social goals. The CBRC is widely-respected and has demonstrated its willingness to act in pursuit of its safety and soundness mandate. It urgently needs to have a plan to enhance its experience and expertise, ensure progress to date is sustainable, and needs continued support of government in that endeavor.

90. This assessment of the current state of the implementation of the Basel Core Principles for Effective Banking Supervision (BCP) was undertaken between June 7 and June 25, 2010. It reflects the regulatory and supervisory framework in place as of the date of the completion of the assessment. In line with the BCP methodology, the assessment focused more on the major commercial banks and their regulation and supervision, given their importance to the system.

B. Information and Methodology Used for Assessment

91. The assessment team reviewed the legal framework for banking supervision, held extensive discussions with the staff of the CBRC and two of its regional offices. The assessors also met with officials of the central bank—the PBC, the MoF, the National Audit Office (NAO); several commercial banks, audit firms, rating agencies, and the China Bankers Association. The team examined the current practice of on-site and off-site supervision of the CBRC. The assessment team had the benefit of working with a comprehensive self-assessment completed by the CBRC, enjoyed excellent cooperation with its counterparts, and received the information it required.

92. Reaching conclusions required judgments by the assessment team. Banking systems differ from one country to another, as do their domestic circumstances. The banking system has undergone tremendous change in China in the recent period and this process is still ongoing. The CBRC is a relatively young agency, having been created in 2003 from the PBC as part of the major banking sector reform instituted by the Chinese authorities. In addition to the strengthening of financial sector regulation and supervision, these reforms have also led to the conversion of four large state-owned banks into joint-stock companies; reform of rural credit cooperatives; restructuring of joint-stock banks and securities companies; and reform of the insurance sector.

C. Institutional Setting and Market Structure—Overview

93. The Chinese financial system is dominated by the rapidly-growing banking sector, with nonbank financial institutions accounting for only a fraction of the system. The banking system accounts for nearly 80 percent of the net new lending every year. China's capital markets remain relatively shallow, and over 60 percent of outstanding bonds issued by the government and the majority of the remaining being issuances by the large financial institutions, with policy banks (which are state owned and provide a range of development finance services in support of infrastructure, agricultural development, export insurance, etc.) and China Development Bank being the second largest issuers. The insurance sector, however, is rapidly growing, though, as are linkages between banks and insurance companies.

94. Although the banking sector is extraordinarily large with assets over 200 percent of GDP the financial systems is still relatively new, simple and evolving. Key financial prices remain regulated, which insulates banks from market risk. Despite gradual interest rate liberalization over more than a decade, retail interest rates remain partly regulated—deposit rates are subject to a cap and lending rates to a floor. Banks can price lending above the floor to a degree, and do so in practice.

95. Within the banking sector, the five large commercial banks account for just over half of the banking system assets. The next Tier of banks are the joint stock commercial banks, followed by city commercial banks and rural commercial banks which have been formed by the reform of city credit cooperatives and rural credit cooperatives respectively. These are followed by deposit taking institutions such as rural and city credit cooperatives, postal savings banks, village and township banks. Despite over 200 branches and subsidiaries operating in China, foreign banks remain a small presence with assets less than 2 percent of the total. However, in recent years, overseas financial institutions have made significant equity investments in Chinese banks.

96. The prudential ratios on capital adequacy, NPLs, and liquidity, for instance, for the banking system have improved significantly. A significant amount of the bank assets represent exposures to central bank, and central and local governments, and there remains scope for further gains to be made in wider intermediation.

D. Preconditions for Effective Banking Supervision

97. The legal system in China brings together a number of distinct legal traditions within the overarching framework of a civil law system. The structure of the legal framework has undergone a series of phased transitions, first to enable complete state ownership until the 1970s, and more recently to facilitate China's move towards a more market-oriented economy within a socialist political and economic framework.

98. In lieu of a Commercial Code, China enforces a series of commercial laws, providing a mechanism to regulate commercial activities. In its place, the government legislated a series of distinct measures to regulate commercial relations. More recently, a number of symbolically and legally important measures have been passed, notably the Property Law of 2007, that further recognizes private property rights, as well as the Enterprise Bankruptcy Act 2007, which seeks to give greater protection to secured creditors than has otherwise been accorded under Chinese law (e.g., by giving secured creditors priority over worker's wages on winding up). There is little data with reference to enforcement of bank debts, but available data suggests that that enforcement of contracts in general by Chinese courts has improved dramatically in some urban centers to keep pace with economic reform.

99. China is gradually building up an infrastructure that promotes and supports market discipline. The *Company Law, Law on Commercial Banks, Law on Banking Regulation and Supervision, Securities Law, and Insurance Law* all provide specified requirements on information disclosure. The CBRC was established in 2003 as a stand-alone prudential authority and is widely credited with having made significant achievements in its short existence, having been the key driving force in improvements in risk management, corporate governance and internal control and disclosure in Chinese banks. In practice, all banks are required to publicly disclose their information in their annual reports, including audited financial statements, corporate governance, capital adequacy, risk exposures, risk management strategies and practices, and other quantitative and qualitative information. In addition, the listed banks are subject to information disclosure requirements set forth by the CSRC. Considerable efforts have also been made by the financial regulatory agencies to improve the corporate governance of financial institutions. Under corporate governance rules banks have a dual board. There is a full-time board of directors. There is also a supervisory board which oversees the performance of the board and senior management. It is not involved in strategy formulation, but receives reports from audit and control functions to ensure that the board and management are performing as expected and following the board-approved strategy.

100. Since 2005, China accounting standards have substantially converged with International Financial Reporting Standards (IFRS) and International Standards on Auditing, respectively. In February 2006, the MoF which sets accounting and audit standards promulgated the *Accounting Standard for Business Enterprises*, which replaced the previous *China Accounting Standards* and became effective in January 2007. The new accounting standards consist of one basic standard and 38 specific standards, which have substantially converged with the international standards and were recognized by the International Accounting Standards Board (IASB). Currently, all listed companies, financial institutions and non-listed large and medium-sized enterprises have adopted the new accounting standards. Also, in 2006, the MoF issued a new set of auditing standards; one review engagement standard; two other assurance engagement standards; two related service standards; and one quality control standard, which have also converged with the international standards and were thus recognized by the International Federation of Accountants.

101. Accounting and auditing professions have grown considerably, though certain areas need improvements. Over the past three decades, China's Certified Professional Accountant (CPA) industry has been growing steadily. Currently, there are more than 7,000 accounting firms registered in China, with more than 97,000 CPAs in practice. The MoF is responsible for regulating the accounting and auditing professions, with the regulatory responsibilities including qualification review and approval, professional performance supervision, and overseeing the activities of relevant industry associations. Coverage of bank audits is adequate, as the CBRC requires banks with total assets exceeding RMB 1 billion to receive financial statement audits; however, some weaknesses exist. Earlier reports and market participants interviewed by assessors have cited that the audit quality of smaller accounting firms needs improvements. The credibility of the audit profession would be enhanced as the authorities implement the standard auditor independence regulation recently incorporated in the *China Code of Professional Ethics for Certified Public Accountants* and increase their oversight of the profession by performing regular and more frequent review of accounting firms' audit quality.

102. In recent years, the PBC has carried out a major reform of the National Payment System (NPS), by launching the China National Advanced Payment System (CNAPS). The CNAPS consists of the High Value Payment System (HVPS) and the Bulk Electronic Payment System. The HVPS is a real time gross settlement systems and mainly used for large value transfers. It is used to provide fast, efficient, secure and reliable payment clearing services to banking institutions, private and public entities and financial markets. Currently the system has more than 1,600 direct participants. China is also evolving to a more intensive use of non-cash payment instruments, especially cards.

103. China does not have an explicit public safety net in the form of deposit insurance but is considering its introduction. Given the high level of government ownership of banks, there may be a public perception that the State would stand behind all depositors in the case of a closure. The central bank has authority to make lender of last resort loans to banks.

104. There have been restructurings of several banks with serious financial difficulties. These have tended to involve "whole bank," going concern solutions whereby another bank has been convinced to take over the assets and liabilities of the problem institution (or at least the deposit liabilities). There is no explicit resolution framework for such eventualities but the authorities have demonstrated the ability to achieve such solutions using the existing bankruptcy and other laws. There are several aspects of the bankruptcy laws that deserve consideration in order to increase systemic protection and reduce contagion risk in the event of bank failures. The authorities should consider whether a separate insolvency regime for banks may serve them better especially given the increasing internationalization of the large banks and the current global focus on developing more compatible cross-border resolution frameworks.

E. Main Findings

Objectives, independence, powers, transparency, and cooperation (CP 1)

105. The objectives and responsibilities of authorities involved in banking supervision are clear. CBRC's mandate has enabled it to focus on a single mission of safety and soundness and that has helped it become a high-quality organization. Using this mandate, CBRC has been very successful in articulating to banks and the public the need to achieve both safety and soundness and the needs for economic and social progress through the banking system. Indeed, safety and soundness contributes to development goals. CBRC has pushed for high-quality risk management by banks as part of their delivering on economic and social objectives. Following its mandate, and as a result of observed or potential deficiencies in risk management practices, CBRC has recently introduced a range of prudential measures, including more stringent credit risk management of loans to local government platforms and real estate lending. It has also successfully pushed banks to hold more capital and more provisions in the face of rapid loan growth as part of the stimulus package.

106. The potential conflict between safety and soundness objectives and other objectives exists in many countries but can be more acute in China because of the predominant use of the banking system, much of which is state owned, to achieve economic and social goals. The 12th plan for the financial sector being developed as part of the 12th Five-Year economic plan under the SC for the NPC should reinforce the importance of safety and soundness and CBRC's early intervention to resolve potential problems before they become serious. It should also make a priority for continued improvement in banks' risk management with a focus on assuring all banks, not only the most advanced, make needed improvements and ensure that improvements already made are well entrenched in their operations. The importance of safety and soundness and high quality risk management to economic and social objectives should be explicitly recognized by the authorities. Current CBRC leadership has played a key role in promoting prudential goals and dealing with issues of possible conflict of safety and soundness objectives with national economic policies. It will be important to continue this.

107. The arrangements for resourcing in CBRC leads to potential independence issues, and hampers effectiveness, particularly as banks become more complex and innovative, and expand abroad. So does the potential ability for the SC to override CBRC rules, though this has never been exercised. The CBRC law mandates it to take decisions free from interference from any party, and CBRC reports that no interference has occurred since its creation. However the existing arrangements could be problematic in future. The laws, rules and guidance that CBRC operates under generally establish a benchmark of prudential standards that is of high quality and was drawn extensively from international standards and the BCP themselves.

108. However, much of the guidance is relatively new and the issues raised in assessment of various CPs are often ones of better implementation. In many ways, the strength of CBRCs regulation to date lies in the deliberately simple, conservative approach it has taken, often relying on specific prudential ratios that banks must meet. This is true for liquidity and for capital adequacy, for example. The challenge going forward is that this approach, by itself, will not be sufficient as markets and banks evolve. CBRC is well governed within the constraints it faces and has steadily and materially increased its transparency. There is need for: more forward resource planning; an urgent government-supported strategy for material upgrading of skills especially specialist skills; and more flexibility in budgeting and pay to support this strategy and attract and retain talent. CBRC's performance reporting has greatly improved but more is possible.

109. The legal framework for banking supervision has been revised to incorporate legislation, guidelines and rules (which all have legal standing) based on international standards. CBRC has authority to take a wide range of corrective and remedial actions, and is clearly willing to use them. CBRC staff is legally protected from the consequences of acts committed in good faith. CBRC also has the legal authority to share information with other regulators, domestically and internationally and does so through networks of Memorandum of Understanding (MOUs).

Licensing and structure (CPs 2–5)

110. China defines the permissible activities of banks and operates an extensive licensing and approval process for banks. Considerable staff is involved in approving new institutions, new branches or sub-branches of existing institutions, new products, as well as changes in ownership. Fit and proper criteria apply to board and senior management, but also extend to many other positions in a bank. The use of the name "bank" is properly controlled and shell banks are not permitted. Minimum capital requirements to start a new bank depend on the type of bank and are in line with or higher than international norms.

111. CBRC implements an appropriate approval process for changes in ownership and major acquisitions. However, the Chinese system is evolving from a system of state ownership to more private ownership, opening up the possibility of more complex ownership structures for banks. In this context CBRC's lack of legal authority could impede their ability to review beneficial owners or indirect changes of control. They report that they do usually get information on beneficial/indirect owners through the direct acquirer or through other indirect means. The assessment team did not come across instances where supervision effectiveness has been compromised because of this issue but this legal authority should be bolstered. Other CBRC rules that also involve potentially more complex bank ownership structures (e.g., related party rules) should also be reviewed to ensure that such structures are clearly covered by the rules. Investments by banks, including in overseas branches, require approval as part of the general approval system. While banks are generally prohibited from investing in nonbank activities, in the recent past exceptions have been permitted for investment in financial leasing and asset management. Bank-insurance and bank-fund management company investments have not been allowed until recently, when four cross-ownership pilots are in process. In those cases CBRC imposes firewalls between the banks and the other entity. Among other considerations, there are also explicit provisions that these pilots must earn at least average industry returns or they are to be dissolved.

Prudential regulation and requirements (CPs 6–18)

112. The capital adequacy rules are based on Basel I. Basel II is being introduced over the 2011–2013 period for six banks that must adopt it on a mandatory basis. Some other banks have also decided to adopt it on a voluntary basis. Basel II was not formally assessed as it was not in place at the time of the mission. The choices China has made in implementing Basel I have generally been conservative, and result in Chinese banks uniformly having capital ratios above the Basel minimum. Banks' capital is composed primarily (approximately three-quarters) of high-quality core capital. The minimum required capital is 8 percent. Recent measures have raised expected capital ratios above the Basel minimum to 11.5 percent for the five major banks and 10 percent for all other banks, as part of a move to counter-cyclical buffers. How these buffers will work in a counter-cyclical way has not been specified. CBRC needs to review and communicate what its ongoing expectations are for banks to hold capital above the minimum and the criteria it will use to decide how to alter the buffer. There are a few aspects of the rules that are less conservative than the Basel I provisions, that should be reviewed.

113. Risk management is evolving in Chinese banks. CBRC has played a major role in the significant and impressive improvements that have occurred. Less than fully compliant ratings in certain areas in this assessment generally reflect deficiencies in the legal framework, which can be amended, or that banks have yet to fully implement CBRC guidance. CBRC itself is performing excellently in a challenging and fast-changing environment. It is on the right track with its reform agenda and needs to persevere in a sustained way in its current direction. It will need the full support of all other parties in the government to succeed in the goals it has set for itself. Most major banks have developed risk management systems for each of the major individual risks they face, though improvements are required in certain cases. CBRC guidance is generally of high quality and was often developed directly from Basel documents. Framework guidance in some risk areas is relatively new, with some being issued as recently as the last half of 2009. A period of settling in is required for effectiveness to be enhanced, for those banks who are not the most advanced to catch up, and for CBRC to ensure that all banks have risk management systems commensurate with the risks they are assuming.

114. The new risk governance, risk measurement and risk management systems have not been tested under stress and some areas for material improvement are clearly evident. Board-approved strategies are often too focused on target loan growth in various sectors and not enough on targeted risk measures linked to the bank's own risk systems, as opposed to regulatory requirements. Comprehensive, enterprise-wide risk management that takes account of interactions between risks in measuring, managing and stress testing, and that relates capital to risk is at an early stage in some banks, including some major banks. For many banks the priority is not to move to this stage quickly, but rather to ensure that a sound risk management framework is fully in place, imbedded in their culture and group-wide operations, and sustainable. While much of banking in China is deposit taking and lending, major Chinese banks are some of the largest in the world, and the Chinese lending market is complex by virtue of its scope and diversity, and banks are getting into new areas of lending and other activities. So risk management needs to be commensurate with these realities. China is considering introducing explicit deposit insurance arrangements. It will be important as it does so that it carefully considers the roles of the various organizations in a resolution.

115. Credit risk is the most important risk facing Chinese banks and will remain so for some time. It has received the most focus by banks and CBRC and is generally well controlled. However there is intense focus on NPL experience by banks, policy makers and by a considerable part of CBRC staff. This is understandable given the serious bad-loan experience in the early part of the decade. But this almost sole focus sometimes is at the expense of attention to other early, forward-looking measures of credit risk that need to be responded to. Senior leadership in CBRC and some banks understand the need for forward-looking judgment but assessors sensed that this message has yet to flow fully through their organizations. The rules and practice for problem assets, provisioning for listed banks are otherwise adequate. They are based on IFRS-equivalent accounting rules and regulatory requirements for classifying loans. CBRC does regular, extensive and in-depth reviews of asset quality and replication of the provisioning system. Major audit firms audit the majority of listed banks. The regulatory system has encouraged additional provisions and requires further buffers to be held as part of firm's equity.

116. Traded market risk in the Chinese banking system is low in aggregate and for major banks individually. This will likely increase as market liberalization occurs. The exchange rate liberalization announced recently could increase foreign exchange (FX) risk for banks and their customers. Risk management tools, information technology (IT) and data infrastructure to support them are generally commensurate with the level of risk, though there are areas for improvement. However, sophistication will likely need to increase considerably in the near future. The move to Basel II will assist. Interest Rate Risk in the Banking Book (IRRBB) is a more-prevalent risk for a wide number of banks. These will also likely rise as further liberalization occurs. Tools need to move rapidly beyond the static gap analysis based on contractual maturities of assets and liabilities that many banks are now employing. CBRC could also enhance its outlier analysis for this risk. This affects more than just the listed banks, and the improvement does not require adoption of models.

117. Operational risk has been a focus of banks for a number of years. The two main operational risks have related to possible internal control breakdowns and fraud, and IT risk. These have received considerable focus at banks and they and other observers reported that such incidents have trended down significantly in recent years. The challenge now is to put in place more comprehensive frameworks to deal with all elements of operational risk relevant to individual banks, which has started. More bank business units should be doing regular risk and control self assessment (RCSA) and developing, monitoring and refining key operational risk indicators. Again, a move to complex advanced measurement approaches (AMA) models for capital purposes is not required to make improvements.

Methods of ongoing banking supervision (CPs 19–21)

118. Supervisory approaches are increasingly risk focused. However, use of the CAMELS+ rating system and various other aspects of the supervisory methodology (including its newness in some respects) mean that supervisory assessments are not as forward looking as desirable. As well, heavy reliance on the few basic simple ratios, while appropriate, may discourage more judgment-based assessment of inherent risk and the quality of individual bank's risk management and governance. There is need to maintain the benefits of simple basic indictors while reinforcing banks complying with CBRC guidance which requires use of more sophisticated approaches than some banks are using. That would also encourage more of a risk culture in banks as well, rather than them relying excessively only on complying with regulatory requirements.

119. More attention may need to be placed on mid-size and smaller banks to ensure that they upgrade their risk management and governance performance. CBRC has all the necessary tools of on-site and off-site supervision. There is an extensive system to capture frequent and periodic information from banks. However, disclosure by banks or CBRC of important safety and soundness information, such as capital and liquidity position is less than in a lot of other markets. This should be examined and improved.

Accounting and disclosure (CP 22)

120. China has developed an accounting system that has substantially converged with the IFRS. A recent World Bank study also commended China's effort though certain areas of improvements were identified. Continued attention will need to be given to the development of the private accounting and audit profession in China to ensure that financial statements are professionally prepared and audited. The CBRC should be empowered to reject and rescind the appointment of an external auditor who is deemed to be unfit to perform a reliable and independent audit.

Corrective and remedial powers of supervisors (CP 23)

121. CBRC has the authority and demonstrated willingness to act to resolve problems. Dealing with problem banks has been on the basis of going concern solutions. Capability to close institutions may need to be enhanced going forward.

Consolidated and cross-border banking supervision (CPs 24–25)

122. Consolidated supervision of banks and their direct subsidiaries and branches on the mainland or offshore is of high quality. However, existing laws may permit more complex structures where consolidated supervision may not be possible. On occasion, CBRC has used indirect and informal means to deal with the situation and bring about needed changes in structure. The mission's recommendations (CP 4) to amend laws to formally require CBRC approvals of ultimate beneficial ownership and indirect changes in control would also help address this issue. Reliance by one supervisor on the work of others in mixed corporate groups (bank/insurance/fund management/pilots) may not always work well in practice and has yet to be tested. In terms of home-host relationships, CBRC has a wide network of formal and informal arrangements and has used these effectively as both a home and host.

Table 14. China: Summary of Compliance with the Basel Core Principles

Core Principle	Comments
1. Objectives, independence, powers, transparency, and cooperation	
1.1 Responsibilities and objectives	CBRC has clear safety and soundness goals in legislation, but the authorities have recently also emphasized loan growth, particularly in certain sectors to assist development and macroeconomic recovery. The CBRC message of balancing this growth with prudence needs to be continuously emphasized. The 12th plan for the financial sector being developed as part of the 12th Five-Year economic plan under the SC for the NPC should reinforce the importance of safety and soundness. CBRC leadership should continue to emphasize that banks follow sound practices in implementing national economic policies.
1.2 Independence, accountability and transparency	Budgeting arrangements, external headcount approval requirements and authority (though not used to date) for SC overrides of CBRC rules and decisions compromise CBRC effectiveness and could affect operational independence. CBRC needs to continuously upgrade its staff, including developing more specialist expertise to be effective in the emerging more complex, more innovative and more international environment. It needs government support for a targeted strategy to achieve this goal that will have to include more flexibility in budgeting and salaries and incentives to attract and retain the people it needs to supervise increasingly complex banks, and meet its other objectives. A more forward-looking approach to resource planning and greater transparency around performance measures is also desirable.
1.3 Legal framework	The legal framework for banking supervision has been revised to incorporate sound practices based on international standards. Some legal provisions (mentioned elsewhere) need strengthening and some overlaps clarified in the next round of amendments.
1.4 Legal powers	CBRC has been empowered to take a wide range of corrective and remedial actions to deal with non-compliance and imprudent actions by banks.
1.5 Legal protection	CBRC staff is protected from the legal consequences of actions taken in good faith.
1.6 Cooperation	There exist a plethora of agreements and arrangements for sharing information and coordination between the domestic agencies but the Interagency Financial Coordination Meetings led by the SC are viewed by many as being the most effective.

Cont

Core Principle	Comments
2. Permissible activities	The permissible activities of banks are well defined and the authorities lay particular emphasis on preventing unauthorized deposit taking. While banks are prohibited from undertaking nonbank activities, some pilots have been permitted to test the waters. Banks' transactions with trust companies, which manage individual and institutional wealth have increased significantly in recent times and are believed to reflect both a search for yield and a sale of loans to meet regulatory ratios.
3. Licensing criteria	The CBRC devotes significant resources to the licensing and approvals regime which is comprehensive and covers prior authorization for all activities, services and products.
4. Transfer of significant ownership	CBRC is inhibited in its formal legal ability to identify the ultimate beneficial owner or controlling shareholder while approving transfers of significant ownership in banks and employs indirect and/or informal approaches towards this end.
5. Major acquisitions	More clarity to be provided on the criteria by which to judge major acquisitions of domestic banks by other domestic banks.
6. Capital adequacy	CBRC has adopted a generally conservative approach to implementing Basel I with few exceptions. There are expectations of banks holding capital above the Basel minimum with three quarters of capital required composed of core capital. CBRC's recent adoption of their expectation of a capital buffer as a counter-cyclical measure could be further articulated to be effective. There is a lack of a permanent well-understood cushion above minimum required capital. Implementation of Basel II is pushing major banks to further improve risk management but resources within CBRC for effective implementation on the current timetable may be strained.
7. Risk management process	While much of banking in China is deposit taking and lending, major Chinese banks are some of the largest in the world, and the Chinese lending market is complex by virtue of its scope and diversity, and banks are getting into new areas of lending and other activities. So risk management needs to be commensurate with these realties. CBRC has put in place high-quality internationally-compliant guidance (some relatively recently). Banks have not yet fully complied, the gaps are material for some banks, and practice will likely take time to be in place.
	Major banks and mid-size banks have processes for management of credit/market/operational risks. However, true enterprise-wide risk approaches that integrate strategy setting, monitoring, management and stress testing in ways that consider interactions among risks are at an early stage in some banks, including some major ones. Guidance on some risks is recent and so could not be expected to be complied with as yet (e.g., comprehensive risk management, liquidity risk, reputation risk). A period of settling in is required for existing and newly-developed processes to be fully effective and be assessed by the supervisor. Processes for banks to relate the capital they hold to their risks are at an early stage in banks and the supervisor. For major banks this will be enhanced over time by the move to Basel II. Some further more-detailed guidance for smaller banks on relating capital to risk may be needed.
8. Credit risk	This is the key risk in the Chinese banking system and will remain so for some time. Recent success in cleaning up banks portfolios is impressive. But credit risk is likely rising. CBRC guidance is appropriate. Credit risk management in many banks has improved greatly recently, and assessors saw many examples of excellent practices. However assessors saw clear evidence that the enhancements in governance related to credit risk and credit risk management is not

Cont

Core Principle	Comments
	fully embedded across all banks (and have not been tested under stress). Many banks appear to be relying more on the regulatory NPL ratios in setting credit strategies. CBRC has had to take a variety of action to push banks to improve underwriting and credit-risk management processes that would not have been necessary if bank risk management practices were more fully reliable.
9. Problem assets, provisions, and reserves	Assessors spent considerable time reviewing this principle. Most banks follow relevant accounting principles in determining loan loss allowance and comply with regulatory minima set by CBRC. A lot of efforts are made by CBRC and auditors of major banks to ensure that provisioning meets accounting and regulatory requirements. Smaller banks appear to face challenges in following accounting principles relating to determining individual and collective impairment. Banks' ability to write off loans in a timely way has been negatively impacted by the strict -write-off criteria laid out by MoF.
10. Large exposure limits	CBRC lays great emphasis on identifying large exposures through a dedicated off-site system. However, it should also consider developing a more comprehensive framework for assessing risk across connected/related-parties.
11. Exposure to related parties	While a robust regime is prescribed for identifying related parties and requiring that transactions with them be undertaken at arm's length and be subject to limits, it does not take into account common ownership by local governments, which may be a risk factor for some banks owned by local governments.
12. Country and transfer risks	Country and transfer risks are gaining in materiality for Chinese banks. While the major banks with the bulk of the exposure have systems in place, this is still work in progress for the others. CBRC has recently consolidated its supervisory expectations in this regard and is monitoring progress in implementation.
13. Market risks	The extent and complexity of market risk is low given market structure and absence of approval for complex products, and banks strategies being more client-driven than proprietary. While existing risk management approaches are reasonable for the current environment, there are weaknesses in execution and a material upgrade will be needed if any further interest rate or exchange rate liberalization occurs or if banks adopt more aggressive strategies.
14. Liquidity risk	Use of simple regulatory rules such as maximum loan/deposit ratio and minimum current assets ratio, as well as reserve requirements, mean banks are highly liquid. Banks should be encouraged to adopt more sophisticated liquidity risk management methods to prepare for further market liberalization.
15. Operational risk	Banks and the supervisor have considerable history of detailed high-quality internal control processes (focused on reducing fraud) and attention to IT risks. The current challenge is to move beyond that to a more-complete measurement and management of operational risk. Progress is occurring but this varies across larger banks. Guidance that covers all elements of the CP is recent and upgrading of specialist skills in CBRC will be required. Practice of banks doing RCSA across businesses or developing key risk indicators (KRI) for various business lines needs further development.
16. Interest rate risk in the banking book	This is a risk that is meaningful for a wide variety of banks of all sizes. The need for active management will likely grow as and when further interest rate liberalization occurs. Currently many banks are using static gap analysis based on contractual maturities to measure and manage this risk. It is desirable to move to more dynamic analysis based on

Cont

Core Principle	Comments
	projected cash flows, non-parallel shifts in interest rates and incorporating assumptions about how the behavior of various categories of assets and liabilities might be affected in these scenarios. There is room for CBRC to enhance its analysis of possible outliers.
17. Internal control and audit	Internal control awareness has been heightened and the CBRC has strong supervisory focus in this area. Publicly listed banks will face the challenge of implementing "C-SOX" which requires external auditors to opine on the adequacy of their self assessments of internal controls.
18. Abuse of financial services	The supervisory responsibilities for addressing the abuse of financial services in (and by) banks are divided between the PBC and the CBRC. There are opportunities for improving cooperation and information sharing between the two as they carry out this shared responsibility.
	CBRC is making material strides in dealing with fraudulent practices in banks but some work remains to be done. A few Anti-Money Laundering (AML) related recommendations relevant for banks as identified in the 2006 FATF assessment are to be addressed.
19. Supervisory approach	While the supervisory approaches are increasingly risk-focused and incorporate good practices, supervisors should consider focusing on incorporating more examiner judgment in ratings and lessen reliance on quantitative formulaic approaches.
20. Supervisory techniques	To further the risk-based approaches in place, CBRC should reconsider its focus on examination of branches which are largely compliance focused. Resources could then be allocated to other higher priority supervisory activities.
21. Supervisory reporting	There is an extensive system to capture frequent and periodic information from banks and CBRC should consider making banks' quarterly financial information available to the public to foster greater transparency in the banking industry.
22. Accounting and disclosure	The CBRC does not have the authority to reject or rescind the appointment of an external auditor who is deemed unfit to perform a reliable and independent audit. The October 2009 *World Bank Report on the ROSC–Accounting* and Auditing identifies weaknesses in the audit quality of the smaller and mid-sized accounting firms and the oversight of the accounting profession. The lack of published financial data on aggregate and individual bank data reduces the transparency of the banking system.
23. Corrective and remedial powers of supervisors	CBRC has the ability to act to take corrective action if prudential rules are not observed and data on enforcement actions suggest that it also has the willingness to act in this regard. Bank closing experience has been very limited though there have been large-scale mergers as part of banking system consolidation in which CBRC has been involved.
24. Consolidated supervision	Consolidated regulation and supervision of groups composed of banks and their mainland or offshore subsidiaries and branches is of high quality. Laws and rules permit more complex structures where CBRC would be challenged to meet the key elements of the principle. With cross ownership by banks of fund management companies and insurers (pilots exist) reliance on firewalls and institutional regulation by each regulator of their part of the group may not be sufficient.
25. Home-host relationships	CBRC has laid emphasis on developing and maintaining a wide network of formal and informal arrangements with overseas supervisory authorities and has used these effectively as both a home and a host. It has also launched a supervisory college for one large international bank and will shortly launch a second one.

Table 15. China: Recommended Action Plan to Improve Compliance with the Basel Core Principles

Reference Principle	Recommended Action
CP 1.1 Responsibilities and Objectives	Ensure upcoming revised 12th Five-Year plan developed by the SC for the financial sector emphasizes importance of safety and soundness including early intervention by the regulator to get potential problems resolved and the contribution safe and sound banks make to achieving economic and social goals. Make improving banks' risk management as a way of supporting economic and social goals a priority over the next five years— not just in leading banks but in all banks. Consider amending CBRC objectives to emphasize early intervention. Reduce focus on NPLs and increase focus on more forward-looking monitoring and measurement of risk. CBRC leadership to continue to emphasize the importance of prudential goals in implementation of national economic policies.
CP 1.2 Independence, Accountability and Transparency	Give CBRC authority for staffing and budgeting within broadly-set targets. Consider moving to model where industry fees directly fund CBRC to enhance independence. Develop a SC supported plan to upgrade CBRC staff expertise including more budget flexibility and allowing CBRC more flexibility in remuneration to better attract and retain specialist resources. Address potential independence issues.
CP 4 Transfer of Significant Ownership	The law should clearly require evaluations of ultimate beneficial owners and shareholders exercising indirect control in all cases of acquisition and transfers of significant ownership in banks.
CP 6 Capital Adequacy	Reconsider the few areas where capital rules are less conservative than Basel I. Consider ways to draw out implementation of Basel II to ensure success, such as a longer parallel run period. Secure more specialist resources on an ongoing basis to effectively supervise Basel II banks. Enhance disclosure of capital position of banks.
CP 7 Comprehensive Risk Management	Persevere in current direction to improve bank compliance with CBRC guidance. Ensure adequate focus on risk management capabilities of the banks, not just the Basel II banks. Encourage banks to have more risk-related measures in their annual board-approved strategy setting. Perform cross-bank targeted review of risk management practices with focus on enterprise-wide approach, benchmark banks and provide feedback on areas for improvement. Encourage use of more enterprise wide scenario stresses such as how a slowdown would affect all risk areas. Encourage more relating of capital banks hold to their risks. Consider targeted review of this across major banks, benchmark, and provide feedback. Consider more detailed guidance on relating capital to risk for non-Basel II banks.
CP 8 Credit Risk	Further develop more forward-looking assessment of credit risk in CBRC risk rating system. Encourage banks to use more of their own risk metrics in setting their annual credit risk strategies. Make sure all major banks have implemented CBRC credit risk guidance.
CP 9 Problem Assets	Establish a less burdensome mechanism to facilitate the loan write-off process.
CP 10, 11 Large Exposures and Related Party Lending	Bring common ownership of enterprises by local governments into the definition and discipline of large exposures and related party transactions.
CP 12 Country and Transfer Risk	Ensure implementation of country and transfer risk management guidance (issued in June 2010) in all major banks. Have banks submit an action plan to deal with deficiencies by year-end 2010. Perform a supervisory review of policies and practice for these banks within the next 18 months.
CP 13 Market Risk	Develop and implement an effective strategy to increase specialist resources in this area. Repeat the 2006 cross-system review of market risk management at regular intervals as a means of assessing progress, benchmarking and pushing for continuous improvement. Review appropriateness of threshold for exemption from market risk capital determination.
CP 14 Liquidity Risk	Put additional supervisory focus on this area as a means of reinforcing implementation of the guidance issued in 2009. Signal to banks at senior levels the desire for more sophisticated liquidity risk management. Put high priority on performing an assessment of all major banks against the new guidance.

Cont

Reference Principle	Recommended Action
CP 15 Operational Risk	Ensure all major banks have a plan to develop at least RCSA and KRI across their businesses. Enhance expertise of CBRC resources to permit cross-system review of major banks progress against 2007 guidance. Priority is less than for liquidity and IRRBB. Guard against pressure for premature moves to AMA.
CP 18 Abuse of Financial Services	Improve coordination and information sharing between CBRC and PBC through more regular and frequent information including those arising from AML inspection findings; and large and doubtful transaction reports. Develop an information sharing protocol between CBRC and PBC. Continue progress on dealing with fraudulent transactions in and by banks. Make it legally binding on banks to identify beneficial customers.
CP 22 Accounting and Disclosure	Develop an auditor independence requirement to enhance the credibility of the auditing profession. Prioritize implementation of policy recommendations identified in the October 2009 *World Bank ROSC Report on Accounting and Auditing* focusing on improving the audit quality of the smaller to mid-sized accounting firms and stronger oversight of the accounting profession. Empower CBRC to reject or rescind the appointment of an external auditor who is deemed unfit to perform a reliable and independent audit by them. Enhance the transparency of the banking system by publishing aggregate banking data, key financial ratios, and peer group averages quarterly. The frequency of audit oversight inspections should be increased.
CP 24 Consolidated Supervision	Amend legislation to give CBRC authority to force banks in all cases to be held in corporate structures that permit consolidated supervision. Use new authority regarding beneficial ownership and indirect control (CP 4) to ensure corporate structures permit consolidated supervision. Give CBRC authority to examine fund management and insurance affiliates of banks if concerns regarding risk and risk management capabilities exist.

F. Authorities' Response

123. The Chinese authorities welcome and support the BCP assessment as an opportunity for reflection and improvement for banking regulation and supervision according to international standards. The assessment team has undertaken excellent work, demonstrating high quality professionalism, dedication and the ability to cut through complex issues in a constrained timeframe. The authorities appreciate the opportunity to provide the following comments on the assessment.

124. The CBRC, with strong support from the Chinese government, has actively pursued its statutory mandate for safety and soundness of the banking sector through promulgating a prudential framework benchmarked to international standards and continuously improving supervisory effectiveness. This effort is facilitated by substantial enhancement in corporate governance and risk management in the Chinese banking industry through three decades of reform and opening up. These achievements and progress have been largely recognized in the assessment report. The assessment demonstrates that the banking supervision in China is broadly in compliance with the BCP.

125. There are a number of issues in the assessment for which the authorities would like to provide further clarification. The assessment identifies the potential ability for the SC to override CBRC rules as a potential threat to CBRC's operational independence. The CBRC does not see this as an independence concern that would

compromise its effectiveness. According to the Law on Banking Regulation and Supervision, the CBRC shall, in accordance with applicable laws and administrative regulations, formulate and promulgate supervisory rules and guidelines for banking institutions. And according to the Legislation Law, only under the circumstances of violating laws and regulations, or existence of inconsistencies between rules issued by different ministries or commissions, the SC may alter or annul "inappropriate" rules issued by the ministries or commissions. Therefore, the CBRC can perform its rule-making authority independently unless its rules and guidelines contravene relevant laws or administrative regulations. Such an arrangement serves as a check and balance on the CBRC and other government agencies to exercise authority in accordance with law. This also helps maintaining the integrity and consistency of the legal framework in China. In practice, the SC has never altered or annulled the rules and guidelines issued by the CBRC.

126. The assessment also indicates that the CBRC's current budgeting and headcount arrangements could lead to potential independence issues and hamper supervisory effectiveness. Since its establishment, the CBRC has received unrelenting support from the SC and relevant ministries in undertaking banking regulation and supervision. The CBRC has upgraded the efficiency and quality of its staff through continuous recruiting, training and development efforts, while the efficiency of supervision has also been enhanced through effective application of IT. However, the CBRC acknowledges that, like many banking supervisory agencies around the world, it faces challenges in attracting, developing and retaining supervisory talent in an increasingly competitive and complex industry environment. By working closely with relevant government agencies, the CBRC aims to further increase supervisory resources where appropriate, upgrade staff skills and retain high-quality front-line supervisors, in order to fulfill its mandate for safety and soundness in a fast changing industry environment.

127. The CPs revised in 2006 place a greater emphasis on risk management, and the methodology requires assessors to consider the practices of banks as well as supervisory agencies. The CBRC, since its establishment, has made great efforts to improve its risk-based supervision capacity, while requiring banks to enhance their corporate governance and risk management capabilities. To this date, the main business of Chinese banks is still traditional deposit-taking and commercial and retail lending. It is only in recent years that a few banks have been allowed to enter into non-bank financial businesses on a trial basis and these operations remain very small. As a result, China's banking sector is much simpler than those of developed markets, where the risk environment is much more challenging due to greater complexity and interconnectedness. The assessment acknowledges that the CBRC has played a major role in the significant and impressive progress that banks have made in improving their risk management, while identifying a number of areas for further improvement. The authorities' view differs from the assessment in the degree to which banks' risk management is commensurate with the current risk environment they operate in. However, the authorities concur that continued improvements in banks' risk management are needed, as financial reform deepens and liberalization creates greater interconnectedness and complexities in the Chinese financial system. For example,

looking ahead, comprehensive enterprise-wide risk management that takes account of interactions among risks and effectively relates capital to risks will need to be further strengthened at the Chinese banks. Meanwhile, the CBRC will also continue to enhance its capability in evaluating banks' risk profiles and risk management processes together with the increase in size and complexity of the Chinese banking sector.

128. The assessment has proven to be valuable and rewarding in generating insights and suggestions that will contribute towards the improvement of banking supervision in China. The CBRC appreciates the recommendations made in the assessment, and will take actions on those that are considered appropriate and applicable. Some of them are already being implemented and others taken into account in the CBRC's medium- and long-term plans to improve supervisory effectiveness. The CBRC will also continue to push forward the reform and opening-up of the Chinese banking sector, which has proven a key driver in enhancing the safety and soundness of Chinese banks. In the meantime, the CBRC will continue to actively engage in the activities of the FSB and the BCBS to develop and reform international banking supervisory standards, so as to contribute towards the enhancement of the resilience of the global banking system.

Annex II. Observance of Financial Sector Standards and Codes—IAIS Insurance Core Principles: A Summary

A. Introduction

129. Insurance companies in China are closely supervised and generally subjected to appropriate regulation. The CIRC, employs a rules based framework and has achieved a high level of regulatory compliance from supervised companies. Generally, a high level of observance with the core principles can be seen on those core principles where a rules based approach and control can be exercised. In contrast insufficient regulation exists on market exit and portfolio transfers. Supervision should be strengthened on the adequacy of reserve levels, the insurer's observance of solvency requirements and the strictness with which CIRC ensures compliance with capital requirements. A shift from rules based to principles based supervision is likely to become necessary if resources are to meet growing demands. However in the immediate future rules based approach seems most appropriate.

130. This assessment of compliance with International Association of Insurance Supervisors (IAIS) Insurance Core Principles (ICP) was carried out as part of the 2010 FSAP. The assessment is based on the 2003 version of the IAIS Insurance Core Principles and Methodology. It took into account relevant IAIS standards and guidance in addition to the ICPs.

131. The CIRC conducts its duties through its headquarters in Beijing and 35 regional branches, the insurance bureaus. Insurance regulations issued by the CIRC are guided by high level regulations issued by the SC (including on compulsory motor insurance) and the basic law issued by the People's Congress. In addition to formal regulations, CIRC has issued a range of directives, guidance notes etc under its mandate to develop the SC's commercial and social policy objectives for the insurance market.

132. This assessment is based upon information made available to the assessor in preparation for and during the June 2010 FSAP mission. CIRC contributed a self-assessment and further information in response to requests before and during the mission. Requested documentation, including relevant laws and a number of key regulations were supplied in English. However many of the 42 key CIRC regulations and supporting directives and explanations were only available in Chinese. The assessment has been informed by discussions with regulators and market participants. The assessors met with staff from the CIRC Headquarters (HQ), two large regional insurance bureaus, insurance companies and intermediaries, and with the accounting and actuarial professions. The assessors are grateful for the full cooperation extended by all.

B. Institutional and Market Structure—Overview

133. The Chinese insurance market is the six largest in the world. At the end of 2009 there were 59 life insurers, 52 non-life (Property and Casualty (P&C) or property) insurers, and nine reinsurers, including one specialist credit insurer, and four specialist agricultural insurers (one of which is a mutual). The four specialist heath insurers are classified as part of the personal (life, etc.) insurance sector. Non-life insurers may now also write short term medical coverage. Eight insurance groups have been formed under holding company structures and 10 insurers have established asset management companies. Life insurance premium income in 2009 was US$109.2 billion, a penetration of 2.3 percent of GDP and a metric typical of a relatively advanced economy. In 2009 non life insurance generated US$ 53.9 billion of premium, a penetration of 1.1 percent of GDP. The P&C sector is dominated by motor insurance (which accounted for 70 percent of gross written premium) a metric more characteristic of an emerging market. This unusual pattern is likely to reflect both cultural and historical roots.

134. China's life insurance market is highly concentrated. The top 10 insurance companies account for nearly 90 percent of gross premium. With the exception of American International Assurance Company (AIA), life insurance business is not open to foreign funded companies except through joint ventures where the foreign shareholder may have up to 50 percent of the equity.[9] The non-life business is also highly concentrated and continues to be dominated by the leading P&C Insurance Group the People's Insurance Company of China (PICC).

135. The life insurance business mix has changed significantly in the last half of this decade. The traditional guaranteed return business has dropped from 42 percent to 23 percent of life policies and being replaced by Universal Life and Investment linked business. Participating business[10] throughout the decade has held approximately 55 percent of the market as it has provided a reasonably consistent and stable profit margin for the insurers and offers the possibility of an enhanced return to the policyholders.

136. The non life business mix has remained largely static. Motor and commercial property accounts for 80 percent and liability, Marine Aviation and Transit (MAT) and accident jointly account for another 11 percent. The only clear upward trend in share of premium has been in the agricultural and medical insurance lines. Household insurance accounts for only 1 percent of non-life premium and China, unlike other countries, is not seeing a boost in insurance sales from the development of the mortgage markets. It appears in part this may be due to banks not being prepared to monitor and enforce policy continuance.

---

[9] Two foreign shareholders other than American International Group (AIG) have 51 percent shareholdings reflecting special circumstances.

[10] Participating business has a low guaranteed return and offers the opportunity for additional participation in emerging profits.

C. Main Findings

137. The preconditions for effective supervision are generally met. Where principles are not full observed, generally one of two reasons applies:

- CIRC or other empowered official agencies have intentionally decided that the full implementation of the respective core principle would not fully take into account the current development phase of the Chinese insurance market or would be in conflict with constitutional arrangements. This observation may be applicable to principles on: supervisory authority, supervisory objectives, investments, derivatives and AML.

- CIRC has—in contrast to its overall comprehensive regulations—insufficient rules for some important areas of supervision. China takes a fairly pragmatic approach to regulation and will often wait for the actual emergence of business cases demanding new rules before acting. It is responsive rather than proactive and has thus missed important areas. This observation is applicable to principles on: change in control and portfolio transfer, exiting the market and insurance activity.

138. There also areas, where CIRC has strong and explicit regulation in place but its application or implementation is assessed as being too loose and also bearing substantial reputational risks for CIRC. This observation would be applicable to principles on: liabilities and solvency regime.

- CIRC has implemented a comprehensive supervisory framework and strong emphasis has been given to the implementation of suitable corporate governance rules and sufficient risk management systems for all insurance companies. The conditions for effective insurance supervision are largely met with some impediments stemming from the continuing battle of Chinese officials against corruption and bribery.

- The supervisory system is strong and well organized but CIRC has a compelling need for additional resources in its core supervisory departments. CIRC is responsible for a wide range of tasks in a very large and diversified market. It also has to be prepared for the continuing rapid growth of the scale and scope of China's many and diverse insurance markets. Today, its qualified staffing in some departments may not be adequate to permit it to carry out its responsibilities in a growing and changing market.

- The principles regarding the supervised entities are largely observed. Further regulation should be issued to facilitate portfolio transfers and to disconnect licensing arrangements from the registration of the legal entity.

- CIRC's ongoing supervision of insurance companies and the supervision of markets and consumers are tight and display a strong level of control. Most principles in these sections are fully observed. In fact, some of the supervisory reporting requirements seem almost too comprehensive and are reported too frequently. Disclosure and consumer protection are adequate and have recently been improved.

- The application of prudential requirements needs to be strengthened substantially, especially the liabilities and the solvency regimes. There are also some deficiencies in the regulation regarding quantitative investment requirements, but the authority has signaled that further regulation will be issued shortly. CIRC should also review its current arrangement with PBC on fighting Money-Laundering. The shared responsibilities are not reflected in the activities carried out solely by PBC. The lack of adequate reporting back to CIRC is not acceptable and bears a reputational risk for CIRC. Processes and responsibilities should be reviewed and restructured to address this weakness.

Table 16. China: Summary of Observance of the Insurance Core Principles

Insurance Core Principle	Comments
ICP 1 – Conditions for effective insurance supervision	The preconditions for effective supervision are largely met. Stronger enforcement is needed to eliminate a general perception of the acceptance of corruption and to minimize unethical behavior in the financial sector. CIRC bureaus have recently been engaged in an active campaign to reduce fraudulent behavior and to enforce ethical behavior of insurance company management and staff. The influence of the Chinese authorities over business development and companies' strategies is potentially hampering the desired growth of the market. China has to resolve the contradiction between a controlled market including tight control over the entry and expansion of foreign funded companies and the need to develop the life insurance market to provide sufficient coverage and innovations to facilitate the overall growth of the Chinese markets.
ICP 2 – Supervisory objectives	CIRC's supervisory objectives are defined in broad terms. Financial stability, consumer protection and fair competition could be translated into operational goals and form the basis for a mission statement of CIRC. That statement could also help new staff to engage more quickly with the authority's tasks. The CIRC's second objective and related responsibilities for the development of the domestic market (as implemented) are rather unique for a supervisor. It was made clear to the assessor that both sets of objectives are essential to the controlled and sound growth of the sector and the need to supply insurance coverage to consumers and domestic industries. Generally supervisors support the development of the sector through ensuring a level playing field and adequate and prompt supervision. As such, the more hands on developmental objectives and responsibilities of CIRC are not in line with the ICP. Moreover, the range of commercial and social objectives almost inevitably will lead to conflicts with the supervisory objectives. Possible scenarios include decisions on adequacy of pricing, product design and consumer protection and licensing in the context of regional and social development. The regulatory and commercial objectives each require very distinct mindsets and skills. It is recommended the two mandates be separated and a suitable agency be identified to take ownership of the developmental, commercial and social objectives. This would help to ensure the supervisor has a clear objective and is able to undertake its role without conflict. This would help the government and the industry to understand better the risks to safety and soundness of actions taken.
ICP 3 – Supervisory authority	CIRC is not entirely independent and free from political process. It became apparent, that the Chinese regulatory framework is based on strict control, cascading down from the state council to CIRC HQ to the insurance bureaus. In addition, the staffing levels of CIRC are not adequate. In particular, the areas of off-site monitoring, inspection, international cooperation, accounting and auditing and the staffing levels of key units

Cont

Insurance Core Principle	Comments
	in the insurance bureaus should be substantially strengthened through increased suitable staffing. As in ICP 2, it is recommended the commercial and social development objectives be disconnected from CIRC and consideration be given to establishing a development agency for the financial sector as a whole. As such, that agency could ensure a closer alignment of development in the banking, securities and insurance areas while also looking to the specific needs of each sector.
ICP 4 – Supervisory process	At this time in the development of the sector the rules based approach for supervision undertaken by CIRC is appropriate and it is not recommended that CIRC should shift to a principle based system. In fact, interviews with staff and industry, including auditors and actuaries, have confirmed that the prescriptive system currently corresponds to the business culture in China. This should be reexamined going forward to determine the feasibility and appropriateness of the rules based approach as the industry continues to change. In addition, in the future it will be necessary to consider the potential impact on the CIRC which under the rules based system requires staff sufficient to undertake the labor intensive processes. Albeit that staff for CIRC will have to increase under both a rules and principles based system, staffing levels will need to be increased substantially under a rules based system in order to adequately manage the expected enormous size of the market and the diversity of the provinces and market players.
ICP 5 – Supervisory cooperation and information sharing	The information sharing with authorities exists on an as-needs basis. It is recommended to establish information sharing in a pro-active manner and to provide those authorities supervising insurance groups with related business in China with information on the Chinese market on a regular basis. Reciprocally, CIRC should ask for respective information.
ICP 6 – Licensing	The licensing process should not be restricted to control the market entry of insurers but must also facilitate changes of insurers' strategy and ability to underwrite business. The separation of the formation of a company and insurance licensing should be made clearer. CIRC must be able to ensure that a company may be prohibited from writing new policies but still is liable and able to administer its current liabilities and contracts.
ICP 7 – Suitability of persons	An insurance company has to apply for approval before changing its external auditor. In doing so, only the firm but not the responsible partners name will be submitted to CIRC. Without further inquiries, CIRC would not be aware of a potential mismatch between the complexity of the insurance company and the experience of the responsible auditor. It is recommended, that CIRC should request more detailed information on the background and function of the external auditor. Such approach would be more in line with the general attitude to control within the regulatory approach. CIRC maintains high requirements for the suitability of key personnel. The growth of the insurance market and the demand for highly qualified and experienced management skills should be monitored. Further development of the market should not be limited by the supply of suitable personnel or worse, lead to undesirable compromises. Hence, CIRC should ensure that a general awareness exists on the need of suitable output from universities and professional bodies and should encourage insurers to facilitate adequate training courses.
ICP 8 – Changes in control and portfolio transfers	CIRC must develop a suitable regulation to facilitate the transfer of portfolios. Specific attention must be given to the transfer of liabilities, the adequacy of reserves and technical provisions, the ability of the recipient of the portfolio to meet requirements on suitability, license and internal control. A transfer should not be dependent upon the acceptance of policyholders or beneficiaries but timely notification of the intended transfer should be provided to them. A transfer of life insurance business should require the separation of the existing life policy business from the transferred business in the recipient's company.
ICP 9 – Corporate governance	CIRC has issued sufficient regulation to ensure that corporate governance is recognized as one of the key fundamentals of the Chinese supervisory framework. Given the size of the country itself, the size of the market (already large at this early phase of its development) and the low quantity of insurance companies, regulating governance and enforcing its application is paramount to a sound and safe market environment. Preparatory research for this mission, interviews with insurance companies and further

Cont

Insurance Core Principle	Comments
	conversations have raised concerns on the robustness of the system against corruption, including bribery. It is believed that a stronger effort to reduce corruption is needed. This would especially address the distribution of insurance products, the handling of insurance claims, general trustworthiness of the legal system, accessibility of courts and protection of consumer rights.
ICP 10 – Internal controls	The focus on internal control is rules based and sufficiently detailed. Reports to CIRC, both HQ and bureaus, are regularly and timely. Minutes of the various committees are submitted and analyzed. CIRC could consider asking external auditors to include in their regular audits an inspection of the risk managements systems and the internal control procedures at least for the large companies, where a full scope inspection cycle of five year might be too infrequent.
ICP 11 – Market analysis	The monthly submission required by CIRC is very substantive in size and level of detail. It is unclear to what extend the amount of data can actually be meaningfully analyzed in time: especially as data on technical performance usually does not vary significantly in that short a time period. CIRC should consider whether the monthly submission should be significantly reduced. Certain technical performance data could be required on a quarterly basis as is already the case for reinsurers.
ICP 12 – Reporting to supervisors and off-site monitoring	CIRC has established a comprehensive classification system and can now allocate supervisory resources efficiently according to the risk profile of each supervised entity. The criteria within the classification system could be further enhanced to also reflect the technical performance of life business through the usage of embedded value accounting. Moreover, impact and probability of risks should be better reflected.
ICP 13 –On-site inspection	On-site inspections should also be used to verify whether assumptions made off-site turned out to be accurate. There are merits in concentrating inspections in one department. However, the experience and understanding of how the insurance company operates and what its processes and business model are, is very important for all of CIRC's staff involved in the operational supervisory process.
ICP 14 – Preventive and corrective measures	The prevention process is thorough and comprehensive. It almost contains more rules than needed given the business culture explained above and has to be enforced in all areas, especially the prudential principles need to be enforced more rigorously. Corrective actions are solvency based and there is evidence of forbearance.
ICP 15 – Enforcement or sanctions	
ICP 16 – Winding-up or exit from the market	Specific regulation under which a voluntary exit from the market via run off (for non life insurers) or portfolio transfer/ merger can be facilitated still needs to be produced. This is relatively urgent given current market conditions including the single insurer rule. Portfolio transfers should be subject to actuarial clearance and supervisory approval but not policyholder approval.
ICP 17 – Group-wide supervision	The Chinese market has been developed with a distinct aim to limit and restrict the quantity of companies in order to maintain manageable levels. China already ranks as the six largest insurance markets in the world. Most of the developed markets within the top 10 would have at least three times the quantity of companies. It is expected that the role of insurance groups will become more significant, requiring CIRC to further develop regulation to facilitate the supervision of insurance groups. This will certainly involve centralized risk management functions and group solvency requirements allowing for diversification.
ICP 18 – Risk assessment and management	The implementation of the risk management function requires substantial efforts from both companies and CIRC. Progress and adequacy of the systems are not easily measured through off-site monitoring and supervisory reporting. The cycle for on-site inspections extends to five years. CIRC should agree to changes in regulation and require adequate audited reports for at least those companies with substantial market share or specific exposures.

Insurance Core Principle	Comments
ICP 19 – Insurance activity	The insurance activity is sufficiently well defined. CIRC assumes a high level of control over the market. Limitations on the ability of the insurance companies to further develop products or business procedures in order to gain competitive advantage exist. CIRC should prevent insurers from taking loans and pledging assets covering capital requirements or technical provisions. Product approval and off-site monitoring must lead to early recognition of shortfalls and must lead to rectification plans with immediate effect and short response times.
ICP 20 – Liabilities	CIRC should not allow insurers to maintain inadequate reserve levels. Policyholder and beneficiaries must expect CIRC to ensure minimum reserve levels at all times. Product approval and off-site monitoring must lead to early recognition of shortfalls and must lead to rectification plans with immediate effect and short response times. CIRC should also prevent insurers from writing new business for as long as reserve levels are inadequate. CIRC should prevent egregious cross-subsidizing of policies. The introduction of new accounting standards should have been applied with precautionary measures. Effects from re-measurement should have been deferred to other comprehensive income as part of equity and should have not been disbursed to shareholders for at least three years.
ICP 21 – Investments	Chinese insurers face a very narrow range of investment categories and opportunities to invest their assets. Whilst quantitative and qualitative restrictions appear to ensure a safe and sound environment, it also overly exposes the insurers to domestic interest rate and credit risks. As described under ICP 22, CIRC should issue regulations to allow for macro and portfolio hedging CIRC has to assume that investment management must be capable of engaging in hedging activities. Analysis of the financial performance of Chinese insurers has shown a strong volatility of the investment income. The performance of traditional and with profit products in particular depend on reliable and stable investment returns. Insurers should have more flexibility to achieve those returns. Micro hedges are deemed to be insufficient and not flexible enough to provide suitable protection. CIRC should issue distinct regulations governing the quality of assets covering technical provisions and capital requirements. For those categories, related party transactions should not be permitted.
ICP 22 – Derivatives and similar commitments	At the time of the assessment, insurers as a whole were not allowed to write or purchase derivatives. Thus there is limited scope to hedge investment risks. However selected exceptions were granted to six domestic insurers with adequate internal controls. Those insurers were allowed to purchase interest rate swaps on RMB as part of a pilot study. CIRC is has now issued a rule on stock index futures and is considering implementation procedures.
ICP 23 – Capital adequacy and solvency	The solvency regime is rather static and insufficiently risk based. There are two main concepts of solvency frameworks at the centre of international regulatory debate: Solvency II, a European development, taking specifics of an insurer's business model into account and also allows for a recalculation of assets and liabilities under a concept of full economic values. The second concept is the refinement of a risk-based-capital (RBC) approach, as applied in the U.S. markets. Conceptually, Solvency II might be more sophisticated but it is also far more complex in its application to insurer and supervisors. China is currently investigating what direction it should take between the two general approaches. Taking CIRC's current rules and control based approach into consideration; a move towards Solvency II might not be recommendable. In line with its current development stage a refinement of its current solvency regime would build on the current principles of static analysis of claims and premium development, assessment of asset risk, recognition of growth developments and allowances for inflation and specifics of business lines. Furthermore, a re-measurement of liabilities for solvency purposes is strongly recommended. CIRC has currently five companies operating with solvency margins below 100 percent. Those companies are still allowed to write new business but might be limited in their geographical growth. Inadequate solvency levels have existed for some of these companies for more than two quarters.

Cont

Insurance Core Principle	Comments
	As a supervisory principle, no licensed entity should be allowed to write new business for as long as the solvency levels are not above 100 percent. If management of shareholders cannot with in very limited timeframes provide capital injections, the company should be declared insolvent and be placed under the administration of the supervisor. The current situation with eight companies operating below 100 percent solvency ratios signals to the markets that breaches of capital requirement will not have serious consequences such at revocation of licenses or publicly warnings. The recognition of loadings for bank deposits with inadequately capitalized banks is paradoxical. The adequate measure would be to require companies to immediately withdraw the deposits, in order to secure policyholders and companies interests. CIRC should be aware of its potential reputational risks by failing to have an adequate solvency regulation. It also faces a reputational risk for failing to demonstrate adequate enforcement measures by permitting excessive forbearance. The forbearance is in contradiction with the overall hands-on approach and control over the supervised insurance companies. CIRC should prevent insurers from taking loans and pledging assets covering capital requirements or technical provisions.
ICP 24 – Intermediaries	
ICP 25 – Consumer protection	CIRC could introduce the disclosure of complaints per company to further enhance companies' discipline and to increase the awareness on customer satisfaction. The complaint function should be moved from the insurance association to a more independent source to enhance creditability of the process.
ICP 26 – Information, disclosure and transparency towards markets	Since the regulation on disclosure only recently has been introduced, a review process should be established to allow for modification and refinements within a timeframe of the next two years.
ICP 27 – Fraud	CIRC has increased substantially its efforts against fraud. Staffing levels should be increased to address fraud at a more appropriate level. Corruption and bribery are a concern A stronger effort and adequate staff will allow CIRC to contribute more effectively to an overall enhancement of market discipline in the financial sector.
ICP 28 – Anti-money-laundering, combating the financing of terrorism	Currently the share of responsibility for AML between PBC and CIRC and the lack of active involvement and influence of the CIRC over the process results in a significant reputational risk to the CIRC, particularly as the current system as operated by PBC is not complete. A clear accountability is needed to respond in a timely manner to the specifics of AML. The rather opaque involvement of CIRC in conjunction with the lack of influence and involvement on inspections and sanctions is not satisfactory. A decision is needed as to where the AML function will be housed and then to ensure it is carried out effectively. If it is not with the CIRC, then it is essential that CIRC be adequately informed so as to properly supervise the sector. In addition the thresholds for the reporting of suspicious transactions should be more in line with those with income levels.

D. Key Recommendations

139. The assessment team found several improvement opportunities, summarized in the Table below:

Table 17. China: Recommended Action Plan to Improve Observance of the Insurance Core Principles

Principle	Recommended Action
ICP 2 – Supervisory objectives	Financial stability, consumer protection and fair competition could be translated into operational goals and form the basis for a mission statement of CIRC. That statement could also help new staff to engage more quickly with the authority's tasks. CIRC's second objective and related responsibilities for the development of the domestic market (as implemented) are rather unique for a mainstream supervisor. It is recommended the two mandates be separated and a suitable agency be identified to take ownership of the developmental, commercial and social objectives. This would help to ensure the supervisor has a clear objective and is able to undertake its role without conflict.
ICP 3 – Supervisory authority	The staffing levels of CIRC are not adequate. In particular, the areas of off-site monitoring, inspection, international cooperation, accounting and auditing and the staffing levels of key units in the insurance bureaus should be substantially strengthened through increased suitable staffing.
ICP 6 – Licensing	The licensing process should not be restricted to control the market entry of insurers but must also facilitate changes of insurers' strategy and ability to underwrite business. CIRC must ensure that a company will be prohibited from writing new policies but still is liable and able to administer its current liabilities and contracts.
ICP 8 – Changes in control and portfolio transfers	CIRC must develop a suitable regulation to facilitate the transfer of portfolios. Specific attention must be given to the transfer of liabilities, the adequacy of reserves and technical provisions, the ability of the recipient of the portfolio to meet requirements on suitability, license and internal control. A transfer should not be dependent upon the acceptance of policyholders or beneficiaries but timely notification of the intended transfer should be provided to them. A transfer of life insurance business should require the separation of the existing life policy business from the transferred business in the recipient's company.
ICP 14 – Preventative and corrective measures	Corrective actions in line with Section 6 of the insurance law need to be applied more vigorously to insurers breaching solvency.
ICP 16 – Winding-up or exit from the market	CIRC should develop specific regulation under which an exit from the market can be facilitated via portfolio transfer or merger and which allows for run off of non life business.
ICP 20 – Liabilities	Product approval and off-site monitoring must lead to early recognition of shortfalls and must lead to rectification plans with immediate effect and short response times. CIRC should also prevent insurers from writing new business for as long as reserve levels are inadequate. CIRC has to prevent cross-subsidizing of policies. The introduction of new accounting standards should have been applied with precautionary measures. Impacts from re-measurement should have been deferred to other comprehensive income as part of equity and should not have been available to shareholders as dividends for at least three years.
ICP 23 – Capital adequacy and solvency	CIRC has to facilitate the rectification of solvency margins for five companies operating with solvency margins below 100 percent. As a supervisory principle, no licensed entity should be allowed to write new business for as long as the solvency levels are not above 100 percent. If management or shareholders cannot with in very limited timeframes arrange for capital injections, the company should be declared insolvent and be directed under the administration of the supervisor. The recognition of loadings for bank deposits with inadequately capitalized banks is paradoxical. The adequate measure would be to require companies to immediately withdraw the deposits, in order to secure policyholders and companies interests.

Cont

Principle	Recommended Action
ICP 28 – Anti-money laundering, combating the financing of terrorism	A clear accountability is needed to respond in a timely manner to the specifics of AML. The rather opaque involvement of CIRC in conjunction with the lack of influence and involvement on inspections and sanctions is not satisfactory. A decision is needed as to where the AML function will be housed and then to ensure it is carried out effectively. If it is not with the CIRC, then it is essential that CIRC be adequately informed so as to properly supervise the sector.

F. Authorities' Response

140. We appreciate the FSAP assessors' recognition of what the CIRC has achieved in supervisory enforcement, categorized supervision, market analysis, regulatory cooperation, information sharing, and consumer protection.

141. The assessors have also acknowledged the CIRC's efforts and progress made in corporate governance, internal control, group supervision, solvency regulation, risk management, and off-site supervision.

142. The assessors understand that, in the few areas where full observance has not yet been achieved, the CIRC has taken appropriate regulatory measures and approaches based on China's own conditions including its unique market environment and development stage. The regulatory philosophy we follow is consistent with IAIS's core principles for insurance regulation. We focus on prudential supervision, emphasize risk prevention, make vigorous efforts to maintain the market order and to protect consumer interests, thus we have effectively maintained the stability of the market.

143. As a response to the assessor's comment on solvency supervision, the CIRC attaches great importance to this task. Drawing upon the solvency supervisory standards of the European Union (EU) and the U.S., we have established a solvency supervisory system tailored to China's realities. The current system reflects the status quo of China as an emerging market and facilitates the stability of our insurance market. The fact that China's insurance industry remained resilient to the global financial crisis proves the risk-control ability of our solvency supervisory system. Specifically, the current system takes into account the underwriting risk, investment risk, interest rate risk, credit risk and asset liability matching risk of insurance companies. The system has the basic features of a risk-based solvency supervisory system and provides a good foundation for the transition to a comprehensively risk-based system. Currently the CIRC is studying the solvency supervisory systems in the world and dedicated to further improve its own system.

144. With respect to AML, it should be seen that China has its unique mechanism for this function. As provided by China's Anti-Money Laundering Law, the PBC leads the work of AML and other authorities should actively assist it in its work. The division of responsibilities among relevant authorities is clear. The CIRC bears its

share of responsibility and carries it out in its daily supervision. In practice, insurance institutions observe the AML rules put in place by both the PBC and the CIRC. They have established complete internal controls and other relevant measures for this purpose, and are actively carrying out the AML obligations. In order to supervise the risks of insurance companies, the CIRC carries out inspections on their internal controls, which include AML controls, and exchanges information with the PBC (the AML Bureau) through adequate channels.

145. To address the emerging issues and changes as market develops, the CIRC has been improving its rules and regulations and striving to enhance effective supervision. Since the newly revised Insurance Law was promulgated on October 1, 2009, the CIRC has formulated and introduced new rules and revised old rules covering personnel qualification, information disclosure, asset management, equity management and other aspects. Efforts have been made to further enhance industry order, strengthen corporate governance and internal control, promote risk management capabilities of insurance companies, and fundamentally safeguard the legitimate interests of the stakeholders.

146. We also appreciate the recommendations of the assessors. We will carefully study these recommendations and take them into consideration in our regulatory practices and the formulation of rules and regulations.

Annex III. Observance of Financial Sector Standards and Codes—IOSCO Objectives and Principles of Securities Regulation: A Summary

A. Introduction

147. This assessment was performed in 2010 as part of the FSAP of China. The assessment used the IOSCO Objectives and Principles of Securities Regulation (May 2003) and the Methodology for Assessing Implementation of the IOSCO Objectives and Principles of Securities Regulation (February 2008). It was assisted by a self-assessment prepared by the CSRC, public information contained on the CSRC website and the websites of other entities in China, and a review of relevant Chinese laws and regulations.

B. Institutional and Market Structure—Overview

148. The CSRC performs centralized supervision and regulation of the securities and futures markets on the Chinese mainland. China has adopted a sectoral supervision model for its financial industry, with securities market under separate supervision by CSRC. In accordance with the laws, and as duly authorized by the SC, the CSRC performs centralized and unified supervision and regulation of the nation's securities and futures markets, with the aim both of promoting soundness in the markets and promoting market development.

149. Under this arrangement, the CSRC headquarters undertake the following responsibilities: formulating, amending and revising rules and regulations concerning the securities and futures markets, making market development plans, processing key reviews and approvals, guiding and coordinating efforts in risk disposals of insolvent securities or futures companies, organizing investigation of and enforcement against material violations and non-compliances, and guiding, inspecting, promoting and coordinating the nation-wide regulatory efforts. Under the supervision of the CSRC headquarters, its 36 regional offices are responsible for front-line supervision within their respective jurisdictions.

150. SROs are critical components of the regulatory system. To supplement the regulatory activities of the CSRC, SROs including the stock and futures exchanges, SD&C, Securities Association of China (SAC), China Futures Association (CFA) are responsible for self-regulation and front-line supervision over securities/futures trading activities of their members or listed companies. In addition, the National Association of Financial Market Institutional Investors (NAFMII) was established in 2007 to oversee the trading of fixed term instruments through the inter-bank lending and bond market.

151. The CSRC is subject to the general authority of the SC which appoints the Chairman. The Chairman holds Minister rank in the Chinese Government, on the same level as the Chairmen of the CBRC and CIRC. The responsibilities of the CSRC are clearly articulated in the *Securities Law and the Law of the Peoples Republic of China on Securities Investment Funds (*henceforth the *Fund Law)* and in a series of related laws that have expanded the duties and powers of the CSRC.

152. The CSRC has broad regulatory authority over the stock and futures exchanges, the SD&C and other clearing and settlement institutions, securities companies, futures companies, and collective investment scheme (CIS) operators. Other governmental agencies in China have responsibility for discrete regulatory functions that are included in the IOSCO principles. The major authorities are described below. Others are mentioned in the detailed principle-by-principle assessment. Of particular relevance to the IOSCO assessment the Peoples Bank of China is primarily responsible in China for AML regulation, guiding and organizing the AML work of the financial sector and regulators including the CSRC and monitoring relevant fund flows. It also regulates the inter-bank lending market and inter-bank bond market, and was the Government entity which provided seed funding for the Securities Investment Protection Fund (SIPF), which was established to assist with the resolution of a large number of failed securities companies and compensate investors earlier this decade.

153. The SSE was established in 1990. At the end of 2009, SSE had a total of 870 listed companies, 1,351 listed stocks with US$ 2.78 trillion market capitalization, and US$ 5.22 trillion stock turnover. It has 107 securities firm members and seven domestic and overseas special members. Securities listed on SSE are traded through an electronic bidding system with automatic price matching according to price and time priority through the SSE's mainframe. The Shenzhen Stock Exchange was also founded in 1990, and has a Main Board, SME Board, Growth Enterprise Board (GEB) and the stock transfer agent system. The exchanges' trading and business rules are subject to the approval of the CSRC.

154. There are three commodities futures exchanges and one financial futures exchange in mainland China. These consist of the Shanghai Futures Exchange (SHFE), the Dalian Commodity Exchange (DCE), the Zhengzhou Commodity Exchange (ZCE) and the China Financial Futures Exchange (CFFEX). The CFFEX, which is owned by the other commodity futures exchanges, recently commenced trading in stock index futures, China's first financial derivative contract, and it is intended to launch other market-oriented derivatives such as options and potentially futures and options on treasury bonds and foreign exchange to diversify the financial derivatives market. The commodity exchanges' trading and business rules are subject to the approval of the CSRC.

155. The SD&C was founded in 2001 and establishes rules for participants in the clearing and settlement process, in particular for managing clearing and settlement accounts. The SD&C is required as a securities registration and clearing institution to establish securities and clearing accounts, clear and settle securities and the cash associated with securities transactions, and distribute entitlements as instructed by the issuer (Article 157 of the *Securities Law*). It has developed detailed rules to ensure its members' compliance with the relevant laws and regulations, including rules related to the administration of securities accounts, administration of clearing participants, and the administration of securities reserve funds, which are subject to the approval of the CSRC. The disciplinary powers include restricting or cancelling the use of participating accounts, and suspending or terminating the clearing participants' clearing rights.

156. There are two primary types of CIS business in China: securities investment funds managed by fund managers, and collective asset management business conducted by securities companies. Wealth management products have grown considerably in size in recent years—at the end of 2009 wealth management products of banks totaled US$ 147.6 billion, of which, investment grade products accounted for more than US$ 96.4 billion. In addition, some funds, specifically private equity style funds administered through a trust company, are regulated by the CBRC; and some other funds, specifically private equity funds linked to industry development, are regulated by the NDRC.

157. The SAC and the CFA are national SROs for the securities and futures industries respectively. They aim to implement self regulation over the securities and futures industry under the centralized supervision and regulation of the CSRC; to serve as a bridge between the government and the securities and futures industries; and to maintain fair competition in the securities and futures industries, promote transparency, fairness and equitability of the market and its healthy and steady development. The SAC and CFA are responsible for frontline supervision of members and under delegation from the CSRC conduct initial qualification examinations for members of the securities and futures industries.

158. The Chinese securities sector has seen considerable volatility but overall has grown very quickly, especially in the last five years. At the regulatory level, there have been a number of important regulatory reforms to support the movement towards a more modern capital market. The reform of non-tradable shares introduced a market-based pricing system for so-called non-tradable shares in listed companies closely held by government and semi-government authorities. The securities sector also underwent a significant overhaul in the early part of this decade following widespread solvency problems and misappropriation of funds held on behalf of clients in securities firms and funds management companies. This overhaul included introducing extensive third party custodian requirements for handling client property and risk-adjusted capital requirements for securities firms. These reforms appear to have been successful in providing greater stability to securities firms and in protecting client assets.

C. Preconditions for Effective Securities Regulation

159. The Chinese regulatory regime has adopted a clear set of accounting and auditing standards. These are well advanced in the process of converging with IFRS and IAS and which are of high and internationally acceptable quality. The accounting and audit profession is growing and developing in professional competence and capacity. Similarly, the private legal profession and the capacity of the judicial system to handle commercial disputes has also been developing, but the involvement of institutional and retail shareholders in corporate governance is less well developed. As a result, more of the burden of dealing with commercial failures that involve regulatory breaches falls onto the CSRC than in jurisdictions with more active shareholders and easier access to litigation to resolve serious disputes.

160. There are various levels of law making within China. The highest levels are laws developed by the National People's Congress (NPC) or its Standing Committee, which include the *Securities Law* and the *Fund Law*. At the next level there are Administrative Regulations promulgated by the SC subject to the Constitution and other laws. At a third level, there are rules and regulations developed and promulgated by the CSRC in accordance with (and subordinate to) the laws and regulations of the SC. These CSRC rules and regulations may be described as "Tentative" or "Trial" where they are new regulatory requirements or relate to innovations, but they have the same status as other rules or regulations promulgated by the CSRC and are enforceable as such.

161. In some cases the strict letter of the law has been buttressed by opinions issued by the Supreme People's Court, and these appear to have been effective. For example, the Supreme Court has issued opinions that establish the legality and enforceability of Article 139 of the *Securities Law* and similar provisions which establish that in the insolvency of a securities firm funds held on behalf of a client shall not be treated as part of the liquidation but remain the property of the client: see the *Circular of the Supreme People's Court on Relevant Issues Concerning the Freeze and Transfer of Funds in the Clearing Accounts of Stock or Futures Exchanges (1997)*. In the bankruptcy case of Minfa Securities, the insolvency administrator had proposed that around US$ 11.29 million worth of clients' transaction settlement assets it had secured should be regarded as property in the liquidation. The Supreme People's Court ruled that such funds did not belong to the liquidation and should be used to cover the shortfall in clients' transaction settlement funds.

D. Main Findings

162. As noted above the Chinese securities and futures industry and their regulation has undergone considerable development since the establishment of the CSRC less than 20 years ago. Reforms in recent years, in particular the non-tradable shares reforms, the introduction of stock index futures trading in 2010, and the overhaul of third party custodian and risk-based net capital requirements for securities firms, have enhanced the transparency of the market, broadened the range of available products and improved the financial soundness of intermediaries, to the considerable benefit of investor protection in China. These reforms have been carefully planned and implemented, and have been welcomed by market participants. They provide evidence of an active and strategic approach to regulation of the Chinese securities markets on

the part of the CSRC and other authorities. These reforms have built on an extensive
set of regulatory provisions which have drawn on the experience of other more
developed securities markets, the United States and Hong Kong amongst others. There
are few areas in which the regulatory framework needs further work in order to fully
meet the IOSCO standards. Some of the areas for improvement identified in this report
look to further improvements in the legal and accounting environment.

163. The Regulator: The responsibilities of the regulator responsible for securities
regulation, the CSRC, are clearly set out in three primary pieces of legislation: the
Securities Law, the *Fund Law*, and the *Regulations on the Administration of Futures
Trading*. A sectoral approach to regulation applies in China, under which the CBRC
regulates banking and banking institutions and the CIRC regulates insurance and
insurance companies. Where banking or insurance companies engage in securities
type activities, such as establishing and distributing wealth management products,
the CBRC and CIRC have corresponding regulatory authority. In addition, some
entities such as hedge funds and private equity funds are either not regulated or lightly
regulated by other entities. In the interests of avoiding regulatory arbitrage, products
performing a similar function should be regulated in a similar way, and the authorities
should pay particular attention to wealth management products in this regard. With
respect to hedge funds and private equity funds, the IOSCO Principles as in force at
the date of this assessment do not require their regulation. However, given the rapid
growth in these funds (especially private equity funds) and the potential for them to be
used as retail investment vehicles, the authorities should consider placing them under
the regulatory authority of the CSRC. The CSRC has power to develop rules and
regulatory documents within the authority granted by laws and the *Legislation Law*
for the purpose of performing its functions. It operates in practice as an independent
agency free from political or commercial interests, but as a SC administrative organ
it is required to follow civil service staffing and budgetary procedures which do not
necessarily keep pace with developments in the regulated population, and some greater
flexibility in this regard would help it discharge its regulatory functions. The CSRC's
budget is not sufficient to enable it to exercise its powers and responsibilities, given
the rapid growth in the market and the nature of other market discipline mechanisms
at this stage of China's capital market development. There is considerable attention
devoted to investor education, but significant further efforts are required to address
retail investors' understanding of the market and risk.

164. SROs: The regulatory arrangements in China place significant reliance on SROs
to perform regulatory functions, under the authority and supervision of the CSRC.
These SROs include the exchanges, clearing and settlement institutions, and industry
associations. Given the growth of the Chinese capital markets and in particular in listed
companies, retail investors and regulated entities, the SROs will need to give continued
attention and resources to their regulatory functions. While the CSRC exercises
significant authority and oversight over the SROs and communicates regularly with
them, it should consider instituting a formal program whereby it conducts regular
comprehensive inspections of the exchanges.

165. Enforcement: The CSRC has comprehensive powers related to inspection, investigation, surveillance and enforcement, and in particular has a useful power under which it can freeze assets by administrative order for the purpose of safeguarding them during the completion of an investigation. The laws and regulations provide a range of private rights of action for compensation and other action in the event of non-compliance causing damage to investors, but the legal system (in particular, the commercial courts) and the effect of market discipline provided by institutional investors and other participants on corporate governance is not as significant in China as in other jurisdictions. While private enforcement action is not a substitute for public enforcement action, supervision and regulation, it can supplement and support it. In combination, these factors undermine the capacity of private legal action to have a meaningful practical impact on compliance. Given the very high level of retail participation in the market, this means that the CSRC and authorities a greater share of the burden of ensuring compliance than in other markets. Arrangements for surveillance of abnormal trading are extensive and some substantial enforcement actions have been taken to deter market manipulation and insider trading, but there is need for continued attention and resources to enforce the laws with respect to illegal investment activity (including Ponzi schemes and bucket shops).

166. Cooperation: The CSRC has the ability to share public and non-public information with both domestic and foreign counterparts without other external process, for the purpose of performing regulatory and supervisory functions. The CSRC has established formal information sharing arrangements with the CBRC and CIRC, and with a large number of foreign securities and futures regulators. The CSRC and other domestic regulators should give more consideration to the efficacy of their cooperative arrangements, especially with respect to ensuring that products or activities that have a similar function are regulated similarly to avoid the potential for regulatory arbitrage. The CSRC is a signatory to the IOSCO Multilateral Memorandum of Understanding on Exchange of Information (MMOU) and actively makes and responds to requests for information and assistance with foreign regulators.

167. Issuers: The regulatory regime contains detailed requirements and follow-up mechanisms of the CSRC and exchanges for the disclosure of comprehensive information about financial results and risks of listed companies and other investment offers. The CSRC should promulgate a clearer requirement that advertising refer potential investors to the prospectus, similar to the requirement for CIS. The regulatory regime adequately addresses the rights and equitable treatment of shareholders, including with respect to mergers. However, the timeframes for the provision of annual and semi-annual financial statements, and the thresholds for reporting changes in substantial shareholdings, appear long by the standards in place in other major markets and should be reviewed. The regulatory regime has adopted a clear set of accounting and auditing standards which are well advanced in the process of converging with IFRS and which are of high and internationally acceptable quality. Continued attention will need to be given to the development of the private accounting and audit profession in China, and the level of fines for the provision of false or misleading financial statements should be reconsidered, to ensure that financial statements are professionally prepared and audited.

168. CIS: There are clear regulatory requirements for those that wish to operate
or market a CIS, which provide reasonable entry requirements, ongoing eligibility
and conduct rules, and requirements aimed at managing conflicts of interest. The
regulatory regime adequately provides rules governing the legal form and structure of
CIS. Segregation and protection of client assets is assured through a mandatory system
of third party custodianship, and there are comprehensive disclosure requirements
to enable a prospective investor to evaluate the suitability and prospects of the
scheme. There are adequate provisions governing valuation requirements including
audit requirements, and specific requirements concerning the pricing of subscription
to or redemptions from funds. However, the provisions related to the professional
qualifications and experience of fund managers should be reviewed as the industry
develops. Given the high level of retail participation in the market, it is very important
that all information should be provided in clear and simple language, and the CSRC
will need to monitor this closely. The CSRC should be wary of the potential for
unlicensed CIS activity, such as Ponzi schemes, to arise in the Chinese market and
give attention to detecting and deterring it.

169. Market Intermediaries: The Chinese regulatory regime requires that market
intermediaries must be licensed with the CSRC, and are subject to initial and ongoing
capital and experience and qualifications requirements. The CSRC should consider
amending its rules on investment consultants to require such consultants to disclose in
detail to clients their personal backgrounds and career records, working experience,
compliance record, investment strategies and fee structure, as the development of
an independent financial advising capacity can be an important part of markets with
significant levels of retail participation. The regulatory regime in China provides
appropriate prudential controls with respect to market intermediaries and that relate
to the risks involved in the particular businesses that market intermediaries undertake.
The initial registered capital requirements and the ongoing risk-based net capital
requirements provide a significant level of prudential buffer in respect of risks. As
the system of risk-based net capital is relatively new, the CSRC should continue to
monitor it carefully to ensure that it captures all relevant risks. The regulatory regime
requires market intermediaries to have an internal risk management function and
controls to protect the interests of clients. The CSRC could consider some extensions
of technical aspects of the regulatory regime to cover existing parts of the industry,
such as whether the concept of suitability included in the requirements for trading
in stock index futures should be more generally applied, in light of the broad retail
participation in Chinese capital markets and the need for investors to be informed
about the risks of products appropriate to their circumstances, and whether some
form of third party custodianship should apply to the management of client margins
currently held by futures companies. The Chinese regulatory regime makes adequate
provision for dealing with the failure of an intermediary, building on experience with
significant failures of securities companies in the early part of this decade. However,
the authorities should consider altering the threshold in the relevant regulations, that
in the absence of a failure to observe a rectification order that the failure "severely

threaten the order" of the market, to ensure that the CSRC can act promptly before the problem becomes too large.

170. Secondary Markets: The Chinese regulatory regime makes adequate provision for authorization and oversight of entities which wish to operate a stock or futures exchange, covering the exchanges themselves, admission of products to trading, trading information, and execution procedures. The regulatory regime provides for market authorities to monitor the risk of large and open positions that pose a risk to the market or clearing. In the event of default, there are procedures in place to ensure that the problem is isolated and does not affect other market participants, and for apportioning any loss appropriately. While CSRC staff maintain regular dialogue with the stock exchanges especially on listed company disclosure and trading issues, and membership and trading rules of the exchanges are subject to approval by the CSRC, instituting a formal program whereby it conducts regular comprehensive on-site inspections like for other exchanges should also be considered. The CSRC and exchanges have implemented systems for the ongoing surveillance and supervision of trading to ensure market integrity, and have devoted considerable human and technological resources to detecting and deterring insider trading and market manipulation. At the same time, given the size of the market, its rapid growth, and the enormous interest generated by new listings, the number of abnormal trades detected and on which action is taken seems low. The CSRC should consider some extra and continuing efforts to detect and deter unfair trading practices.

Table 18. China: Summary of Observance of the IOSCO Principles

Principle	Findings
Principle 1. The responsibilities of the regulator should be clearly and objectively stated	The responsibilities of the regulator responsible for securities regulation, the CSRC, are clearly set out in three primary laws: the *Securities Law*, the *Fund Law*, and the *Regulations on the Administration of Futures Trading*. The CSRC has power to develop rules and regulatory documents within the authority granted by laws and the *Legislation Law* for the purpose of performing its functions. It is required to follow the legal principles established by the *Legislation Law* and the *Constitution of the Peoples Republic of China*, including principles of transparency. In practice, the CSRC has developed several rules, regulations and statement of guidance or opinion related to its functions, and market participants express satisfaction with the transparency of the consultation process.
	A sectoral approach to regulation applies in China, under which the CBRC regulates banking and banking institutions and the CIRC regulates insurance and insurance companies. Where such institutions engage in securities type activities, such as establishing and distributing wealth management products, the CBRC and CIRC have corresponding regulatory authority. There is potential for gaps and inequities to arise where products with similar characteristics are not regulated in the same manner, so a review of the requirements across the banking, insurance and securities sectors with respect to wealth management products should be conducted to ensure consistent regulatory approaches and avoid any unjustified differential treatment.

Cont

Principle	Findings
Principle 2. The regulator should be operationally independent and accountable in the exercise of its functions and powers	The CSRC operates in practice as an independent agency free from political or commercial interests. The reforms that it has introduced in recent years, including the tradable shares reform, introduction of stock index futures, and reforms aimed at redressing solvency and conduct problems of securities and fund management companies provide strong indications of its independence. However, it is not entirely operationally independent in form from political process. The Chairman is appointed by the State Council and subject to its oversight with respect to the operating and governance structure. The provisions concerning the potential liability of staff should be made clearer that they do not bear any liability for the bona fide discharge of their functions and duties and that their protection is not subject to the discretion of the CSRC. The CSRC's budget is not sufficient to enable it to exercise its powers and responsibilities, having regard to the rapid growth in the market and the nature of other market discipline mechanisms at this stage of China's capital market development, notwithstanding positive developments in the accounting and legal framework, There is a strong system of accountability in place for regulatory and administrative decisions.
Principle 3. The regulator should have adequate powers, proper resources and the capacity to perform its functions and exercise its powers	The powers and authorities of the CSRC are sufficient, taking into account the nature of China's capital markets. However, the CSRC's budget has not kept adequate pace with the growth in regulated entities and activities and its salaries are a very small proportion of comparable industry standards, which constrains the CSRC's ability to retain staff with industry experience.
Principle 4. The regulator should adopt clear and consistent regulatory processes	The CSRC adopts clear and consistent processes in making regulatory and administrative decisions and provides adequate opportunities for review. There is some considerable attention given to investor education, but significant further efforts are required to address retail investors' understanding of the market and risk.
Principle 5. The staff of the regulator should observe the highest professional standards	The CSRC staff observes high professional standards including avoiding conflicts of interests and preserving the confidentiality of information obtained in the course of their duties. The CSRC staff is subject to legislative provisions and a written code of conduct, which requirements not to hold to trade in securities and futures, not to hold any positions in regulated entities, and not to misuse information.
Principle 6. The regulatory regime should make appropriate use of SROs that exercise some direct oversight responsibility for their respective areas of competence and to the extent appropriate to the size and complexity of the markets	The regulatory arrangements in China place appropriate and significant reliance on SROs to perform regulatory functions, under the authority and supervision of the CSRC. These SROs include the exchanges, clearing and settlement institutions, and industry associations.
Principle 7. SROs should be subject to the oversight of the regulator and should observe standards of fairness and confidentiality when exercising powers and delegated responsibilities	The SROs are subject to appropriate authorization and oversight arrangements exercised by the CSRC to provide assurance of their ability to perform their functions. Given the growth of the Chinese capital markets and in particular in listed companies and regulated entities, the SROs will need to give continued attention and resources to their regulatory functions. The CSRC should consider instituting a formal program whereby it conducts regular comprehensive on-site inspections of the exchanges.
Principle 8. The regulator should have comprehensive inspection, investigation and surveillance powers	The CSRC has comprehensive powers related to inspection, investigation and surveillance.

Cont

Principle	Findings
Principle 9. The regulator should have comprehensive enforcement powers	The CSRC has comprehensive enforcement powers, and in particular has a useful power under which it can freeze assets by administrative order for the purpose of safeguarding them during the completion of an investigation. The threshold for exercise of its formal investigation powers should be amended to provide the regulator with more discretion on when to bring those powers to bear. The laws and regulations provide a range of private rights of action for compensation and other action in the event of non-compliance causing damage to investors, but the legal system (in particular the commercial courts) and the effect of market discipline provided by institutional investors and other participants on corporate governance is not as significant in China as in other jurisdictions. In combination, these factors undermine the capacity of private legal action to have a meaningful practical impact on compliance. Given the very high level of retail participation in the market, this means that the CSRC and authorities a greater share of the burden of ensuring compliance than in other markets.
Principle 10. The regulatory system should ensure an effective and credible use of inspection, investigation, surveillance and enforcement powers and implementation of an effective compliance program	The CSRC oversees a credible and active inspection, surveillance, and investigation system which provides adequate oversight of the market. The CSRC should consider means of encouraging investors who have a problem to raise their concerns with the CSRC, both to bolster the market intelligence available from this source and to boost investor confidence in the regulatory framework. Arrangements for surveillance of abnormal trading are extensive and some substantial enforcement actions have been taken to deter market manipulation and insider trading, but there is need for continued attention and resources to enforce the laws with respect to illegal investment activity (including Ponzi schemes and bucket shops).
Principle 11. The regulator should have the authority to share both public and non-public information with domestic and foreign counterparts	The CSRC has the ability to share public and non-public information with both domestic and foreign counterparts without other external process, for the purpose of performing regulatory and supervisory functions.
Principle 12. Regulators should establish information sharing mechanisms that set out when and how they will share both public and non-public information with their domestic and foreign counterparts	The CSRC has established formal information sharing arrangements with the CBRC and CIRC, and with a large number of foreign securities and futures regulators. The CSRC and other domestic regulators should give more consideration to the efficacy of their cooperative arrangements, especially with respect to ensuring that products or activities that have a similar function are regulated similarly to avoid the potential for regulatory arbitrage.
Principle 13. The regulatory system should allow for assistance to be provided to foreign regulators who need to make inquiries in the discharge of their functions and exercise of their powers	The CSRC is a signatory to the IOSCO MMOU and actively makes and responds to requests for information and assistance with foreign regulators.
Principle 14. There should be full, timely and accurate disclosure of financial results and other information that is material to investors' decisions	The regulatory regimes contains detailed requirements and follow up mechanisms of the CSRC and exchanges for the disclosure of comprehensive information about financial results and risks of listed companies and other investment offers. The CSRC should consider promulgating a clearer prohibition on advertising unless it refers potential investors to the prospectus, similar to the requirement for CIS. The timeframes for the provision of annual and semi-annual financial statements appear long by the standards in place in other major markets and should be reviewed. In addition, continued attention will need to be given to the development of the private accounting and audit profession in China, and the level of fines for the provision of false or misleading financial statements should be reconsidered, to ensure that financial statements are professionally prepared and audited.

Cont

Principle	Findings
Principle 15. Holders of securities in a company should be treated in a fair and equitable manner	The regulatory regime adequately addresses the rights and equitable treatment of shareholders, including with respect to mergers. While the Law makes adequate provision for these matters, the extent to which a private institutional shareholder or group of retail shareholders can practically take action through the Court system appears to be constrained by the cost and by the capacity of the courts. Hence, the practical effect is that market discipline is inadequate to enable enforcement of these rights or compliance with these obligations, which places more burden to deal with cases of non-compliance on the CSRC or the SROs. The reporting obligation for changes in substantial shareholding (currently for changes of 5 percent) should be reviewed, in keeping with the standards in other major markets.
Principle 16. Accounting and auditing standards should be of a high and internationally acceptable quality	The Chinese regulatory regime has adopted a clear set of accounting and auditing standards which are well advanced in the process of converging with IFRS and which are of high and internationally acceptable quality. There is a need to continue to develop the size and experience of the accounting and audit profession in China, given the significant role that accountants and auditors play in providing assurance on the accuracy and completeness of financial statements of listed companies and other investment vehicles.
Principle 17. The regulatory system should set standards for the eligibility and the regulation of those who wish to market or operate a CIS	There are clear regulatory requirements for those that wish to operate or market a CIS, which provide reasonable entry requirements, ongoing eligibility and conduct rules, and requirements aimed at managing conflicts of interest. The provisions related to the professional qualifications and experience of fund managers should be reviewed as the industry develops. The CSRC should be wary of the potential for unlicensed CIS activity, such as Ponzi schemes, to arise in the Chinese market and give attention to detecting and deterring it. The provisions relating to delegations, and in particular a requirement that the fund manager, custodian or securities company maintain adequate oversight of the actions of delegates, should be made clearer.
Principle 18. The regulatory system should provide for rules governing the legal form and structure of CIS and the segregation and protection of client assets	The regulatory regime adequately provides rules governing the legal form and structure of CIS. Segregation and protection of client assets is assured through a mandatory system of third party custodianship.
Principle 19. Regulation should require disclosure, as set forth under the principles for issuers, which is necessary to evaluate the suitability of a CIS for a particular investor and the value of the investor's interest in the scheme	There are comprehensive disclosure requirements for CIS which provide the information necessary to enable a prospective investor to evaluate the suitability and prospects of the scheme. There are adequate provisions governing valuation requirements to enable an investor to determine the value of their investment. Given the high level of retail participation in the market, it is very important that all information should be provided in clear and simple language, and the CSRC will need to monitor this closely.
Principle 20. Regulation should ensure that there is a proper and disclosed basis for assets valuation and the pricing and the redemption of units in a CIS	There are detailed regulatory requirements governing the valuation of CIS assets including audit requirements. There are also specific requirements concerning the pricing of subscription to or redemptions from funds.
Principle 21. Regulation should provide for minimum entry standards for market intermediaries	The Chinese regulatory regime requires that market intermediaries must be licensed with the CSRC, and are subject to initial and ongoing capital and experience and qualifications requirements. The CSRC should consider amending its rules on securities and futures investment consultants to require such consultants to disclose in detail to clients their personal backgrounds and career records, working experience, compliance record, investment strategies and fee structure, as the development of an independent financial advising capacity can be an important part of markets with significant levels of retail participation.

Principle	Findings
Principle 22. There should be initial and ongoing capital and other prudential requirements for market intermediaries that reflect the risks that the intermediaries undertake	The regulatory regime in China provides appropriate prudential controls with respect to market intermediaries and that relate to the risks involved in the particular businesses that market intermediaries undertake. The initial registered capital requirements and the ongoing risk-based net capital requirements provide a significant level of prudential buffer in respect of risks. As the system of riskbased net capital is relatively new, the CSRC should continue to monitor it carefully to ensure that it captures all relevant risks.
Principle 23. Market intermediaries should be required to comply with standards for internal organization and operational conduct that aim to protect the interests of clients, ensure proper management of risk, and under which management of the intermediary accepts primary responsibility for these matters	The regulatory regime requires market intermediaries to have an internal risk management function and controls to protect the interests of clients. The concept of suitability included in the requirements for trading in stock index futures should be more generally applied to trading in both futures and securities, given the need for retail investors to be provided with sufficient information about products and services to be able to make an informed investment decision. The recently introduced "Know-your-client" regulations for securities companies should be carefully monitored to ensure that they are resulting in investors making better informed investment decisions, given the growth of the market and the level of retail participation in it. In light of the apparent effectiveness of the third party custodian requirements for securities firms and fund management companies in preventing problems of misappropriation of client assets, the CSRC should consider whether some form of third party custodianship should apply to the management of client margins currently held by futures companies.
Principle 24. There should be a procedure for dealing with the failure of a market intermediary in order to minimize damage and loss to investors and to contain systemic risk	The Chinese regulatory regime makes adequate provision for dealing with the failure of an intermediary, building on experience with significant failures of securities companies in the early part of this decade. However, the authorities should consider altering the threshold in the relevant regulations, that the failure "severely threaten the order" of the market, to ensure that the CSRC can act promptly before the problem becomes too large.
Principle 25. The establishment of trading systems including securities exchanges should be subject to regulatory authorization and oversight	The Chinese regulatory regime makes adequate provision for authorization and oversight of entities which wish to operate a stock or futures exchange, covering the exchanges themselves, admission of products to trading, trading information and execution procedures. While CSRC staff maintains regular dialogue with the stock exchanges especially on listed company disclosure and trading issues, annual inspections like for other exchanges should also be considered. The CSRC should also consider providing more autonomy to the stock exchanges in choosing its chief executive.
Principle 26. There should be ongoing regulatory supervision of exchanges and trading systems, which should aim to ensure that the integrity of trading is maintained through fair and equitable rules that strike an appropriate balance between the demands of different market participants	The CSRC and exchanges have implemented systems for the ongoing surveillance and supervision of trading, to ensure market integrity. Membership and trading rules of the exchanges are subject to approval by the CSRC.
Principle 27. Regulation should promote transparency of trading	The regulations require the provision of pre- and post-trade information to market participants on a timely basis, including requirements to provide such information to all participants on an equitable basis.
Principle 28. Regulation should be designed to detect and deter manipulation and other unfair trading practices	The CSRC and exchanges have devoted considerable human and technological resources to detecting and deterring insider trading and market manipulation. At the same time, given the size of the market, its rapid growth, and the enormous interest generated by new listings, the number of abnormal trades detected and on which action is taken seems low. The CSRC should consider some extra and continuing efforts to detect and deter unfair trading practices.

Cont

Principle	Findings
Principle 29. Regulation should aim to ensure the proper management of large exposures, default risk and market disruption	The regulatory regime provides for market authorities to monitor the risk of large and open positions that pose a risk to the market or clearing. In the event of default, there are procedures in place to ensure that the problem is isolated and does not affect other market participants, and for apportioning any loss appropriately.
Principle 30. Systems for clearing and settlement of securities transactions should be subject to regulatory oversight, and designed to ensure that they are fair, effective and efficient and that they reduce systemic risk	Not assessed. Please refer to the separate CPSS/IOSCO assessment of payment, clearing and settlement systems.

E. Key Recommendations

171. The assessment team found several improvement opportunities, summarized in the Table below:

Table 19. China: Recommended Action Plan to Improve Implementation of the IOSCO Principles

Principle	Recommended Action
Principle 1	Where banks or insurance companies engage in securities type activities, such as establishing and distributing wealth management products, they should be regulated in the same manner as wealth management products regulated by the CSRC, to avoid regulatory arbitrage. A review of the requirements applying to wealth management products across banking, insurance and securities should be conducted to ensure consistent approaches and to avoid gaps or unjustified differential treatment.
Principles 2 and 3	The operational budget of the CSRC should be adjusted according to the size of the regulated population, and some freedom should be provided to allow the CSRC to structure itself and pay salaries which enable it to retain staff with appropriate qualifications and industry experience. The provisions concerning the potential liability of staff should be clarified to ensure that staff does not bear liability for the bona fide discharge of their functions and duties.
Principle 4	The CSRC, SIPF, and SROs should increase their efforts to educate investors about the market and risk.
Principle 7	Given the growth of the Chinese capital markets and in particular in listed companies and regulated entities, the SROs will need to give continued attention and resources to their regulatory functions. The CSRC should consider instituting a formal program whereby it conducts regular comprehensive on-site inspections of the exchanges.
Principle 9	It would be useful and provide greater legal certainty to the CSRC in its enforcement role if the threshold for exercise of its formal statutory investigation powers were amended to provide greater discretion on when it may bring those powers to bear.
Principle 10	The CSRC should consider means of encouraging investors who have a problem to raise their concerns with the CSRC, both to bolster the market intelligence available from this source and to boost investor confidence in the regulatory framework. In addition the CSRC needs to devote continued attention and resources to enforcing the laws with respect to illegal investment activity (including Ponzi schemes and bucket shops).

217

Cont

Principle	Recommended Action
Principle 12	The CSRC and other domestic regulators should give more consideration to the efficacy of their cooperative arrangements, especially with respect to ensuring that products or activities that have a similar function are regulated similarly to avoid the potential for regulatory arbitrage.
Principle 14	The CSRC should consider promulgating a clearer prohibition on advertising unless it refers potential investors to the prospectus. The level of fines for the provision of false or misleading financial statements should be reconsidered. The statutory timeframes for the provision of annual and semi-annual reports by listed companies should be reviewed.
Principle 15	The obligation to report changes in substantial shareholdings (currently only for changes of over 5 percent) should be reviewed, in keeping with the standards in other major markets.
Principle 16	Continued attention should be given to the development of the private accounting and audit profession in China, to ensure that financial statement are professionally prepared and audited.
Principle 17	The provisions related to the professional qualifications and experience of fund managers should be reviewed as the industry develops. The CSRC should be wary of the potential for unlicensed CIS activity, such as Ponzi schemes, to arise in the Chinese market and give attention to detecting and deterring it. The provisions relating to delegations, and in particular that the fund manager, custodian or securities company maintain adequate oversight of the performance of a delegate, should be made clearer.
Principle 21	The CSRC should consider amending its rules on investment consultants to require such consultants to disclose in detail to clients their personal backgrounds and career records, working experience, compliance record, investment strategies and fee structure, as the development of an independent financial advising capacity can be an important part of markets with significant levels of retail participation.
Principle 22	As the system of risk-based net capital is relatively new, the CSRC should continue to monitor it carefully to ensure that it captures all relevant risks.
Principle 23	The concept of suitability included in the requirements for trading in stock index futures should be more generally applied to trading in both futures and securities, given the need for retail investors to be provided sufficient information about products and services to be able to make an informed investment decision. In light of the apparent effectiveness of the third party custodian requirements for securities firms and fund management companies in preventing problems of misappropriation of client assets, the CSRC should consider whether some form of third party custodianship should apply to the management of client margins currently held by futures companies. The recently introduced "Know-your-client" regulations for securities companies should be carefully monitored to ensure that they are resulting in investors making better informed investment decisions, given the growth of the market and the level of retail participation.
Principle 24	The authorities should consider altering the threshold in the relevant regulations for intervention in the failure of a market intermediary, that the failure "severely threaten the order" of the market, to ensure that the CSRC can act promptly before the problem becomes too large.
Principle 25	Annual inspections of the stock exchanges should be instituted, as they are for futures exchanges. The CSRC should consider providing more autonomy to the stock exchanges in choosing its chief executive.

Cont

Principle	Recommended Action
Principle 28	The CSRC should consider some extra and continuing efforts to detect and deter unfair trading practices, including: • Educating company officers, officers of securities and futures companies and related parties that insider trading and other market manipulation is a criminal offence; • Educating prosecutors and judges about the impact that insider trading has on investor confidence in the market; • Redoubling efforts at investigating suspicious trading around events likely to involve it, like initial public offerings (IPOs) and merger announcements, and lowering the thresholds for investigating or making enquiries; • Considering whether special rules should be developed to suspend or quarantine the proceeds of suspicious trades, including considering lowering the threshold of the level of suspicion (for freezing or quarantining actions) or altering the definition of abusive or suspicious trades to facilitate taking civil or disciplinary action; and • Considering measures related to product design, especially in relation to futures products, to make them sufficiently broad-based that it is difficult for insider trading or market manipulation to be successful.

F. Authorities' Response

172. CSRC appreciates the immense time, efforts and resources devoted by the FSAP Assessors, the World Bank and the International Monetary Fund, to the FSAP assessment, and to the compiling of the *Report of Observance of Standards and Codes: IOSCO Assessment of Securities Markets* (hereinafter: *the Report*). *The Report* has, in a general sense, managed to reflect the implementation of the IOSCO objectives and principles by China's securities and futures regulatory system. We fully understand how challenging and complex it was to conduct such a project as to review China's capital market, the world's largest emerging market in transition. Therefore, we marvel at and are moved by how much the Assessors managed to accomplish in relatively limited amount of time. They held scores of meetings with the CSRC headquarters and regional offices. They met with various regulated entities, SROs, service providers and local governmental officials. They also went through colossal volumes of reading materials. The Assessors have not only conducted comprehensive reviews of China's capital market and its regulation, but also put forward many valuable comments and recommendations.

173. We are grateful for the opportunity to make a formal response to *the Report*. We identify with most of *the Report*, including its major Findings and part of the Recommendations. To start with, *the Report* highly recognizes the development and achievements of China's capital market over the past two decades, as well as the regulatory efforts thereof, noting "Reforms in recent years, in particular the nontradable shares reforms, the introduction of stock index futures trading in 2010, and the overhaul of third party custodian and risk-based net capital requirements for securities firms, have enhanced the transparency of the market, broadened the range of available products and improved the financial soundness of intermediaries, to the considerable benefit of investor protection in China. These reforms have been

219

carefully planned and implemented, and have been welcomed by market participants. They provide evidence of an active and strategic approach to regulation of the Chinese securities markets on the part of the CSRC and other authorities." Meantime, *the Report* also points out that these reforms have built on an extensive set of regulatory provisions which have drawn on the experience of other more developed securities markets, and that there are few areas in which the regulatory framework does not meet the IOSCO standards. In addition, *the Report* acknowledges that "the Chinese regulatory regime has adopted a clear set of accounting and auditing standards which are well advanced in the process of converging with the IFRS and IAS and which are of high and internationally accepted quality."

174. After reading the Recommendations of *the Report*, we recognize that all of them are worthy of immense attention and some of the Recommendations have already been incorporated into our work plans. For example:

a. *Regarding the regulator*

175. With lessons drawn from the latest financial crisis, we identify with relevant Recommendations in *the Report*, such as strengthening regulatory coordination among different Regulators (i.e., the CSRC, the CBRC, and the CIRC), placing unregulated markets and products under regulation, allowing greater flexibility for the Regulator in terms of staffing and budget, clarifying relevant provisions to ensure that regulatory staff do not bear liability for the bona fide discharge of their functions and duties, etc. In response to these Recommendations, China's regulatory authorities will take further measures to enhance the efficacy of the CBRC-CSRC-CIRC MOU to avoid potential regulatory gap. Meantime, China's regulatory authorities are taking active measures that will cover the previously unregulated institutions and products (e.g., private equity funds). With regard to Recommendations to increase regulatory resources and to exempt staff from liability for the bona fide discharge of duties, the CSRC will further consult with relevant government agencies, as well as legislative and judicial authorities. We believe more regulatory resources that are proportionate to China's political system, economic status and the overall income level of its financial industry will manage to satisfy the regulatory demand of an ever-expanding market.

b. *Regarding SROs*

176. We agree with *the Report* that the SROs will need to give continued attention and resources to their regulatory functions; and that the CSRC, SIPF, and SROs should increase their efforts to educate investors about the market and risk. We recognize that given the rapid growth of the Chinese capital market and in particular in listed companies and regulated entities, the functions of SROs need to be further tapped into. The CSRC will enhance its regulation of and communication with the SROs, and will seriously consider relevant Recommendation to conduct regular comprehensive onsite inspections of the stock exchanges.

177. However, we cannot agree with some Findings and Recommended Actions in

the Report, which we think are misunderstandings and erroneous. We feel that such misunderstandings and errors are partly due to the lack of sufficient understanding of China's capital market, its features and mechanisms; and partly due to the failure to acknowledge the remedies that have already been put in place, or perhaps to the lack of trust in the efficacy of existing mechanisms and measures. In some cases, *the Report* even denies, without sufficient proof that such regulatory practices are ineffective, some tried-and-trusted practices that are unique to the Chinese market. We would like to express our concerns.

c. *Regarding enforcement*

178. We do not think *the Report* has sufficiently reflected CSRC's efforts and achievements in cracking down on illegal investment and insider-trading. In 2006, the Steering Group on Cracking Down upon Illegal Securities Activities was jointly established by the CSRC and Ministry of Public Security. With the aim to organize and coordinate domestic efforts in combating illegal securities activities, the work of this Steering Group has yielded visible results. In our daily work, the CSRC monitors various public news media including the internet, in order to timely detect clues of securities violations for prompt handling. In 2001, the CSRC enacted the *Notice on Implementing an Incentive Mechanism for the Reporting of Illegal and Fraudulent Securities and Futures Trading,* encouraging investors to blow whistles on illegal securities and futures activities. Pursuant to China's securities laws, any securities or futures violation that exceeds RMB 300 thousand constitutes a crime, and shall be referred by the CSRC to public security authorities. To sum up, illegal investment activities akin to Ponzi schemes and boiler rooms have been effectively detected and punished.

d. *Regarding intermediaries*

179. *The Report* recommends that there should be initial and ongoing capital and other prudential requirements for market intermediaries that reflect the risks that the intermediaries undertake. *The Report* also recommends that "as the system of risk based net capital is relatively new, the CSRC should continue to monitor it carefully to ensure that it captures all relevant risks." However, we believe that CSRC's supervision of net capital is sufficient and appropriate. The risk-based net capital system, featured by off-site supervision and on-site inspection, and timely and effective regulatory measures taken against problematic intermediaries, has proved to capture risks very well. Moreover, ever since 2007, the CSRC has been continuously monitoring and assessing the net-capital based risk regulatory system via IT monitoring platforms, and requires regular stress-test thereof.

180. In recent years, the CSRC has made a series of improvement on market infrastructure, and the futures market has achieved a great progress. The monitoring system of the secured custody of futures margins has taken into full consideration of the characteristics of futures trading, and the status quo of the market. It has played a significant and indispensable role in securing a healthy and stable development of the

futures market. We wish to share the experience of our innovative regulatory system with regulators from other countries, and to enhance financial regulation through strengthening communication.

e. *Regarding accounting and auditing standards*

181. We regret to say that we cannot identify with the Rating result of IOSCO Principle 16. In order to ensure high quality auditing for listed companies and other market players, the CSRC has established a qualification license system, allowing only accounting firms that have obtained the qualification license to perform auditing for listed companies and other market players. The CSRC conducts all-round regulation including onsite inspection to the accounting firms with relevant qualifications (currently 53 firms), listed companies and other major market players. Judging from the reality, the size and professional capability of accountants and auditors are enough to satisfy the needs of the capital market.

f. *Conclusion*

182. While we may not agree with everything *the Report* says, we fully agree with what the Assessors kindly reminded during one of our numerous meetings—that we should not take pride in the findings, nor rest on our past laurels. In this sense, the FSAP Assessment stands as a good chance for us to retrospect the past and take a prudent look into the future. After all, given the tremendous changes that the world is undergoing, China's capital market is exposed to profound changes and challenges, both home and abroad, while its regulators are encountered with an increasingly complex market and ever-growing tasks of maintaining sound and steady growth. An incomplete list of the challenges that we are facing include issues such as how to further build and improve the market legal framework, enhance enforcement and deterrence, so as to better protect the lawful rights of investors; how to strengthen regulatory coordination and function-based regulation with regard to various wealth management products offered to the public, so as to minimize potential regulatory gaps; how to regulate the once unregulated markets and products, striking appropriate balance between financial innovation and regulation; how to prevent and resolve systemic risks, strengthen the oversight of cross-border capital flow and sound early warnings of risks from abroad; how to cultivate sophisticated investors and encourage institutional investors, etc. We recognize that they are but some of the challenges we are faced with, that call for our unremitting effort and commitment. As regulators of China's capital market, we have a long and promising way ahead of us.

Annex IV. Observance of Financial Sector Standards and Codes—Assessment of Observance of CPSS Core Principles for Systemically Important Payment Systems: A Summary

A. Introduction

183. The assessment was conducted in June 2010. In addition to the 2001 CPSS-CPSIPS Report, the methodology used follows the Guidance Note for Assessing Observance of CPSIPS prepared by the IMF and the World Bank in collaboration with the Committee for Payment and Settlement System (CPSS) in August 2001.

184. The information used included all relevant laws, rules and procedures governing the systems, the abundant material available on the issue inside and outside the central bank.[11] In addition, extensive discussions were held with regulators—PBC, MOF, CSRC, CBRC, and SAFE; several stakeholders in the Chinese Payments System, including the big four commercial banks, joint stock commercial banks, city commercial banks, policy banks, foreign banks, and rural banks,[12] funds management companies, the card operator (China Union Pay), the China Foreign Exchange Trade Center (CFETC) and securities depositories—China Central Depository & Clearing Co., Ltd. (CCDC) and China Securities and Clearing Corporation Limited (SD&C). A self assessment by the PBC of the country's SIPS with the CPSS Core Principles as well as of the central bank's responsibilities in applying the Core Principles (CPs) was provided prior to the mission. The self-assessment was prepared by the PBC Payment and Settlement Department, in close consultation with the major stakeholders of the China National Payments System (CNPS).

B. Institutional and Market Structure

185. In recent years, the PBC has carried out a major and comprehensive reform of the CNPS. The PBC implemented the CNAPS, which consists of the HVPS and the Bulk Electronic Payment System (BEPS). The HVPS system currently operates in a tiered way (multi-entry point) with a national processing center (NPC) and 32 local processing centers (LCFs). The HVPS system is interconnected to many trading, payments, and securities settlement systems (SSS) to allow for central bank money settlement. In addition, there are numerous cheque clearing houses around the country administered by the PBC local offices or delegated to banks. China Union Pay (CUP) handles the clearance of cards transactions whose balances are settled in the HVPS.

---

[11] The China Payment System Development Reports, 2007, 2008, and 2009, prepared by the PBC Payment and Settlement Department were particularly relevant.

[12] Bank of China (BoC), Industrial Commercial Bank of China (ICBC), China Construction Bank (CCB), Agricultural Bank of China (ABC), Bank of Beijing (BOB), China Development Bank (CDB), Bank of Communication, Shanghai Pudong Development Bank, Standard Chartered Bank, HSBC, Bank of East Asia (BOEA), JP Morgan-Chase, and Shandong United Rural Cooperative

Also automated clearinghouses (ACHs) and other systems handle clearance and settlement for a variety of payment instruments.

186. The HVPS is a systemically important payment system, as it is the backbone of the national payments system in China. The HVPS handled transactions for a value of CY 804 trillion in 2009, approximately 24 times the GDP value. Thus, the HVPS is being assessed against the ten CPSIPS of the CPSS and the four responsibilities of the central banks in applying the CPSIPS. The BEPS is not currently a systemically important payment system. However, its importance for an efficient settlement of the interbank payment system is growing.

187. The cheque clearinghouses around the country also handle an important value of transactions. The gross value of cheques issued in 2009 reached a value of CY 248 trillion in 2009, about 7.4 times the GDP. However, of this amount, 350 million cheques are interbank cheques valued at about CY 62.5 trillion. This means that the majority of the cheques issued in the country are "on us" cheques. Also, ACHs handled CY 69 trillion in 2009, about two times the GDP, relatively important (though not major) for a big country like China. Thus, neither the cheque clearinghouses nor the ACHs have been considered systemically important in this assessment but their relative importance has been taken into consideration in the assessment of Responsibility B and C.

188. Regarding the use of payment instruments, China is evolving to a more intensive use of non-cash payment instruments, especially cards. The relationship of cash (M0) to GDP has been declining since the beginning of the 2000 from a level of 14.8 percent of GDP in 2000 to 11.2 percent in 2009. Bank cards issuance have been increasing at a high pace and approximately 2.07 billion had been issued at end-2009, of which 1.88 billion were debit cards. Bank cards have therefore become the primary non-cash payment instrument in China accounting for over 90 percent on the total non-cash volume in 2009.

189. Domestic foreign exchange (FX) transactions are mostly executed at the CFETC. The majority of participants settle their transactions bilaterally while 26 participants use a net clearing model and the CFETC acts as CCP at end-2010. Settlement of the CY leg occurs through the HVPS and settlement of the foreign currency leg with domestic settlement banks, at which participants hold FX accounts. The mission was not provided with complete data of the transactions cleared and settled through the multilateral arrangement nor has the PBC conducted an assessment of this payment system. However, in light of the nature of these transactions and the potential systemic importance of the system, the PBC is urged to assess the compliance of this system with international standards as soon as possible.

190. The China Domestic Foreign Currency Payment System (FCPS) was launched in April 2008 to handle the clearing and settlement of domestic foreign currency denominated transactions. The FCPS is a Real-Time Gross Settlement (RTGS) system and currently handles payment transactions in seven foreign currencies. The values settled in the system do not show a systemic importance of the system.

C. Payment Systems Oversight

191. The PBC powers to oversee payment and settlement systems have a sound and clear legal basis, CSRC has overlapping oversight powers on the securities settlements. The PBC oversight and regulatory powers over retail payments, interbank payments, securities settlements and related functions are recognized in the legal framework. These powers are articulated in the Article 4 of the "Peoples Bank of China law." The securities commission also has oversight powers over securities settlements, including government securities, derived from Article 179 of the "Securities law." A formal memorandum of understanding (MoU) defines general cooperation arrangements among the PBC, MOF and other authorities, such as the CSRC and the CBRC. There is no specific MoU defining the modus operandi of these authorities over payment and settlement systems, however, there have been frequent coordinated actions and regular meetings at the technical level.

192. The PBC carries out its oversight function over all payment arrangements in the country. In addition to overseeing the systemically important payment systems in the country, the PBC has played a catalyst role in reforming interbank payment arrangements in China. Recently, The PBC oversight has been extended to nonbank payment service providers. However, the PBC has not issued a comprehensive document covering the objectives, scope, instruments and institutional arrangements of its oversight function as yet.

193. The PBC has implemented a data analysis platform to assist in its oversight activities. The Payment Management Information System (PMIS) gathers payment and settlement information from various systems including HVPS and BEPS. This system provides various standard analytical reports and various ad-hoc analysis features which assist the PBC in its oversight activities. PMIS also enabled the PBC to monitor the liquidity position of the participants in real-time.

194. The PBC has not yet formally established any national payments council. The central bank has legal authority to establish a self-regulated China payments and clearing association, but it has not yet established one, although it is working on a project to create the China National Payment and Clearing Association.

195. The PBC, in cooperation with other authorities and relevant stakeholders, is working on a number of projects to further improve the safety and efficiency of the CNPS. They include: the launch of a "second generation" version of the CNAPS; a reform of key aspects of the legal and regulatory framework; and initiatives to further increase the penetration of retail payment services, in particular in rural areas and through the use of innovative channels and modalities.

D. Main Findings

196. The assessment team found the payment systems in China to be operated in a safe way. However, several improvement opportunities, summarized in Table below, were identified.

Table 20. China: Recommended Actions to Improve Observance of CPSS Core Principles and Central Bank Responsibilities in Applying the CPs

Reference Principle	Recommended Actions
Legal foundation *CP 1*	Chinese authorities should accelerate the legislative process to complete the reform of the legal and regulatory framework for payment and securities settlement. This will include: • The enactment of a payment system law to give full legal protection, among other things, to settlement finality and netting arrangements. • The introduction of the Interpretation of Enterprise Bankruptcy Law or revision of the Enterprise Bankruptcy Law to exempt the payment system sector from the "zero-hour rule." • The upgrade of payment system rules and procedures to the level of PBC regulation.
Understanding and management of risks *CPs 2 and 3*	As it is not clear whether participants are fully aware of the potential legal risk associated with settlement finality, the PBC might want to inform participants about the measures it took to mitigate this risk and the projects under way to eliminate it. The PBC should further monitor the credit risk and liquidity risk of the system by improving relevant rules and building the second-generation payment system. Relevant actions mainly include: • Provide participants with more comprehensive queuing and account monitoring functions, "package" liquidity real-time inquiry functions and large-value payment system queuing matching. • Apply more active mark-to-market mechanisms for the collateral used in the intra-day liquidity facility. • As liquidity conditions evolve, maintain flexibility in the conditions applied to intra-day liquidity facilities and consider the removal of charging for collateralized credit.
Settlement *CPs 4, 5, and 6*	-
Security and Operational Reliability, and Contingency Arrangements *CP 7*	The second-generation payment system will have a more efficient operation and maintenance mechanism, which realizes automatic upgrading of the system application software; it will: • improve the real-time operation monitoring function, which carries out comprehensive and automatic monitoring of the IT resources of the payment system; • improve the risk warning capability, effectively analyzing the potential risks of the system and giving timely warning; • realize automatic handling of system failures to the maximum degree; and • reduce the system maintenance work load, increasing the operation monitoring efficiency and upgrading the operation maintenance level. The second-generation payment system will build the backup system with complete production recovery capability, business switching capability and data searching capability on the framework of the production center, remote backup center and the data backup center in the same city to ensure the continuous processing of payment and the security and integrity of information and data in case of emergency. The above measures are strongly encouraged.

Cont

Reference Principle	Recommended Actions
Efficiency and Practicality of the System *CP 8*	Notwithstanding the important progresses achieved since the launch of the CNAPS, some features might be adjusted to increase efficiency and practicality to the users, such as: 1) The "multiple access point" feature of the system might impact the efficient management of liquidity and adds to the cost of participating in it. 2) High value electronic transactions might still be perceived as relatively more expensive vis-à-vis large value cheque transactions, although it is noted that commercial banks are gradually switching their customers to other electronic payment options. 3) Operating hours could be extended to reflect the growing importance of the system.
Criteria for Participation *CP 9*	To further strengthen supervision and management of the payment system participants and guarantee the secure and stable operation of the payment system, the PBC plans to revise the *Administrative Measures for Accessing to and Exiting the Payment System by Banking Financial Institutions*. For instance, it plans to specify and detail the mode for examining the access applicants in the Administrative Measures: • testing relevant personnel on knowledge about the payment systems; • onsite check of the payment settlement processing environment; and • calling the top management together for prudent talks so as to increase the operability of access review and approval. These measures are strongly encouraged.
Governance of the Payment System *CP 10*	As mentioned, the PBC is already addressing most of the existing shortfalls of the system and should be commended for the extraordinary effort to launch and operate a sophisticated and reliable payment system, which constitutes the backbone of China's financial system. Involving more and more system participants in the 'second generation" project and, eventually creating a formal users' group will facilitate cooperation and foster the systems' performance over time. Also, the regular rehearsal of crisis procedures for all types of emergency occurrences and not just for operational matters, both within different departments of the PBC and with system participant, would certainly increase the PBC capacity to respond to unforeseen events. Over time, the PBC should strive to achieve full observance of the other CPs.
Central Bank Responsibilities in Applying the CPs *Central Bank Responsibility A, B, C, and D*	The PBC should clarify in detail its policy stance in payment system oversight in a publicly available document, which would expand on the scope of its actions and its plans to achieve its public policy objectives in payment system matters. With regard to policy objectives, the PBC might want to clarify that its oversight extends beyond the two traditional main objectives of efficiency and reliability of payment systems to a wider set of issues including the promotion of competition in the payment services market and the protection of consumer interests. With regard to the scope of its oversight role, the oversight policy document would explicitly state the PBC decision to apply its powers over all payments and SSS in the country those that are systemically important and retail systems, since the latter are especially important in supporting economic activity, broad access to payment services and the public trust in money. The oversight policy document should also cover in detail the PBC major policies and instruments. Major policies would touch upon the main aspects of payment systems including, risk control, access, governance, transparency, pricing, system reliability and business continuity, efficiency, etc. Instruments would range from moral suasion to on-site inspections, from regulation to cooperation, from sanctions to the direct provision of payment services. Also, the oversight document should elaborate on the criteria used to determine when a system is systemically important. A list of these systems should be provided and constantly monitored and updated. Finally, the policy document would elaborate on institutional arrangements and cooperation in the payment system arena (see Responsibility D below). The HVPS does not fully observe all CPSIPS and actions to achieve its full compliance should be completed by the PBC as a priority.

Reference Principle	Recommended Actions
	A thorough evaluation of the risks associated with the cheque clearing and proactive actions to remove large value payment items from the cheque clearinghouse should be carried out as a matter of urgency.
	Some clarification of the roles of the Payment and Settlement Department and the internal audit department in the oversight of the PBC operated payment systems might be necessary.
	The mission considers that a more proactive oversight by the PBC over the CFETS and the ACHs might be advisable. In particular, an assessment of the safety and efficiency of these systems with relevant international standards is recommended.
	The PBC should consider a further refinement of its cooperative framework at the domestic level, by activating and implementing Memoranda of Understanding on payment and settlement issues and a structured oversight working framework with all relevant authorities and creating the China National Payment Association
	At the international level, the PBC is encouraged to continue its commendable effort of cooperation with relevant central banks and international organizations.
	A thorough application of the CPSS cross-border cooperative framework is also recommended.

E. Authorities' Response

197. The Chinese authorities welcome and support the CPSS assessment as an opportunity for reflection and improvement for China payment and settlement system according to international standards. The assessment team has undertaken an excellent task, demonstrating high quality, professionalism, dedication and the ability to cut through complex issues in a constrained timeframe. The authorities appreciate the opportunity to provide the following comments.

198. Over the past decade, China has continuously pushed forward the development of China payment and settlement system, which constitute the backbone of China's financial system. We have built a payment network consisting of the central bank inter-bank payment systems, the banking institutions' internal payment system, the security settlement system, the FX settlement system, the bankcards payment system and other retail payment systems run by private sectors. Non-cash payment instruments have been widely used and met various payment requirements. Commercial drafts have been underwritten and transferred in an electronic way. Bankcards penetration ratio has been on a fast track and bankcards have been the most widely used payment instrument by Chinese residents. Online payment, mobile payment and telephone payment have been developing dramatically. The application of non-cash payment instruments has greatly facilitated economic production and civil life, reduced cash circulation and transaction costs. Payment providers have been diversified. These include the central bank, banking institutions, nonbanking institutions and securities settlement institutions as payment organizations. The payment services have been market-driven. Modern payment means have also found their way in rural areas. The pilot cross-border trade settlement in RMB has developed in an orderly way. The management system of bank settlement accounts has improved on a gradual basis. The PBC has promulgated regulations on bank settlement accounts and established the bank settlement account management system to implement regulations. At the

same time, the PBC launched a nationwide identity authentication system of accounts with the Police Bureau to implement the "know your customer" scheme. The payment system oversight has been strengthened, with safety and efficiency as the priority. The PBC has also improved supervision techniques and realized the DVP mode in the bond market.

199. The Large Value Payment System (LVPS) run by the PBC has been designated as the systemically important payment system and has been assessed against the CPs. The assessment concluded that the system observes (observed or broadly observed) all the CPs except CPI (legal basis). The PBC pays high attentions to the assessment results and appreciates valuable recommendations of the IMF and the WB. In implementing the recommendations, the PBC has realized one point entry in CNAPS1, e.g., the treasury centralized booking system and China postal savings bank's internal payment system have been connected to CNAPS1 from one point and settled their transactions with one account.

200. Measures will be taken to strengthen our legal foundation, management and supervision of China payment systems, so as to improve its practicality and efficiency in the future.

- *CP I legal Foundation*. The PBC has been aware of the shortcomings in the legal framework, and has decided to draft a payment system act to avoid the effects of the "zero hour rule" and give the legal recognition of netting arrangements and settlement finality. But the process of establishing legislation will take time and may involve many authorities.

- *CP VIII Practicality and Efficiency*. The PBC is launching the 2nd generation of CNAPS to increase efficiency and practicality. CNAPS2 will be designed to extend the opening hours of settlement to meet the needs of users in different areas and various financial markets.

- *CP X Governance*. The PBC has decided to improve management, upgrade the payment system and conduct a regular drill of emergency procedures, with an aim to achieving full observance of the CPs.

201. *Central Bank Responsibilities A, B, C, and D*. The PBC fully agrees with the recommendations and will take proper measures to ensure full observances of all CPs. The PBC will clarify in detail its policy stance in the payment system oversight in a publicly available document, and extend its oversight over all payments and securities settlement systems, including the systemically important systems and retail payment systems. The PBC will assess the safety and efficiency of the CFETS and the ACHs with relevant international standards. Besides, the PBC is about to establish the China National Payment Association and strengthen cooperation with relevant authorities, foreign central banks and international organizations.

AnnexV. Observance of Financial Sector Standards and Codes—Assessment of Observance of CPSS-IOSCO Recommendations for Securities Settlement Systems and Central Counterparties:A Summary

A. Introduction

202. This summary is based on the Recommendations of the Committee on Payment and Settlement Systems (CPSS) and the International Organization of Securities Commissions (IOSCO) for Recommendations for Securities Settlement Systems (RSSS) and the Recommendations of CPSS-IOSCO for Central Counterparties (RCCP). This assessment was conducted in September 2010.

203. The information used in the assessment included relevant laws, rules and procedures governing the systems, and other available material.[13] In addition, extensive discussions were held with regulators and overseers: PBC, CSRC, SSE, SHFE, DCE, ZCE, CFFEX, CCDC, SD&C, SAC, CFA; several stakeholders, including banks and broker-dealers active on the SSE, SHFE, and the interbank bond market, participants of the CCDC and SD&C as well as banks that facilitate settlement and funds custody for corporate securities and futures. Three self assessments were prepared by the CCDC for the CCDC settlement system, by the SHFE for the SHFE clearing and settlement system and by the Department of Market Supervision of the CSRC for the SD&C clearing and settlement system. Other relevant information was derived by the assessment process for Systemically Important Payment Systems (SIPS).

204. The assessment was conducted on processes and functions as opposed to institutions. Given that the bonds are mostly traded over the counter (OTC), the processes relating to trades outside the stock exchange were also examined.

B. Institutional and Market Structure

205. The Securities Settlement Systems (SSS) in the PRC are organized around three different types of markets, which are the bond market, the corporate securities market and the futures market. The bond market comprises the interbank bond market, the exchange bond market, and the bank counter market. The interbank bond market is the most dominant market, with more than 97 percent of total bond trading volume. The two stock exchanges, the SSE and the SZSE, were established in 1990 and offer trading in the same type of securities, being shares, bonds, funds and warrants. Turnover on both stock exchanges is relatively high and has grown tremendously during the last decade. According to the World Federation of Stock

---

[13] CSRC Annual Reports 2008 and 2009, CDC Annual Report of China's Bond Market 2009, PBC responses on the FSAP questionnaire for payment systems and securities clearing and settlement; websites from CSRC, SSE, SZSE, SHFE, CDCC/Chinabond; and other relevant documents.

Exchanges, as of 2009, the SSE ranks as the 3rd exchange worldwide in share trading with RMB 34 trillion, and the SZSE as the 6th with RMB 18 trillion. There are also three commodities exchanges: SHFE, DCE, and ZCE. The SHFE ranks as the 10th derivatives exchange worldwide, measured in number of contracts traded and the second largest commodity exchange. A CFFEX was established in 2006 as a joint venture of the SSE, SZSE, SHFE, DCE, and ZCE but still volume and value of transactions are relatively modest.

206. The CCDC is the SSS as well as the central securities depository (CSD) for bonds. It is the only institution entrusted by the MOF to be the depository for government securities. The CCDC was established in 1996 as a Government entity and since then it is regulated by the PBC and overseen by the PBC and MOF. In addition, the CBRC is in charge of the appointment of Executive Managers of CCDC. The CCDC settles bond transactions (spot, repo, forward) on a gross basis for both bonds and funds, though CCDC management under PBC guidance, is currently considering introducing also a netting facility. Securities are held at the end-investor level in most cases (98 percent). The CCDC book entry system is interconnected with the interbank trading system (operated by the China Foreign Exchange Trading System (CFETS)). Cash settlement takes place in the central bank HVPS. Settlement takes place on T+0 for most transactions (82.9 percent of total value settled in 2009). In addition to the commonly used delivery versus payment (DvP) settlement, CCDC allows for other settlement modalities, Payment after Delivery (PaD), Delivery after Payment (DaP) and Free of Payment (FoP).

207. The SD&C is the central counterparty (CCP), SSS, as well as the CSD for all instruments traded on the SSE and SZSE. The SD&C was established in 2001 and is jointly owned by the SSE (50 percent) and the SZSE (50 percent). Securities settlement arrangements for SSE and SZSE are based on front-end availability of securities and funds, otherwise transactions do not take place. Securities are held at the investor level detail in the SD&C while funds are kept through a system of third party custodian banks with the SD&C acting as the settlement agent.

208. The four futures exchanges have their own clearing and settlement departments, which offer the function of a CCP. Settlements can be either in cash (daily mark to market) as well as physical settlements (delivery on expiration). The exchanges operate a pre-margining system, that is, futures contracts can only be purchased under the premise of sufficient margin deposits. In addition to the pre-margining system the exchanges have established other risk management controls including: price limits, limits to speculative positions and large holders, compulsory closed-out of positions, a system of warning indicators, and settlement reserves. Cash settlement is effected through the accounts of five commercial "settlement" banks. The "settlement" banks only operate as custodians for margins and facilitators for transfers of funds with the futures exchanges conducting settlement functions. Also, the China Futures Margin Monitoring Center was established in 2006 as a non-profit company under the sponsorship of the three futures exchanges to guarantee the safety of futures margin.

209. The CCDC, SD&C, and SHFE/DCE/ZCE operate important securities and derivatives settlement systems both, due to the large volume and value of transactions (GDP comparison) and the fact that they support key financial sector markets (interbank bond market, stock exchanges and futures). Therefore, the CCDC and SD&C are being assessed below against the 19 RSSS and the SHFE is being assessed against the 15 RCCP. The SD&C operates as a CCP for most of the market transactions but given the "unique" features of its settlement process (front-end control of securities and funds) it is being assessed against the RSSS. The other two commodities futures exchanges, DCE and ZCE, follow very similar settlement procedures to the SHFE, thus, findings and recommendations for the SHFE are also applicable to DCE and ZCE.

C. Main Findings

210. The assessment team found the securities settlement systems in China to be operated in a safe way. However, several improvement opportunities, summarized in Tables 21, 22, and 23, were identified.

Table 21. China: Recommended Actions to Improve Observance of CPSS-IOSCO RSSS—OTC Bonds Market-CCDC

Reference Recommendation	Recommended Action
Legal risk	
Recommendation 1. SSS should have a well-founded, clear and transparent legal basis in the relevant jurisdiction.	The PBC and MOF should consider an overall review of the legal and regulatory framework to provide a solid legal basis to clearance and settlement of operations of the interbank money market, the OTC bond market and CCDC. The framework should include the main elements at the Law level and not only at the Ministry-level procedures. The efficiency of the collateral disposal should be analyzed and improved as soon as possible. The conflict of law in the cross-border settlement is not currently an important risk source for securities settlement in China. However, as the Chinese financial markets increasingly overact with foreign ones, it is important that the Chinese legal and regulatory framework addresses any potential conflict of laws.
Pre-settlement risk	
Recommendation 2. Confirmation of trades between direct market participants should occur as soon as possible after trade execution, but no later than trade date (T+0). Where confirmation of trades by indirect market participants (such as institutional investors) is required, it should occur as soon as possible after trade execution, preferably on T+0, but no later than T+1.	Efforts should be made to ensure that all OTC transactions are indeed confirmed on T+0.
Recommendation 4. The benefits and costs of a CCP should be assessed. Where such a mechanism is introduced, the CCP should rigorously control the risks it assumes.	PBC should finalize the process to determine if the typology of the market and other legal, institutional and market considerations would justify the establishment of a CCP mechanism.

Cont

Reference Recommendation	Recommended Action
Recommendation 5. Securities lending and borrowing (or repurchase agreements and other equivalent transactions) should be encouraged as a method for expediting the settlement of securities transactions. Barriers that inhibit the practice of lending securities for this purpose should be removed.	CCDC should consider improving securities lending and borrowing mechanisms beyond the current existing bilateral arrangements. Accounting practices and tax rules need to be improved to facilitate securities lending and borrowing.
Settlement risk	
Recommendation 7. CSDs should eliminate principal risk by linking securities transfers to funds transfers in a way that achieves DvP.	The settlement of transactions using DvP has strongly increased since 2008. The CCDC is encouraged to further increase the use of DvP settlement to reach as soon as possible 100 percent settlement on a DvP basis.
Recommendation 8. Final settlement should occur no later than the end of the settlement day. Intra-day or real-time finality should be provided where necessary to reduce risks.	Protection of settlement finality should be included in the legal framework.
Other issues	
Recommendation 13. Governance arrangements for CSDs and CCPs should be designed to fulfill public interest requirements and to promote the objectives of owners and users.	A clear separation should be made between the oversight function of the PBC, the other supervisory tasks of CBRC and MOF, and the operational responsibility of PBC. The interests of participants should be explicitly taken into account.
Recommendation 16. SSS should use or accommodate the relevant international communication procedures and standards in order to facilitate efficient settlement of cross-border transactions.	The CCDC should work to improve the use of relevant communication procedures and standards and, therefore, facilitate cross-border trades.
Recommendation 17. CSDs and CCPs should provide market participants with sufficient information for them to accurately identify the risks and costs associated with using the CSD or CCP services.	The CCDC should disclose the answers to the questionnaire set out in the CPSS/IOSCO disclosure framework or the answers to the key questions set out in the assessment methodology for RSSS.
Recommendation 18. SSS should be subject to transparent and effective regulation and oversight. Central banks and securities regulators should cooperate with each other and with other relevant authorities.	Supervisors and regulators should continue to exercise their action effectively. The PBC should clarify the roles it plays with respect to the CCDC by clearly distinguishing its oversight and supervisory role from its participation in the governance of the system. Further fine tuning is needed in the cooperation arrangements of the different regulators in respect to clearance and settlement issues.
Recommendation 19. CSDs that establish links to settle cross-border trades should design and operate such links to reduce effectively the risks associated with cross-border settlements.	There does not seem to be a comprehensive and standardized procedure to analyze risks in cross-border links. This matter should be addressed as soon as possible by the CCDC and its overseers.

D. Main Recommendations

211. The assessment team found several improvement opportunities, summarized in the Table below:

Table 22. China: Recommended Actions to Improve Observance of CPSS-IOSCO RSSS—Stock Exchange (SSE, SZSE)—SD&C

Reference Recommendation	Recommended Action
Pre-settlement risk	
Recommendation 4. The benefits and costs of a CCP should be assessed. Where such a mechanism is introduced, the CCP should rigorously control the risks it assumes.	SD&C today mostly relies on its clearance and settlement system design and some additional risk control measures to ensure control of risks. For the future, SD&C may consider to evaluate how to strengthen its robustness as a CCP through a review of several elements such as monitoring of exposures, stress tests, availability of financial resources, etc. Exploring experiences from off-shore peers on this may be useful. This may become a more immediate priority if SD&C wants to accommodate a market evolution to a more wholesale market for which the current clearance and settlement design (mostly thought for a retail market) may not be effective.
Settlement risk	
Recommendation 7. CSDs should eliminate principal risk by linking securities transfers to funds transfers in a way that achieves DvP.	CSRC and SD&C should consider to make public a description of SD&C clearance and settlement arrangements to avoid the perception that by not following a more "orthodox" DvP structure they do not comply with the DvP principle.
Recommendation 9. CSDs that extend intraday credit to participants, including CSDs that operate net settlement systems, should institute risk controls that, at a minimum, ensure timely settlement in the event that the participant with the largest payment obligation is unable to settle. The most reliable set of controls is a combination of collateral requirements and limits.	SD&C should perform a comprehensive and deep assessment of its credit risk exposures as soon as possible, including possibility of multiple failures.
Recommendation 10. Assets used to settle the ultimate payment obligations arising from securities transactions should carry little or no credit or liquidity risk. If central bank money is not used, steps must be taken to protect CSD members from potential losses and liquidity pressures arising from the failure of the cash settlement agent whose assets are used for that purpose.	Full compliance of the payment systems used to transfer funds with the CPSIPS should be achieved to ensure that no settlement risks stem from the clearing and settlement process due to the existence of liquidity and credit risks in the payment system. However, the DvP equivalent nature of the SD&C settlement arrangements would eventually limit the risk to market risk.
Other issues	
Recommendation 13. Governance arrangements for CSDs and CCPs should be designed to fulfill public interest requirements and to promote the objectives of owners and users.	The SD&C should develop an action plan to comply with all RSSSs and the Governance of the system must be accountable for it and take the necessary actions to achieve full compliance.
Recommendation 16. SSS should use or accommodate the relevant international communication procedures and standards in order to facilitate efficient settlement of cross-border transactions.	It is advisable that the SD&C in cooperation with the exchanges and market participants and in consultation with the CSRC activate a process to constantly evaluate the benefits of developments on relevant international communication procedures and standards and act promptly to implement the necessary changes to meet market needs.
Recommendation 17. CSDs and CCPs should provide market participants with sufficient information for them to identify and evaluate accurately the risks and costs associated with using the CSD or CCP services.	The SD&C should disclose the answers to the questionnaire set out in the CPSS/IOSCO disclosure framework or the answers to the key questions set out in the assessment methodology for RSSS.

Cont

Reference Recommendation	Recommended Action
Recommendation 18. SSS should be subject to transparent and effective regulation and oversight. Central banks and securities regulators should cooperate with each other and with other relevant authorities.	Supervisors and regulators should continue to exercise their action effectively. Although a high level cooperation framework among relevant authorities does exist, cooperation at the technical level might be structure more formally. In addition to existing mechanisms, authorities should also foster cooperation between them and the private sector and other relevant stakeholders by creating an appropriate forum to discuss payment and settlement matters.
Recommendation 19. CSDs that establish links to settle cross-border trades should design and operate such links to reduce effectively the risks associated with cross-border settlements.	In light of the potential internationalization of the Chinese market, links are likely to become the norm rather than the exception. The SDC&C, the exchanges and market regulators might want to work on a standardized framework to assess the risks associated to such links, when the need materializes.

Table 23. Recommended Actions to Improve Observance of CPSS-IOSCO RCCP—SHFE

Recommendation 1. Legal risk	
A CCP should have a well founded, transparent and enforceable legal framework for each aspect of its activities in all relevant jurisdictions.	Most key concepts of clearing and settlement are covered by the SHFE rules and regulations, however, not in statutory law. In order to observe this recommendation statutory law should contain provisions on derivative trading, e.g., the enforceability of trades, finality, netting, novation, investor protection and collateral protection.
Recommendation 4. Margin requirements	
If a CCP relies on margin requirements to limit its credit exposures to participants, those requirements should be sufficient to cover potential exposures in normal market conditions. The models and parameters used in setting margin requirements should be risk-based and reviewed regularly.	No clear legal basis exists for the acceptance of warehouse receipts as collateral to deposit as margin for the coverage of market risk exposure. This threatens the stability of the CCP.
Recommendation 13. Governance	
Governance arrangements for a CCP should be clear and transparent to fulfil public interest requirements and to support the objectives of owners and participants. In particular, they should promote the effectiveness of a CCP's risk management procedures.	The SHFE is urged to engage in a self assessment with the new standards under preparation by the CPSS and IOSCO which will be released in 2011. A workshop on these standards might be organized with the participation of local authorities and market participants, as well as international practitioners from both the public and the private sector.
Recommendation 14. Transparency	
A CCP should provide market participants with sufficient information for them to identify and evaluate accurately the risks and costs associated with using its services.	In order to observe this recommendation the SHFE should publish the disclosure framework for the CPSS-IOSCO RCCP.
Recommendation 15. Regulation and oversight	
A CCP should be subject to transparent and effective regulation and oversight. In both a domestic and an international context, central banks and securities regulators should cooperate with each other and with other relevant authorities.	Given concentration of risks in a CCP and its potential effect on financial stability CSRC and PBC should establish a cooperative oversight framework for CCPs.

E. Authorities' Response

212. The PBC and CSRC appreciate the significant undertaking associated with the FSAP review by the IMF and the World Bank in a comprehensive assessment of the SD&C, CCDC, the SHFE against the *CPSS-IOSCO RSSS* and *for Central* Counterparties (RCCP). We would like to pay a high tribute to the great efforts made by all parties involved in the assessment process and the professionalism of the assessors as demonstrated. We recognize the positive and far-reaching influence the assessment has on the stability and effective regulation and oversight of SIPS, clearing and settlement systems.

213. The assessment well objectively reflects the status of the settlement system in China's security market, bond market and futures market as well as the compliance of the SD&C and CCDC with the *RSSS*, the compliance of the SHFE with the *RCCP*. The PBC and CSRC will share and analyze the comments and recommendations in the assessment with the SD&C, CCDC and SHFE, and consider absorbing and adopting the comments and recommendations in the future. All relevant parties will work together to ensure that SSS in China can operate in a secure, efficient and transparent environment.

214. Meanwhile, the CSRC still holds reservations about certain parts of the assessment of SHFE on its compliance with the RCCP (i.e., Recommendation 1 and Recommendation 4), for the following reasons:

- **On the issue of legal basis.** Regarding China's legislative system, laws are promulgated by the National People's Congress (NPC), and administrative regulations are issued by the SC. Administrative regulations constitute an important part of China's legal system, providing legal basis for not only administrative regulation, but also the settlement of disputes and cases by judicial authorities. However, it is not an explicit clause after all. The *Regulations on the Administration of Futures Trading,* which is the administrative regulation governing futures trading, is the legal basis for China's futures market. We do not believe legal gaps exist in China's futures settlement system.

- **On the legal recognition of the use of dematerialized warehouse receipts as margin contributions.** The use of standardized warehouse receipts as margin contributions is clearly stipulated in the *Regulations on the Administration of Futures Trading*, the *Measures for the Administration of Futures Exchanges* and the relevant business rules of futures exchanges. The *Property Law* also contains clearly-stated provisions on pledge right. In practice, the SHFE designates delivery warehouses to serve as the registration authority for the pledge of dematerialized warehouse receipts. There have never been any controversies or disputes in this regard.

215. The PBC holds reservations about certain parts of the assessment of CCDC on its compliance with the *RSSS*, i.e., Recommendation 1 and Recommendation 8.

Since bond is a kind of security, the Securities Law applies to interbank bond market. Also the finality has legal certainty. The regulations issued by PBC indicates, "bond transaction settlement cannot be revoked once completed," "the cash and bonds with the status of waiting for transfer in the settlement process and the collateral regarding to the settlement can only be used for completing the settlement and shall not be enforced compulsorily for other purposes." The spirit and principles of the *Securities Law* apply to domestic securities market in China, including inter-bank bond market; despite that the *Securities Law* contains specific provisions more on the exchange market. Regulations promulgated by PBC, which are in accordance with the spirit and principles of the *Securities Law* and mainly applied to inter-bank bond market, are the special provisions in Chinese legislation system on securities. According to the *Law on Legislation,* regulations issued by PBC belong to broadly defined laws and have legal enforceability. Owing to these, inter-bank bond market has been operating smoothly and safely these years since its establishment.

216. The PBC, together with CCDC, will seriously analyze the opinions and suggestions raised in the Assessment Report and keep improving the depositary and settlement system of China's inter-bank bond market.